La Galgada, Peru

A PRECERAMIC CULTURE IN TRANSITION

La Galgada, Peru

A PRECERAMIC CULTURE IN TRANSITION

By Terence Grieder, Alberto Bueno Mendoza, C. Earle Smith, Jr., and Robert M. Malina

Published with the assistance of the Getty Grant Program

UNIVERSITY OF TEXAS PRESS ◆ AUSTIN

First edition, 1988

Requests for permission to reproduce material
from this work should be sent to:
  Permissions
  University of Texas Press
  Box 7819
  Austin, Texas 78713-7819
ISBN: 978-0-292-74106-5

Library of Congress Cataloging-in-Publication Data
La Galgada, Peru: a preceramic culture in transition /
    by Terence Grieder . . . [et al.].—1st ed.
        p.   cm.
    "Published with the assistance of the Getty Grant
      Program."
    Bibliography: p.
    Includes index.

        1. Galgada Site (Peru) 2. Indians of South America—
Peru—Galgada Region—Antiquities.   3. Excavations
(Archaeology)—Peru—Galgada Region.   4. Galgada
Region (Peru)—Antiquities.   5. Peru—Antiquities.
I. Grieder, Terence.   II. Title: Preceramic culture in
transition.
F3429.1.G34G35 1988   88-10305
985—dc19   CIP

First paperback printing, 2012

Contents

Preface and Acknowledgments *vii*

1. Introduction *1*
   Terence Grieder

2. The Geography of the Tablachaca Canyon *4*
   Alberto Bueno Mendoza and Terence Grieder

3. The History of La Galgada Architecture *19*
   Terence Grieder and Alberto Bueno Mendoza

4. Radiocarbon Measurements *68*
   Terence Grieder

5. Burial Patterns and Offerings *73*
   Terence Grieder

6. Skeletal Materials from La Galgada *103*
   Robert M. Malina

7. Floral Remains *125*
   C. Earle Smith, Jr.

8. Fiber Arts *152*
   Terence Grieder

9. Petroglyphs *182*
   Alberto Bueno Mendoza and Terence Grieder

10. Ceramics *185*
    Terence Grieder

11. La Galgada in the World of Its Time *192*
    Terence Grieder, Alberto Bueno Mendoza, C. Earle Smith, Jr., and Robert M. Malina

12. Art as Communication at La Galgada *204*
    Terence Grieder

APPENDIX A
Description of Skeletal Material by Tomb *217*
Robert M. Malina

APPENDIX B
Catalog of Tomb Contents *242*
Terence Grieder

APPENDIX C
La Galgada Textile Specimens *249*
Terence Grieder

Bibliography *271*

Index *279*

Preface and Acknowledgments

This study was inspired by Teodoro E. Ló-pez Trelles, governor of the village of La Galgada in 1969, when it was a busy mining town at the end of the northern branch of the Santa Railway. As I was returning from Cabana at the end of the first season of work on the ruins of Pashash, I was given a brief tour of the ruins at La Galgada by López Trelles, who had been protecting them from looting and hoped to interest someone in a serious study of them. Although I found the desolate environment of the canyon floor uninviting, I was impressed by the fine walls visible then and I planned to make a study when the work at Pashash was completed.

In 1976, with the work at Pashash done, Alberto Bueno Mendoza and I visited La Galgada and spent a week examining ruins in the vicinity. Since the great earthquake of 1970 had destroyed the Santa Railway and closed the mines, the village had become almost a ghost town, although several families continued to live there to farm the lower terrace of the river and work the coal mine on a small scale. Alfredo Giraldo maintained a small hotel there, where we lodged throughout the project. Since 1970 La Galgada has been reached by a dirt road bulldozed over the old railroad roadbed. In 1975 the bulldozer improving the road departed from the railroad line and made its cut slightly higher as it passed through the ruins. It thus sliced off the upper levels of the western half of the low South Mound and set the road directly against the southwestern corner of the North

Mound. Our inspection of the road cut in 1976 showed us several things: the site was much older than we had previously guessed and was almost certainly Preceramic; a program of archaeological salvage was imperative and could not be delayed very long; and, finally, the site was worth a major effort.

The following year was spent in an effort to raise funds sufficient to gather a group of specialists for a large cooperative study. Shortage of funds reduced the scale of the project in its earlier seasons, but in 1978 Bueno and I carried out a twelve-week field season, with help from Ponciano Paredes Botoni, concentrating on salvage excavations of the road cut through the South Mound. In 1979 and 1980 Bueno and I continued our work, expanding to include the North Mound, and in 1981 C. Earle Smith, Jr., and Robert M. Malina joined the project to make special studies of the botanical material and the human skeletal remains, respectively. We did laboratory studies in 1982, 1983, and 1984, and a survey of related sites in the canyon in 1985.

The project was envisioned from the beginning as thirty-six weeks of fieldwork, with whatever additional periods of analysis the collections might require. That work has been accomplished. Like any important site, La Galgada offers much more than can be studied in one lifetime. It is also vital that it be studied by various investigators with different points of view and over a long period of time. The site is currently under the supervision of the director of the National Site Museum of Cerro Sechín, Lorenzo Samaniego Román, for the Peruvian National Institute of Culture.

All of us who took part in the project owe a debt of gratitude to numerous individuals and organizations who supported the work in various ways. The investigation was authorized by the Commission on Technical Qualifications of Archaeological Projects of the National Institute of Culture in Acuerdo No. 03/25.04.78. Financial support was provided by the University Research Institute of the University of Texas at Austin, the Wenner-Gren Foundation for Anthropological Research, and Margaret B. Moore and Herschel T. Moore of Austin, Texas. We acknowledge gratefully this indispensable help. The project has benefited by the help of many more people than can be named here, but Alfredo Giraldo in La Galgada and Louise Pierucci-Holman in Austin deserve special thanks. Others, who are not listed among the authors of this report, made important contributions to the fieldwork, notably Bernardino Ojeda and Ponciano Paredes. We are grateful to Dr. Fernando Cabieses, director of the Museum of Health Sciences in Lima, for provision of laboratory and storage space and for his constant sympathy and encouragement.

C. Earle Smith, Jr., died October 19, 1987, in an automobile accident. At that time his contribution to this volume was complete; since he did not have the opportunity to participate in editorial revision it is published here as he submitted it. Professor Smith, who preferred to be called Smitty, was a leader in the field of archaeological botany and a perfect colleague in fieldwork. His pleasure in the work and in his contacts with the people and the environment enriched the fieldwork experience for all of us.

T.G.
January 1988

La Galgada, Peru

A PRECERAMIC CULTURE IN TRANSITION

1. Introduction

TERENCE GRIEDER

This is a report on a study of the cultural remains found at a site on the east bank of the Tablachaca River in the highlands of northern Peru (Fig. 1). The nearest modern village, about 2 km to the north, is the coal-mining town of La Galgada. We have referred to the area of our study by the name of the village, although the local people call the area of the ruins "San Pedro." There are a great many ancient sites of occupation belonging to various periods near La Galgada village (Fig. 5) and throughout the canyon of the Tablachaca, few of which have been studied or previously named in writing. The two mounds we are calling "the La Galgada site" (Fig. 2) are among the most impressive in the lower levels of the canyon and seem also to be among the oldest.

During the third millennium B.C. the people of the central Andes were in a technical period which can be called truly preceramic in that their northern neighbors were making pottery and they were not. Lack of pottery has been assumed to define small bands of hunting and foraging people with the very limited material culture required by a life of wandering. But that is not the situation in Peru, where monumental public architecture, permanent houses, irrigation agriculture, fine textiles, and the working of stone, bone, and shell have all been found in the last forty years, in various combinations, accompanied only by gourd and stone vessels. Moreover, the region of northern and central Peru where those features are found also had an art style

sufficiently unified, despite local variations, that we cannot identify by style trade items from one center in the ruins of another. In the present state of our knowledge, La Galgada, which has all the features mentioned above, makes an important contribution to our understanding of Preceramic culture and its transition to the Initial Period.

The site was apparently first occupied about 3000 B.C. by settled agricultural people who began to build small chambers apart from their houses for ceremonies around a firepit. The following twelve centuries tell the story of the "rise and fall" of La Galgada, as the chambers coalesced into imposing temples, each level of building converted to tombs as it was buried by a later level of building. A system of canal irrigation was constructed and trade and cultural connections expanded. Before about 2000 B.C. there is evidence of connections with the advanced cultures of Ecuador in imported seashells, in technical changes in textiles, and in the first imported pottery. During the following centuries La Galgada went through a rapid process of adaptation, changing the style of its temples and tombs, its cloth and its art, but before 1500 B.C. the center was abandoned and its population had moved elsewhere.

This study focuses on several large questions:

What were the physical characteristics of the people, and what plant resources nourished and supplied them?

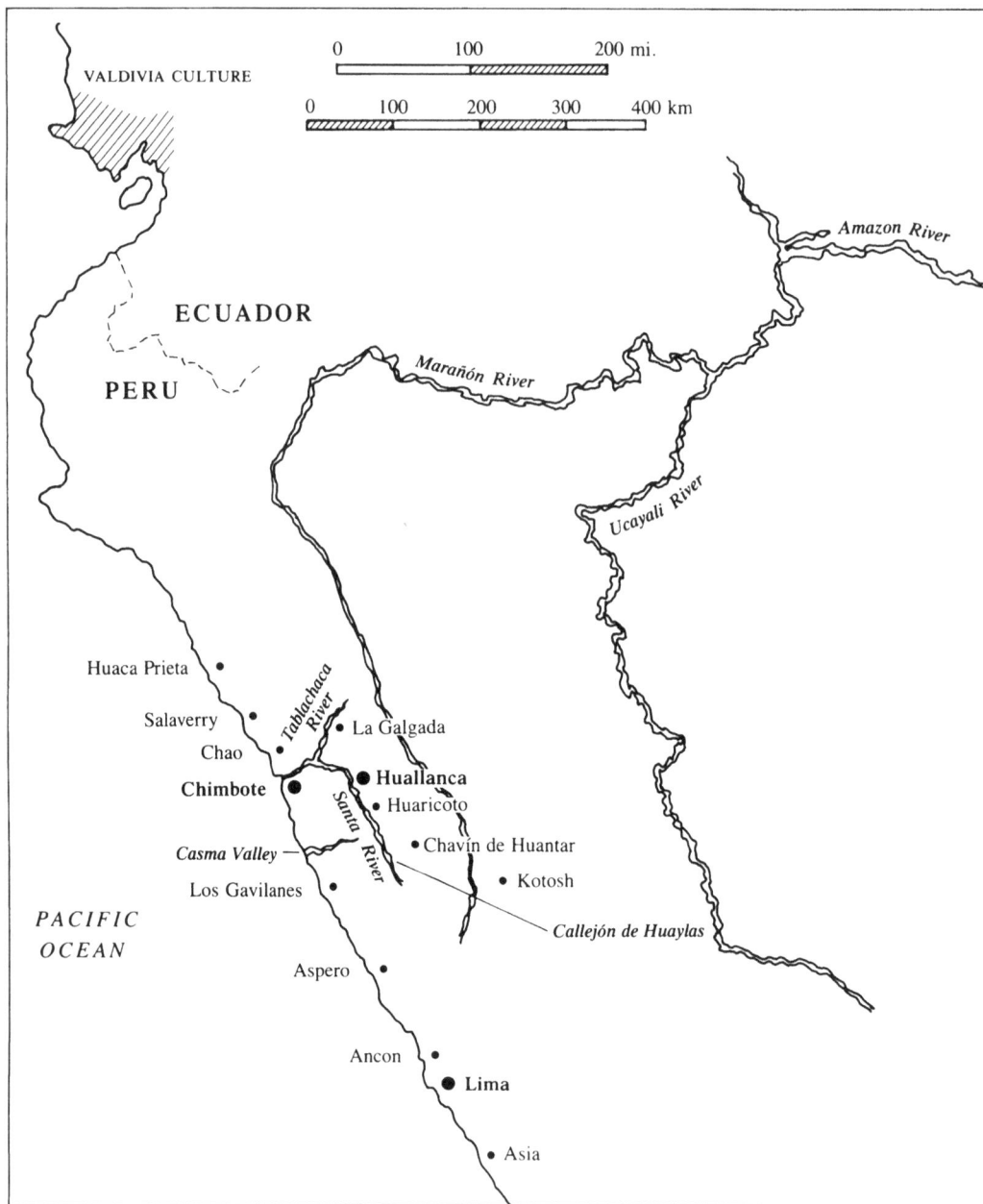

1. Northern Peru and southern Ecuador. La Galgada is located at 78°9′ west longitude, 8°28′ south latitude, in Pallasca Province of the Department of Ancash. Sites indicated are some of the most important contemporaries of La Galgada.

What are the characteristics of the architectural remains, and what do they suggest about the aims and style of the builders?

What were the highest levels of technical skill reached by the ancient inhabitants in each phase of their history, and in what technical traditions did they participate?

What ideas and attitudes were held by the ancient inhabitants, and what traditions and contacts affected the symbols and styles of their expression?

These are the kinds of questions we ask continually about our own culture, and they have limitless ramifications. They are not, however, questions arbitrarily imposed on the site by the investigators. They are responses to prior expressions made by the ancient inhabitants who designed the buildings, learned the skills, held the ideas, and invented forms for their expression. We decided to study this site, rather than some other, because we were predisposed to the study of architecture, technology, and styles and symbols at their highest levels of expression. Communication ends when the audience goes away, as it did at La Galgada centuries ago; yet many of the messages were encoded in very enduring forms which continue to transmit. These messages provide the answers for which we are seeking the questions. Thus, we reconstitute ourselves as an audience for the builders and artisans of La Galgada, to try to understand what they made and what they meant.

2. View of La Galgada site in 1978 before excavation, looking northwest, with South Mound in foreground, North Mound in right background, road newly cut in 1975 at left.

2. The Geography of the Tablachaca Canyon

ALBERTO BUENO MENDOZA and TERENCE GRIEDER

The La Galgada site is located at 8° 28' south latitude and 78° 9' west longitude in Pallasca Province in the Department of Ancash of the Republic of Peru. Although its altitude is a mere 1,100 m, it lies near the center of the Andes Mountains 74 km by air from the Pacific Ocean and 70 km by air from the Marañón River, a principal tributary of the Amazon. Pallasca Province (Fig. 3) lies across that highland zone, its borders mainly defined by some of Peru's largest rivers: the Marañón flowing north into the Amazon on the east; the Santa, the largest river on Peru's west coast, on the southwest, and the Tablachaca (or Chuquicara), the principal tributary of the Santa, on the northwest.

In modern times the province faces Tablachaca Canyon (Fig. 4), all the major centers of population spread along the east side of the canyon at more or less 3,000 m altitude. The lower elevations are very sparsely inhabited because they are much drier than the regions above 3,000 m. The canyon floor supports agriculture only where water is drawn from the permanently flowing Tablachaca River. Those conditions do not seem to have changed significantly in the past 4,500 years, to judge by the plant remains and the differences in preservation of organic materials at the various altitudes. But the ancient patterns of land use differed markedly from those of today. The dry lower elevations were much more densely inhabited in Pre-Columbian times than they are now, and

the higher elevations may also have been more populous, although the vegetation and destruction of ruins by moisture make the traces less easily seen.

It is no accident that the canyon was densely inhabited in Pre-Columbian times, since it provided one of the easiest routes between the Pacific Coast and the Amazon Valley to be found within the borders of modern Peru, with only 7 km of the whole route at an elevation of more than 4,000 m. The numerous ruined settlements of various periods along the canyon, including an Inca town and road, may be presumed to bear some relation to the use of the canyon as a communication route between Peru's three environmental zones, the desert coast, the temperate and frigid zones of the mountains, and the tropical forest of the Amazon Basin. La Galgada, at the halfway point on that route, surely benefited from that special location.

The western half of Pallasca Province is a great mountain spur between the two canyons of the Santa river system. The Santa, whose source is Laguna Conococha, more than 200 km south of La Galgada, runs northwestward through the Callejón de Huaylas and breaks through the coastal range in the narrow Cañón del Pato, where it begins to turn westward. Joined by the Manta River, which drains Corongo Province, south of Pallasca, the Santa forms a large, fast-flowing river when it is joined by its main tributary, the Tablachaca. The full-grown Santa waters the long Santa Valley, where it supports

Southeast corner of North Mound showing the
revetment wall supporting the Initial Period constructions. Foundations are in place below it for a
larger wall which was never built.

South Mound excavations of 1978 showing
D-11:C-3 (left foreground) and C-11:I-3 (right
center). Just behind the right niche of C-11:I-3 is
the opening to C-11:F-5. Floor 5 is at upper left.
View is toward the southeast.

F-12:B-2 tomb, with Burial I, a male over fifty flexed on right side. Cotton bags, baskets, and gourd vessels deposited as offerings are visible.

Stone cup and mortar; cup is from C-12:D-1, mortar from C-10:E-10.

Firepit in Floor 30 of central chamber
(H-11:E-10, opening on the right) with the opening of the later firepit toward the left.

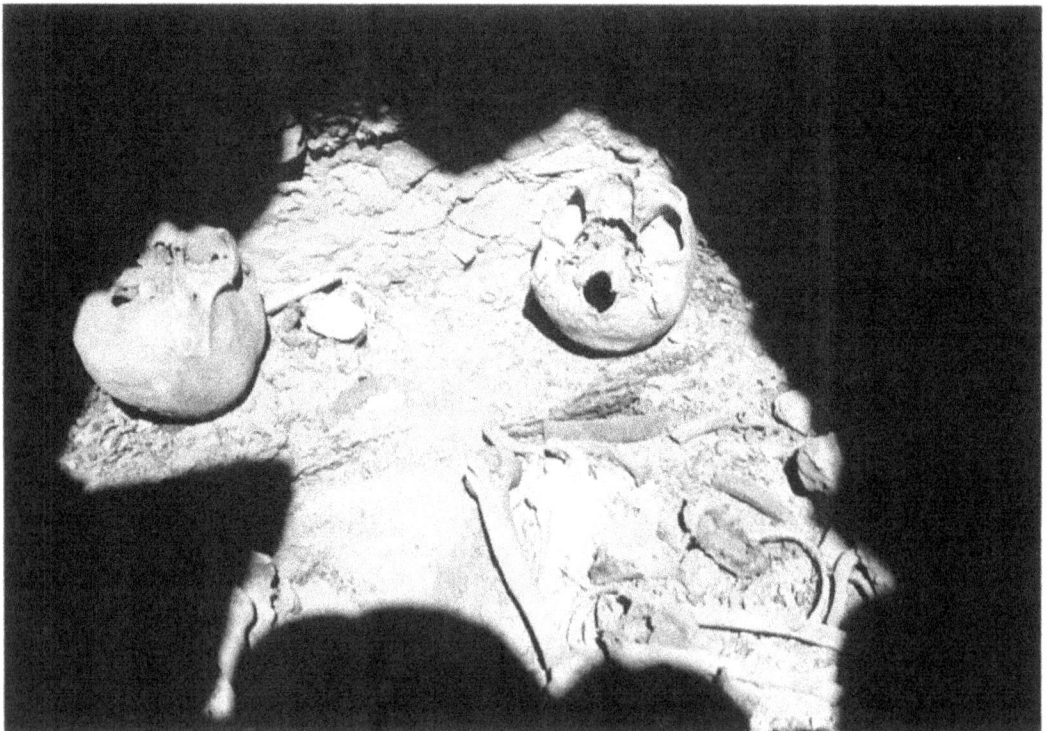

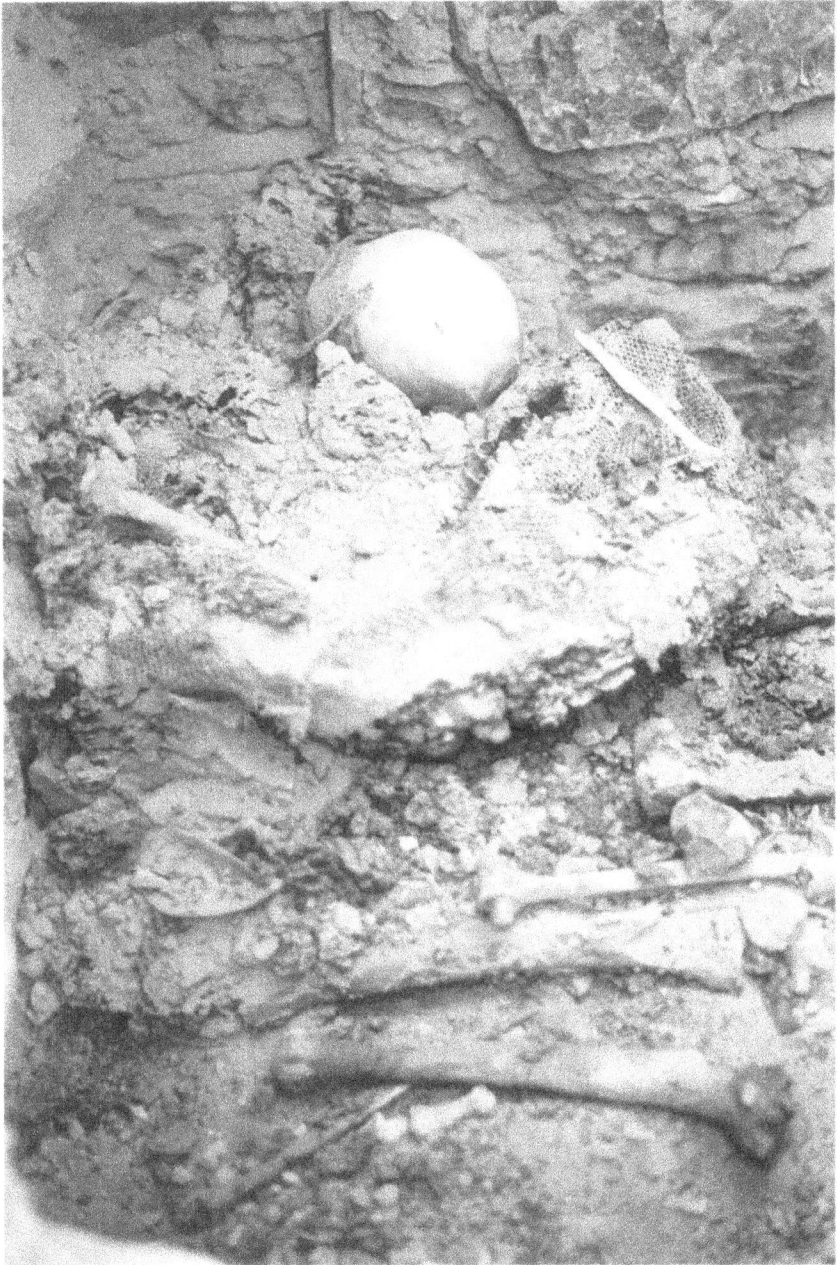

D-11:C-3, Floor 24, Burial III, flexed bundle burial of an adult male. Under the bundle are visible the legs of extended Burial II.

D-11:C-3, Floor 24, extended Burials I (at right) and II, viewed toward the south. Note fragment of infant skull at left center, clam shell, and red diatomite necklace at right.

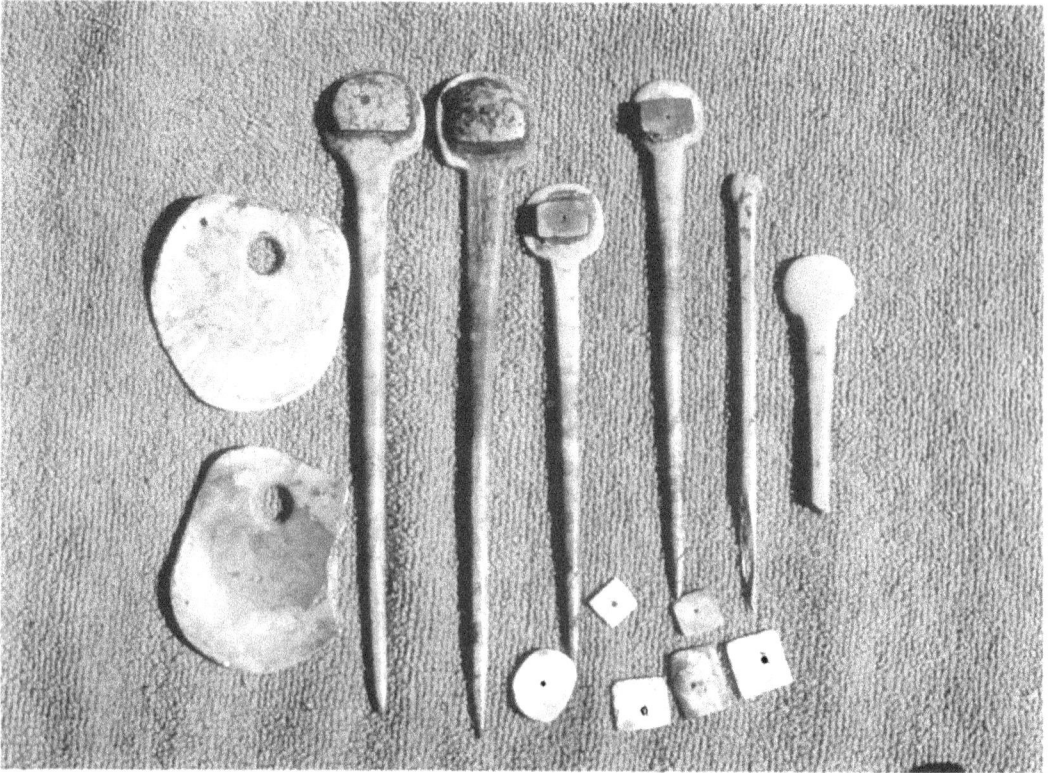

Selection of personal ornaments from the late Preceramic burials in tomb C-12:D-1. At left are a pair of shell ear pendants 5 cm. in diameter which accompanied a male body. The small shell beads at bottom were sewn on a net cap worn by a man, the cap solidly covered with beads. The bone pins, some with turquoises attached, were hairpins worn by a woman.

Rabbit pendant with turquoise eye and shell inlays from tomb D-11:C-3, 5.8 cm. long. (Compare Figs. 74gg, 77.)

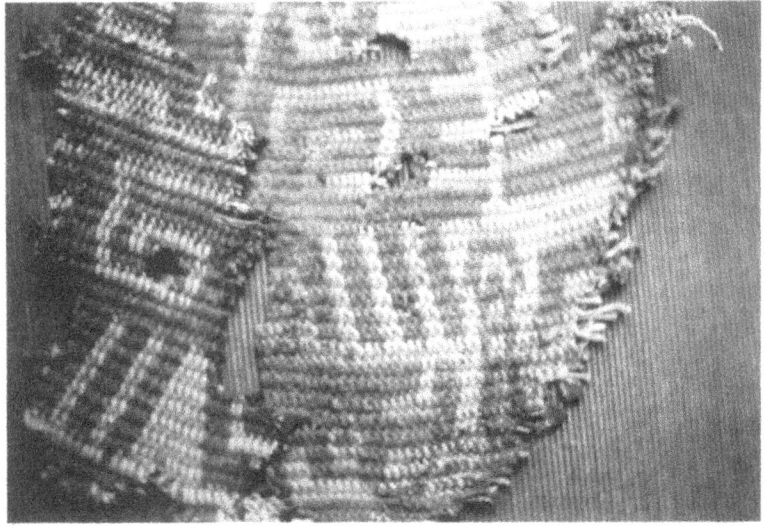

Textile Specimen 90, a looped cotton bag with double birds and one small snake (lower right) from C-11:F-5. (Compare Fig. 139.)

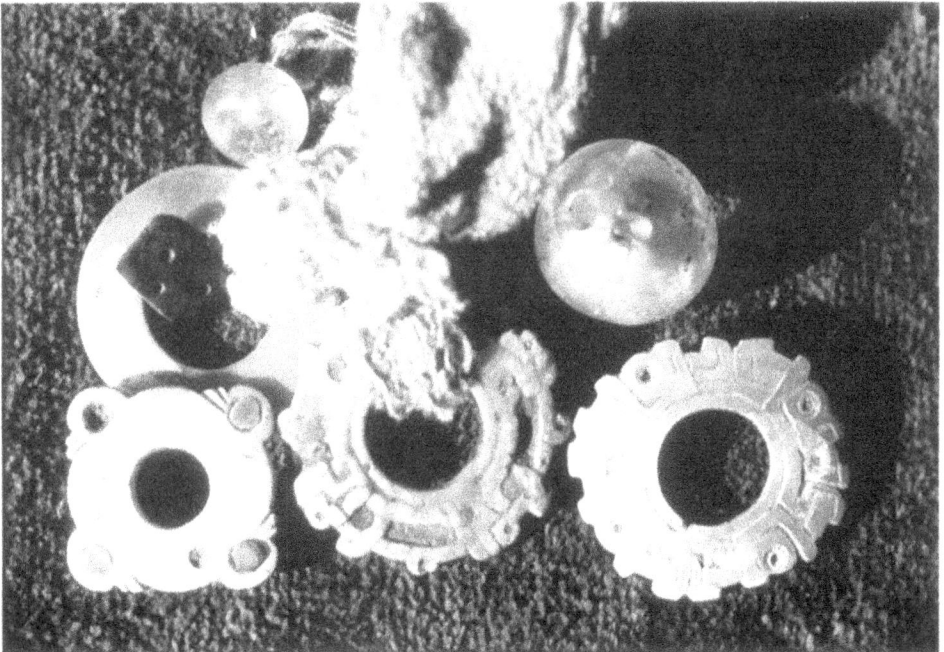

Items from the Initial Period cache H-11:G-10. The cloth has been dated by radiocarbon 3320 B. P. ± 270. (Compare Figs. 83–84.)

Detail from Textile Specimen 14, a looped cotton
bag from a male burial in F-12:B-2 tomb. (Compare Figs. 128–129.)

Offering 13 in tomb C-12:E-10, consisting of
nested baskets, cotton bags, and a gourd bowl. It
is turned upside down to show Textile Specimen
66, with a snake design in black on yellow.
(Compare Figs. 145–146.)

3. Pallasca Province.

large-scale agriculture and finally flows into the Pacific near the town of Santa.

The Tablachaca River has a total length of only a little over 80 km from its source in the Pelagatos Range at 4,950 m altitude on the continental divide to its junction with the Santa at Chuquicara. The lower part of the river used to be known by the name Chuquicara, probably best translated "river which reveals precious metals" (chuqui, "gold"; kcara, "naked"), but recent maps of the Peruvian Instituto Geográfico Militar designate it Tablachaca (tabla, "wood"; chaca, "bridge"), the name taken from the bridge which spans the river at Mollepata, which in recent years has been extended from the upper part to the whole river.

Precipitation, in the form of snow and hail on the mountain peaks and rain on the tundra levels, nourishes the glacial lakes which give rise to the river. The Tablachaca is identified as the stream which drains Laguna Pelagatos to flow through the highlands of Pampas, where it is joined by the Plata, the Sarín, and the Conchucos. There is great sea-

sonal difference in the flow, heaviest in the rainy season of January–March and declining to a minimum in August–December. But the Tablachaca always remains a considerable stream even at low water. At Mollepata, on the north bank in Santiago de Chuco Province, it passes under the Tablachaca Bridge and begins its long, nearly straight descent southward through its deep canyon. From that point it receives water from only a few small or intermittent tributaries: the Huandoval, Cabana, and Ancos on the Pallasca bank and the Angasmarca, Santiago, and Chorobal from the Santiago de Chuco side.

From Allayamucha to Quiroz the river passes through dramatically folded and tilted metamorphic rock with strata of crystalline anthracite which have been one of the principal economic assets of the region in this century. Erosion of those strata blackens the stream, which everywhere carries a heavy load of sediment since it has an average gradient of about 4 percent. It also carries gold, which has been the motive for placer mining operations at several places.

4. Aerial photograph of Tablachaca Canyon taken in 1962. White arrow marks La Galgada site. Courtesy Servicio Aerofotográfico Nacional.

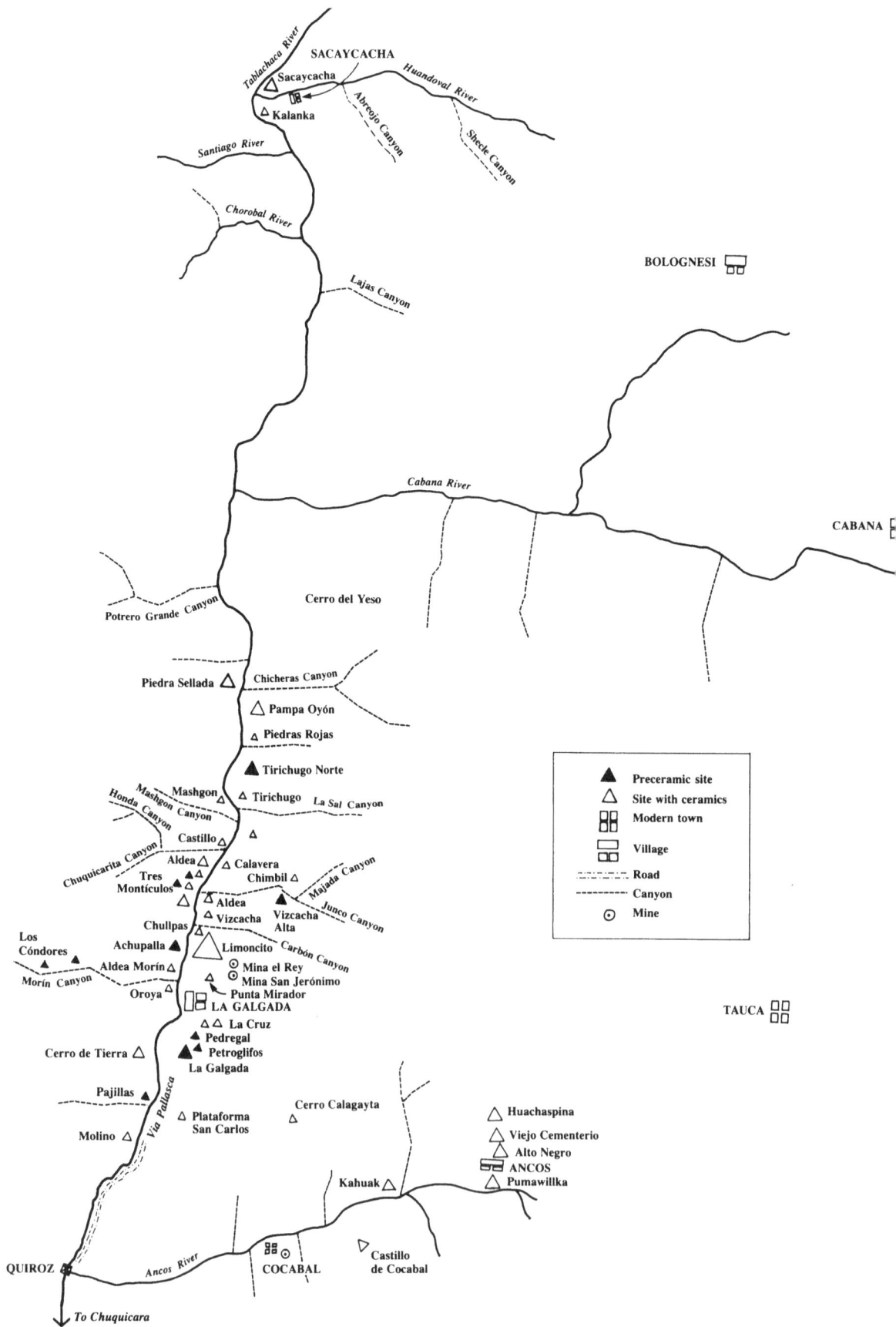

SACAYCACHA

Tablachaca River

Sacaycacha

△ Kalanka

Huandoval River

Abrojo Canyon

Shecle Canyon

Santiago River

Chorobal River

Lajas Canyon

BOLOGNESI

Cabana River

CABANA

Potrero Grande Canyon

Cerro del Yeso

Chicheras Canyon

Piedra Sellada △

△ Pampa Oyón

△ Piedras Rojas

▲ Tirichugo Norte

Mashgon △   △ Tirichugo   La Sal Canyon

Mashgon Canyon

Honda Canyon

Castillo △   △

Chuquicarita Canyon

Aldea △

△ Calavera

Tres △ ▲   Chimbil △   Majada Canyon

Montículos   △

Junco Canyon

△ Aldea

Chullpas   △ Vizcacha   Vizcacha
                              ▲ Alta

Los   △
Cóndores ▲   Achupalla ▲   △ Limoncito   Carbón Canyon

Aldea Morín △   ⊙ Mina el Rey

Morín Canyon   ⊙ Mina San Jerónimo

Oroya △   Punta Mirador

LA GALGADA

△ △ La Cruz

Cerro de Tierra △   ▲ Pedregal

▲ Petroglifos
La Galgada

Pajillas ▲

△ Plataforma
San Carlos

Molino △   Cerro Calagayta
            △   △ Huachaspina

△ Viejo Cementerio

△ Alto Negro

ANCOS

Kahuak △   △ Pumawillka

TAUCA

QUIROZ   Ancos River

▽ Castillo
de Cocabal

COCABAL

To Chuquicara

▲	Preceramic site
△	Site with ceramics
🄳🄳	Modern town
▭	Village
·-·-·	Road
- - -	Canyon
⊙	Mine

In its upper parts the canyon is slightly broader, with terraces on which some agriculture is pursued. There is a sparse natural vegetation of guarango (*Acacia macracantha*), molle (*Schinus molle*), algarrobo (*Prosopis juliflora*), carrizo (*Arundo donax*), chillca (*Baccharis* sp.), pájaro bobo (*Tesaria integrifolia*), etc., on the margins of the river and the lowest terraces. On the higher terraces grow giant cactus (*Curis: Cereus macrostibus*), chimbal (*melocactus: Echino cactus*), pitahaya (*Cactus pitahaya*), chuná or ovinas cactus (*Novoespostoa lanata*), spiny achupallas (*Puya* sp.), and other widely spaced stunted plants.

The steep canyon walls are punctuated at intervals by *huaycos,* deep narrow ravines through which the seasonal rains carry flash floods loaded with mud and rock, racing down from the heights at great velocity with a thunderous roar. As the canyon narrows at Quiroz, just below the basin in which the Preceramic ruins lie, the walls become more precipitous and rocky, with zones of sliding gravel—*graneros* to the local people—and rock falls, or *galgas,* which give La Galgada its name. While the depth of the canyon is less in this lower course, it is also narrower, with an igneous dike nearly damming the river at one point. Even in the narrow parts of the canyon there are numerous ruins of ancient settlements, with house walls and agricultural terraces. Anciently a major trail must have followed the canyon, as an Inca road did at the end of the prehispanic period. In the twentieth century a narrow-gauge railway was built from Chimbote, on the Pacific coast, with two branches, one to Huallanca, on the Santa, the other to La Galgada, principally to serve the anthracite mines. The catastrophic earthquake of 1970 destroyed

the railroad, and it was replaced by a narrow shelf road following the rail line and using its tunnels in the narrowest parts of the canyon.

A survey of about 25 km of the lower terraces at about the middle of the canyon, from Sacaycacha to Quiroz, from the Huandoval River to the Ancos River, shows an abundance of sites of various periods (Fig. 5). This complements Alberto Bueno's earlier survey of sites on the east rim of the canyon at higher elevations in the district of Cabana and Huandoval (Grieder 1978:10). Preceramic sites are concentrated on both banks of the river for at least 8 km near the modern village of La Galgada. Of the eleven Preceramic sites indicated on the map, sketch maps and photographs have been made of three: Pedregal (Fig. 6), Pajillas (Fig. 7), and Tirichuco Norte (Fig. 8). These sites all fall within that 10-km-long basin between Piedra Sellada and Molino in which the canyon widens sufficiently to offer some agricultural opportunities. Judging by the material excavated at the La Galgada site, many of these sites were occupied into the Initial Period. Subsequently, in the Early Horizon Period, the major center in this area seems to have been the Castillo de Cocabal (Fig. 9) overlooking the fertile Ancos River valley. In the Early Intermediate Period, when Pashash dominated the heights around Cabana (Grieder 1978), many sites, large and small, were found throughout the canyon. Based on its preference for locating its temples on the tops of hills, we have called this Early Intermediate culture Cerritos Culture. Its characteristic pottery, with a high percentage of white or cream ware bowls, is found at the ruined town dominating the mouth of the Huandoval River, at Pampa Oyón and Piedras Rojas, at Calavera, at a temple and town protected by a defensive ditch at Vizcacha, and on the Ancos River at a town (Alto Negro), temple (Viejo Cementerio), and

5. Archaeological sites in central part of Tablachaca Canyon. Map by Alberto Bueno Mendoza.

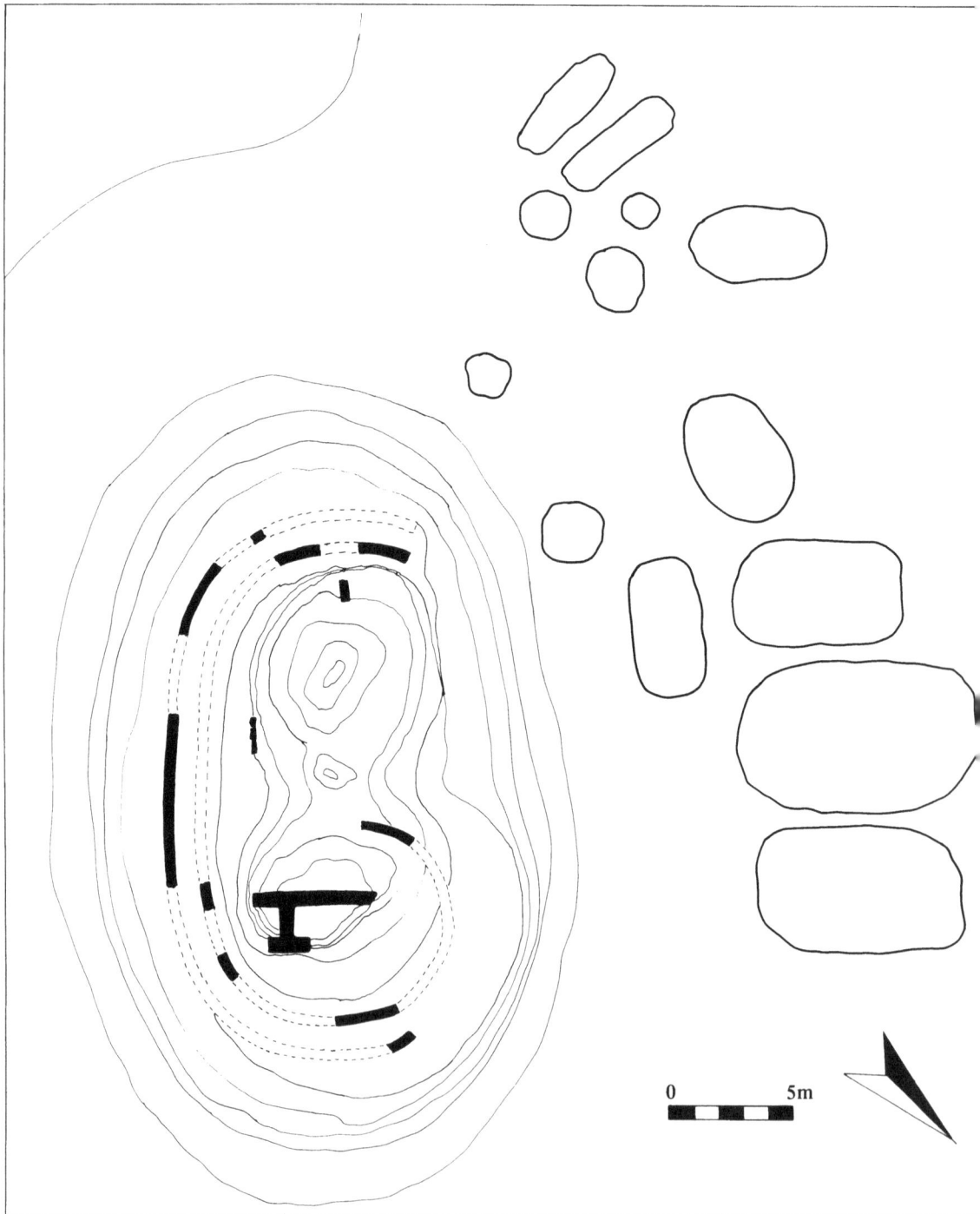

6. Pedregal site. Plan by Alberto Bueno Mendoza.

large circular structure (Pumawillka). The later periods are not surely identified until the Inca remains at Kalanka, at a small burial site near the mouth of the Cabana River, and in the well-preserved town with a tambo, road, and chullpa burial towers at Limoncito.

The individual sites named are an attempt to identify discrete sites of occupation, but more significant is the fact that even these numerous sites do not come close to exhausting the identifiable places with ancient remains. Throughout the whole canyon there are clear and abundant vestiges of ancient habitation, but in that 10-km sector in which the known Preceramic sites are located, both banks were largely or completely occupied, at least in the late Preceramic and Early Intermediate periods.

It is against this background that we must see the La Galgada site, as one of the most important ceremonial and burial areas in a larger, well-populated district, which in Preceramic terms must be considered virtually a metropolitan center (Fig. 10).

What made special the spot on which the Preceramic La Galgada village and mounds were erected? Examination of its geography gives us several different kinds of answers. Although it is entirely within the highland Andean region, the site is low in altitude, with the climatic advantages that provides for agriculture. The basin in which the ruins are located, narrow as it is, is the lowest area in the canyon with the combination of reasonably broad river terraces and abundant permanent water (Fig. 11). The canyon has a special attraction for people who understand canal irrigation because its steep grade allows canals to carry water high above the riverbed in a very short distance, so the wider basins in the canyon could provide a considerable area of irrigated land with a minimum of effort. It is hard to believe that the earliest settlers at La Galgada were not already aware of this advantage, consider-

7. Pajillas site. Terraced platform in center faces east toward Tablachaca River.

8. Tirichuco Norte site. *Above,* sketch of site, which faces west toward river. *At right,* looters' pit in top of upper platform.

9. El Castillo de Cocabal. View is west.

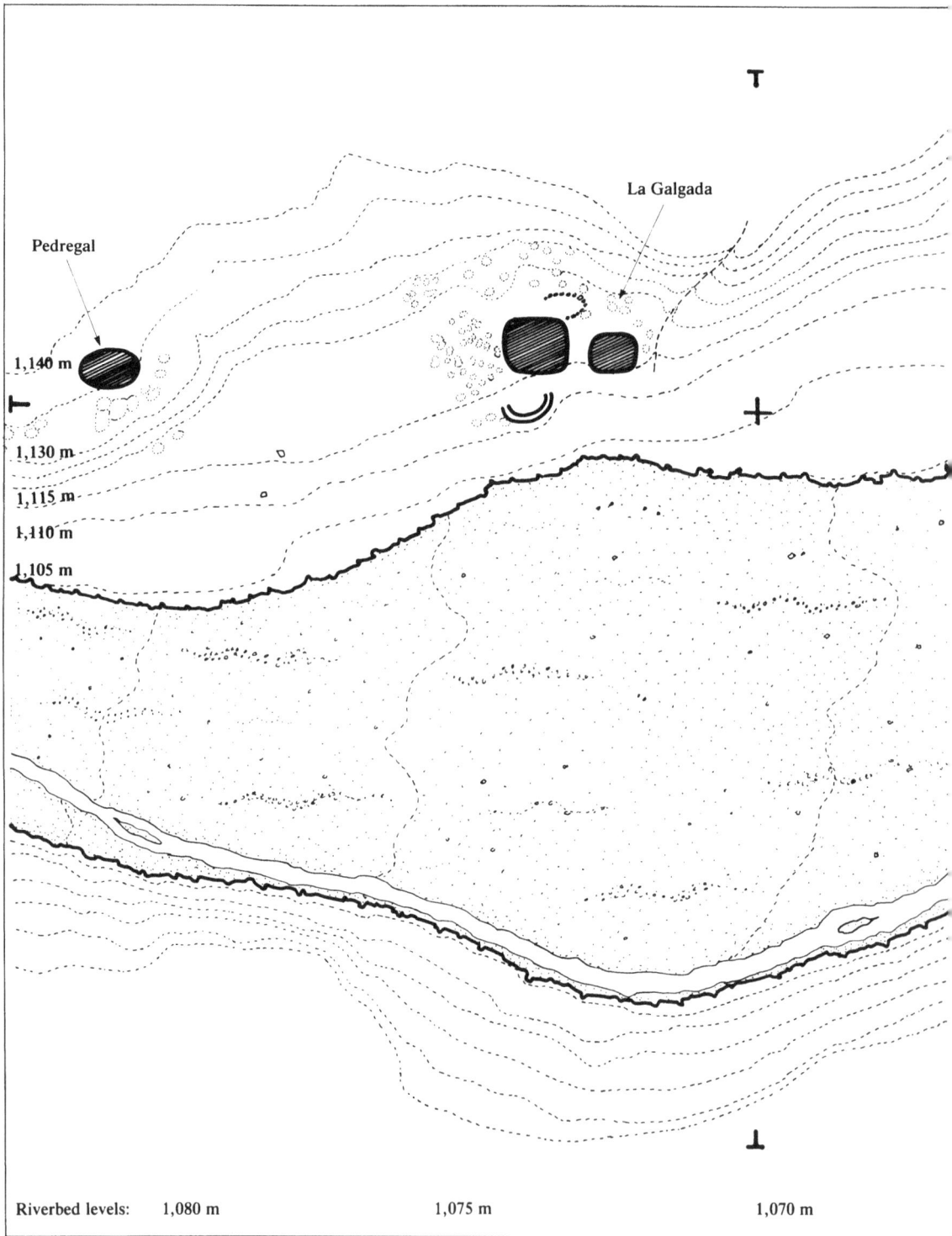

La Galgada

Pedregal

1,140 m

1,130 m

1,115 m

1,110 m

1,105 m

Riverbed levels: 1,080 m   1,075 m   1,070 m

San Carlos

1,130 m
1,120 m
1,110 m
1,105 m
1,100 m
1,095 m

1,100 m
1,120 m
1,130 m

Pajillas

N

0   50   100 m

1,065 m

1,060 m

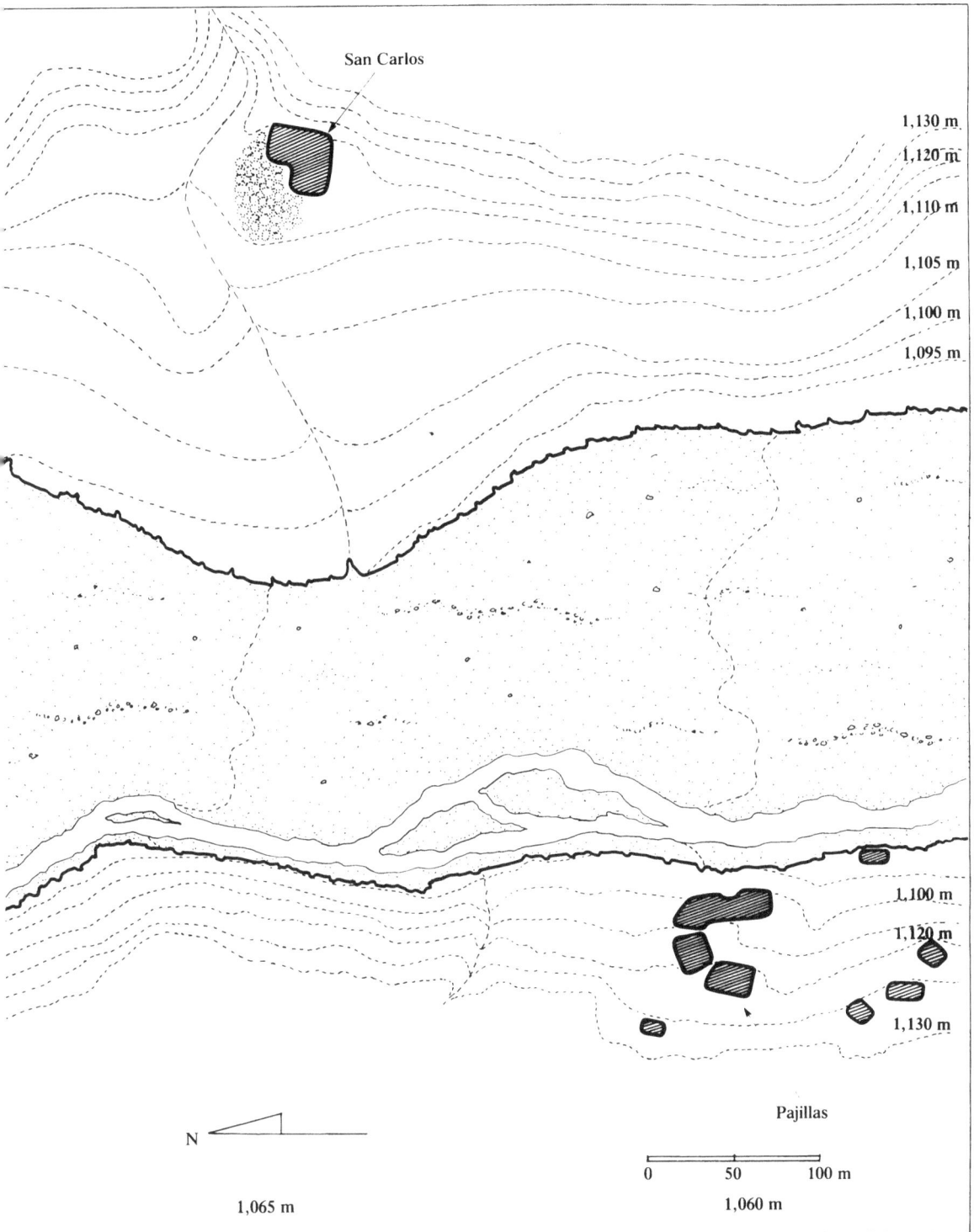

10. Basin of La Galgada site. Map by Bernardino Ojeda.

11. View northward up the Tablachaca River; La Galgada site in center between line of trees on riverbank and mountain ridge.

ing their subsequent agricultural history (Fig. 12).

The agricultural potential was one attraction, another would appear to have been the location on a major trail linking environmental zones. Unlike agriculture, which seems to have been a factor from the start, the role of the site as a center of economic or cultural interaction seems to have become effective later, after the ceremonial area was already constructed. There is no question that in the later part of the Preceramic—about 2500–2000 B.C. according to calibrated radiocarbon measurements—La Galgada was trading in luxury goods with the Pacific coast and probably also with the highlands and the Amazon basin. Our knowledge of other contemporary highland sites is too scant to permit comparisons, but from the evidence at La Galgada alone it appears that this place

was an important center for the diffusion of coastal and northern techniques and ideas, including some whose ultimate source lay in the advanced cultures of Ecuador. Probably the early settlers at La Galgada already perceived that the location was central even in their day.

A third factor seems certain to have played a role throughout the history of the site and may help account for the particular location of the ceremonial buildings. Looking due west from the tops of the mounds the observer sees the peak of Cerro Pajillas ("Straw Mountain") rising high above the other bank of the river. Casual local lore of uncertain antiquity identifies another part of that mountain as a head or face, which would make the central peak the left breast of a great human form which sprawls across the western horizon. Such terreforms are popularly identified

12. Irrigation canal and field at entrance to basin where ruins are located. Collapsed area is behind photographer.

13. Cerro Pajillas terreform west of La Galgada. Head is at right.

in a number of places in modern Peru, perhaps reflecting the ancient personification of mountains as divine beings described by ethnologists working in the southern Peruvian highlands. "The mountain had a head on the summit, a chest and shoulders on the central slopes, and, where two rivers diverge from below the central slopes, a crotch and legs," Joseph Bastien tells us of the Qollahuaya (1973:xviii). Mountains are personified as either male or female; the sacred mountain "Apu Saqro is female; she is the wife of Apu Wañumarka and their children are Apu K'otin (in the southwest) and Apu Quisqamoko (in the south)," Gary Urton tells us (1981: 51). Once the head of the Cerro Pajillas figure is identified, the human image is visible, not merely conventional (Fig. 13). The hollow of the eye is formed by a deep cleft, the chin by a precipice, two peaks mark the breasts and a rounded hilltop the belly, with a distant outcrop indicating the feet. This terreform of mother earth conforms to widespread ancient beliefs that west is the direction dominated by the feminine power

of the earth, where all celestial bodies are swallowed up by the earth, their setting taken as an analogy for death (cf. Reichel-Dolmatoff 1971:46). But since the heavenly bodies spring forth again in the east, each reborn from the earth in its own proper time, the analogy suggests that people may likewise follow that path into the earth with the hope of springing again into renewed life at the appointed time. The building of small circular ceremonial chambers centering on a firepit, most of them oriented to the peak, or breast, of Cerro Pajillas, and converted to tombs, gives support to the idea that the principal Preceramic temples and tombs were located at this particular spot because it was only here that the earth revealed herself anthropomorphically in the mountain on the west.

Thus geography offered ancient people several inducements to settle at La Galgada and, as will be shown, they took advantage of many of the opportunities provided by the nature of the landscape.

3. The History of La Galgada Architecture

TERENCE GRIEDER and ALBERTO BUENO MENDOZA

INTRODUCTION

The ancient inhabitants of La Galgada had various needs which were met by building: shelter for the living, disposal of the bodies of the dead, retention of agricultural land and the channeling of water to it, and the provision of places for ceremonies and rituals. From a utilitarian point of view it is surprising that the greatest efforts went into provision of places for ceremonies and the disposal of the dead, in that order. Building related to agriculture ranks next, with shelter for the living the lowest priority. One might infer from this that building was not viewed as principally a utilitarian activity, but as a means to express a philosophy or religion. In this utilitarian age we sometimes forget that building was viewed in that way by practically all preceding ages.

The site was mapped on a grid of 10-m-square sectors designated by letters of the alphabet from south to north and by numbers from west to east. Each sector could be identified by a letter and number, e.g., C-15 (Fig. 14). Within each sector the same pattern was followed, each square meter being designated by a letter from A through J south to north and by a number from 1 through 10 west to east. This system provides a reference on the horizontal plane for any particular square meter of the site, for example, C-15:E-8. Vertical location within this grid is given by an elevation above sea level or by measurement from a numbered floor to be

found on the section drawings.

Our studies conform to the ancient priorities in that agricultural and domestic constructions were given less attention than ceremonial buildings and tombs. In this chapter we will look first at the domestic and agricultural works and then go on to examine the ceremonial buildings and tombs in greater detail.

HOUSES, CANALS, AND FIELDS

The area of houses around the North and South Mounds (Fig. 14) was mapped by tracing the curvilinear piles of stone which once formed the walls of what we interpret as domestic structures. Three of these buildings were excavated by Ponciano Paredes Botoni in June 1978, and a fourth was studied at the end of the 1981 season. All these studies reached the same conclusion. The houses were round or oval, averaging about 14 m^2 of floor area. Walls were random fieldstone laid in mud mortar. The highest preserved wall was 65 cm high, but the amount of fallen stone suggests that walls were typically about a meter high. We have no evidence of the upper parts, but it would seem likely that they were of thatch on poles. Floors were natural earth, covered with ash to a considerable depth, often 30 cm or more. A possible fireplace was defined inside one of the buildings studied (Fig. 15), but ash was abundant on all the floors. There were also areas of ash deposit outside the

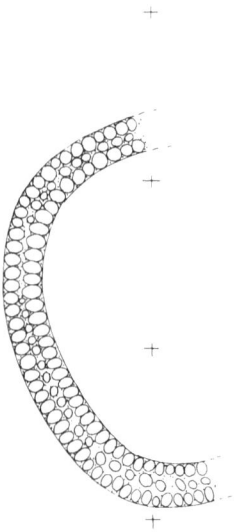
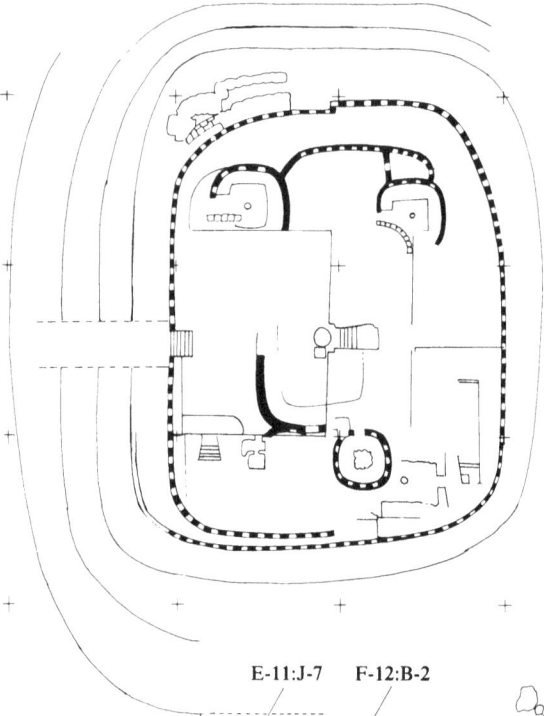
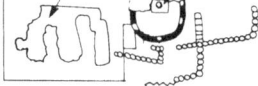
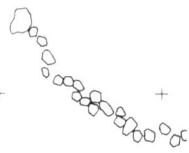

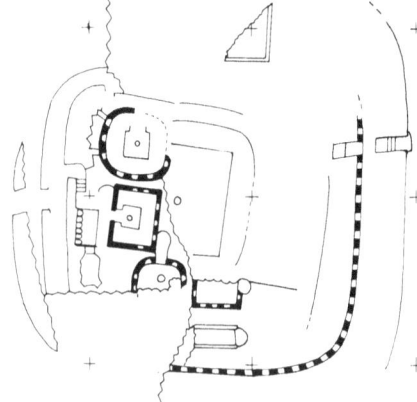

7 8 9 10 11 12 13

K

house

J

I

North Mound

H

G

F

E-11:J-7   F-12:B-2

N

10 m

0

E

D

South Mound

C

B

7 8 9 10 11 12 13

14. Map of La Galgada site on its letter/number grid. (Grid was begun at C-10 in order to allow for extension in all directions.)

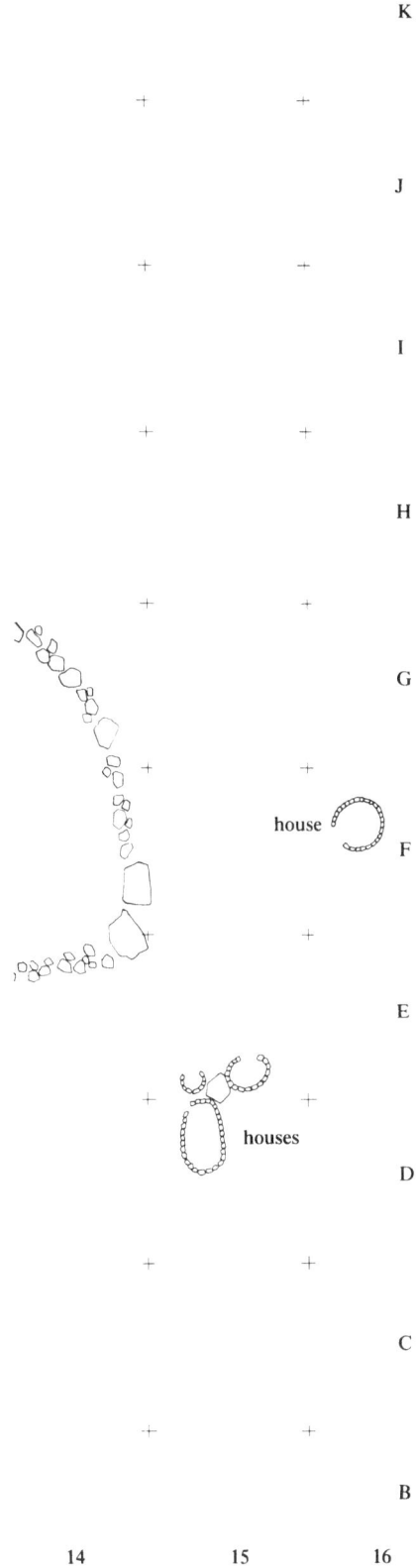

J

I

H

G

house

F

E

houses

D

C

B

15. Excavation of D-15 house by Ponciano Paredes. The whole floor is ashy, but the standing stones are original and seem to mark a hearth.

16. House area DE-15; view southwest. Scale rod is 2 m.

houses, especially in the area just east of the South Mound (Fig. 16), suggesting that cooking may also have been done outside the houses. No particular floor areas dedicated to specific activities could be determined. The appearance of the houses seems to have been much like that still seen in remote parts of the highlands today, with a thick circular fieldstone wall and a deep roof of thatch. The houses at La Galgada would appear to be closer to modern types than to that excavated on the coast at Chilca by Christopher B. Donnan (1964), which represented an earlier period as well as a different environment.

A detailed study of the houses might permit an estimate of the ancient population. At this point we are not certain how many houses were occupied at the same time and are not able to differentiate houses from structures which might have served other purposes.

The other large category of utilitarian construction was agricultural: canals, terrace walls, and field divisions (Figs. 12, 17). Two canals enter the area of the ruins at the north, or upstream, end where the collapse of large sections of the hillside has left the canals some 20 m in the air. To judge by the elevation of the canals, the original intake for the irrigation system must have been in the same location used today for a canal which waters fields at the base of the modern village, in the next basin north of the ruins. The collapse of the river bank at Pedregal (Fig. 17), between the ruins and the modern village, cut the canals and destroyed the supply of water to the fields below the ruins. Smith's study of the floral remains (Chapter 7 in this volume) makes it clear that the Preceramic inhabitants were responsible for the system, which was surely used by later people, just as part of the system remains in use today. Two canals (Fig. 18), a narrower one higher and a wider parallel one about a

17. North end of site basin: *a,* house platform of
Pedregal site; *b,* Inca road; *c,* modern auto road;
d, ancient irrigation canal (note its collapse at
left); *e,* ancient field terrace; *f,* ancient field
pattern.

18. The pair of ancient irrigation canals south of
the mounds.

half-meter lower, follow the natural contour at about the 1,108 m elevation. Presumably the wider canal was the later one, set at a lower level to speed the flow or counteract elevation of the land. Charles R. Ortloff, Michael E. Moseley, and Robert A. Feldman (1982:575–576) describe tectonic uplift as affecting canal building, as it might have happened at La Galgada. Although the canals have not been traced beyond the ruins, it seems probable that both the canals and the field system extended farther south in the basin.

Field patterns and cultivation patterns are still clear in the area below the mounds, but we cannot be certain about the period they represent. Local residents confirm that there has been no modern use of this area for agriculture, so the field patterns are probably prehispanic, as they appear to be. Back-and-forth furrows mark the fields, which are divided into terraces, with stone walls dividing field areas within the terrace levels.

THE CEREMONIAL BUILDINGS

The most important buildings to the ancient builders, to judge by their careful planning and construction, their fine finish, frequent rebuilding, and eventual dedication as tombs, were those which formed and stand on the North and South Mounds (Fig. 19). The absence of tools and food in them and the presence of parrot feathers, deer antlers, and other exceptional items on their floors, as well as their eventual re-use as tombs, all encourage the belief that they served ceremonial functions. Similar structures at other sites—Kotosh, Huaricoto, Los Gavilanes (Izumi and Terada, eds. 1972; Burger and Salazar Burger 1980; Bonavia 1982)—have been considered temples or public structures by previous investigators. Richard L. Burger and Lucy Salazar Burger have defined, on the basis of buildings similar to those found on the La Galgada mounds, a "Kotosh Reli-

gious Tradition" and suggested the kinds of ritual practices which might have been carried out in such buildings (1980).

Our knowledge of the architectural history of the mounds was obtained by excavation, which requires the destruction of the upper layers to obtain information about the lower. The great importance of the buildings of the later Preceramic, which were found relatively intact, militated against their destruction and leaves us largely ignorant of the deeper and earlier levels. We judge that there remain about 13 m of construction, presumably superimposed buildings or mound fill, below the parts excavated and reported here.

Early Buildings of Waterworn Stone

The earliest constructions are in general easily identified by the waterworn boulders or cobblestones of which their walls were built. The sequence found at La Galgada, in which waterworn stone is early, to be replaced by quarrystone, is the opposite of that found in the similar Preceramic structure at nearby Tirichuco B, and also opposite to that found by Robert Alan Feldman (1980:47, 95) at Aspero, on the coast. The usefulness of these technical practices for relative dating does not extend beyond the individual sites. Waterworn stones were easily available in the wide bed of the river and were used occasionally in all periods as fill, but among the earliest dated structures and the deepest excavated layers at La Galgada, walls built of cobblestones are the principal type. Stones vary from the size of large watermelons, probably too large for one person to lift, to the size of grapefruit. They appear to be an unstable material with which to build a wall, but the lowest course was made of large boulders and successive courses were held in place by a large amount of mud mortar.

The largest structure made of waterworn stone, and also built of the largest boulders, is the ring platform surrounding the circular

19. Reconstruction of the ceremonial area during the late Preceramic Period, showing Floor 30 on the North Mound.

20. Ring platform of circular plaza, HI-7, viewed from North Mound. Foreground is the modern road built in 1975.

21. North Mound, west front, showing the Black Chamber (H-10:F-4) at arrow. Scale (30 cm) rests on bench level.

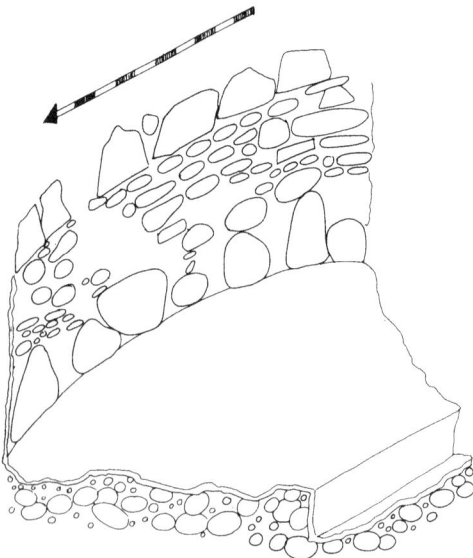

22. Black Chamber (H-10:F-4). Scale 1 m.

plaza west of the North Mound (Fig. 20). The boulders were laid in gravel, rather than mud, but the structure was presumably originally sealed in a layer of mud plaster. The eastern half of the circle is now beneath the road, and the visible western half has been damaged by construction of two Early Intermediate Period houses against its western margin and by twentieth-century railroad and road building, not to speak of millennia of erosion. Since waterworn boulders do not occur naturally on the high river terrace, and particularly not in semicircular patterns, the existence of the structure is certain, but we can say little about its original appearance beyond the facts that it had a diameter of about 18 m and its top surface was about 2.5 m wide. The circle is the most westerly construction in the North and South Mound group. Subsequent to its construction two successive irrigation canals were built curving along its west wall to bring water to the fields on the river terraces.

Facing the circle, and now remaining as a fragment just east of the road, was a small chamber built of river cobbles (Figs. 21–22). This chamber was engulfed by later building and was largely destroyed when the main stairway was constructed. Excavation showed that it was set on a layer of river cobbles resting on a deeper layer of large quarrystones—that is, broken stone unsmoothed by water, laid as coarse fill for the cobble level, which was conceived as part of the structure. That excavation did not reach sterile soil.

The remains of this chamber, at H-10: F-4, nicknamed the Black Chamber for its unique wall color, consist of just 1.80 m of the curving east wall preserved to the height of 1 m. The base of the wall was built of large waterworn stone, then a series of breadloaf-size (about 20 cm long) cobbles laid parallel to the wall surface, and finally a course of quarrystone, which may have been

interrupted by niches. The surface was covered with mud plaster and painted black. Although there are fragments of mud plaster bearing black or blue paint in other places in fill, this is the only standing wall which was painted black. Considerable areas of mud plaster with its paint layer were found intact.

The black wall belonged to a type of building we have called a "ritual chamber," the commonest building type in these two mounds. A bench level extended outward from the wall about 95 cm, ending in a 20-cm step down to the floor level, of which just a small piece remains. This is an early example of the use of the bench level, for some of the other early chambers have flat floors without the bench. If this chamber resembled the others, it had a firepit in the center of the floor, probably vented by a horizontal channel under the floor in the direction of the door. If the chamber was oriented toward the circular plaza, the door would have been on the west.

Belonging to the same early period of building with river cobbles is a set of buildings which now lie between the two mounds in sectors EF-11/12 (Fig. 23). The deepest, with its floor at 1,118.90 m altitude, and thus presumably the earliest, is the ritual chamber F-12:B-2, which had been converted into a tomb by removing its original roof, filling the northern half of the chamber with stone, and laying flat stones for a new ceiling. Bueno discovered the circular stone cover of the tomb entrance at the end of the 1980 field season, recognized its significance, and prudently covered it until it could be studied in 1981. Raised, that cover revealed a small antechamber of quarrystone with cotton cords running like umbilical cords from the surface down into the tomb, where three bodies were laid (see Figs. 66–67). The radiocarbon tests on the contents of the firepit (TX-4450) gave an uncorrected reading of 3820 ± 100 B.P., presumably

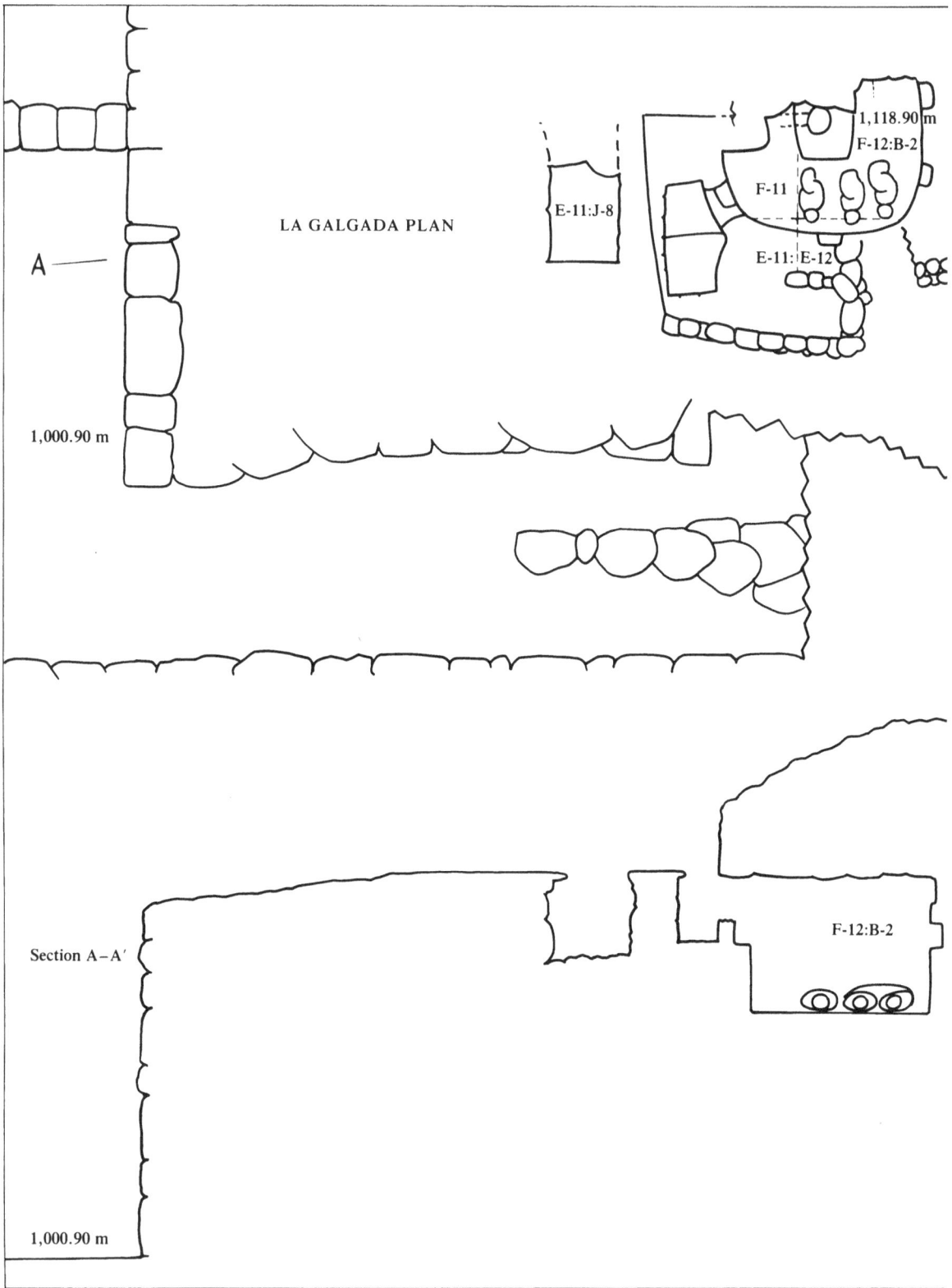

LA GALGADA PLAN

A ————

E-11:J-8

1,118.90 m
F-12:B-2

F-11

E-11: E-12

1,000.90 m

Section A–A′

F-12:B-2

1,000.90 m

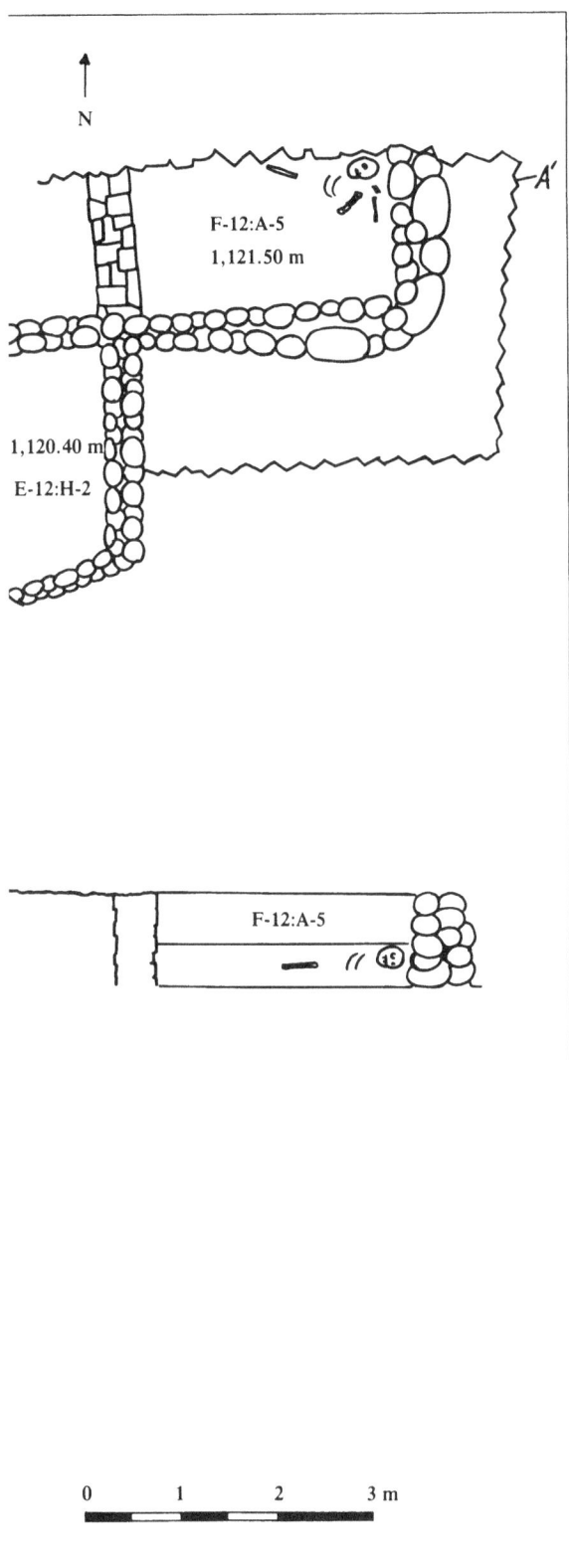

marking the final use of the firepit. That age measurement may be calibrated to the period 2625–1980 B.C. (see Chapter 4, especially Table 2).

Figure 24 is a reconstruction drawing of the building before its conversion to a tomb. Since the southern half of the building is intact, the drawing is not speculative. This building has a bench level of an unusual sort. In later buildings the entrance through the door was onto the floor level with its firepit, the bench being interrupted by the doorway. In F-12:B-2 the bench really serves as a floor, with the firepit in a small sunken area in the center. The design of the walls is also different from the common pattern of later chambers, which divide the wall in half with a narrow setback on which the niches were set. In F-12:B-2 the niches are in the flat surface of the wall, the setback being near the top of the wall. Despite its unconventional use of these elements, this small chamber employs the elements which La Galgada builders took as the definition of their style: the subcircular outer wall, west

23. Sector EF. Section is on line A–A'.

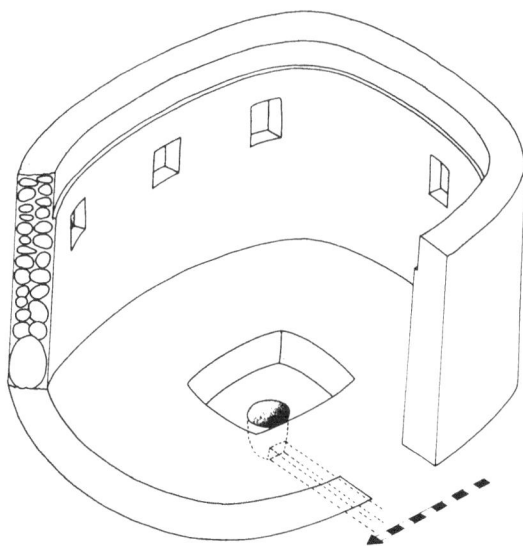

24. F-12:B-2 chamber. Scale 1 m.

or north orientation, floor and bench, firepit and vent, niches and a setback or dado. The original chamber was about 2.30 × 2.85 m. At the center is a firepit about 30 cm in diameter with a ventilator shaft extending westward from the bottom of the pit. The ancient doorway is covered by the massive stones of the tomb wall, but in all discovered cases the ventilator shaft passed under the center of the doorway, which allows us to presume that this chamber was oriented westward. The height of the walls is 1.62 m, with rectangular niches 30 cm high set halfway up the wall. Halfway between the top of the niches and the top of the wall a narrow setback articulates the wall. The walls and floors were covered with a coat of brown mud plaster and finished with a thick coat of pearly white paint, which is still in excellent condition. This white is the common finish of ceremonial buildings at La Galgada; its material has not been analyzed, but deposits of white mineral, perhaps talc, are found in the canyon and appear likely sources for the white wall finish.

To the south and east of F-12:B-2 there are other constructions of river cobbles (Fig. 23). Since their floors are at higher levels (1,120.40 and 1,121.50 m altitude), they are presumably of slightly later date. Burned wood from the floor of the deeper chamber (E-12:H-2; sample TX-4449) gave a calibrated date range of 2540–1960 B.C. The cobblestone walls are preserved to only 1.20 m height. They join the longer and more massive wall of F-12:A-5, again a double-face wall set on large waterworn boulders. Both of these buildings had several floor levels, and the later floor of F-12:A-5, which covered a burial without offerings, accompanied a dividing wall built of quarrystones, good evidence of the change of building materials at this site.

The last of the river-cobble buildings is a buried ritual chamber in the North Mound identified as I-11:B-8, the presumed location of its original firepit, now buried under the massive stone pier that supports a stone roof. Its floor, at 1,124.17 m altitude, was largely destroyed when looters discovered the chamber in 1928 (a date given by newspaper scraps in the chamber). When we examined the chamber in 1979 nothing remained of burials or offerings which were entombed in the converted chamber.

The chamber can be studied, however, as it was before conversion to a tomb (Fig. 25). It was about 3.80 m square, all the walls curving to rounded corners. The doorway was in the middle of the west wall, flanked by a pair of niches. There were also four niches in each of the outer walls, although only two remain visible in the east wall. The walls are 1.90 m high, divided in half by a setback on which the slightly trapezoidal niches were set. The walls are double-face, of river cobbles in mud mortar, plastered with brown mud painted plain white inside and out.

The original lintel of the door is still in place, four wooden poles 5–6 cm in diameter, two of maguey and two of algarroba, both locally available. This suggests that the original ceiling may have been of wooden beams, probably covered with mud and painted white. That roof would necessarily have been replaced when the chamber was buried under fill for later constructions. Also destroyed, but probably by the twentieth-century looters pitting the floor, was the vent for the firepit, which presumably passed under the door on the west side.

This early phase of building is of special interest because in it we find established several features with wider connections: two distinctive building types—the circular plaza and the firepit chamber—the preference for waterworn stone in building, and the subcircular plan. Each of these traits is worth a long analysis, but the general range of each

25. I-11:B-8 chamber, interior north wall. Note waterworn stones in wall, abundant mud mortar, mud-plastered dado and wall around niche, and white paint.

type will just be noted here.

The circular plaza first appears in Preceramic buildings (from north to south) at Alto Salaverry in the Moche Valley (Pozorski and Pozorski 1979:37–39), two examples at Salinas in the Chao Valley (Cárdenas 1979: Figs. 14, 37, 39), at Piedra Parada near Supe (Pozorski and Pozorski 1979:56), and perhaps Sechín Alto in the Casma Valley, where it lies between the arms of a U-shaped temple (Alan Sawyer, personal communication), which may place it in the Initial Period, in which that combination is common on the north and central coasts of Peru (Feldman 1980:211). The circular plaza is found

as well at Chavín de Huantar in the Early Horizon (Lumbreras 1977).

The firepit chamber has a still longer history, perhaps going back to Asian sources of the widely used American pit house. Ceremonial versions include the British Columbian wooden clan house with a firepit in the central sunken floor surrounded by benches, the Southwestern kiva, which had subfloor ventilators similar to those at La Galgada (Fewkes 1908), and the Aztec rock-cut ceremonial chamber at Malinalco. It appears in the Peruvian Preceramic contemporaneously at Kotosh and its neighbors, at Huaricoto, and at Los Gavilanes, as well as at La Galgada. These relationships will be examined further below (see the section "Some Preliminary Conclusions about the Chambers").

Waterworn stone was widely used as a building material in early periods, especially as a facing for platform revetments. There are interesting examples in Mesoamerica at San Lorenzo (Coe and Diehl 1980:1:34), in Mound 12 at Chiapa de Corzo (Mason 1960: 9), and in the earliest level at Cuicuilco (Vaillant 1944:59). In Peru it was widely used where it was easily available, mostly for fill, but also as single-face walls of semi-subterranean houses or as revetments. Both those uses are found at Huaca Prieta (Bird 1948a:22–23). La Galgada currently appears to be the only one with freestanding double-face walls of river cobbles.

The subcircular plan of the chambers has connections in a narrower region, restricted to the Santa and Casma valleys. Among the other Preceramic sites it is found only at Huaricoto. A little later it is found in the Casma Valley in the important temples of Moxeke and Cerro Sechín. The numerous ritual chambers at Kotosh and its neighbors are all rectangular in plan, as is the example at Los Gavilanes.

A Series of Quarrystone Chambers in the North Mound

By about 2200 B.C. (judging from radiocarbon measurement TX-2463), building walls with waterworn stone had gone out of style and angular broken stone quarried in the hills was used for all wall construction. Stones were usually roughly squared into rectangular blocks, sometimes as small as modern bricks. They were laid in mud mortar and were probably always covered with a finish of mud plaster, although in many cases the stone masonry is so handsome it is hard to imagine covering it. In addition to making the stones easier to lay up into walls, the flat surfaces also permitted sharper

articulations of the walls and a smooth surface with a thinner and evener coat of mud plaster than was possible on the cobble walls.

The tendency to begin walls with a first course of very large boulders, seen in the walls of waterworn stone, was retained in the quarrystone walls. The first course was made of large blocks set upright with a flat surface on the face of the wall. The spaces between these upright blocks were filled with smaller stones making three or four courses (Fig. 52). This pattern of wall building became a basic element in the Andean tradition, with important later examples in Tiahuanaco and Inca architecture.

Around 2200 B.C. the top of the North Mound had at least five ritual chambers, and in the areas we did not excavate there is room for another one or more. Of the five known examples, all were accessible at the same time, although the oldest could be reached only through a shaft. The pattern was a large central chamber with its firepit at H-11:E-10, facing west, with smaller chambers and tombs clustered around it (Fig. 26). There are traces of quarrystone buildings earlier than this group; for example, the east wall of the later tomb H-12:C-2 is an old white-finished quarrystone wall, and the floor and east wall of the square firepit of the large central chamber are white quarrystone constructions. (There are also older examples of quarrystone building in the South Mound which will be discussed below.) Our excavations in the North Mound stopped at this level, which we call Floor 30, in order to leave a coherent set of structures intact. Structures below Floor 30 were investigated only when they could be reached without excavation, as in the cases of I-11:B-8, G-12:I-1, and H-12:C-2, all of which could be reached through ancient shafts.

The main chamber appears always to have faced west, but the subsidiary chambers flanking it could be oriented either north

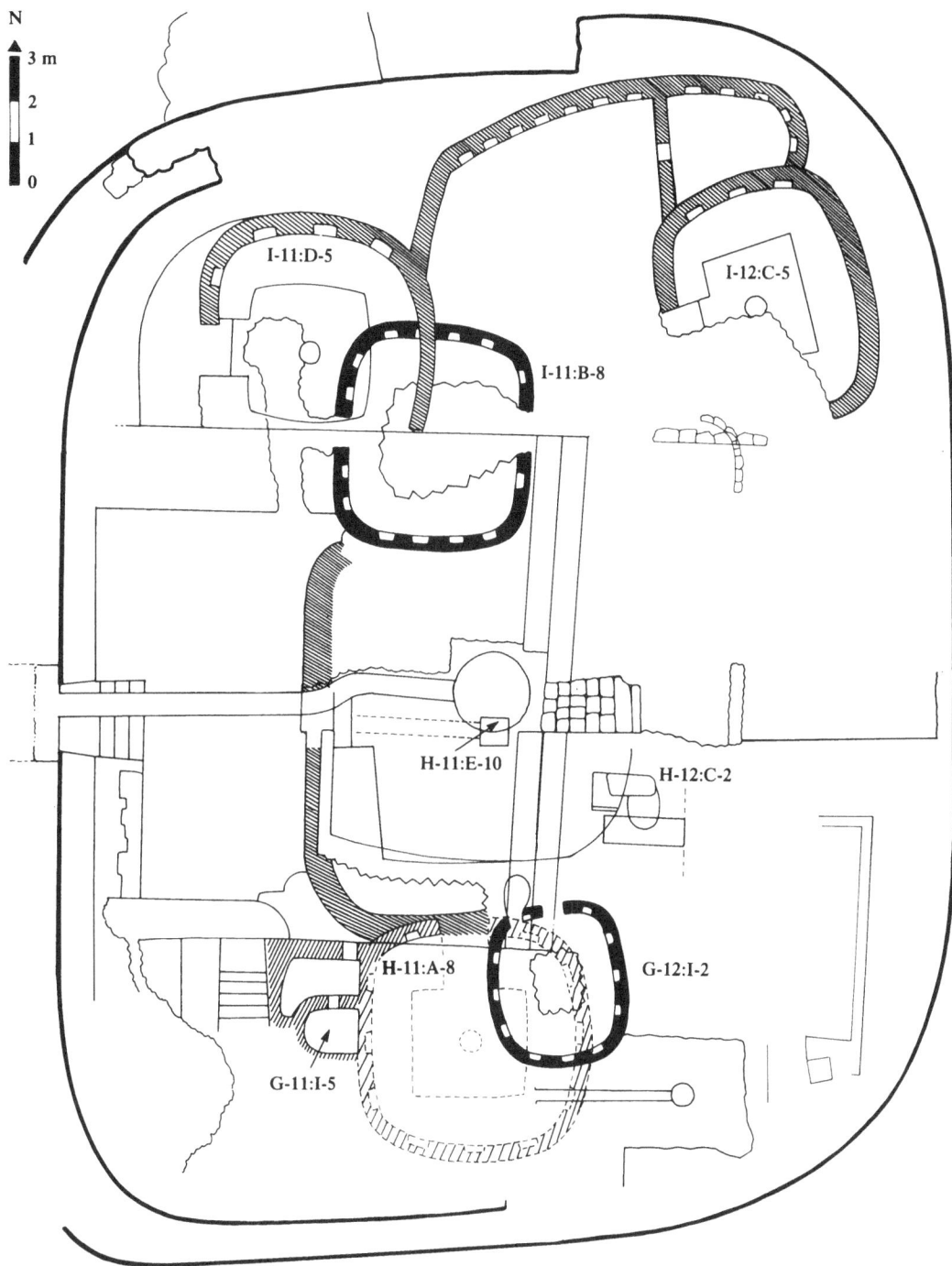

26. Plan of structures on North Mound, GHI-11/12. Solid black walls are earliest (Floor 40 level and earlier), hatched are late Preceramic (Floor 30 and associated structures), and outlined areas are Initial Period (Floor 20 and later). Dotted lines show hypothetical former structures inferred from what remains.

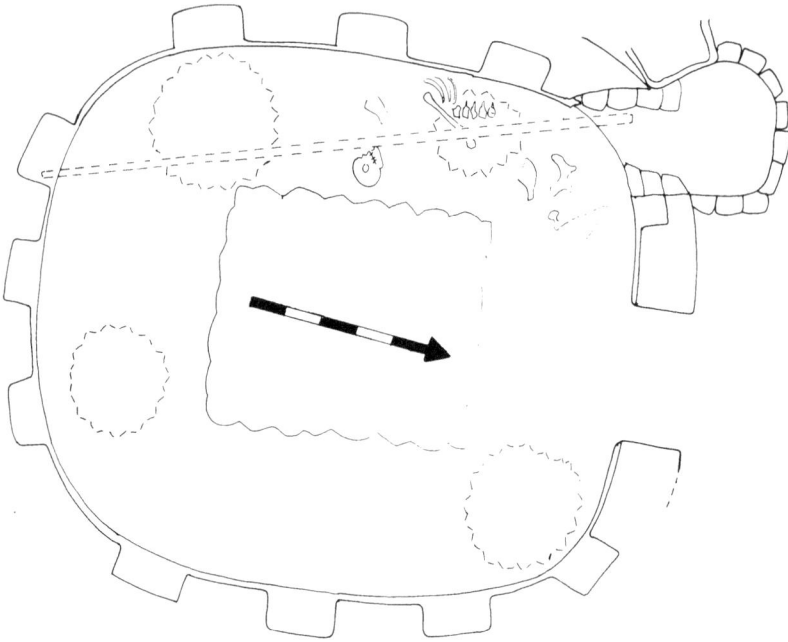

27. G-12:I-2 chamber. Scale 1 m.

28. Interior wall of G-12:I-2 with quarrystone (above niche).

29. Small black handprints on wall of G-12:I-2.

or west. The earliest quarrystone chamber of which we have evidence on the North Mound (Fig. 27) is on a slightly lower level than the last river cobble building, I-11:B-8. The floor of this new chamber (identified as G-12:I-2 for the presumed location of its firepit, which is now covered by the stone column which supports the stone roof of the tomb), is at 1,123.83 m altitude. The walls are of small, roughly squared stones laid to make flat surfaces, articulations, and lintels on niches (Fig. 28). The chamber measures 3.10 × 2.70 m, with three niches in each wall except the north, where the doorway is flanked by niches. The 35-cm-thick walls are finished both inside and out with mud plaster painted white, which indicates that the chamber was originally freestanding, not subterranean. Just to the east of the inside of the doorway there are two small black handprints, both hands of a child or small adult (Fig. 29), but they may have been placed there when the chamber was converted to a tomb. At that time the doorway was blocked with rubble fill and a new entrance was cut through the northwest corner which led through a 1.90-m shaft to the main chamber, on Floor 30. After the conversion of this chamber to a tomb, four bundle burials were placed on its floor, as shown by indentations purposely made to hold them. The bundle in the northwest corner had broken, leaving the bones scattered; these bones have not been catalogued. All the other bundles had been removed entirely, presumably by modern looters who reached the chamber through a deep hole which evidently exposed the old doorway, but which later caved in and concealed the chamber.

Although the G-12:I-2 chamber remained accessible from the main chamber, it evidently could no longer fulfill its ritual functions, since its firepit had been buried under the stone roof support, so a new chamber was built at a higher level, partly overlapping the earlier chamber, and like it in facing north into the main chamber. This structure is known only by a fragment of wall showing the doorway and part of the northwest wall with one niche. That fragment is unusual in having the articulation of the dado continue vertically as a frame for the doorway. This wall is identified as H-11:A-8.

The G-12:I-2 chamber was part of a complex on top of the North Mound before about 2200 B.C. We have only hints about the central structure on the mound at that time— that it was built of quarrystone and finished white is suggested by the walls in the Floor 30 firepit and the H-12:C-2 tomb—but the G-12:I-2 chamber flanked the central space on the south and faced north, into the center, and the old cobble-walled I-11:B-8 chamber flanked it on the north and faced west, probably parallel to the central chamber (see Fig. 26). If that reconstruction is correct then these buildings established the pattern which we find later when the Floor 30 group was built at a level about 2 m higher.

We ordinarily expect a temple floor to be on the same level as or a higher level than the floor of its entrance courtyard, but in these early building groups the opposite is the case (Fig. 30). The floor of the central chamber on Floor 30 is 30 cm lower than the courtyard floor west of it. When Floor 20 was built in the central chamber and the courtyard they were on exactly the same level, but subsequently the courtyard floor was rebuilt at a higher level, with two white-finished steps leading from the new court floor (Court Floor 18) down into the central chamber. Court Floor 18 remained in use as a later building raised the floor levels in the central chamber until with Floor 13 the chamber and the courtyard were on the same level and merged into a single space. Later building eliminated the chamber form entirely, substituting a central stairway to a higher platform, of whose buildings we have only traces.

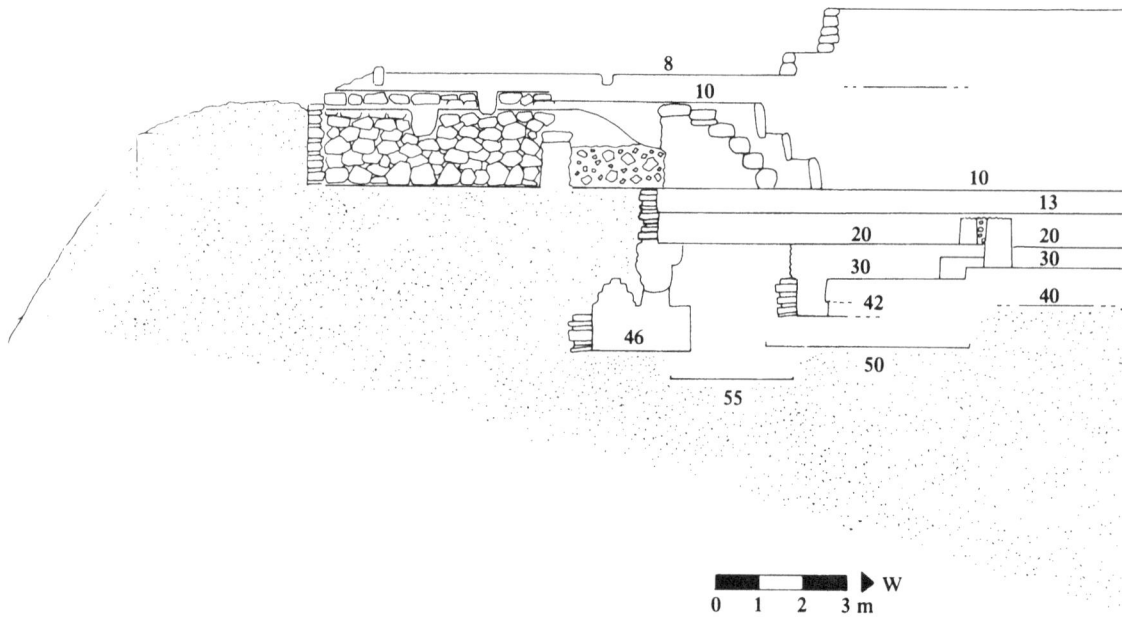

30. Numbering of floor levels in North Mound. Synthetic section.

That pattern of climbing a platform or mound and then stepping down into an enclosed chamber was standard at La Galgada for centuries and surely expressed a basic religious concept. The sacred was set apart from the level of daily life, as on a hill or mountain, but was down and inside, not in the sky. This interpretation of the architectural form must be combined with other evidence, which includes feathers, depictions of birds, and a preference for green or blue-green stone, all of which have celestial implications, to give a picture of the builders' complex religion.

The central chamber on Floor 30 seems to be an orthodox ritual chamber with thick, curving walls, a small, deep firepit, and a bench which defined a rectangular floor. Our excavations revealed about one-third of this chamber, from the firepit to the doorway on the west to the center of the south bench and wall (Fig. 31). That 6 × 6 m excavation gives grounds for reconstruction drawings of the other two-thirds without the destruction of the later levels in those areas.

The outer dimensions of the chamber were approximately 9 × 12 m, with the square firepit as the focal point. The firepit had been set against an earlier wall, and a mud-plaster cap had been added around the rim to convert it from square to round (Fig. 33, lower right; Fig. 34). This is the earliest chamber on top of the North Mound to have a preserved bench, in this case 50 cm high and approximately 125 cm wide. (The Black Chamber had a low bench earlier and the floors of I-11:B-8 and G-12:I-2 had been destroyed, so we cannot be sure whether they had benches or flat floors. In the South Mound we can trace the development of the

31. Excavated area of central chamber on Floor 30 (H-11:EF-10).

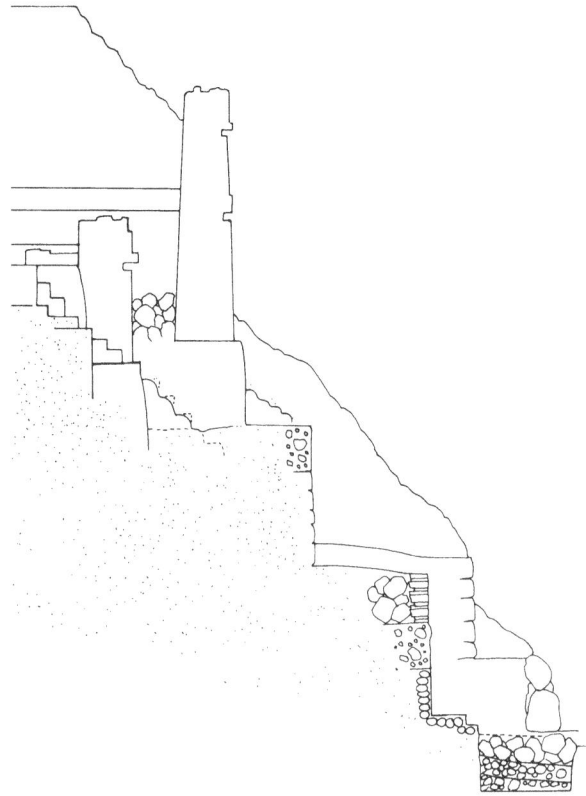

bench in more detail.) At the doorway there was a 30-cm step up to the court level. All the surfaces were built of quarrystone finished with mud plaster and painted a smooth, brilliant white.

The central chamber on Floor 30 (Fig. 32) is flanked on the north by two smaller chambers, I-11:D-5 near the front of the mound and I-12:C-5 (Fig. 33) near the back. Both chambers face approximately west, but their floors are at different levels, the one near the front 1.30 cm higher than the central chamber and the one at the back 2 m higher than the central chamber, its floor being at the level of the central chamber's roof. On the south the central chamber still had a shaft open down to the tombs built in G-12:I-2 and a doorway opening from its bench level into another chamber at H-11:A-8, the bench level acting as the higher courtyard

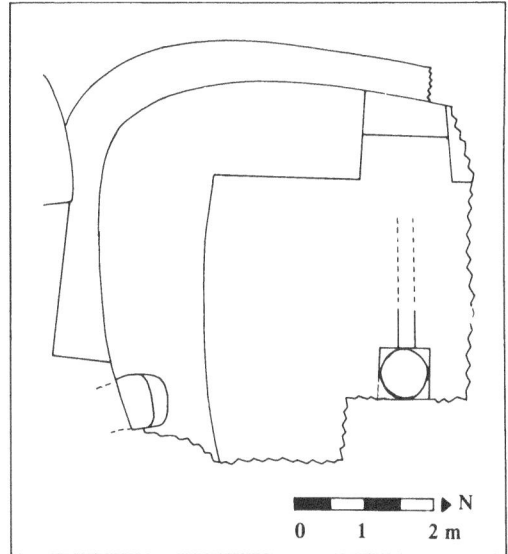

floor for the side chamber. It is apparent from this layout that there was already a tendency for the two sides of the platform to rise to higher levels than the center, with the flanking temples set on platforms which made the central chamber semisubterranean. The northeast corner of the central chamber's outer wall could not have been freestanding, but must have served as a revetment for the platform of I-12:C-5. Court Floor 20 was added while Floor 30 was still in use in the chamber, making one more step up from the chamber to the court (Fig. 30).

When Floor 30 was buried, about 2150 B.C., that pattern began to shift toward a symmetrical U-shaped platform which covered the whole top of the mound. We find that pattern in its mature phase, with all the forms rectangular, at Huaca de los Reyes (Moseley and Watanabe 1974:155) and

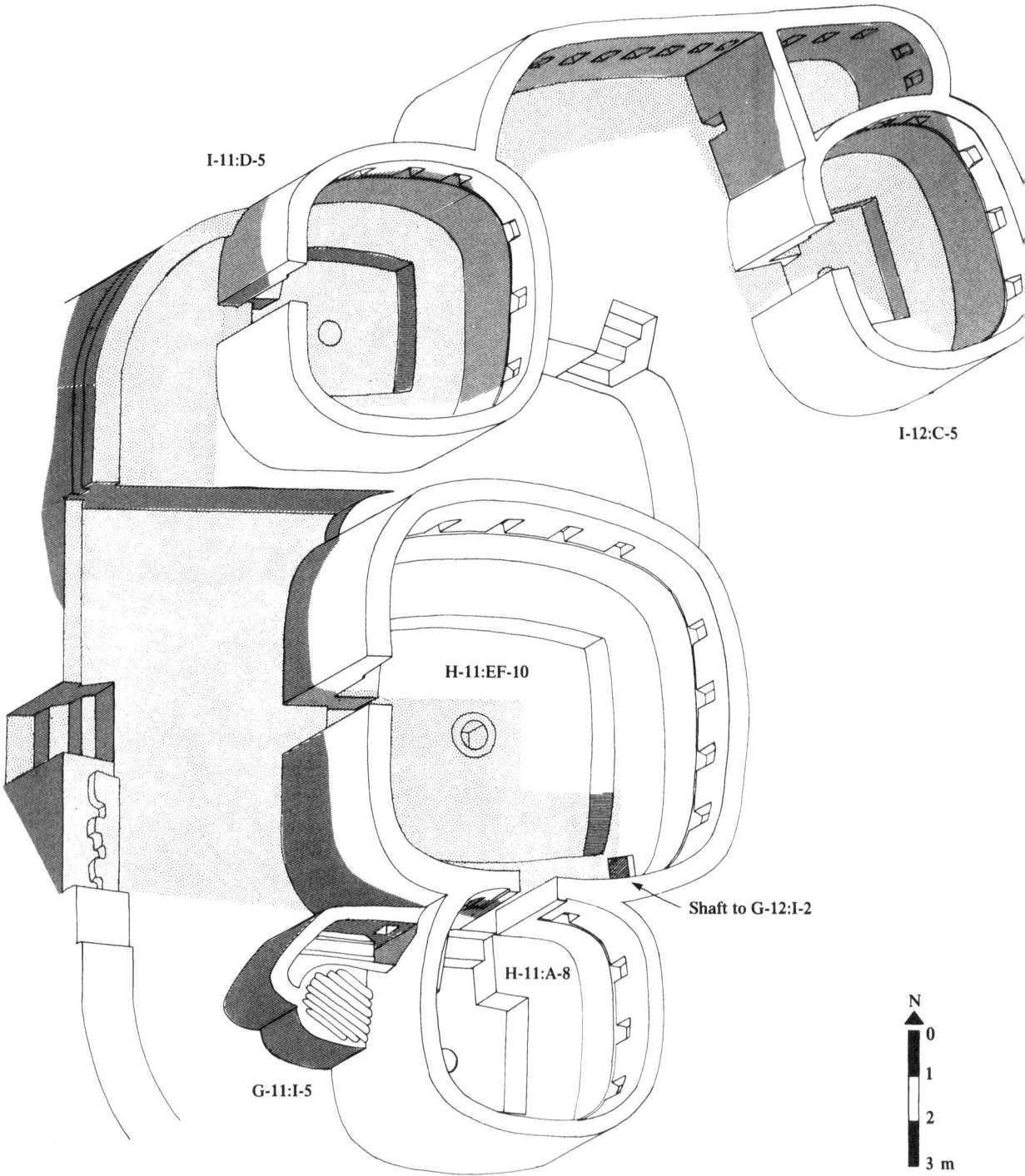

32. Late Preceramic level of North Mound associated with Floor 30. Shaded areas have been excavated; unshaded areas are speculative reconstruction.

33. I-12:C-5 chamber.

Chavín de Huantar (Rowe 1962a:9), a pattern characteristic of the Early Horizon.
Since the curving outer walls of the North
Mound at La Galgada were never buried, it
never attained the standard Early Horizon
form, but it shows a long series of transitional steps built over several centuries.

The pattern began to change with the laying of Floor 20, when the firepit was moved
65 cm north, adjoining and slightly overlapping the firepit of Floor 30 (Figs. 34, 35).
The new firepit was sunk into Floor 30, and
a vent was built using Floor 30 as the vent
floor. This new pit established the location
for all the subsequent firepits in this area,
through three later floors. We can only guess
at the location of the west wall of the new
chamber, since it was entirely dismantled
during later building campaigns, but traces
of its bench level are found 50 cm west of

the Floor 30 bench, making the chamber
slightly larger (Fig. 36). It was similar to
its predecessor in having a high platform
against its northeastern quarter supporting
the I-12:C-5 chamber, which was still open.
As the central chamber continued to grow
larger it becomes increasingly doubtful that
it was roofed, and there is no roofing material in the fill. The smaller chamber on the
south, behind the doorway at H-11:A-8, was
also still open during this period and was almost certainly roofed in the same manner as
the small tomb complex adjoining it on the
west (see discussion of the Log-Roofed
Tomb later in this chapter).

The next phase was the building of fan-
shaped vents (Fig. 37) on top of Floor 20 in
association with Floor 15, a plain brown
mud floor. The vents are hard to explain.
Smoke may have emerged from their ends if

34. Firepits at H-11 : EF-10 in Floor 30 of Main
Chamber. Numbers at right margin identify floor
levels.

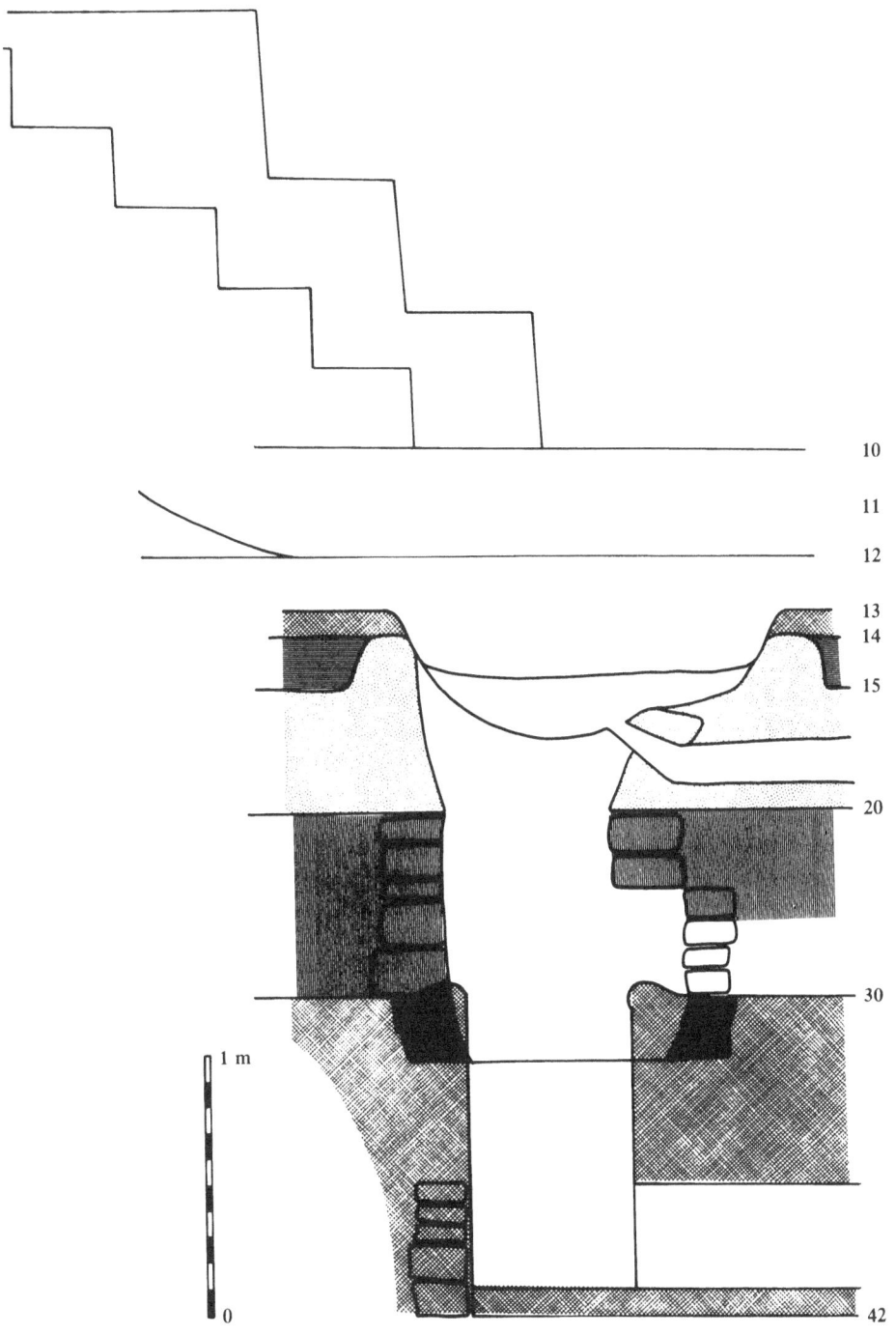

35. Levels in the firepits at H-11:EF-10.

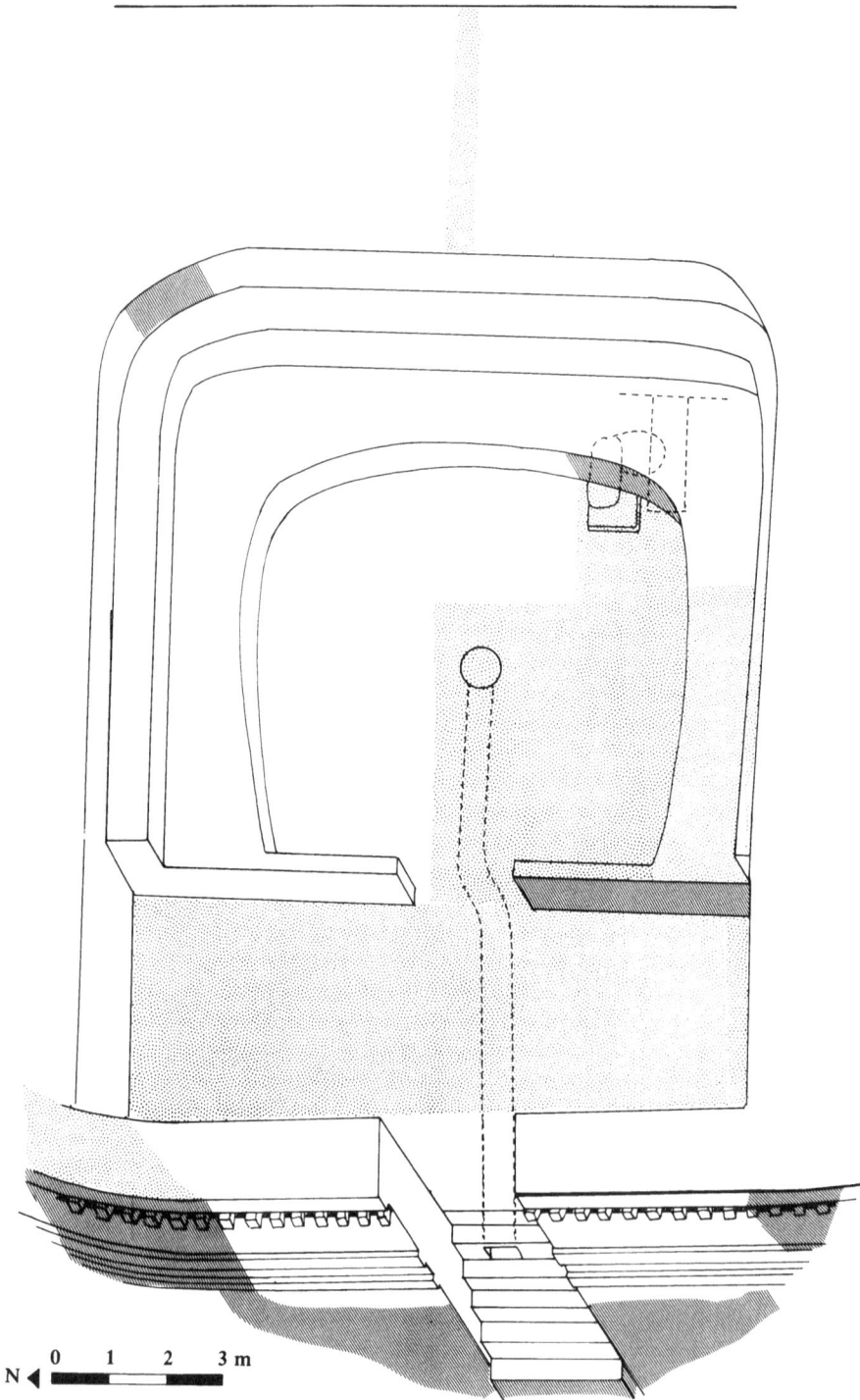

36. Early Initial Period chamber on Floor 20,
North Mound. Shaded areas have been excavated; white areas are speculatively reconstructed.

the fire in the pit was kept low enough, but the inflow of air to the fire must always have tended to counter the flow of smoke and make the presence of the vents hard to perceive. Perhaps they did not function as expected, since they were soon sealed, along with Floor 15, under a well-finished white floor, Floor 13, laid on fill which included a bed of red ash from the firepit.

The firepit for Floor 13 was the same as for Floor 20, using the same vent, but with the addition of a much wider basin, 1.40 m across the inside of the basin with a 20-cm-wide rim of mud-plastered stones. If the firepit was actually in an unroofed space, as seems likely judging by the size of the chamber, this larger firepit would have been impressive for people standing in the open air on the top of the mound (Fig. 38).

The white Floor 13 sealed not only the fan vents but also the top of the old firepit, not filling it in, but placing a shallow basin-like mud floor over the deep pit (upper left in Fig. 34). A small opening was retained to draw air from the main vent resting on Floor 20. Raising the floor under the fire would have further enhanced the visibility of the fire in an outdoor ceremony.

A unique burial or offering was placed at the edge of the exposed bench of Floor 20 as the new fill for Floor 13 was laid: the body of a small monkey, lying on its side, without other offerings.

Floor 13 was the complete expression of the local compromise between the old firepit chambers and the emerging U-shaped temple (Fig. 38). It retained the firepit in a white floor, but it adopted the new elements of an open courtyard at the center of the complex with elevated platforms on three sides. It was the first radical departure from the tradition of the firepit chamber because it eliminated the enclosing walls of the chamber and it unified the whole top of the mound around one enlarged firepit. By this time the 2-m-

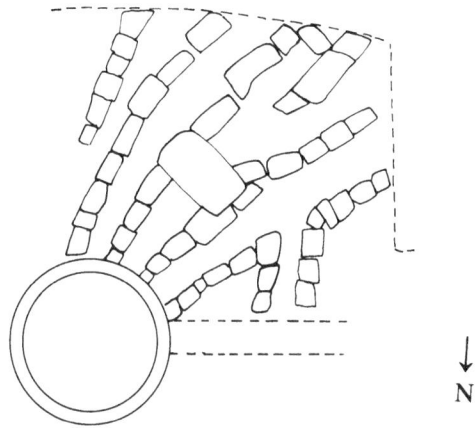

37. Vents from main firepit laid under Floor 15.

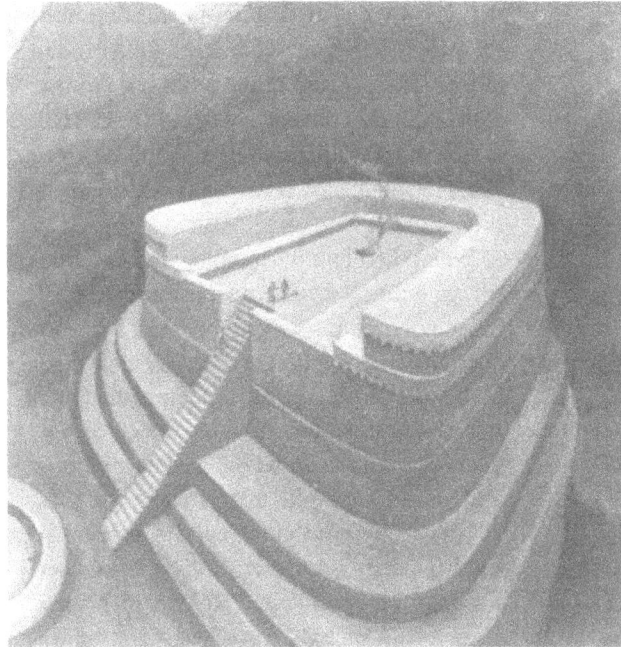

38. The North Mound as it might have looked at the time of Floor 13.

deep fill covering the north and south wings was in place and the construction of the upper part of the outer revetment wall must have been accomplished. Later construction and looting have destroyed almost all traces of building on the wings during this period, although there are 35-cm-high fragments of walls of this period in the south wing. The reconstruction (Fig. 38) shows the top of the U-shaped platform as devoid of structures, which was probably not the case.

Masonry construction grew coarser and more massive in the period of Floor 13, although still distinct from the extremely rough style used for tombs, since temple walls were plastered smooth. The rough, massive style is evident in the curving north-eastern corner of the Floor 13 chamber found at I-12:BC-3/4 and in the axial wall of the same period in the eastern sector at H-12: F-6/9, whose function remains unknown since the southeast corner was not excavated to that depth.

When the Floor 13 temple was buried in fill, an entirely new form was adopted for the temple, eliminating the central fireplace and replacing it with the entrance to a higher platform, which supported rectangular build-ings. At first the brown mud surface desig-nated Floor 11 covered the earlier temple and rose in a ramp to the center of the U. A 1-m-deep firepit in the eastern part of Floor 11 does not appear to have been used for long; Floor 10 (Fig. 39), in which the mound took its final form, was soon built. The rectangular courtyard with its flanking walls took its final appearance; the axial stairway was built leading to the eastern plat-form (Fig. 40), which rose in three stages. Another stairway led from the central court-yard to the top of the south wing, and it is likely that a matching stairway ascended the north wing. Traces of foundations and piles of stone testify to the rectangular buildings on the eastern platform at the center of the

U. Later additions included Floor 8, with its small rectangular firepit chamber at the southeast corner of the mound about 1500 B.C., and 2 m of platform building which raised the level of the south wing to the level of the roofs of the buildings in the center.

The Revetments of the North Mound

Throughout these periods the massive revet-ments surrounding the North Mound were undergoing constant rebuilding (Fig. 41). The earliest wall exposed by our excavations (the dotted area in Fig. 42) was part of the retaining wall for the platform around the earliest chambers we have discovered on the mound, whose floors are at altitudes of 1,123.83 m (Floor 55, in G-12:I-2), and 1,124.17 m (in I-11:B-8). That early wall is now evident only within the stairway, where it formed one step. The top of that wall was at 1,124.70 m. With the building of Floor 30 1.35 m higher, additional steps were built and another massive wall was built to en-close Floor 30 (horizontal shading). It is ex-posed only on the west front, where its upper parts had been destroyed by later building. The appearance of the upper parts is un-known, but the articulated face of the wall around the northwest corner nearest the chambers, which is attached to or at least contemporary with this wall, suggests that the Preceramic walls were already articula-ted. In that respect they would harmonize with the walls of the chambers themselves. A central stairway descending about 10 m must have been in place, but only traces of its foundations remain (Fig. 43).

The next phase of wall-building was inau-gurated with the construction of a 1.20-m-thick wall around the outside of the earliest wall. It may have served originally as a sup-port for the stairway and a reinforcement for the higher wall supporting Floor 30, or it may always have been intended as the foun-dation for the new wall which enclosed Floor

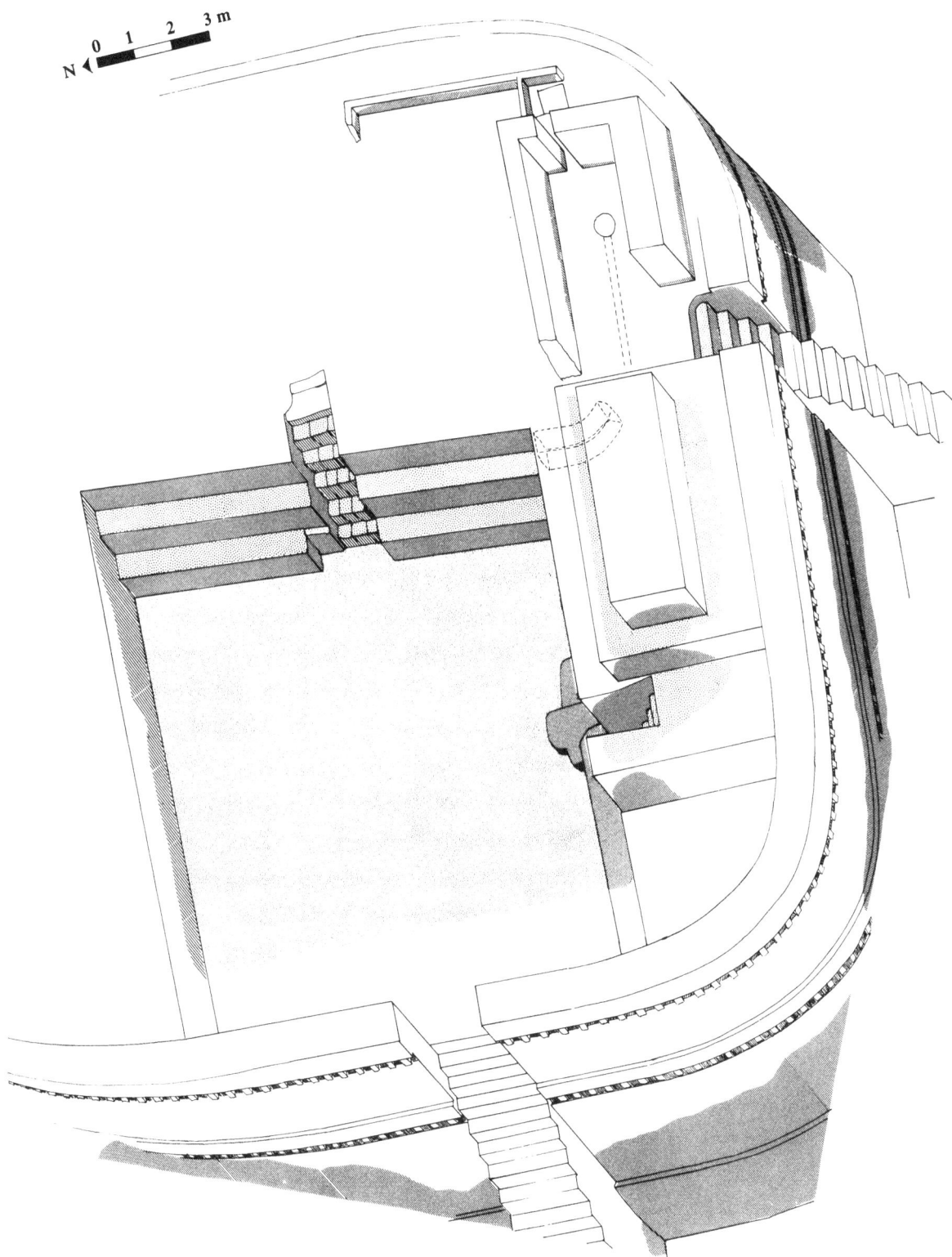

39. Structures associated with Floor 10 of the
North Mound. Shaded areas have been excavated; white areas are speculatively reconstructed.

40. Floor 10 stairs in center of North Mound at beginning of excavation.

41. The North Mound from the southwest.

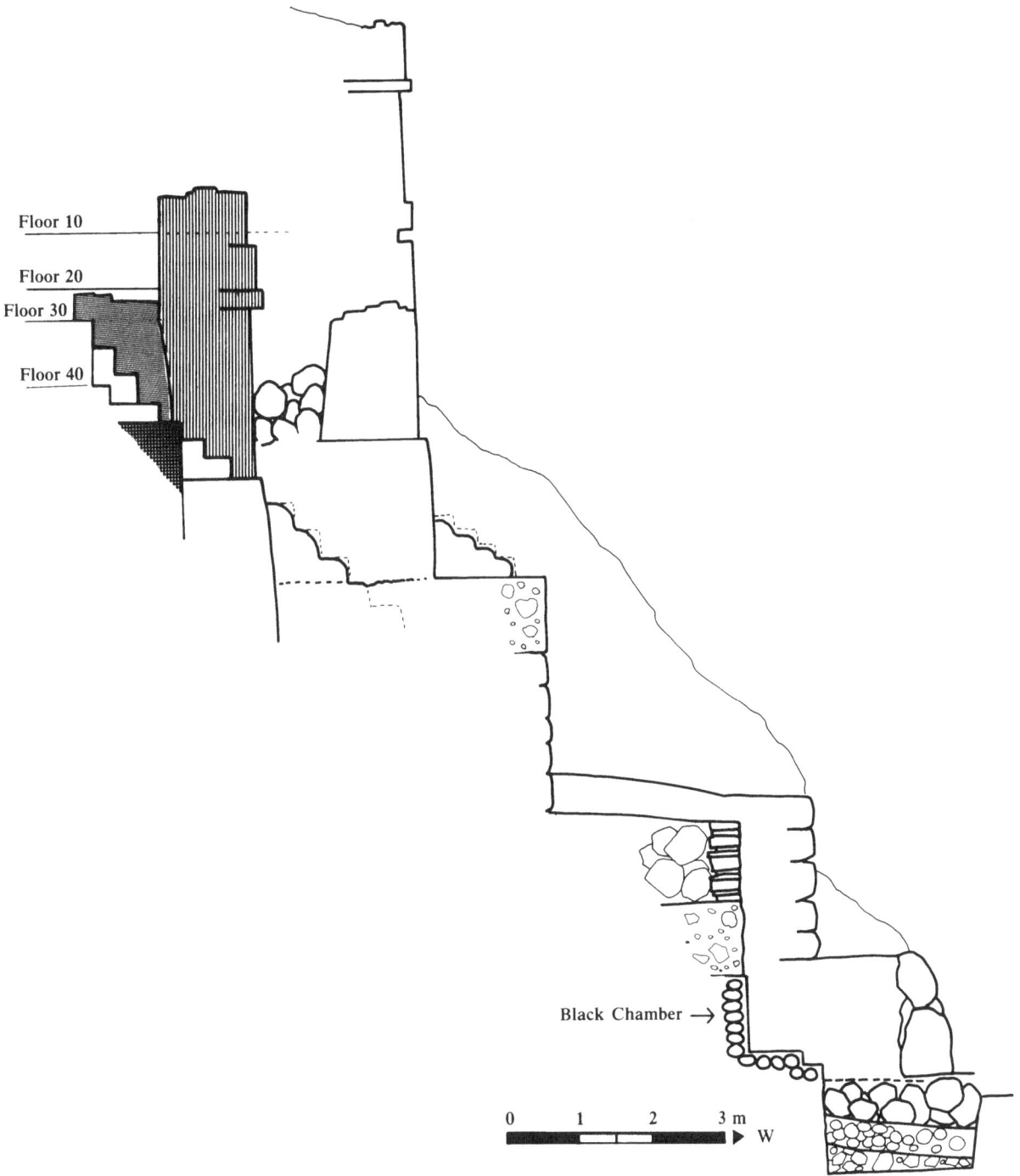

Floor 10

Floor 20

Floor 30

Floor 40

Black Chamber →

0   1   2   3 m

▶ W

42. East-west section through revetments of west front of North Mound, sector H-10.

20 (vertical shading in Fig. 42), the first Initial Period floor and wall. The top of the Floor 20 wall has been destroyed on the west front of the mound, and the finished top is not preserved anywhere, but this is the corbeled wall at the northwest corner of the mound (Fig. 44). Although articulated walls had long been in use for both exteriors and interiors, this is the earliest example of corbeling as far as we know. It conforms to Preceramic attitudes toward building, but was a new form on a larger scale to fit its location. There are traces of a central stairway perpendicular to this wall. That contrasts with later practice in this region, for Early Intermediate Period stairs were ordinarily parallel with the walls they ascended (Grieder 1978: 29, 30).

The walls at the southeast corner, which have a frieze of niches in the foundation and corbels at the top which supported a higher level of the wall (now lost), are the most complete segment of the revetments (Fig. 45). That segment is not continuous with the west front wall that contains Floor 10, there being interruptions in the continuity of the wall on both sides, but it was evidently incorporated in the ring of Floor 10 revetments. It may be that the back half of that ring belongs to a slightly earlier period, probably Floor 13, and was retained for a while as part of the later ensemble. It gives us an impression of the height and quality of the Initial Period structures.

The latest complete ring reached about 1,130 m altitude. It was built in two stages, with a broad foundation and the ornamental wall standing about 6 m high (Fig. 42). Its lower levels are visible across the west front, and the eastern segment mentioned above (Fig. 45) is intact within about 1 m of its top. This colossal construction supported the upper layers of the mound, which belong to the Initial Period. Impressive as the walls were, they do not appear to have been func-

43. West front of North Mound showing the rubble foundations for the Initial Period great wall whose fine face is at left.

tional as a fort. It is clear that their principal function was simply to contain the mass of the platform.

The system for constructing the walls is easily perceived in the excavations. The older wall was first covered with loose stones piled up against the base. Then a colossal wall of unshaped stones was begun outside the wall and leaning back against the loose stones and earth of the dry fill laid between it and the old wall. At the southeast corner the rough wall was begun 2.50 m outside the old fine wall, and the foundations for the next fine wall were built 4 m outside the old fine wall. When the old fine wall was completely covered by the coarse wall and fill,

44. Northwest corner of revetments of North Mound.

45. Southeast corner of North Mound revetments. Note the two remaining corbels at the top. Loose fill at right lay behind next wall.

then the new fine wall was built. The coarse walls above and below the Initial Period fine wall at left center in Figure 43 were the beginning stages of a new casing for the mound. The mound as we see it today is covered with partially constructed coarse walls and masses of loose rock and dirt. When building finally ceased at La Galgada it was not because the inhabitants had lost ambition. An even larger wall to enclose the whole mound was in the first stages of construction when building ended there forever.

Chambers in the South Mound

Although there are no complete buildings made of waterworn stone in the South Mound, the radiocarbon tests place the beginnings of the South Mound in the same period as the earliest excavated structures in the North Mound. Still, the North Mound had at least 10 m of construction at the time the South Mound was begun, and it is probable that the history of the South Mound encompasses only about the last half of the whole sequence of building at the site (Figs. 46–47).

The earliest South Mound chamber is C-11:F-5, Floor 23, built of random quarrystone laid in mud mortar (Fig. 48). The lowest course was built of the largest stones, but they were laid flat, not erect as in later building. C-11:F-5 had a floor without a bench, perhaps because it was so small (about 2 × 2.20 m originally), but it had all the other typical features: a large firepit vented under the door, a dado, three niches in each wall except the north, where the door was flanked by niches. This chamber is somewhat unusual in its orientation toward the north. It was converted to a tomb when the Square Chamber (C-11:I-3) was built northwest of it at the level of its roof. The conversion was accomplished by building a massive green stone vault over the part of the room which remained in use. The tomb was reached by a shaft which opened behind the

Square Chamber, and as later levels were built that shaft remained open as high as Floor 5, by which time it was 5.5 m long (Fig. 49).

The next building was D-11:C-3, Floor 25, a subcircular chamber 3.85 × 3.55 m, with a rectangular floor 1.60 × 2.25 m around the small firepit, and a bench raised just 20 cm (Fig. 50). Like the earlier chamber, this one has the firepit vented toward the north, where the door was presumably located (left unexcavated to retain the walls of the later tomb). Burned wood from the firepit gave the calibrated period 2530–2125 B.C. (TX-3167), which places it in about the same period as F-12:B-2. The walls, of quarrystone laid in courses with fairly large blocks, make much use of thin slabs to level the courses. Thin pieces were also added at all angles for chinking. A thick coat of mud plaster mixed with straw covered all the stone. This was followed by a coat of yellow earth color, probably the original finish. Later a white finish was applied with a brush, whose marks show in some places on the surface. Whether the finish coat was applied to the exterior surfaces of these walls is uncertain; none remains, and the masonry is handsome enough to deserve to be seen, but the probability is that it also was covered.

On the interior the walls were built up to 80 cm where the wall was set back 4 cm, making a dado of the lower wall. Three rectangular niches were built in each of the three exposed walls, and presumably two flanking the door in the north wall. The wall was carried up another 30 cm above the niches, reaching 1.50 m above the bench.

Later the chamber was remodeled (Fig. 47; see Floors 24a and 24) and the floor level was raised 40 cm, the bench 60 cm, and the top of the wall 40 cm, with a new set of niches resting on top of the old wall. The new surfaces were finished yellow. Later the whole remodeled building was refinished white.

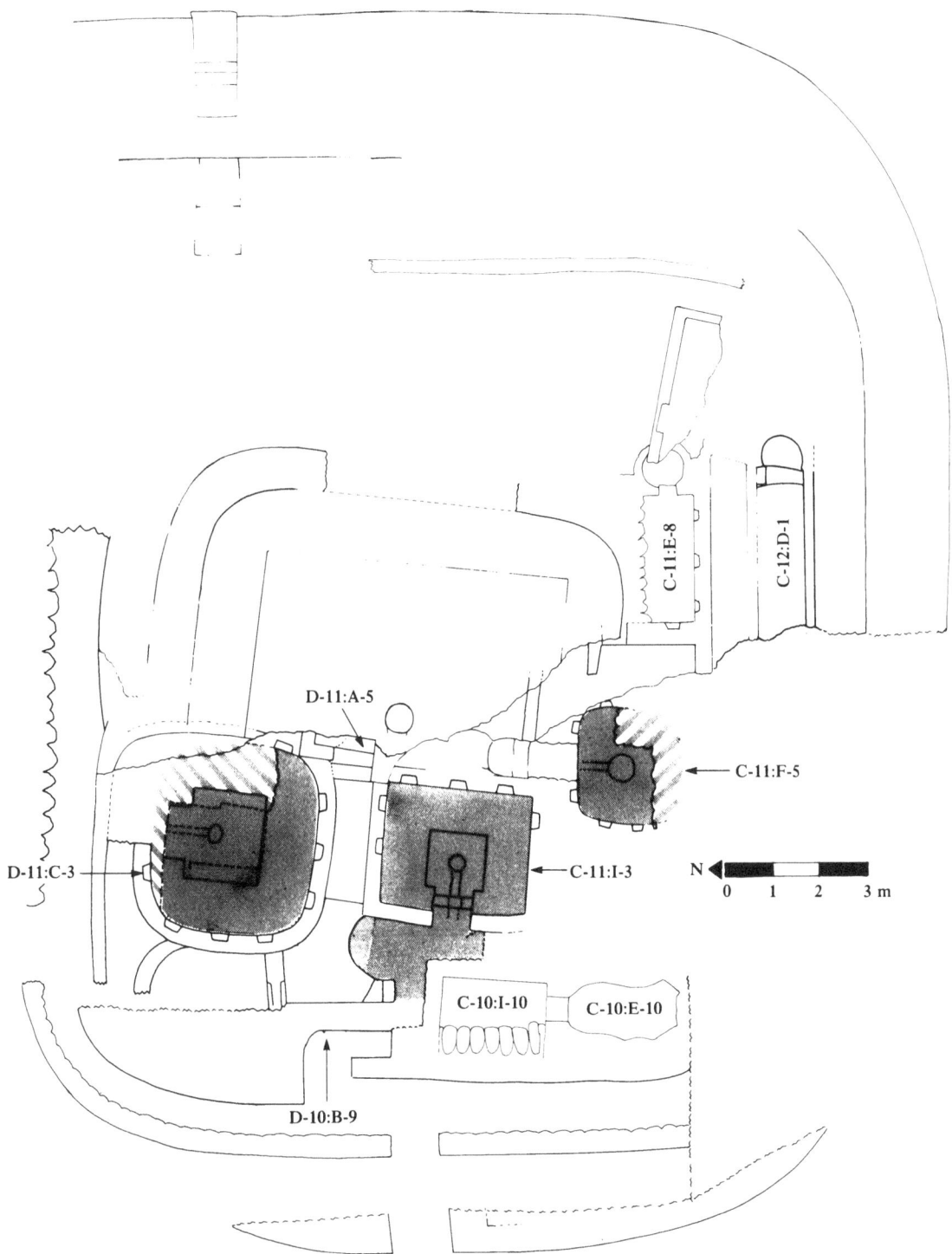

46. Plan of South Mound. Shaded areas are excavated floors of Preceramic chambers; striped areas are presumed floors (unexcavated) of Preceramic chambers; white areas are other structures (tombs and later buildings).

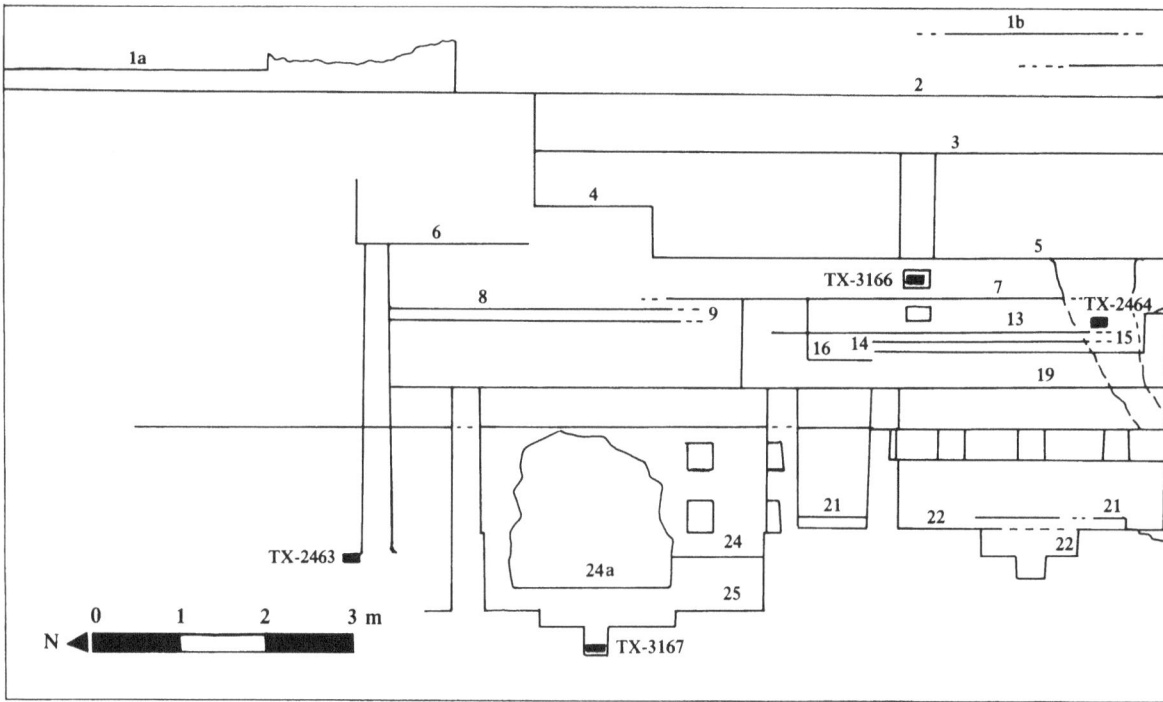

47. Section of South Mound with floor numbering and locations of radiocarbon samples.

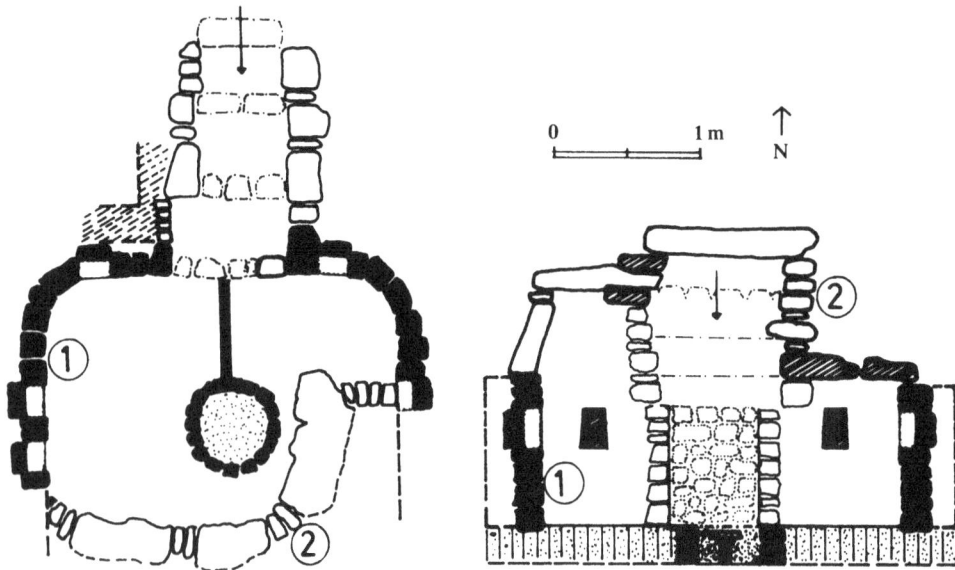

48. C-11:F-5 chamber: plan (left) and profile (right), showing location of white-painted chamber walls (1) and green stone tomb vault (2). Drawing by Alberto Bueno Mendoza.

1c

1e

4

11   10

12

17

18

20

23

26

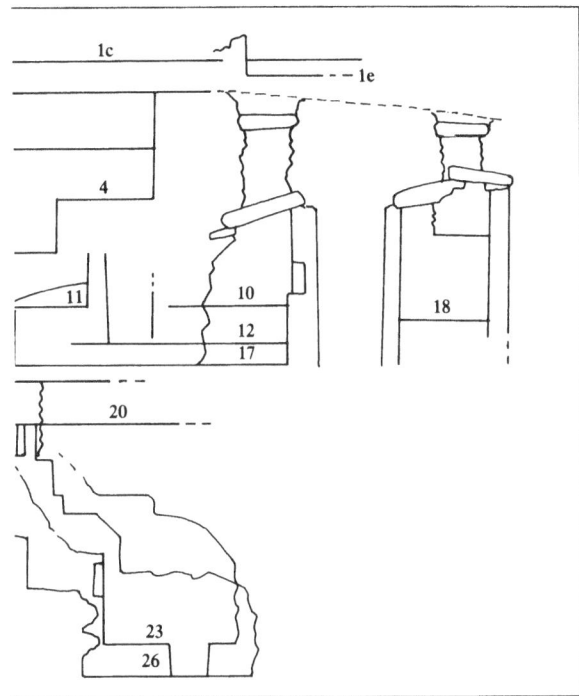

The rebuilding of D-11:C-3 was part of a building campaign that also produced its new neighbor, C-11:I-3, Floor 22, nicknamed the Square Chamber (Figs. 49, 51–53). Its dimensions are 2.90 × 2.60 m. It faces west. Like its older neighbor, it received the unusual yellow finish coat and a later white finish. The niche level in the Square Chamber is indented, the lower part of the wall projecting to form a dado and the part above the niches projecting to match it, a feature found elsewhere only in the G-12:I-2 chamber in the North Mound.

These chambers were in existence about 2300 B.C., surrounded by a wall whose doorway is at D-10:B-9 (Fig. 46). This unusual entrance, through the wall and up steps parallel to the wall, remained in use after these chambers were converted to tombs, probably not later than 2200 B.C., and Floors 20 and 19 were built, the former cutting off the upper

courses of wall from the western halves of both the Square Chamber and D-11:C-3. Floor 19 was the level of the road cut with a bulldozer in 1975. The western half of the South Mound above Floor 19 was entirely destroyed by the roadbuilding.

The existence of roofs on these chambers is mostly uncertain, but chunks of mud imprinted with logs (Fig. 54) were scattered through the various levels of the South Mound, suggesting that all the chambers had roofs like that preserved on the Log-Roofed Tomb (G-11:I-5) in the North Mound, which has natural logs laid tightly at a diagonal and covered with mud. This is the kind of roof Tsugio Matsuzawa (1972:173) describes for the Preceramic temples at Kotosh, basing his argument on "a number of clumps of clay on which the rounded impressions of the surfaces of logs remain in one side," evidence similar to that found at La Galgada. Similar materials found at Huaricoto are interpreted there as having served as roof or walls of wattle and daub, since there are no foundations for masonry walls evident there (Burger and Salazar Burger 1985:122). The smooth, flat mud surfaces of the tops of complete walls found in parts of the South Mound chambers show that whatever type of roof they may have had, it simply rested on the tops of the walls and required no adaptation of the wall. A log and mud roof is the type indicated by all the evidence.

In the eastern half of the South Mound the history can be traced further. Floor 19 (Fig. 47) appears to have served as a courtyard for a chamber on Floor 16 reached by several steps at D-11:A-5. That courtyard would have held the entrances to shafts down to tombs C-10:E-10, C-11:I-3, and D-11:C-3. The middle period in the history of the South Mound, about 2200–2100 B.C., shows evidence of constant building, demolition, and rebuilding, but there was one period during which there was a rectangular white chamber

49. View of South Mound excavations. Note
shaft to C-11:F-5 (at arrow), and chambers D-11:
C-3 and C-11:I-3 (left and right foreground).

50. D-11:C-3 chamber.

51. C-11:I-3 (Square Chamber) viewed from west.

52. West wall of Square Chamber at northwest corner. Scale 30 cm.

on Floor 17 in use in the southern half of the mound and a subcircular chamber on Floor 9 in use in the northern half. The north wall on the exterior of the subcircular chamber remains intact, since it was sheltered by the building of a gallery tomb against it. The radiocarbon test TX-2463 was run on charcoal from the floor of that tomb and should be later than the wall; calibrated it gave a period 2525–1890 B.C., 2207 ± 318 B.C.

About 2100 B.C. the chamber on Floor 17 was converted to a tomb (see C-11:E-8 in the section on tombs) and the first of a series of four large chambers was built covering the whole center of the South Mound. The first two are evident only in partial sections showing the floor and one bench in the road cut (Fig. 47; see Floors 15, 7, 5, and 3). All four appear to have dominated the South Mound in the same way Floor 13 dominated the North Mound during the same period.

None of these four was ever converted to a tomb, as the earlier chambers were, which suggests that the form of the tomb had changed to the massive gallery tombs, such as E-11:J-7 (Fig. 62), outside the old chambers.

Floor 15, the first of this series, had a bench about 45 cm high and 1.10 m wide. The lower part of the wall is preserved and a section of white floor outside the chamber (Floor 12). There are traces of new floors laid within that chamber (Floors 14, 13), but the next new level was Floor 7 with its bench, labeled Floor 6. The front corner of the bench was cut off by the construction of Floor 5, with its bench level, labeled Floor 4. The chamber on Floor 5 may have been a little smaller than its predecessor on Floor 7, but it still reached a maximum width of 9 m, and the next building phase, Floor 3 with its bench on 2, was over 11 m wide. That cham-

53. Firepit, floor, vent, and door of Square Chamber.

54. Mud imprinted with log pattern and log fragment, probably roofing materials of the chambers. Scale length 12 cm.

ber was still using the same firepit, although extended upward 2 m, that had been established in Floor 7. The vents extended west for all these buildings, showing that they all faced west. A new vent was built for Floor 5, but not for Floor 3, which could not have received air from the old vent, since the deep pit was by then clogged with ashes. A later and even larger chamber was built on Floor 2, but later building, erosion, and looting had made its dimensions and details impossible to recover.

Some Preliminary Conclusions about the Chambers

The series of ceremonial buildings at La Galgada stands near the beginning of the history of Andean architecture, but it shows an unexpectedly sophisticated architectural aesthetic, including prototypes for a number of later features. Four phases are evident, spanning the late Preceramic and Initial periods:

(1) In an early phase, small (about 3 m in the widest dimension) subcircular chambers facing west or north were built of waterworn stone in mud plaster, with a vented firepit, no bench or a low bench (20–25 cm high), a setback somewhere on the wall, niches, and a flat roof of logs and mud plaster. These buildings were already raised on a low platform. When they were to be superseded by later building they were converted to tombs by filling half the chamber with stone, removing the roof, and replacing it with a massive roof of stone beams or corbel-vaulted boulders. Tombs were entered through narrow shafts from the new floor surface. A sunken circular plaza accompanied this phase.

(2) Quarrystone chambers, subcircular or rectangular, were articulated as before. The setback in the wall settled at the midpoint, making a dado, with the niches above. Benches increased in height to 30–50 cm. Several chambers of about equal size shared the tops of both mounds, though on the

North Mound the center chamber was dominant and on the South Mound there was a repetition of subcircular/rectangular pairs of chambers. Buried chambers were still turned into tombs, but separate small tombs were also built, with stone corbel vaults, stone beams, or wooden beam roofs. Round or oval houses with low stone walls were surely being built surrounding the mounds by this phase.

(3) A single large firepit chamber dominated the top of each mound. On the North Mound the separation between the chamber and the courtyard was eliminated in the Floor 13 chamber.

(4) Although the outer walls supporting the mound were still circular, the platforms on the North Mound took on a rectangular shape. The rectangular courtyard focused on the central stairway to the U-shaped platform, which was covered with rectangular buildings, at least in the center. At the end of this phase a small rectangular chamber in the southeast corner of the U had a traditional firepit with a vent toward the west. Massive gallery tombs were built throughout this phase.

La Galgada participated in the architectural expression of a widespread religious tradition which required fire in a pit, probably for burnt offerings. Richard Burger and Lucy Salazar Burger (1980) have called this the "Kotosh Religious Tradition" for the site at which its architecture was first studied. At La Galgada only plant remains and no animal remains have been identified in the firepits, but at Huaricoto there is evidence of offerings of meat (ibid.: 28, 31). Probably all that was required architecturally for this ceremony was fire in a pit, so it is doubtful that we will ever be able to trace the full extent of the cult. Improvements were as simple as paving a floor around the pit and painting the pit and floor with colored clay or mud, usually yellow or white. At Huaricoto this was the usual practice in the Preceramic Period. The eight "shrines" at Huaricoto span nearly two thousand years, ending in the mid–Early Horizon with circular chambers with massive stone walls (of which only the base is preserved), no doorway preserved, and a vented firepit in the center of the floor. The sequence at Huaricoto looks like a prolonged version of the general development of the architecture of the fire cult. The simple early type with a pit in a paved floor, but without walls, which has not been discovered at La Galgada or Kotosh, is found at Los Gavilanes, where Duccio Bonavia (1982:63–65, 273) describes a deep pit of ashes in a mud-paved rectangular floor which he calls a public building. It may have had a thatched roof on posts. Formal constructions related to firepits are fairly rare on the coast, but a plastered and replastered firepit in the Huaca de los Sacrificios at Aspero may have been a cult center (Feldman 1980:94), since it seems to have been incorporated in a rectangular walled building.

It is at Kotosh, Shillacoto (see Burger and Salazar Burger 1980:30), and La Galgada that we find the firepit incorporated in its own distinctive architectural complex. There are many common features such as niches in the walls, bench levels on the floors, vents from the firepits, and probably log ceilings roofed over with mud plaster. Differences in wall color (white at La Galgada, yellow at Kotosh) and in plan (circular at La Galgada, rectangular at Kotosh), as well as the unique mud reliefs at Kotosh, separate the two sites. The regions also differ in the early shift to a U-shaped temple at La Galgada, while Shillacoto carried the fire cult on into the Initial Period.

Orientation of the chamber was clearly a matter of some importance at both Kotosh and La Galgada. At Kotosh the chambers all face close to magnetic north or south (Izumi and Terada, eds. 1972:Figs. 84, 85, 106), at

La Galgada north or west. Although hard to interpret, the variations are surely significant. The ability to orient buildings consistently is technically important.

THE SERIES OF TOMBS

La Galgada is as important as a cemetery as it is as a temple center, and the two functions were evidently closely linked in the minds of the ancient inhabitants. Temple chambers were often converted into tombs, and additional tombs were specially built beside the temple chambers or along the revetments of the mounds. Sixteen tombs can be identified, six of them with the original burials completely or largely intact. Of the remaining ten, probably all but one (G-11: I-5) had multiple burials; the intact burials include men, women, and children.

The builders always made a very clear distinction in the manner in which temples and tombs were built. Temples were built of smaller stones, and the surfaces were finished with mud plaster and painted. When the stones were quarried they were squared up and laid in courses and chinked with spalls. Tombs, on the other hand, were always built of the largest stones the builders could handle, laid in a rough manner that looks as if it was intended to appear as a work not of humans but of nature (Fig. 55). As the centuries passed this distinction remained valid, although the massive tomb style tended to be transferred to the building of revetments, where the buttressing effect was especially functional. The later tombs became even more massive, with the largest stones ever used at La Galgada appearing in the Initial Period tomb E-11:J-7.

La Galgada tombs can be divided into two types: those built into buried firepit chambers and those built independently or outside the firepit chambers. The former we have called *chamber tombs*, the latter *gallery tombs* since many of them are similar to the

55. Entrance to I-11:J-2 gallery tomb.

so-called galleries at Chavín de Huantar and Pacopampa. The similarity rests on their rough tunnel or corridor form, although none of the tombs is more than a few meters long and many lumped in that category are small cubicles, but built outside the ritual chambers.

There appears to have been a tendency to shift from chamber to gallery tombs as time passed, but it does not seem to signify a new conception, but merely to reflect the insufficient chamber space to accommodate the demand. The earlier tombs are all in chambers which had been converted and buried. The earliest gallery tombs are inside the revetments and close to the chambers: C-10:E-10, H-12:C-2, I-12:G-4, G-11:I-5, and C-10: I-10 are all members of this category.

But as the firepit chambers grew larger at the end of the Preceramic Period there was less space inside the revetments for additional structures. The larger chambers were also more difficult to remodel into tombs, especially since the large chambers were in the center of the mounds and to completely bury one with a tomb inside would have required rebuilding the entire top of the mound with deep fill. For these reasons the large central chambers on both mounds—Floor 30 and its successors on the North Mound and Floor 15 and its successors on the South Mound— were not converted to tombs as the earlier chambers had been. Instead gallery tombs were built within, between, and outside the revetments. I-11:J-2 and E-11:J-7 are the latest tombs, on both sides of the North

Table 1. Tombs, in Approximate Chronological Order

Sector	Chamber	Gallery	No. Burials	Intact	Looted
1. F-12:B-2	x		3	x	
2. I-11:B-8	x		?		x
3. G-12:I-2	x		4		x
4. I-12:C-5	x		?		x
5. C-10:E-10		x	3	x	
6. C-11:F-5	x		≥14		x
7. C-11:I-3 (Square Chamber)	x		?	anciently destroyed	
8. H-12:C-2		x	?		x
9. I-12:G-4		x	?		x
10. C-12:D-1		x	10–12	x (damaged)	
11. D-11:C-3	x		4	x	
12. G-11:I-5 (Log-Roofed Tomb)		x	1		x
Initial Period (ceramics present)					
13. C-11:E-8	x		3	x (damaged)	
14. C-10:I-10		x	4	anciently burned	
15. I-11:J-2		x	?		x
16. E-11:J-7		x	≥27		x

Note: See Chapter 5, "Burial Patterns and Offerings," for more detail on the content of the tombs. See also Appendices A and B.

Mound, and similar in being true gallery types with low, narrow tunnels of large unworked stones descending into dark, cave-like cubicles. Both had been looted long ago.

The burials and their offerings will be described in Chapter 5; our focus here is on the architecture. Five tombs will serve as examples of the types of buildings in this category.

The earliest of the sixteen tombs, F-12: B-2 (Figs. 24, 56), is a converted firepit chamber which had its last fire in the period 2625–1980 B.C. (radiocarbon test TX-4450). It held the bodies of a man and two women. The chamber had been made into a tomb by tearing off the chamber roof and substituting stone slabs resting on a massive irregular wall that bisected the chamber, leaving the

old firepit in the tomb but covering the door; a new entrance was made through the niche to the left of the doorway. A small quarry-stone antechamber was built outside the new entrance, and a circular slab was laid in place to seal the entrance through the roof of the antechamber.

All the tombs built into the chambers are similar to F-12:B-2 in their materials and general manner of construction. They vary only in the floor plan and entrance. I-11:B-8 is entered through the top half of the original doorway and has the pier supporting the roof attached to the east wall, making a C-shaped plan. C-11:F-5 (Fig. 48) was likewise entered through a shaft to its original door, and the chamber was half filled with a massive wall and vault of specially selected green

56. F-12:B-2 tomb.

boulders. This iron-rich silicified clastic rock turns brown on prolonged exposure, but for the tomb the boulders were broken to reveal their bright green core. The effort to produce a vault of that color means the color is significant, a matter discussed further in Chapter 12. G-12:I-2 is entered through a short shaft leading to an opening cut through the niche left of the door, and the pier fills the center of the chamber (Fig. 27). The four burial bundles were set one in each corner. I-12:C-5 had been damaged by later building, so one cannot be certain of either the tomb plan or its entrance. C-11:I-3 was unusual only in that this square chamber had been made into two small tombs by the building of a thick wall down the center. Later building has destroyed the burials and eliminated the vaults and the entrances, but the basic diagnostic feature of a tomb is present:

57. Entrance to D-11:C-3 tomb.

the massive stone wall. C-11:E-8 was similarly in a rectangular chamber, although we know of only one tomb in it, entered through an opening in the roof at the east end of the vault.

The D-11:C-3 tomb (Figs. 57, 58) was built on a different plan, sharing only the massive stone walls. It measures 130 × 180 cm, with rough stone walls set in the center of an old firepit chamber, using none of the old walls. The corbel vault was sealed with a large flat stone 180 cm above the floor. The entrance, on the west side of the tomb, was reached by a shaft from Floor 19 or higher. The floor of the tomb had been built on a bed of salt crystals about 10 cm thick. The pure white crystals are very striking, many of them as long as a person's finger and curling. Over them was laid a bed of black charcoal powder. This combination of black and

white was clearly intentional and symbolic (probably symbolizing the earth goddess, whose colors in Mexico were black and white; see Grieder 1982:122–123). Finally a thin bed of brown soil was laid and the burial mats were laid on top. Since two pairs of burials were deposited in this tomb, one in the Preceramic and the other in the Initial Period, the entrance must have remained accessible for a long time, but the upper parts of the shaft were destroyed by the road cut.

G-11:I-5 (Figs. 32, 59) was built on the North Mound against the outside of a firepit chamber. The tomb cubicle itself measures only 1.30 × 1 m and 1 m high. The single bundle burial was removed by looters long ago, but its indentation in the floor is visible. This tomb is unique in having a wooden ceiling still in place, made of log beams of the local algarroba 10–12 cm in diameter laid diagonally. A small antechamber curves around the north and west sides of the tomb, a 40-cm-square opening at the floor level communicating between them. The antechamber itself was reached from the central courtyard by another small rectangular opening. The ceiling of the antechamber is another unique example. It has two logs running its length (1.80 m), with slabs of stone laid aslant from the walls to the beams and flat from beam to beam, making a kind of false vault. This tomb is nicknamed the Log-Roofed Tomb.

C-12:D-1 (Fig. 60), like the Log-Roofed Tomb, was built between the outer wall of the South Mound and a firepit chamber. It was a narrow gallery whose entrance was at the east end through the roof, where the short shaft was closed with a shaped stone. Entering, one dropped first to a shelf halfway to the floor. Ten to twelve bundle burials had been set in this tomb, but the burials were badly damaged by falling walls and stone roof beams when the road cut destroyed the west end of the tomb. The ceil-

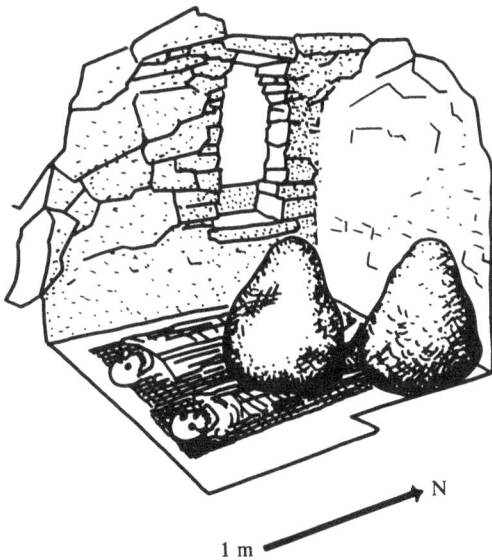

1 m

N

58. D-11:C-3 tomb.

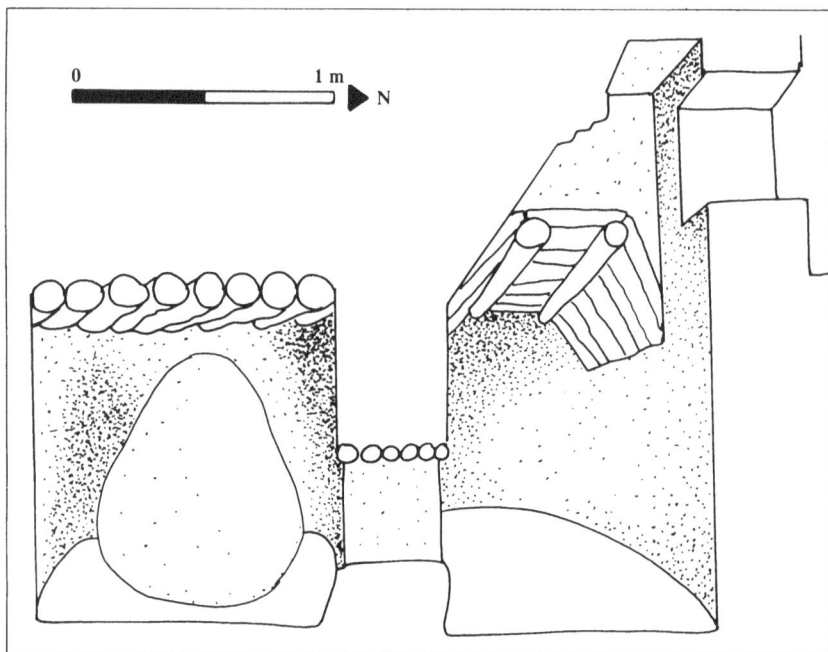

59. G-11:I-5, Log-Roofed Tomb.

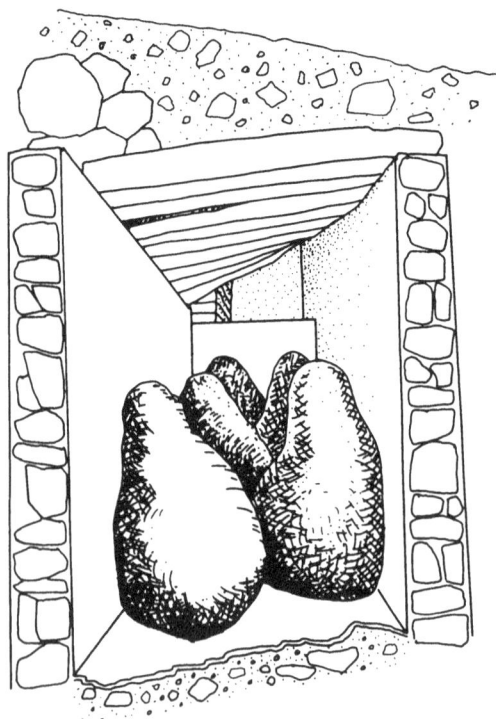

60. C-12:D-1 tomb, showing five of the burials.

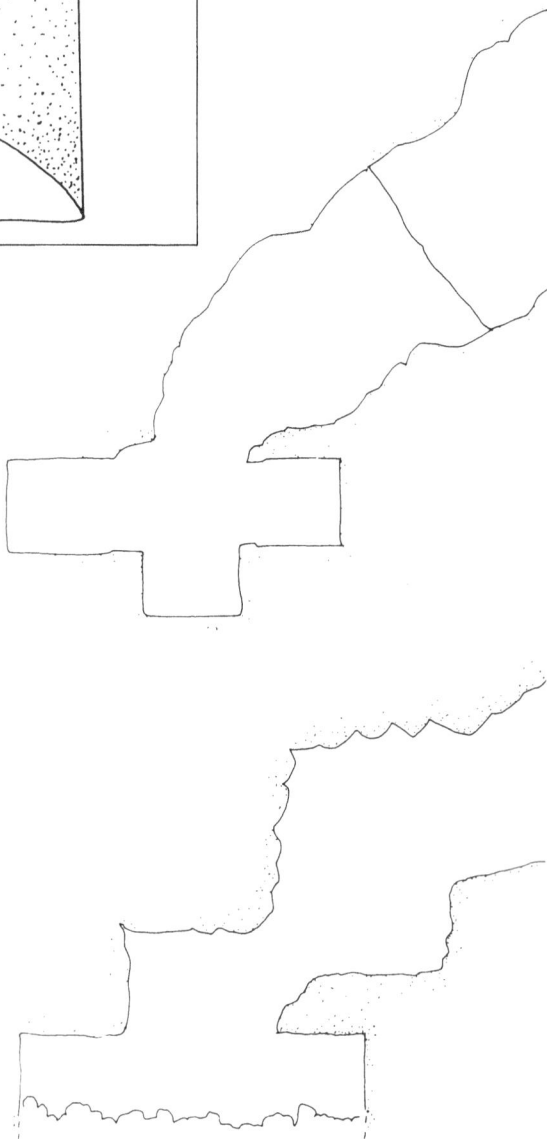

N

0

1 m

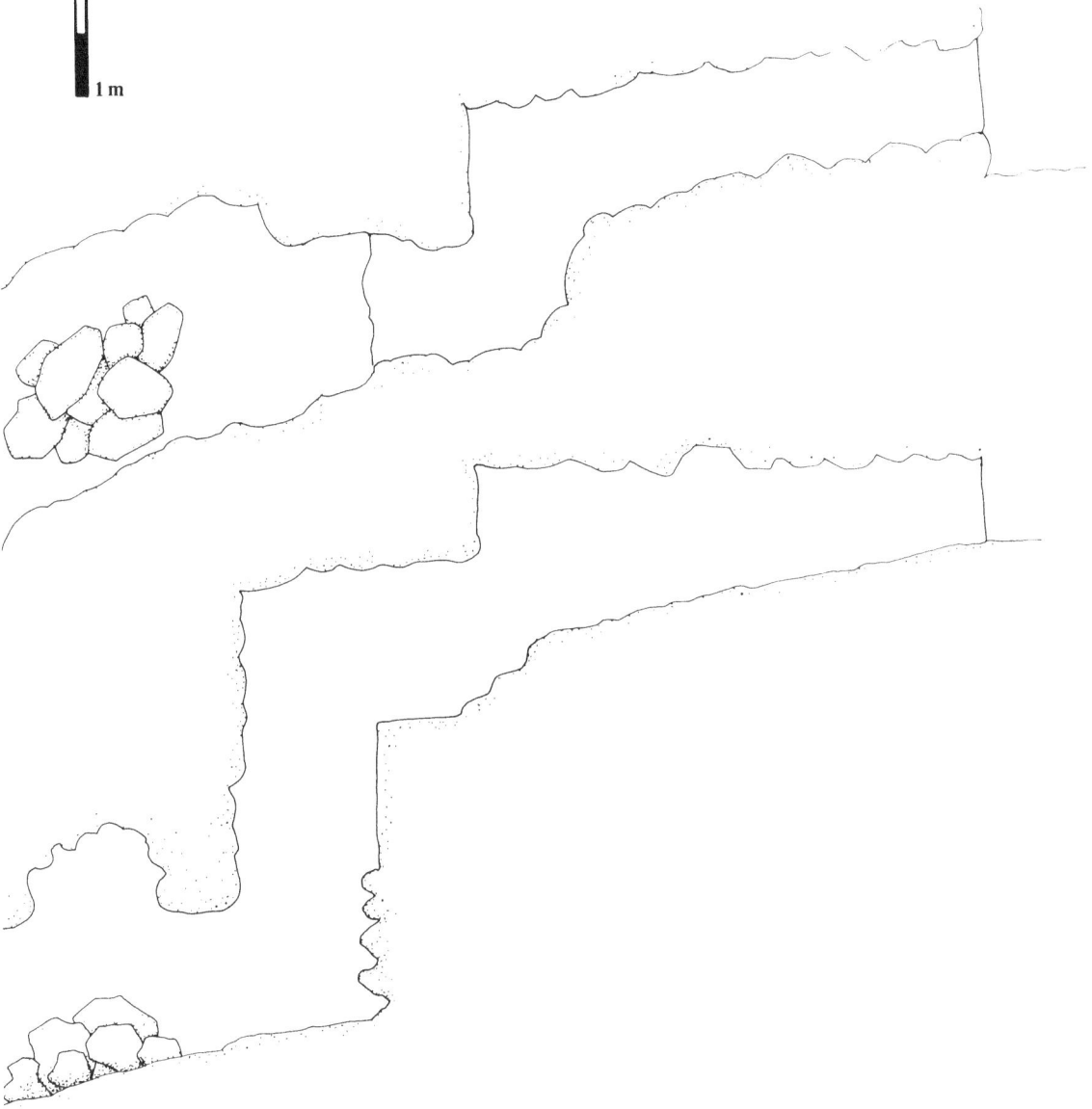

61. I-11:J-2 tomb: plan (*above*) and section (*below*).

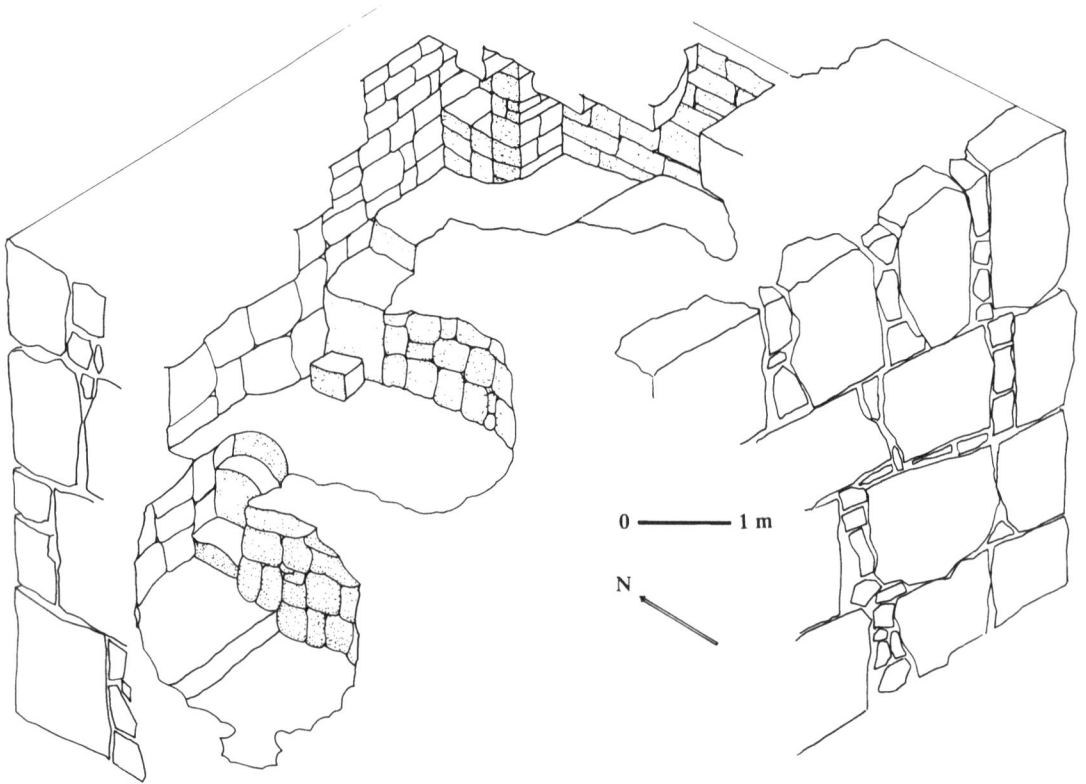

62. E-11:J-7 tomb.

ing was made of large flat stones laid from wall to wall across the 1-m-wide gallery.

The two largest gallery tombs were built on opposite sides of the North Mound and, since they were not hard to find, both had been completely looted. Both are Initial Period structures, but I-11:J-2 (Figs. 55, 61), on the northwest corner of the upper part of the mound, is probably earlier, since it is more closely fitted to the older revetments.

Although E-11:J-7 (Fig. 62) is an independent building, it also abuts against earlier buildings, F-12:B-2 on the east and the lowest, latest revetment of the North Mound on the north. This massive block measures 7.30 m east-west by 6.50 m north-south, and about 4.80 m deep. Except for two chambers and a corridor, it is solid rock. The remain-

ing bones testify that several individuals were buried here. The broad, thick, meter-long stones of the outer walls give a sense of megalithic power similar to that of the earlier tombs, but the stones were cut and shaped, laid in mud mortar and chinked, in a more careful style than was used in the earlier tombs. This tomb might be interpreted as a step in the direction of Chavín style stone masonry of the succeeding period.

These five tombs represent about six hundred years of development, or about twenty-four generations of builders. They show many changes within the general category of the tomb. The earliest tombs required the least amount of effort to build, being the remodeled ritual chambers which were originally constructed for another use. Whether the idea to bury the ritual chambers and build again on top originated from the desire to convert the older chamber to a tomb or from the desire to build a new chamber, or a new chamber on a higher level, or all three, we cannot say, but all three results were accomplished. The ritual chambers were buried by filling them with large boulders and smaller rocks, leaving one or more small chambers for burials. This was gradually formalized to the building of a massive central column or wall and carefully roofing the burial space by laying flat stones from the column or wall to the old walls of the chamber, whose old wooden beam roof had been removed. The majority of the tombs discovered were of this type.

With the Log-Roofed Tomb we see the beginning of special constructions for tombs. It is very small and held only one body, but had a larger antechamber. This tomb gives the impression that the person entombed in it was especially important. D-11:C-3, Floor 24, is a combination of some of these earlier ideas: it was built especially as a tomb, but it lay within an old chamber. The chamber was drastically remodeled twice, once returning it to ritual use, then the tomb built within it. C-12:D-1 was also especially built as a tomb, filling the space between a ritual chamber and a revetment. In that sense the tomb was part of a larger construction with a separate purpose and did not require a great expenditure of energy in itself. E-11:J-7 was by far the largest construction project among the specially designed tombs, containing 228 m^3 of stone masonry. Robert Malina's study of the skeletal materials indicates that it accommodated at least twenty-seven individuals (see Appendix A).

To judge by the size, independence, and complexity of the buildings, tombs gained importance as time passed. Since tombs focus on the occupant, as opposed to the chambers, which focus on the ritual or the deity, the increasing importance of the tombs suggests the increasing importance accorded human individuals during the period La Galgada was inhabited. While the chambers had the firepit at the center throughout their history, a location which could not be occupied by any human being during the ritual, the body (or bodies) of the deceased occupied the center of the tomb. Yet the tombs do not give unambiguous evidence of the way that increasing importance was viewed. The early tombs held very few individual bodies, the late Preceramic Log-Roofed Tomb held just one, and the Initial Period tombs, while larger, may have held more bodies. It does not appear that special distinction was so narrowly limited during these earlier periods as it was, for example, at Early Intermediate Pashash, just a few miles away, where a considerable building and numerous offerings were granted for one single individual (Grieder 1978:52). But the direction of development seems to be toward granting individuals greater distinction.

The ritual chambers always remained the primary category of building. The location and form of the tombs always depended on the chambers, or on the emerging temple of the Initial Period. The tombs clustered in and around the chambers, and the houses and fields of the living around both the chambers and the tombs. It sometimes seems as if the ancient Peruvians were preoccupied with death, the afterlife, and the burial of their dead, but the chambers accommodated the living members of the community, who participated actively (if from an eccentric position) in the rituals. In the choice of spaces for ritual and for burial, at least, the dead gave way to the needs of the living.

4. Radiocarbon Measurements

TERENCE GRIEDER

Table 2 summarizes the radiocarbon measurements made on specimens from La Galgada. All but one were made at the Radiocarbon Laboratory of the University of Texas at Austin; the other was made at the Center for Applied Isotope Studies at the University of Georgia in Athens, as indicated by the TX and UGa sample numbers. The table gives the laboratory identification number of the specimen, the age of the specimen before present (B.P.) on the radiocarbon scale, a "calibrated" date corrected to the conventional solar calendar (B.C.) according to the tables in Klein et al. 1982, and finally the context in the excavations.

Calibrated dates, as given in this table, are the basis for the dates used elsewhere in this report. Klein et al. give a 95 percent confidence range for the conversion of radiocarbon ages to calendar years. Some of the dates used in this report are shorthand references to this range, giving the midpoint of the range, as in Table 3. That single date might seem to imply more precision than Klein et al. would accept, but it is not intended as an exact date any more than an uncorrected radiocarbon age given as a date is intended to imply a precise year. The disadvantage of calibrated dates is that they are inconvenient to compare with dates reported in radiocarbon years, as they have mostly been reported for the past thirty years. The advantage of calibrated dates is that they put all of history on a single time scale. The difference is negligible until one gets back to

about 500 B.C., when radiocarbon ages are about a century too recent, increasing to about four centuries too recent at 2000 B.C. Events that occurred about 2500 B.C. on our standard calendar are dated about 2000 B.C. on the radiocarbon scale. That compounds our natural tendency toward full chronologies in recent centuries and empty ones in ancient times, so that chronological scales tend to use the same space for ancient millennia that they do for recent centuries, or even decades. To develop a sense of history it would seem essential that we have a single scale for the passage of time.

The radiocarbon specimen most seriously out of stratigraphic sequence is the oldest, TX-3664, which was burnt wood on the floor of the small firepit chamber I-11:D-5 at the northwest corner of the North Mound. As this chamber was excavated we were aware of the deep looter's pit just to the south, excavated in 1928, as shown by newspaper scraps in I-11:B-8, Floor 50. A mango seed was found in the fill which produced this specimen, and since the mango is a posthispanic introduction it now seems clear that the backdirt from the looter's pit was piled on the unbroken floor of that upper chamber. If so, then the source of our sample TX-3664 was much lower in the mound, since the looters passed Floor 40 and entered the early chamber. Although the specimen is not securely located, it is reasonable to assign it to the fill on or below Floor 40. The date then may relate to the earlier chamber, I-11:

Table 2. La Galgada Radiocarbon Measurements

Sample	C-14 Age B.P.	95% Confidence Interval, Date B.C.[a]	Midpoint, Date B.C.	Context	Period
TX-4446	3130±80	1670±1120	1395±275	G-12:H-4, Floor 8, firepit	Initial
TX-5606	3320±270	2310±910	1610±700	H-11:G-10, cloth attached to Chavín-related *Spondylus* shell disk	Initial
TX-2464	3440±80	2000±1565	1782±218	Sector C shaft	Initial
TX-3663	3540±50	2130±1705	1917±213	G-11:G-8, Floor 9	Initial
TX-3166	3660±80	2385±1770	2077±308	C-11:J-6, Floors 3, 5, 7, firepit	Initial
TX-4448	3650±60	2300±1870	2085±215	H-11:FG-10, Floor 15, firepit	Initial
UGa-4583[b]	3590±75	2295±1705	2000±295	H-11:EF-10, Floor 30, firepit	Preceramic
TX-4447[b]	3670±70	2390±1775	2082±308	Same as above	Preceramic
TX-2463	3740±90	2525±1890	2207±318	Sector D gallery	Preceramic
TX-4449	3790±70	2540±1960	2250±290	E-12:I-2, Floor 6	Preceramic
TX-4450	3820±100	2625±1980	2302±323	F-12:B-2, firepit	Preceramic
TX-3167	3820±60	2530±2125	2327±203	D-11:C-3, Floor 25, firepit	Preceramic
TX-3664	4110±50	2900±2425	2662±238	I-11:D-5, related to floor 40	Preceramic

[a] According to tables in Klein et al. 1982.

[b] These two specimens are parts of the same sample. They average 2040 for the midpoint of the 95% Confidence Interval.

B-8, Floor 50, a chamber built of waterworn stone in the early technique. The implication of this specimen's age is that the North Mound was the first area to be built in the ceremonial complex and had already reached a height of about 13 m 150 to 400 years before the South Mound was begun and F-12:B-2 was in use.

The next three dates all belong together in the first buildings to the south of the North Mound. These specimens were found in the firepits of D-11:C-3, Floor 25, and F-12:B-2 and in the debris on Floor 6 in the waterworn stone chamber E-12:I-2. The closeness and relative age of these specimens is plausible in relation to the buildings.

TX-2463 is burnt wood from the floor of a gallery accidentally opened by the bulldozer

in 1975. The gallery was a narrow passage outside the wall of the South Mound, roofed with slabs and buried. The midpoint for the range on that test, 2207 B.C. ± 318, is only a century later than the firepit in Floor 25, and taken with TX-3166, from near the bottom of the deep Initial Period firepit related to Floors 7, 5, 3, all the building of the Preceramic Period is compressed into about two hundred years. At the extremes of the standard deviations the time increases to about four hundred years. The truth surely lies somewhere between. The good condition of most of the buried buildings tells us they did not remain long in use, but were products of a nearly continuous process of building and remodeling.

The series of tests on the North Mound

continue with the last great group of Preceramic firepit chambers dated by burnt
wood from the firepit of Floor 30. The sample
was divided between the Texas and Georgia
laboratories, as TX-4447 and UGa-4583. An
average of their results gives an age of 3630
± 75 B.P., which calibrates to about 2300–
1800 B.C. That range, while plausible in itself for a late Preceramic building, is slightly
later than the stratigraphically higher Initial
Period sample TX-4448 from the large firepit on Floor 15, which has a range of 2300–
1870 B.C. These samples reinforce the
conclusion that the pace of building on the
North Mound was rapid.

The last four specimens all come from
Initial Period contexts and, while they appear plausible, they are hard to evaluate.
TX-3663 suggests that the south wing of the
North Mound was already largely in place
before about 1800 B.C., but TX-4446 implies that a firepit in a small chamber on a
slightly later floor level may still have been
in use about five centuries later. The range
on TX-4446 seems late considering the scarcity of ceramics on the site even in late levels. If the Preceramic specimens seem to
give too little time for the amount of construction, the Initial Period dates seem to
give too much time for the construction and
artifact types.

An unburned stick from the wall of the
shaft to C-11:F-5, a late Preceramic tomb
which remained open as late as the Initial
Period Floor 5, gave the date range of 2000–
1565 (TX-2464). That specimen seems to
belong to the Initial Period floors in the
South Mound, but since the shaft had been
open for a long period in antiquity and was

cut by the bulldozer in 1975, this piece of
wood was not a good choice for an unambiguous test result.

TX-5606, taken from a small specimen of
cotton cloth (Fig. 120) tied onto a Spondylus
shell disk carved in a Chavín-related style in
the cache on Floor 11 in H-11:G-10, provides a date which is stratigraphically plausible, though the confidence interval is so
wide that the date could be used to support
almost any argument. It does, however,
strongly support a second millennium B.C.
dating for some Chavín-related monster
heads.

Table 3 shows a series of calibrated dates
(expressed as midpoints with the 95 percent
confidence interval expressed as a standard
deviation) from a set of related sites. In general, the coastal dates, as represented by Aspero and Ancon, are earlier and suggest that
cultural developments were occurring earlier
in that region. But until better comparisons
can be made of cultural material the dates
tell us very little. Architectural types, for
example, developed quite differently in the
highlands and on the coast, but highland
types seem to have influenced later coastal
building. So at this time we still have insufficient evidence to write the history of in-
terregional cultural relations. There is, however, close correspondence among the sites
with firepit chambers: Kotosh, Huaricoto,
Los Gavilanes, and La Galgada. There seems
every reason to be confident that the dates
from those sites do truly reflect the period
when that architectural form was dominant, with the ceremony and philosophy it
expressed.

Table 3. Comparative Radiocarbon Measurements: Calibrated Dates from Eight Sites of the Preceramic and Initial Periods

Preceramic	*Initial Period*

La Galgada

```
        2662±238
            2327±203
                2302±323
                    2250±290
                        2207±318
                            2085±215
                            2082±308
                            2077±308
                                2000±295
                                    1917±213
                                        1782±218
                                            1610±700
                                                1395±275
```

Kotosh Mito Phase (Izumi and Terada, eds. 1972:307)
```
                2455±310
                        2208±317
                            1990±300
                                    1693±217
```

Huaricoto (Burger and Salazar Burger 1980)
```
4085±295
3575±220
    2852±297
            2527±337
```

Huaca Prieta (Bird, Hyslop, and Skinner 1985:51–58)
```
3080±680
    2950±530
        2890±480
            2625±730
                2520±335
                        2085±685
                            2038±483
                                1998±888
                                    1901±331
                                            1615±235
                                            1614±476
                                                    1225±620
                                                    833±428
                                                    788±613
```

Los Gavilanes (Bonavia 1982:74–75)
```
2770±375
                    2215±315
                    2208±418
                            2028±358
                                        1565±315
```

Aspero (Feldman 1980:246–251)
```
3145±595
```

Table 3, *continued*

Preceramic	Initial Period
3030±475	
2898±458	
2775±375	
2600±390	
2523±373	
2508±373	
	2250±290 El Paraíso (Quilter 1985)
	2098±213
	2043±283
	1990±330
	1935±250
	1930±250
	1920±470
	1915±245
	1878±238
	1828±168
	1768±213
	1688±248
	1638±238
	1433±323
	1330±210
	1263±158
3480±300	Ancon (Muelle and Ravines 1973)

Note: Dates are based on Klein et al. 1982. Dates have been converted to midpoints with a ± factor to cover the 95 percent confidence interval.

5. Burial Patterns and Offerings

TERENCE GRIEDER

In this chapter a variety of practices and materials associated with the ritual chambers converted to tombs are examined, beginning with a group of items which were found on chamber floors but seem to antedate the conversion of the chambers to tombs and reflect an earlier use; then the patterns of behavior evident in the burials, and finally the artifacts deposited with the bodies. In the following chapter the skeletons themselves are described.

ITEMS FOUND ON CHAMBER FLOORS

In chambers which may have been used for burials and subsequently filled with dirt and rock and the burials disrupted, it is always hard to differentiate between what was lying on the chamber floor and reflects its use as a ritual chamber and what was in a disrupted burial or was accidentally brought in with fill dirt. There are a few items which were lying directly on the finished chamber floors and represent, as far as we can determine, their original period of use.

Those items and their locations in the excavations are as follows (numbers 1–12 are from Preceramic floors, numbers 13–15 from Initial Period floors):

1. The base of a deer antler 17.0 cm long, broken at the upper end, on Floor 25, D-11:C-3 (Fig. 63).

2. One small green feather fragment, about 2.5 cm long, on the floor of the south half of C-11:I-3 (Fig. 64a). This chamber had been converted to tombs, so the feather

may have been part of the tomb offerings.

3. A piece of white feather down about 5 cm long from the floor of chamber I-12:C-5 in the northeast corner of the North Mound (Fig. 64d).

4. A piece of white feather down about 2 cm long from I-12:C-5.

5. A scrap of green feather, about 2 cm long, from I-12:C-5 (Fig. 64e).

6. Two orange feathers with white down bases, each about 3 cm long, from I-12:C-5 (Fig. 64f, g).

7. Four pieces of white plant down with red spines projecting, each 2.5 cm long, from I-12:C-5 (Fig. 64h–k).

8. A bundle of fine vegetal fiber thread 1 cm in diameter, 2 cm long, from I-12:C-5 (Fig. 64c).

9. A piece of crab claw 1.9 cm long from I-12:C-5 (Fig. 64b).

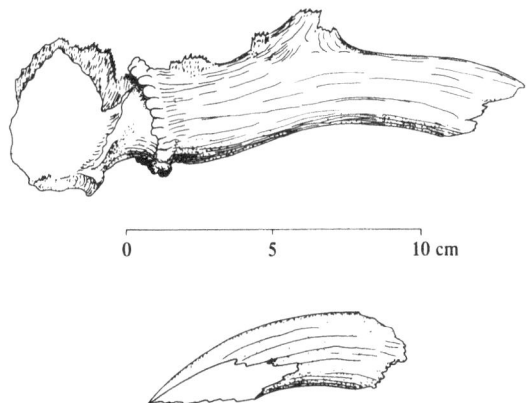

63. Fragments of deer antler from floor of D-11:C-3, Floor 25.

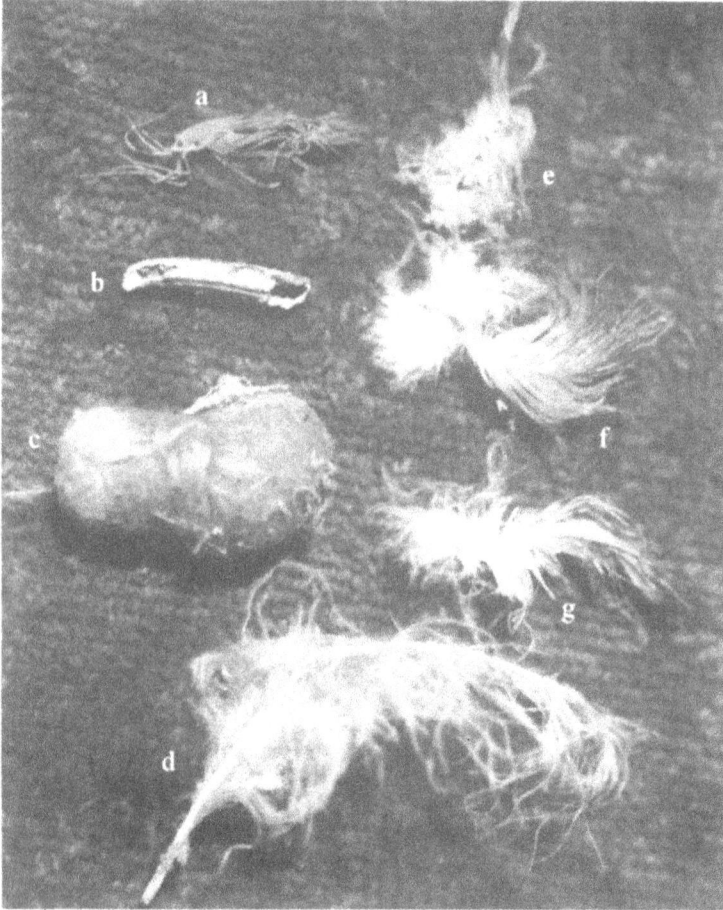

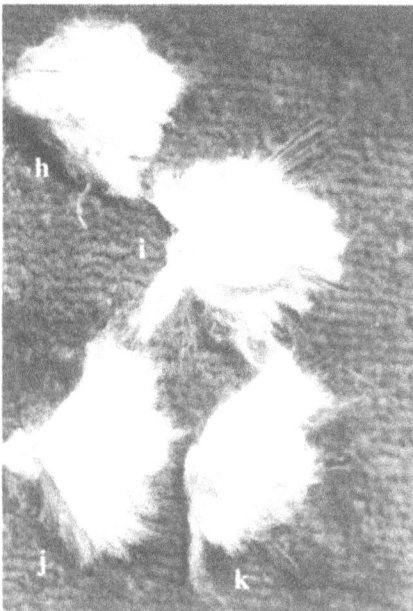

64. Items found on chamber floors C-11:I-3 and I-12:C-5: *a, e,* green feather fragments; *b,* crab claw; *c,* bundle of thread; *d,* white feather down; *f, g,* orange feathers; *h–k,* white plant down.

10. Two pieces of fiber quids, 3.4 and 3.7 cm long, from I-12:C-5.

11. A cylinder 3.2 cm long, 2.3 cm in diameter, with a wooden core and disks of shell on each end and six strips of shell covering the sides, attached with mastic (Figs. 65, 74). There is a 1-cm hole through the cylinder. It was found on Floor 30 in the Main Chamber, at H-11:D-6. This was probably an earplug; it may be compared with a wooden cylinder found at the Asia site in the Omas Valley which was considered an earplug (Engel 1963).

12. Forty-seven white bivalve shells on strings: one alone, thirteen, fourteen, and nineteen on separate strings, but originally presumably on one string. Shells measure 2.8–3.0 cm. Cotton strings are 2 mm thick, S-spun, Z-plied.

13. Small red parrot feathers bound in a bunch, found with black potsherds, plant material, and burnt wood and ashes between two stones set into a white-finished floor in the south wing of the North Mound (at G-11:G-8). The burnt wood gave a radiocarbon age of 3540 ± 50 B.P. (TX-3663). These materials all seem to belong with the floor and possible firepit; no burial is evident.

14. Fragmentary remains of a totora reed basket woven in oblique 2 × 2 interlacing containing some cotton thread, a hank of vegetal fiber containing a turquoise bead, and a wrapped packet of leaves (presumably medicinal), found on Floor 0 in the south wing of the North Mound, at G-11:F-6.

15. An unworked piece of deer antler 9 cm long, broken at both ends, found with the objects in no. 14. There are also black Initial Period potsherds at this level.

The first thing one notes about this collection of things spanning several centuries is that there is much continuity. Two items represented here—deer antlers and feather down—are not found in the burials and may

65. Earplug from H-11:D-6, Floor 30. White shell glued on wooden core.

be presumed to pertain to some other kind of activity. Since the chambers in which they were found are believed to have gone through two phases of use, first as ceremonial chambers, then as tombs, and we have several sets of tomb items, these may be assigned to ceremonial activity. Antlers and feather down are particularly associated with shamanic ritual, antlers being a common insignia on the headdress of the shaman worldwide (Eliade 1964:155) and feather down being a common symbol in shamanic rituals of masculine, or celestial, supernatural power (Grieder 1982:46–48). Although antlers are common in both ancient and recent ritual material from other parts of the Americas, they are not a feature of recent South American shamanic ritual, but feather down is in common use and could provide abundant ethnological analogies for speculation on ancient ceremonies in the chambers at La Galgada.

BURIAL PATTERNS

The burials are an especially rich source of information about the lives, traditions, and techniques of the ancient inhabitants. The tombs in which the burials were placed are discussed in Chapter 3 and the physical characteristics of the skeletons in Chapter 6. The textiles, which are best represented among the burial offerings, are described separately, in Chapter 8. This section examines three other features of the burials: the ways in which the bodies were prepared for burial and laid in the tomb, the personal adornments which were placed on the bodies, and the non-fiber offerings laid beside them.

There are both continuity and variation in the burial practices. The greatest variations are in the position of the body and the manner in which it was prepared for burial. The greatest continuities are in the general character of the textiles and offerings deposited with the bodies. These practices and products are only incidentally related to the fact of death and the emotions it inspires, but are substantial evidence of the techniques, abilities, beliefs, and cultural relationships of the living people who performed the burial and presented the offerings.

The burial groups in Table 4 are listed in what we believe to be chronological order, although there is so little lapse of time between D-11:C-3, Floor 24, Burials I and II, and C-10:E-10 and between the last four groups that we cannot be certain of the order. Thus, the burials fall into four sets: F-12:B-2 is the earliest, with the disturbed traces of D-11:C-3, Floor 25, adding some amplification to our picture of the earliest phase; D-11:C-3, Floor 24, Burials I and II, and C-10:E-10 form a second group; and the remainder, except E-11:J-7, mix late Preceramic and early Initial Period characteristics. E-11:J-7 belongs to a later part of the Initial Period.

The three burials in F-12:B-2 (Figs. 66–67, 69), a man and two women, all over fifty, are the only ones in a tightly flexed position lying on the left side. The position was not a casual choice, since all three are in exactly the same position. All three had their arms crossed on the chest and the legs flexed tightly to the body, and all three bodies were tied tightly into this position with cotton cords around the legs and body. The man's body had been wrapped with forty-nine loops of dark brown cotton cord 1.3 mm in diameter which had been Z-spun and not plied, which is unusual and suggests that Z-spinning for cotton had some special significance in that period. Both the women's bodies had been tied with twenty to twenty-five loops of S-spun, Z-plied yellow cotton string.

Short tufts of human hair, 5–6 cm long, were tucked around the bodies as they were being flexed, tied, and wrapped. All three have the bits of hair, especially around the torso and hips, the largest amount being on woman II, the only one of the three who lacks a mantle. It may be that the hair is the dead person's own, for no hair remains around any of these three skulls, though it is preserved in several of the other burials. Woman III has a swirl of vegetal fiber under the basket she wears as a hat as if to replace lost hair, which further hints that her hair had been removed and cut in short tufts to be packed around her body. Cutting of the hair would also explain the hats on all three heads, hats which appear makeshift, as if they were not hats by original design but were bags and a basket put to this use since bare heads were unseemly. Given the belief found among modern Indian peoples that the soul is especially present in the hair, perhaps we can interpret this practice as a way to keep the spiritually vital hair in contact with the body. Only one later burial followed this practice.

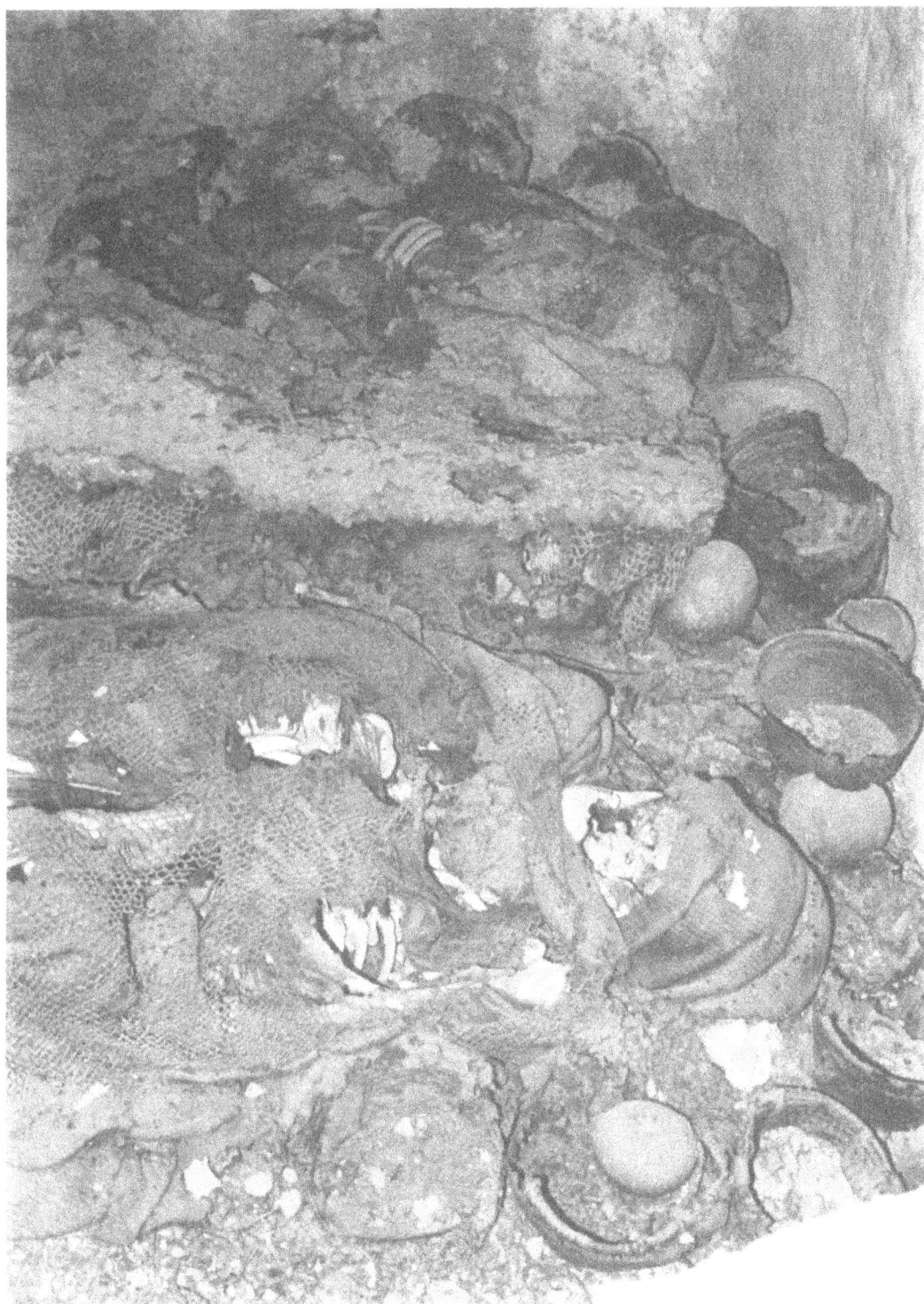

66. Burials in F-12:B-2 tomb. Nearest body is
man (I); farther are two women (II and III).

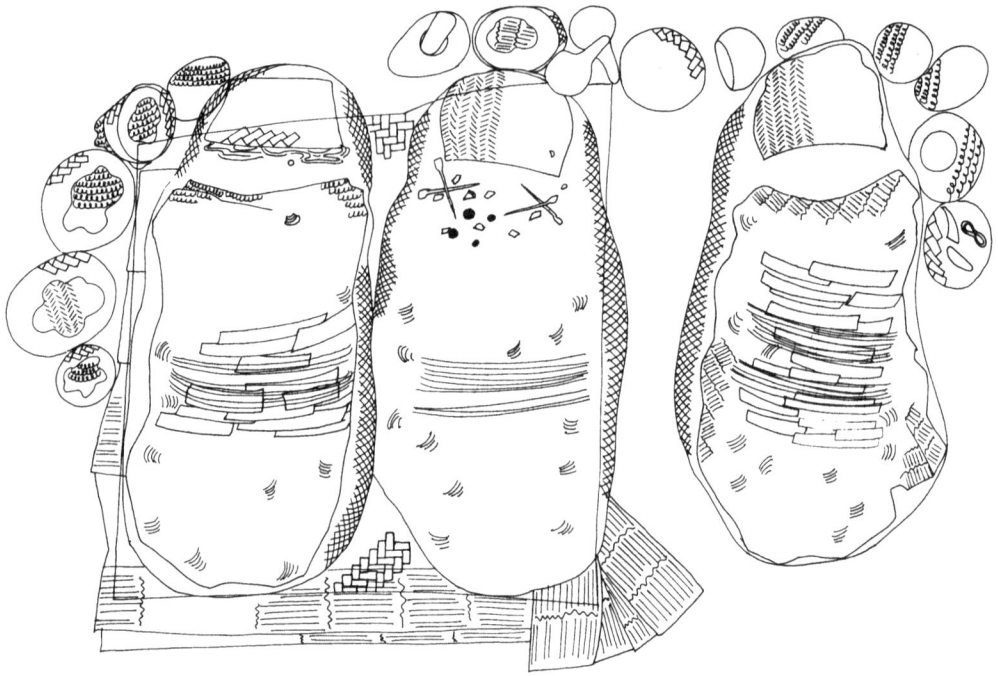

67. Burials in F-12:B-2. See Appendix B for description of offerings 1–18.

68. Burials in C-10:E-10 tomb. See Appendix B for description of offerings. C: cotton.

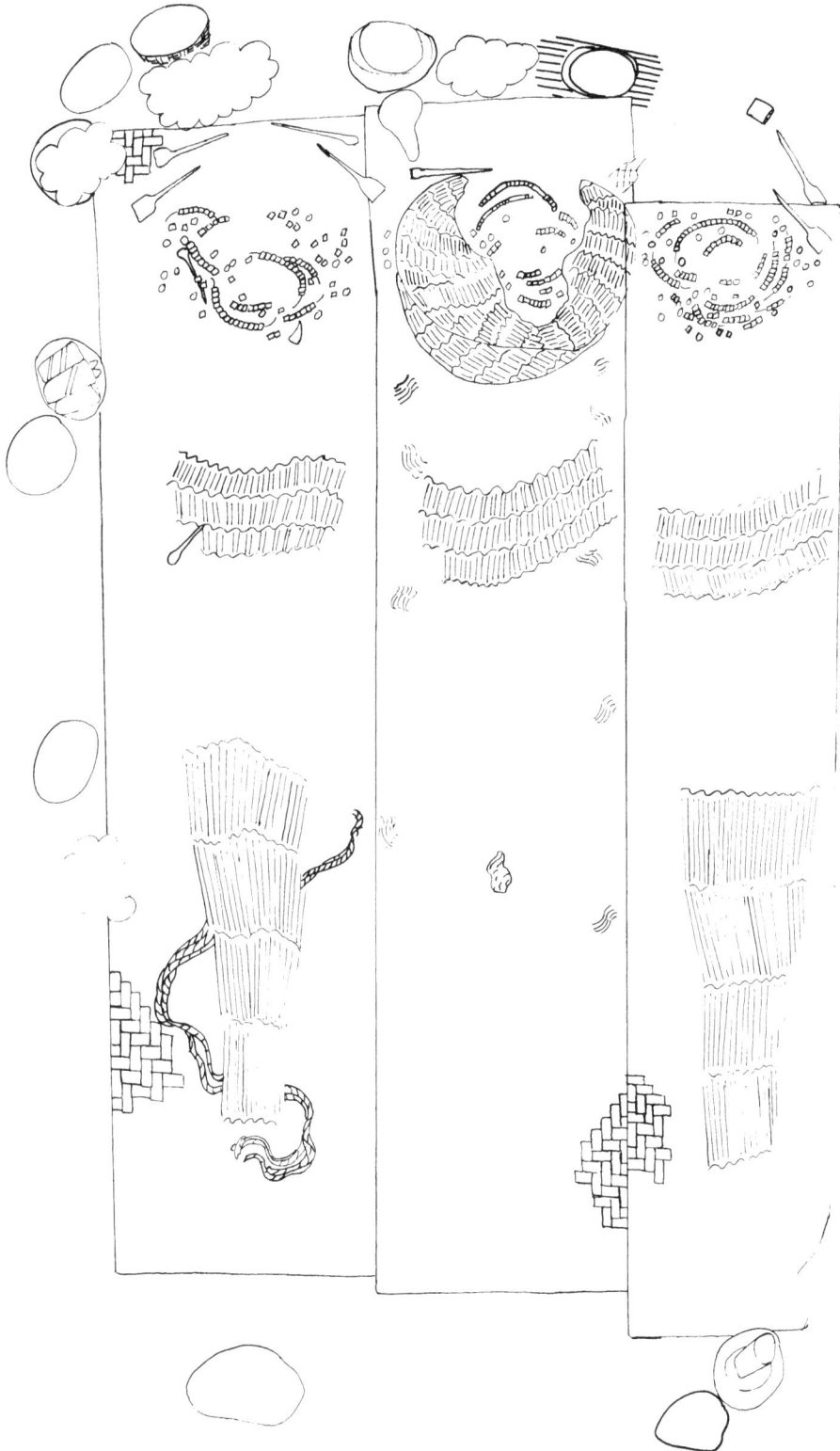

Two of the bodies were also wrapped in strips of barkcloth before the tying was complete but after the body was flexed. The man's body (Fig. 69) had a considerable number of dark brown barkcloth strips 3–4 cm wide, sometimes folded, wrapped around the body and legs inside the strings but outside the bits of hair. Woman III also had coarse, thin brown barkcloth in the same position, but less than the man. The widespread Pre-Columbian belief in the spiritual power of barkcloth (Grieder 1982:81–92) no doubt helps explain its presence here. More than three hundred specimens identified as barkcloth were found in the earlier strata of the excavations at Huaca Prieta and, as at La Galgada, the botanical source remains not certainly identified (Bird, Hyslop, and Skinner 1985:238).

The bodies of the man and woman III were also similar in being wrapped in cotton mantles, the man's twined and the woman's looped. Woman II had no mantle, but lay naked inside a net bag of stiff vegetal fiber similar to the nets covering the other two. All three bodies lay on mats, the two women together on a large twined mat of soft junco, a straw-like reed, and the man on a basket-weave mat of totora reed strips. A totora reed mat was placed over the bodies of the two women.

The materials found on Floor 25, the deepest level in D-11:C-3, appear to represent a burial which was broken up when later building was done. Scraps of net like those on the early burials in F-12:B-2 suggest that the body was flexed, but there are also fragments of a mantle and an interlaced belt, the latter particularly connecting this burial with those in the tomb above, on Floor 24 of D-11:C-3.

The next tomb in which we can determine burial practices is C-10:E-10 (Fig. 68), a small chamber built especially as a tomb with the bodies of three women laid supine,

heads to the south, on totora reed mats. The middle body, that of a woman over fifty years of age, had bits of hair tucked around her body down to the thighs. Unspun cotton was laid around her head, perhaps to replace her hair, but no hat was present. This burial recalls the earliest ones in another feature: between the thighs was a bunched piece of vegetal fiber, perhaps barkcloth. This was the last burial in our sample which included bits of hair and perhaps barkcloth. They are absent from the other bodies (I and III) in this tomb and their presence on that one body may have had something to do with that woman's being especially old when she died and being buried with some old-fashioned practices. Nevertheless, she was buried in the extended position, characteristic of the middle period of burials, and was not covered by a net. All three of these women had twined mantles, and II had a shawl wrapped around her neck and shoulders. The youngest (I), who was pregnant when she died, had a twined junco mat over her body, and coarser totora mats covered both I and III.

Floor 24 in D-11:C-3 (Figs. 57, 58, 70) was an especially built tomb in the center of an old firepit chamber which had been used for two sets of burials following entirely different practices. The earlier set consists of the bodies of a man in his thirties and an old woman, extended supine, heads to the south, their arms crossed on their chests. The largely disintegrated skeleton of an infant lay between their heads. Although the hair of the adults is not preserved, there is nothing, such as a hat, to suggest that it had been cut. Both bodies were wrapped only in twined cotton mantles with interlaced belts. They lay on totora mats, the man's supported by a wooden framework which formed a litter, still evident under the head and shoulders.

The second set of burials in D-11:C-3, Floor 24, were flexed burials set upright.

69. Bones of man from F-12:B-2 wrapped in barkcloth (arrows), cords, twined mantle, and interlaced net.

One, identified as III, was set against the corner of the tomb on top of the feet of the earlier extended body of the woman. The other, IV, was set directly on top of the pelvis of the same body. Both these bundle burials were enveloped in woven cotton mantles and an outer wrapping of bast fiber netting. Burial III was set on a totora mat or basket inside the cloth wrapping. These burials introduce the new position for burials, found also in C-12:D-1, which became one of the standard positions (along with extended) for later Peruvian cultures.

The tombs located at C-11:E-8 and C-12:D-1 are beside each other and are both entered by short shafts from Floor 2. The former is inside the old white, niched walls of a ritual chamber. The latter was added outside the old chamber walls. Although both sets of

burials belong to the period at the very end of the Preceramic and the beginning of the Initial Period and we cannot be certain which set is the earlier, they show different positions for the bodies.

C-11:E-8, the converted chamber, was opened by the road cut but appeared to be largely intact when Alberto Bueno and I examined it in 1976. Our efforts to reseal the opening and hide it until a proper study could be made were unsuccessful, so we have only an incomplete record of this group. It consisted of a man, a woman, and a child extended on their backs, heads to the west. These are the only reclining burials in which the heads were not to the south, and this group is the only one in any of the burials which suggests a nuclear family. The man's body (Fig. 72) lay on a totora mat and

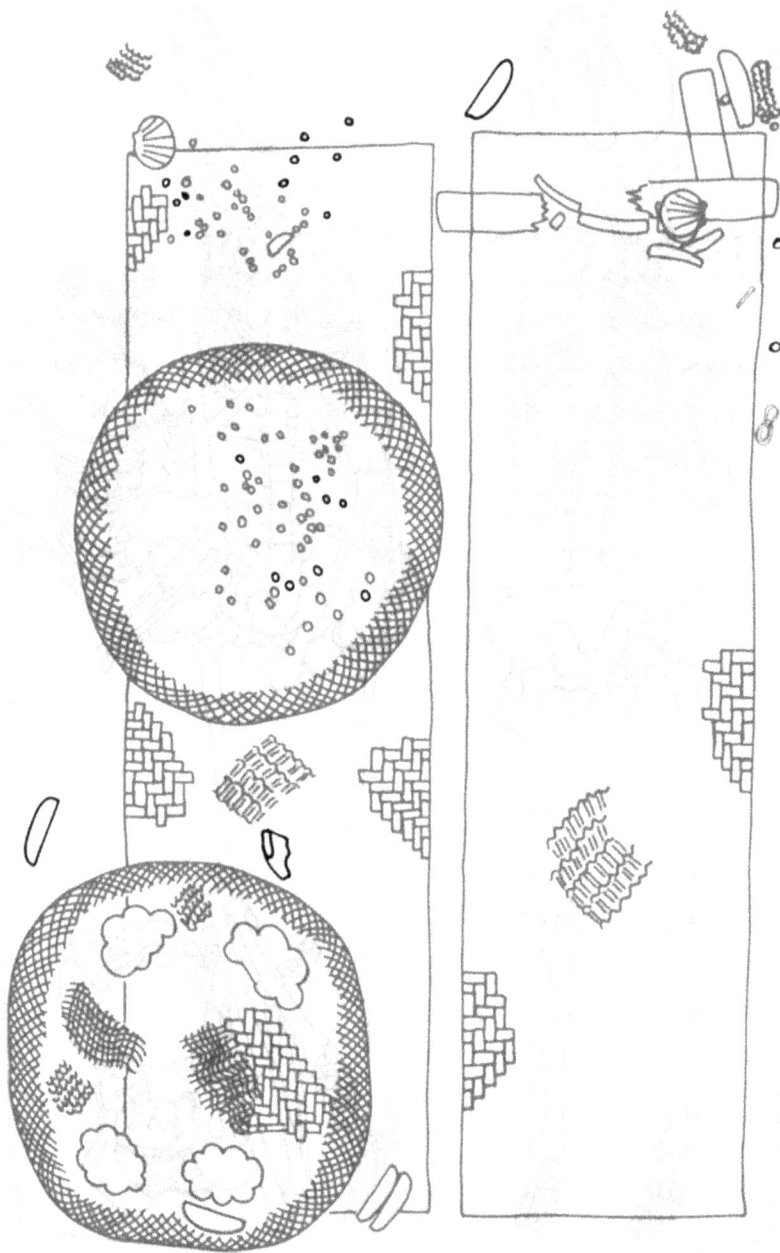

70. Burials in D-11:C-3 tomb.

71. Burials evident during excavation in C-12:
D-1 tomb. West end destroyed by road cut.

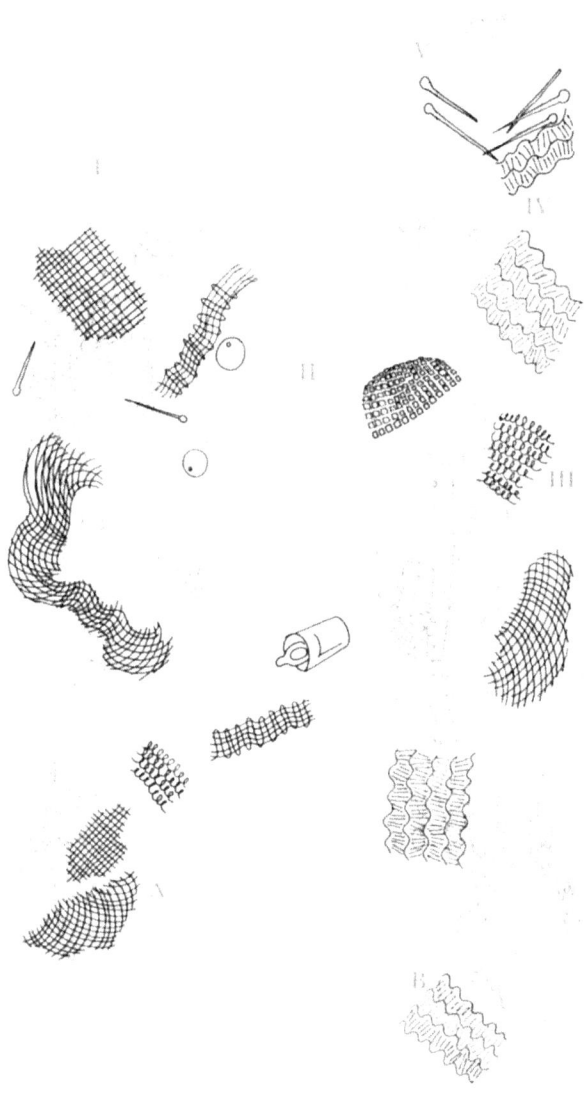

I

II

III

IV

V

B

0   10   20 cm

Table 4. Burial Patterns and Offerings

	F-12:B-2			D-11:C-3 Floor 25	D-11:C-3 Floor 24				C-11:F-5	C-10:E-10		
	I	II	III		I	II	III	IV		I	II	III
Male adult	x				x		x	x	4			
Female adult		x	x			x			3	x	x	x
Adult, sex uncertain									1			
Child									5			
Flexed left	x	x	x									
Flexed sitting							x	x				
Tied	x	x	x									
Extended					x	x				x	x	x
Oriented	S	S	S		S	S				S	S	S
Litter					x							
Totora below	x				x	x	x			x	x	x
Totora above		x	x							x		x
Junco below		x	x									
Junco above										x		
Barkcloth	x	x	x								p	
Twined mantle	x		x	x	x	x				x	x	x
Woven mantle							x	x				
Shawl											x	
Hat	x	x	x									
Hair bits	x	x	x								x	
Net (not body)							x					
Net body bag	x	x	x				x	x				
Belt				x	x	x						
Necklace					x			x	x	x	x	x
Earrings												
Hairpins		p			x					x	x	x
Cloakpin		p			x					p	p	p
Basket	x	x	x							x	x	x
Cloth bag	x	x	x	x	x	x	x		x	x	x	x
Gourd bowl	x	x	x							x	x	x
Stone bowl	x	x	x							x	x	x
Ceramics												
Spindle/thread				x						x		
Unspun cotton							x			x	x	x
Clam shell				x	x	x				x	x	x
Mussel shell				x		x	x					
Crab claws												
Rock crystal		x										
Magnetite		x										
Turquoise			x		x					x		

| C-12:D-1 | | | | | | C-11:E-8 | | | C-10:I-10 | E-11:J-7 |
I	III	V	A	B	Other	I	II	III		
x	x				1	x			1	4
		x			2–3			x	3	6
										5
		x	x		2–3		x			12
x	x	p	x	x						
						x	x	x		
						W	W	W		
						x		p		
								x		
	x	x		x		x			x	
x			x			x				
	x									
						x				
x	x		x							
x	x								x	
						x			x	
x										
p		x							p	
p									p	
									x	
x	x			x		x			x	
										x
	x								x	
						x			x	x
									x	
	x					x				
						x				
									x	
		x								

f: fetus.
x: present.
p: possibly present.

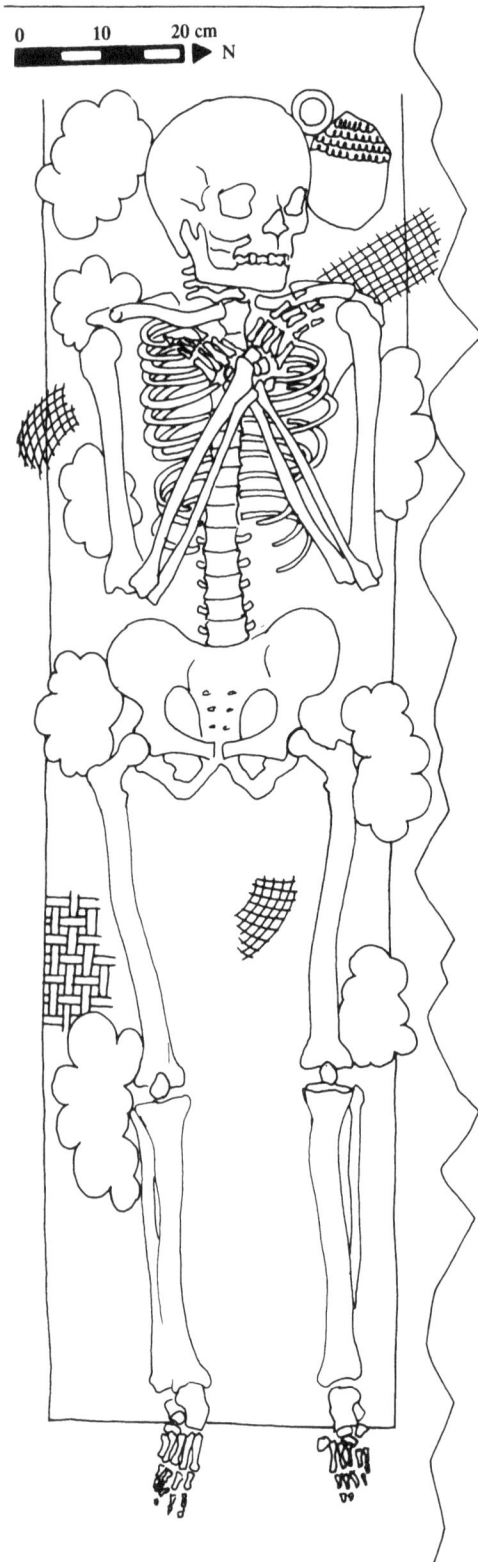

was covered with a twined mantle, the mantle's structure being of the Preceramic type. But beside the man's head, at the left ear, was the only complete pottery vessel found in our excavations, a small Initial Period jar whose lid may be the one found in the disturbed burials in C-10:I-10. The woman's body lay on a junco mat twined in 3-cm-diameter bundles with a vegetal fiber rope 1 cm in diameter. The child's skeleton was extended between the adults'. The skeletons of the woman and child and all associated materials were removed by looters before work was resumed in 1978, so those burials are not described and the skeletons do not appear in Chapter 6 and Appendix A.

C-12:D-1 (Fig. 71) held ten to twelve burials which had been protected from looting by the collapse of the tomb walls when the bulldozer destroyed the western half of the tomb. Although the bodies had all been knocked over by the collapsing walls, they were originally upright flexed bundle burials, the arms crossed on the chest, the knees tightly flexed but apparently not tied into position. There is no evidence that any of these burials were set on mats or baskets. The earliest, to judge by his offerings, was an old man (III) wearing a Preceramic-type twined mantle and accompanied by a stone cup (Fig. 73). He wore a tight net cap covered with flat square white shell beads. Burial I, on the other hand, was wrapped in an Initial-Period-type woven shroud. No trace of pottery was found in this tomb.

C-10:I-10 contains the disturbed and burned remains of four adult burials, a man and three women. We have no evidence of body position from the skeletal remains. The base of a large basket may have been used as the foundation for a flexed burial. Twined mantles and an interlaced belt appear among the textiles, items characteristic of the later

72. Man's body in C-11:E-8 tomb.

Preceramic burials, along with a small ceramic lid which fits the opening of the small jar in C-11:E-8 (see Fig. 158). This tomb's remains contained a number of unusual items, including an amber plumb bob and unusual mineral specimens (Fig. 81). It is probably significant that the whole pottery vessel and the lid which looks as if it belongs to that vessel were both found in burials in which the textiles are late Preceramic types, twined rather than woven. That suggests that pottery was imported in the form of finished trade items before La Galgada began making textiles of Initial Period types. Architecture, however, had already shifted to single large, probably open chambers on the top of each mound. The sequence of development into Initial Period types suggested by these tombs and their contents is (1) architecture, (2) pottery, (3) textiles.

JEWELRY

Personal adornments are found in all the undisturbed burials, as well as in an important Initial Period cache, and it is clear that they constituted an important and developing element in the technology and economy of these cultures. Jewelry became more abundant and varied in the later Preceramic burials. The few surviving items representing Initial Period adornments show different forms and styles from the Preceramic.

Among the three burials in the earliest tomb, F-12:B-2, only the bodies of the two women had jewelry. Body II had the most: two pairs of bone pins (Fig. 74*a–d*) and a broken white stone bead. Other items in that burial (rock crystal, anthracite, pebbles probably of magnetite) seem to have been treasured, but show no special workmanship and were not pierced to be worn. The larger pair of pins lay at the woman's right, the two smaller ones at her left, both pairs beside the head below the ear. The only certain use for such bone pins is as hairpins, in tomb C-12:

73. Burial C-12:D-1(III).

D-1 (IV) (Fig. 75), and in this case their position makes that a plausible suggestion, although the woman's hair may have been cut. They might also have served to fasten clothing, though we have no case in which that use is certain. The other woman, III, had just one green turquoise bead under her head, along with an unworked curling salt crystal. The absence of shell is notable in the jewelry, despite the presence of one marine shell in a basket (offering no. 18; *see* App. B), along with another green bead.

These items—bone pins, beads of stone, especially blue or green stone, and items of shell—formed the basic elements of personal jewelry in the Preceramic Period. The bones have been identified as human. Several types of shell were used: *Ostrea* sp., *Mitillus chorus, Pecten purpuratus,* and

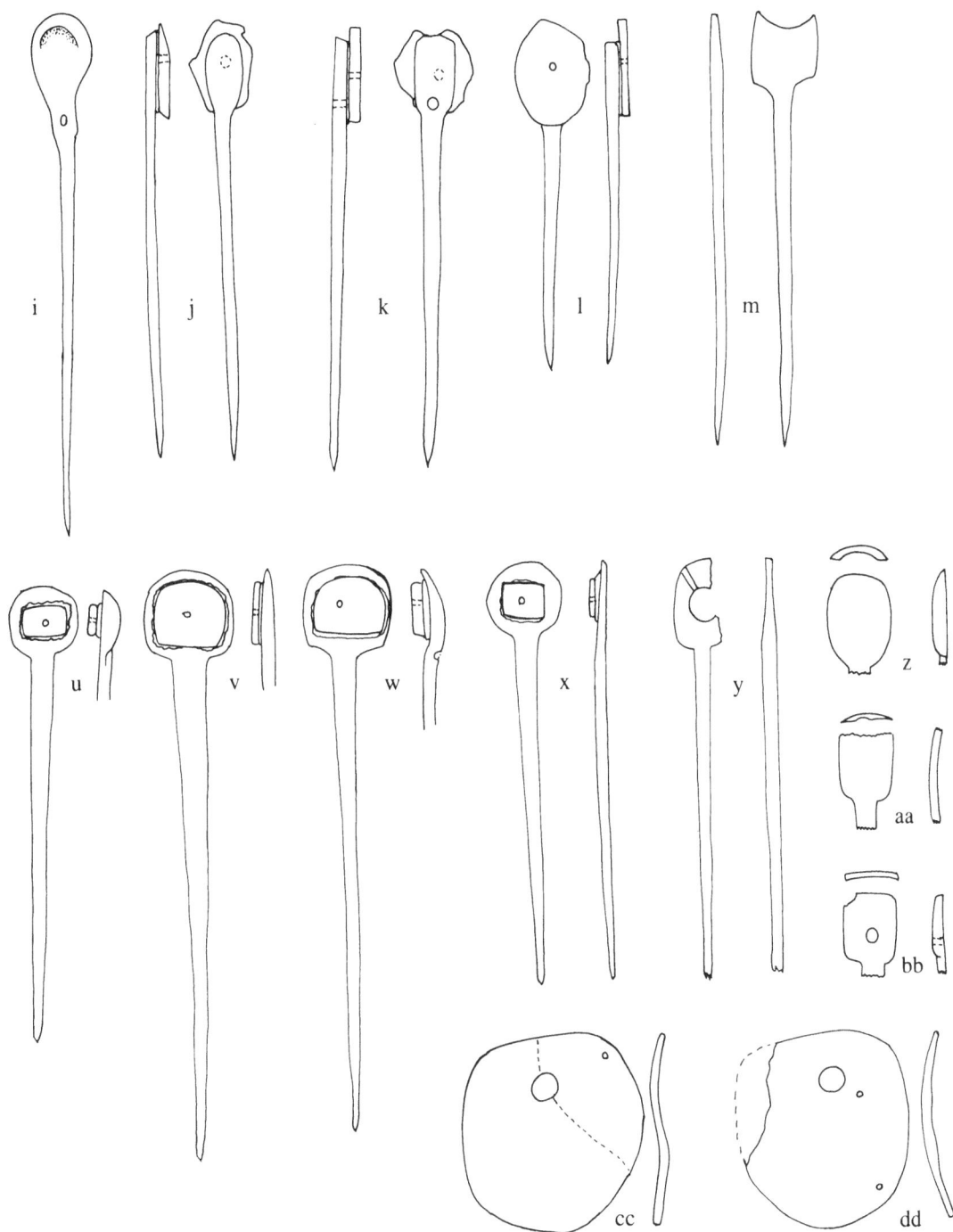

74. Jewelry from burials: *a–d* from F-12:
B-2(II); *e*, from D-11:C-3(I); *f–l* from
C-10:E-10(I); *m*, from C-10:E-10(II); *n–q*,
from C-10:E-10(III); *r–s*, *cc* from C-12:D-1(I);
t–x from C-12:D-1(V); *y–bb*, *dd*, from
C-10:I-10. *Continued on next page.*

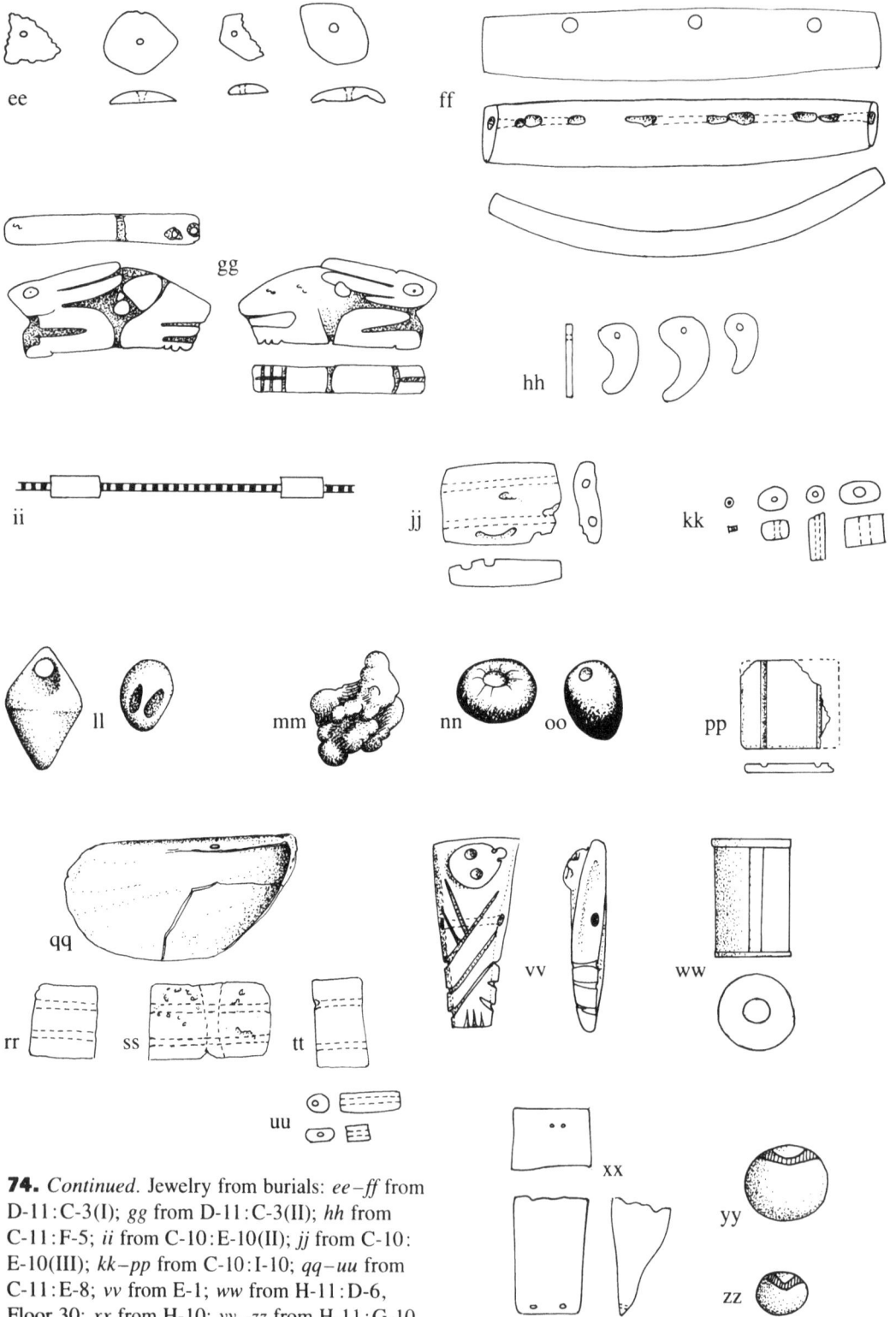

74. *Continued.* Jewelry from burials: *ee–ff* from D-11:C-3(I); *gg* from D-11:C-3(II); *hh* from C-11:F-5; *ii* from C-10:E-10(II); *jj* from C-10: E-10(III); *kk–pp* from C-10:I-10; *qq–uu* from C-11:E-8; *vv* from E-1; *ww* from H-11:D-6, Floor 30; *xx* from H-10; *yy–zz* from H-11:G-10.

Strombus in the Preceramic, with *Spondylus princeps* coming into use at the end of the Preceramic (identified by A. Bueno M.). Any blue or green stone seems to have been treasured and used in jewelry, but the large beads attached to bone pins have been identified by María J. Ojeda Ch. (who identified other mineral and organic materials) of the Spectometry Laboratory of the Universidad Nacional de Ingeniería (Lima) as turquoise: $CuAl_6(PO_4)_4(OH)_8, 5H_2O$, a hydrous basic copper aluminum phosphate.

Through the period represented by the La Galgada burials all those items became more common and more elaborate. The extended burials in D-11:C-3, Floor 24, had much more jewelry, though the numerous offerings of bags and baskets found earlier and later are absent. The man (I) wore a necklace of four red stone beads (Fig. 76) of compacted ferruginous diatomite, all of them slightly curving flat slabs of stone 7, 10, 11, and 11 cm long, 1.9 cm wide, and 0.7 cm thick. They are all drilled longitudinally in short steps so the suspension cord would not show on the front. A single hole probably could have been done except for the curve of the stones. The front faces of the dark red stones were drilled with ten pits for inlays, the pits spaced about 3.5 cm apart, two or three to a stone depending on the length of the stone. Only one of the original inlays remains in place, a green turquoise. This necklace is a remarkable work both technically and aesthetically and must have been a uniquely masculine ornament. Near the head of this man lay one small broken bone pin (Fig. 74*e*), again probably for the hair, and four flat blue-green turquoise beads (Fig. 74*ee*) of the type found attached to hairpins in another burial.

The old woman at his right wore a necklace of white beads with a *Strombus* shell rabbit as pendant (Figs. 74*gg*, 77)—long ears and no tail distinguish it from a vis-

cacha, which has short ears and a long tail. It is uncertain how the rabbit was suspended, since it is not perforated. A thread may have been tied around it, or perhaps the shell plug in the anus provided a way to suspend it, or it may have been simply carried as a fetish. The rabbit is 5.8 cm long, with a pink nose, green turquoise eyes, and varicolored shell and stone inlays. This pair of burials shows a great advance in the working of shell and stone, and the establishment of the Andean tradition of mosaic and inlay in jewelry and figurines. Although the man was accompanied by natural shells, his jewelry was made entirely of stone. We have no way of knowing where the work was done, but the materials could have originated in the highlands surrounding La Galgada. The shell used to make the rabbit and its shell inlays obviously originated on the coast. La Galgada was importing unworked shell, so it is possible that the work was done at La Galgada using techniques perfected in stone. What La Galgada traded for these imported luxuries is not known.

The burials in C-11:F-5 had been entirely destroyed by looters at the time the road cut was made in 1975, but the debris which remained on the floor contained one interesting piece of jewelry. Among the numerous and varied beads on the floor were 106 pieces of bone carved into the shape of claws and drilled for stringing (Figs. 74*hh*, 78). The thin, flat pieces vary from about 1 cm to 2.5 cm long. They are sufficient in number to make a necklace by themselves, but there are also other beads which might have served as spacers. The carved beads clearly represent the claws of birds or animals and are a civilized version of the primitive necklace of natural claws. It is revealing that by this time it was considered acceptable to wear the manufactured substitutes rather than collect the natural claws by hunting. This tends to confirm other evidence that hunting was not

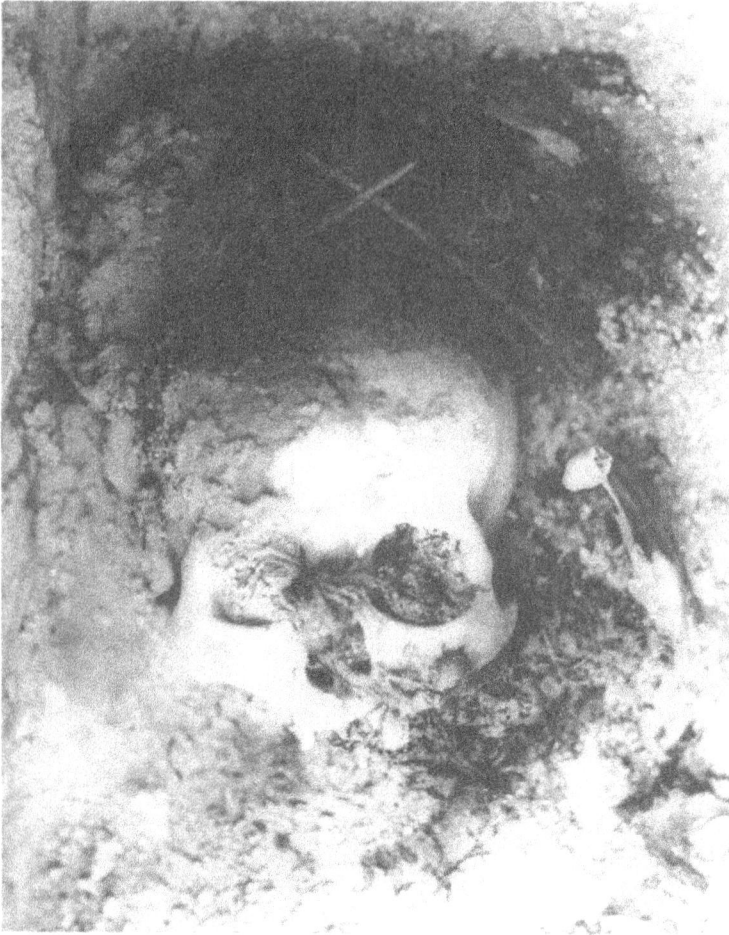

75. C-12:D-1(V) skull with hairpins in place.

76. Red diatomite necklace from man's body, D-11:C-3(I).

77. Rabbit pendant of shell with inlays, D-11: C-3(II). Length 5.8 cm.

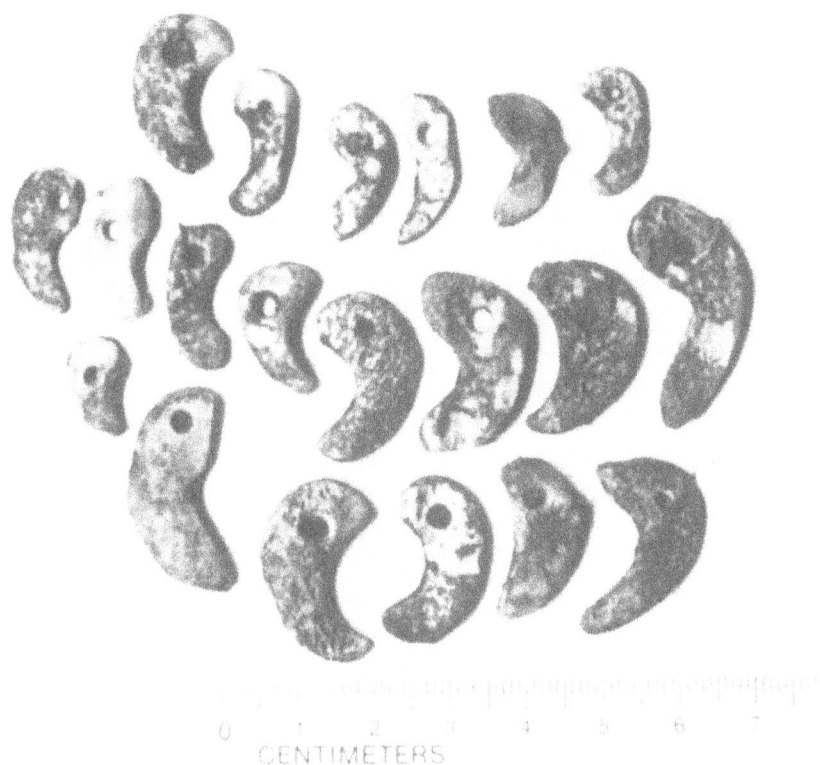

78. Bone "claws" for necklace, C-11:F-5.

a major activity at La Galgada.

The three women's bodies in C-10:E-10 were abundantly provided with bead necklaces and with bone pins. There are three types of pins represented: a plain bone pin (Fig. 74*m*) under the head of the old woman in the middle (II) and two more (Fig. 74*f, i*) with the young woman on her right (I); three bone pins with blue-green turquoise beads attached to the heads with Body I (Fig. 74*j–l*); and a third type, with large flat trapezoidal heads either plain, incised, or with white shells attached, represented by eight examples divided between bodies I and III (Figs. 74*g, h, n–q,* 79). This last group is unique in this tomb; from their position they seem to have been hairpins. The plain pin on body I was near the waist and may have been used on clothing.

Long necklaces were worn by all three of these women, looped in multiple strands around the neck. The young woman, I, wore two necklaces, one of white shell beads 9–11 mm in diameter by 7–9 mm thick, the other alternating dark brown and pink or white shell beads in 10-cm-long groups. Both her necklaces had center pendants, one of *Spondylus* shell, the other of stone. There are some longer (16 mm) beads of stone and bone which may have been mixed into these necklaces. Bodies II and III wore similar necklaces of alternating groups of black and white small beads, interrupted by one long white shell bead at intervals (Fig. 74*ii*). The necklace worn by III centered on a rectangular bead of *Spondylus* shell, drilled laterally twice (Fig. 74*jj*).

That flat rectangular bead with its pair of

lateral perforations is similar to fifteen shell beads (found with two more single-drilled ones) in the debris on the floor of C-11:E-8 (Fig. 80). We do not know whether this was worn by a man or woman.

Among the various items in the burned tomb C-10:I-10 only two kinds seem to be personal ornaments: the fragments of seven bone pins and an amber pendant (Fig. 81)—but other small fetish-like objects of minerals appear (Fig. 74*ll–pp*). Two pins have unusually fancy heads, and the amber pendant, although shaped like a plumb bob, does not hang straight and would not have served any obvious use. It was apparently valued for adornment as a rare material.

The burials in C-12:D-1 contained several distinctive pieces of jewelry—a beaded cap, large shell earrings, and fancy hairpins (Fig. 82). The cap, which was worn by an old man (III), was made of a very delicate bast netting on which were strung as it was made 519 thin square white shell beads. Most of the beads are about 5 mm square, but some are as large as 15 to 17 mm on a side. Two green turquoise beads of the same size and shape were found and may have been part of the same cap.

Two 5-cm shell disks on the floor of this tomb (Fig. 74*cc*) belonged to a man (I) and were probably ear pendants, though how they were worn is not obvious. The off-center hole could have held a string or a rod which passed through a perforation in the ear. These, along with the shell-encased cylinder on Floor 30 of the North Mound (Fig. 65), are the first evidence we have of ear ornaments. The Floor 30 cylinder belongs to the late Preceramic and seems to be quite a different type of ornament from these disks, which belong to the beginning of the Initial Period; the body also wore a woven shroud characteristic of that period. The Initial Period cache to be discussed below also held disks which probably were parts of earplugs. In Inca times the nobility were distinguished by the wearing of earplugs and the higher ranks by larger plugs (Cobo 1979: 208, 245) and it is interesting to note the appearance of earplugs at the same time that architecture begins to change toward more centralized plans. These various changes, which might seem insignificant in isolation, together suggest the formation of a group of high-status people distinguishable by the wearing of ear ornaments who

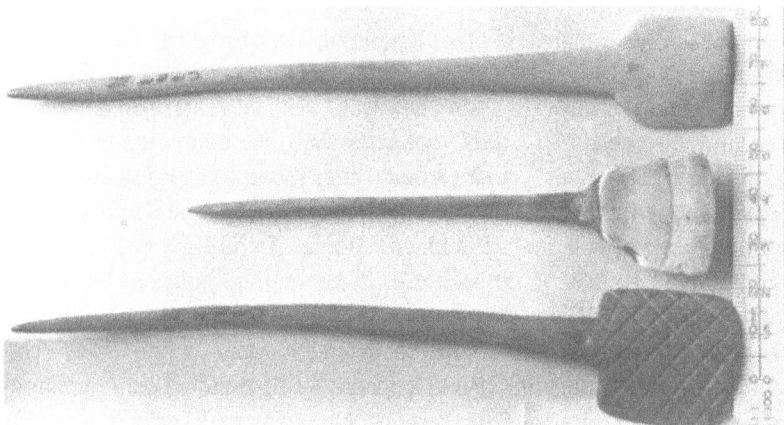

79. Pins, C-10:E-10(III).

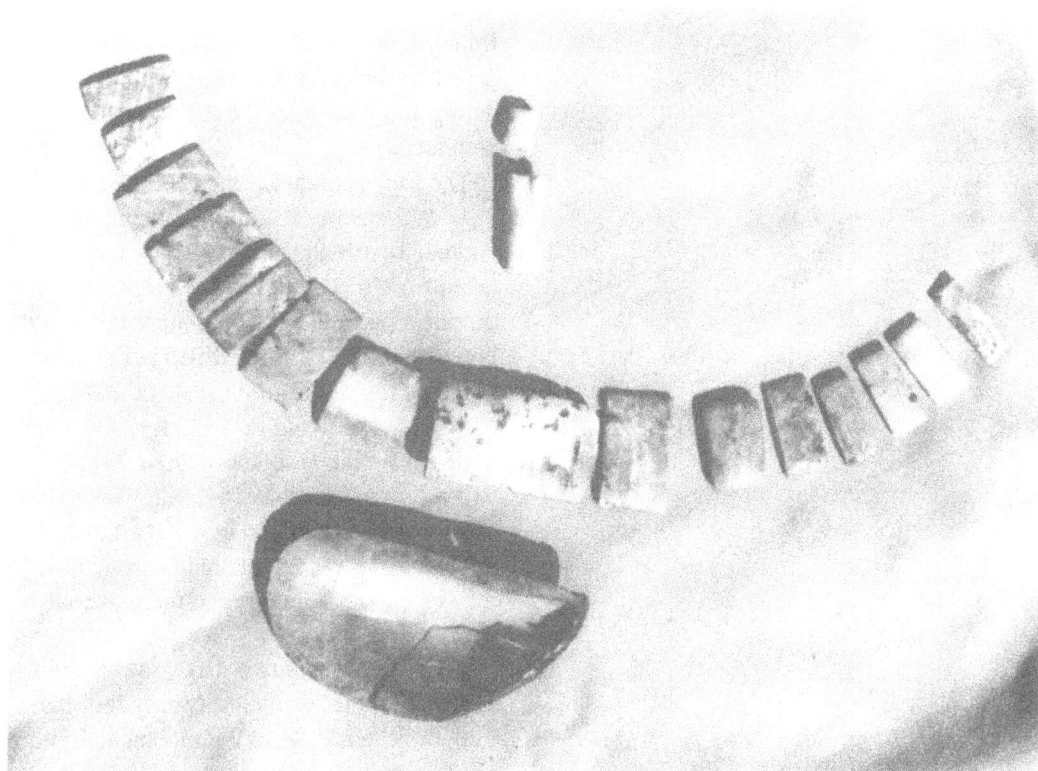

80. Shell necklace, C-11:E-8.

81. Items from destroyed and burned burial
C-10:I-10.

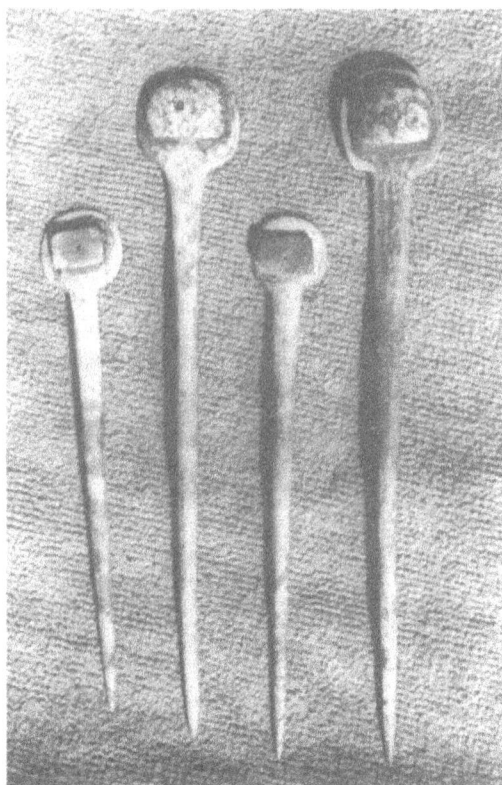

82. Bone hairpins, C-12:D-1(V).

took leadership roles in the society as it centralized.

The set of items found in H-11:G-10 on Floor 11 and under the corner of the stairway which was the centerpiece of Floor 10 are the best sample we have of Initial Period jewelry (Fig. 83, 84). They were a cache, evidently deposited as an offering to sanctify a ceremonial building, rather than a burial offering as in the previous examples. Although the top of the North Mound was heavily pitted by looters, that particular area had not been penetrated and the construction levels of floor and stairs were in their original places. There is no evidence of a pit or any other manner in which the cache could be intrusive. The Floor 10 stairway and the cache should date to the same period. The

architectural evidence indicates a date in the Initial Period. The radiocarbon test (TX-5606) on the cloth in the cache confirms that dating and reinforces the dating of the architecture.

The cache contained the following items:

1. Woven cotton cloth in 20-cm loom widths, Textile Specimen 195. A sample taken from this cloth has been tested for radiocarbon; sample TX-5606 gave a radiocarbon age of 3320 B.P. ± 270. That gives a range on the radiocarbon scale of 1640–1100 B.C., centering on 1370 B.C. On a calibrated scale the absolute range is 2310–910 B.C., centering on 1610 B.C. Since this cloth was tied onto two of the shell disks, items 6 and 8 below, the radiocarbon test may be taken as applying to them as well (Figs. 83, 120).

2. Beads: ninety-two dark gray stone beads, 3–4 mm diameter; twenty-four pale gray stone beads, up to 9 mm long and 5 mm in diameter; six green chrysocolla beads of various small sizes; two rock crystal beads, one 24.0 mm, the other 13.8 mm in their largest diameters. All the beads were drilled biconically and all but the rock crystal beads are faceted on the exterior. There are many traces of red pigment on the green beads and some traces on the others. The smaller rock crystal bead was strung on a brown cotton cord attached to the cloth (item 1 above), which was also tied to two of the shell disks listed below.

3. Five iron pyrite crystals, each about 2 mm on a side.

4. Two unworked pieces of blue turquoise in matrix, both about 1.5 cm in longest dimension.

5. White *Spondylus princeps* shell disk with four bird heads, 3.28 cm in widest dimension (diagonally, across bird heads). The disk is irregular and the shell has a slight twist. The eyes of the birds were drilled and inlaid, two with pink stone or shell, one with

83. Shell disks, mineral disk with shell mosaic, and cloth from H-11:G-10 cache on Floor 11. The cloth is dated by specimen TX-5606. The pattern of the shell mosaic as shown is probably erroneous, but all recovered pieces are shown (compare Fig. 84).

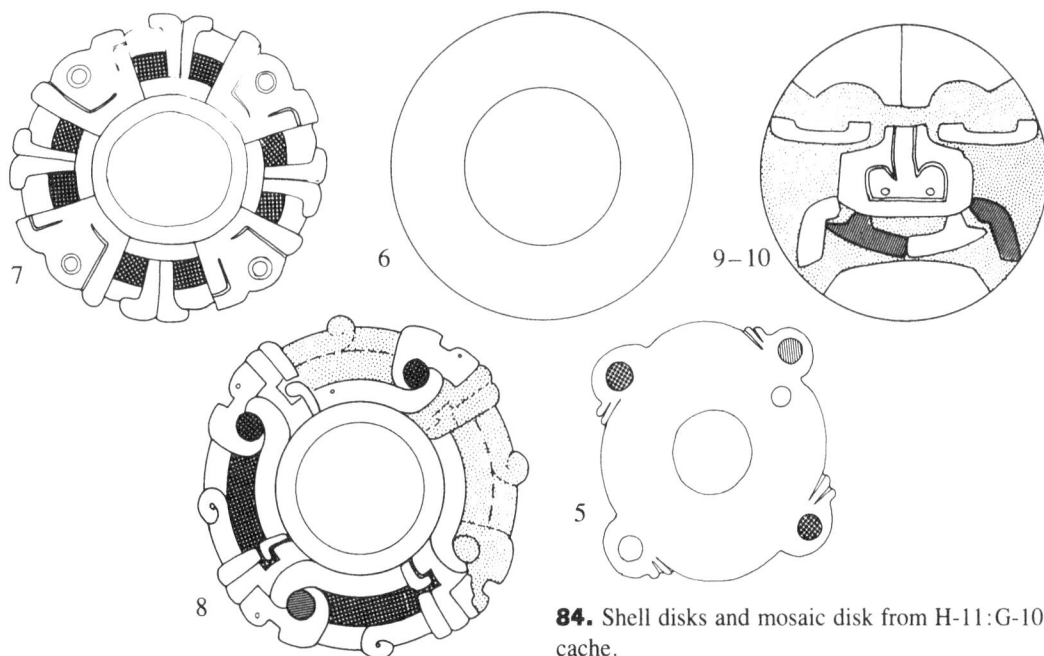

84. Shell disks and mosaic disk from H-11:G-10 cache.

green, and one is missing. (Fig. 83, lower right).

6. Plain iridescent pale orange shell disk, not quite a perfect circle; 3.45 cm in widest dimension. This was tied into the cloth (item 1 above) (Fig. 83, upper center).

7. Disk of iridescent pale orange shell with four heads of raptorial birds with crests incised, 3.68 cm in widest dimension. There is red pigment in the incisions. Eyes were drilled and probably inlaid, but holes are now empty (Fig. 83, upper left).

8. *Spondylus princeps* shell disk, 3.75 cm in widest dimension, carved with four profile monster heads in a Chavín-related style. The eyes are drilled pits, two holding red paste, one a light green stone inlay, the fourth empty. Red paste fills excised areas. Parts of the carved surface were broken off in ancient times. This was tied into the cloth (item 1 above) (Fig. 83, lower center).

9. Slate disk, 3.37 cm diameter at widest, one side smooth gray stone, the other coated with a yellow resinous glue. This is presumed to have supported the items in no. 10 below.

10. Eight pieces of shell mosaic forming a frontal monster mask. The backs of some pieces show traces of yellow glue indicating they were attached to item 9 above. The pattern of the mosaic cannot be securely reconstructed since several pieces are missing (Fig. 83, upper right), but the subject can be securely identified by the piece with a nose incised.

11. Fragments of a small mosaic figurine of a monster with U-shaped white shell eyes, made of wood, resinous glue or paste, white shell, and blue-green turquoise. Eight small strips of bone or antler also seem to have been part of this. The figurine had almost completely disintegrated, but the subject was identified by the eyes, one of which was discovered still adhering to some other pieces. The figurine appears to have been between 2.5 and 3.0 cm tall.

With the exception of most of the beads, the minerals, and the cloth, the items in this cache have no precedent in the Preceramic offerings. Preceramic jewelry took the form of hairpins, or perhaps cloak pins, and necklaces; there are only two cases, noted above, in which there are probable ear ornaments, and one may belong to the early Initial Period. Five of the items here appear to be disks which would be attached to earplugs, the principal doubt being that none of them make pairs. The breaking up of all the pairs might suggest that another cache was deposited simultaneously with the other member each pair. The last item, the decomposed figurine, shared a subject with the mosaic disk, but is otherwise unique at the site in every respect.

The three perforated disks with heads around the rim present us with a particularly provocative set of similarities and differences. All three had circular drilled eye pits, inlaid with stone in at least two cases. Although inlaid eyes are not unknown in Chavín art (see Rowe 1962a: Fig. 27), usually when the eye has a circular pit it represents only the pupil, with the U-shaped white around it. These disks seem to carry on a type of eye with Preceramic antecedents, as in the rabbit pendant. The raptorial birds also appear as a subject on Preceramic textiles, though the motif is not exactly the same. The profile monster heads, however, are entirely new. The Preceramic serpents and monsters on textiles all have frontal faces and none have fangs. But perhaps the newest element of all is the modular banded design of two of the disks. Although the disk with the mosaic monster face and the decomposed figurine may have originated separately from the other disks, given their U-shaped eyes, the three disks with representational designs share a sufficient number of design features that they probably were products of a single workshop and probably do not represent a very long period. The matter of their relationship to the emergence of the Chavín style is discussed in Chapter 12.

Personal adornments are not always taken seriously as indications of cultural history, but they provide us with important information at La Galgada. Three points seem to be of special significance. First is the gradual increase in the number and variety of beads available through the later years of the Preceramic, especially turquoise and shell. Long necklaces of small beads looped many times around the neck seem to have been the admired new style of the late Preceramic. These appear to have been made of imported materials, and perhaps imported as finished products. Second is the sudden popularity of (probable) ear ornaments at the beginning of the Initial Period. The great importance of earplugs in the later Andean cultures and their extreme rarity in the Preceramic burials make this a matter of special interest. Third

is the introduction of *Spondylus* shell in the late Preceramic necklaces and its importance in the Initial Period cache. This warm-water shell was imported by the later Andean societies from the Gulf of Guayaquil for use in rituals associated with feeding the gods of nature and with ceremonies associated with the ruling class (Davidson 1981: 76). Its appearance at the transition between Preceramic and Initial Period is surely another indication of the centralization of the society around rulers who introduced new symbols.

WOODEN ARTIFACTS

The most interesting wooden artifacts all come from the earliest levels. The uses of wood evident in the later contexts vary from a litter (Fig. 85) to the rafters of roofs (Fig. 54), but little evidence of worked wood survives in those levels.

From the antechamber of F-12: B-2, which was built and sealed at the time of the

85. Remains of wooden litter from a looted burial.

burial in that tomb, comes a very small worked stick 7 cm long, with one side flat, the other curved (Fig. 86*d*). It tapers at the broken end; if it was symmetrical it must have been about 10 cm long. It is much smaller than the typical weaver's batten, but its shape suggests that it was used in cloth-making, perhaps on some narrow pieces such as interlaced belts. That same shape is found in two other worked pieces of wood, both from Floor 25 in D-11:C-3 (Fig. 86*a, b*). The smaller is only 6.4 cm long but it may originally have been longer than the previous example, since it does not taper at the broken end. The other is 13 cm long and may have reached more than double that length. Both look as if they might have served as clothmaker's battens. Floor 25 may have the remains of a disturbed burial, and the wooden artifacts may have been offerings with that burial. Their broken condition might be interpreted as "killing" of an artifact in that case, but such intentional breakage is not evident in other burial offerings at La Galgada. Floor 25 does not have any trash, so these artifacts were part of some intentional deposition and the breakage may have occurred when the original deposit was disturbed by the building of Floor 24. This deposit is somewhat unusual in containing tools; the nearest we come to that in other burials is yarn on a spindle (T.S. 67, C-10:E-10) and mortars, baskets, and gourd bowls in several tombs.

From that same deposit on Floor 25 comes a wooden tool 41.6 cm long, broken at the thicker end (Fig. 86*c*). This looks more like an agricultural tool because of its large size, thickness, and curve.

The continuity of La Galgada culture is manifested by items found in Initial Period levels of the south wing of the North Mound (Fig. 87). Two wooden slats (*c* and *d*) appear to have been parts of a litter similar to that on which the man (I) lay in D-11:C-3.

The totora mat (*e*) is identical to those in earlier levels. The other two objects may have served as weaving tools, *b* as a batten, and *a* as a heddle rod or a shed divider. The only item in this group not duplicated in earlier levels is *a,* a very simple slender stick, but one which might have served in the new harness loom.

All these examples were smoothly worked and show no tool marks. One of the battens has three transverse cuts on the curved side, but they were not part of the woodworking process. The largest piece has a tapering section, but it has been worked smooth.

Wood was not an abundant material at La Galgada and all the pieces found there appear to be of woods still available in the canyon.

GROUND STONE ARTIFACTS

Few inhabited sites rival La Galgada for stoniness, and the ancient inhabitants used this resource in various ways: as a building material in its natural state from the river or the hills, roughly broken, shaped by percussion, pecked into shape or into petroglyphs, or abraded into mortars and pestles. Although a workstation for coarse bifacial tools has been identified across the river from La Galgada and may have been used during the occupation of this site, no tool of the type has been identified in the ruins of La Gal-

87. Wooden and matting items found in Initial Period levels in sector G-12, *top to bottom:* wooden shaft 45.3 cm long, 1.0 cm diameter, broken at upper end, has traces of red paint, use unknown; possible weaver's batten, broken and burned at one end, 18.5 cm long, 2.9 cm maximum thickness; wooden slats with square-cut ends, 29.8 and 29.9 cm long, 4.0 and 4.9 cm wide, 1.2 and 1.6 cm thick, similar to slats found in burial debris probably serving as frame for a litter; fragment of totora reed mat, 45 × 20 cm, made of strips 7–9 mm wide.

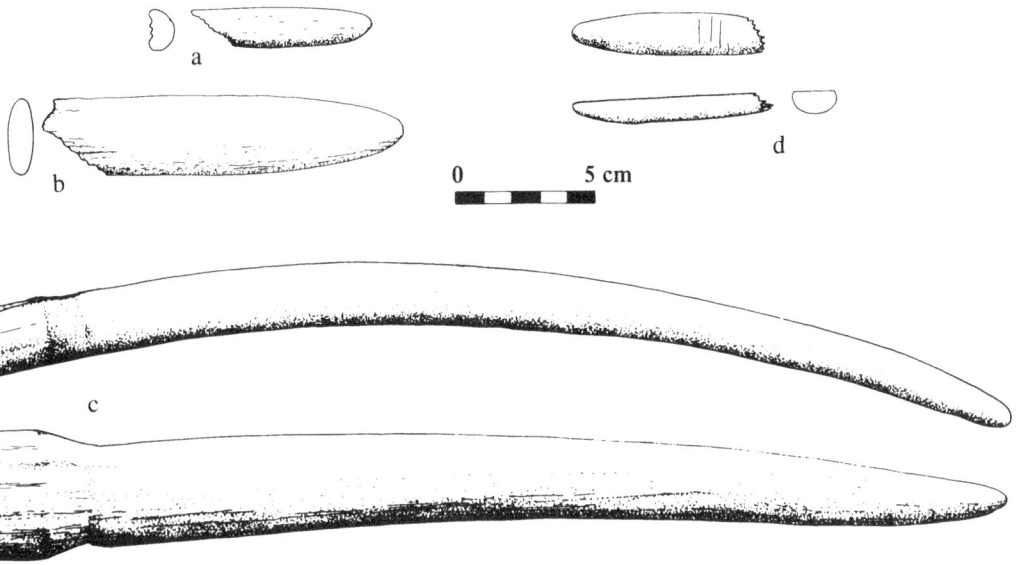

86. Wooden tools: *a–c* from D-11:C-3, Floor
25; *d* from F-12:B-2.

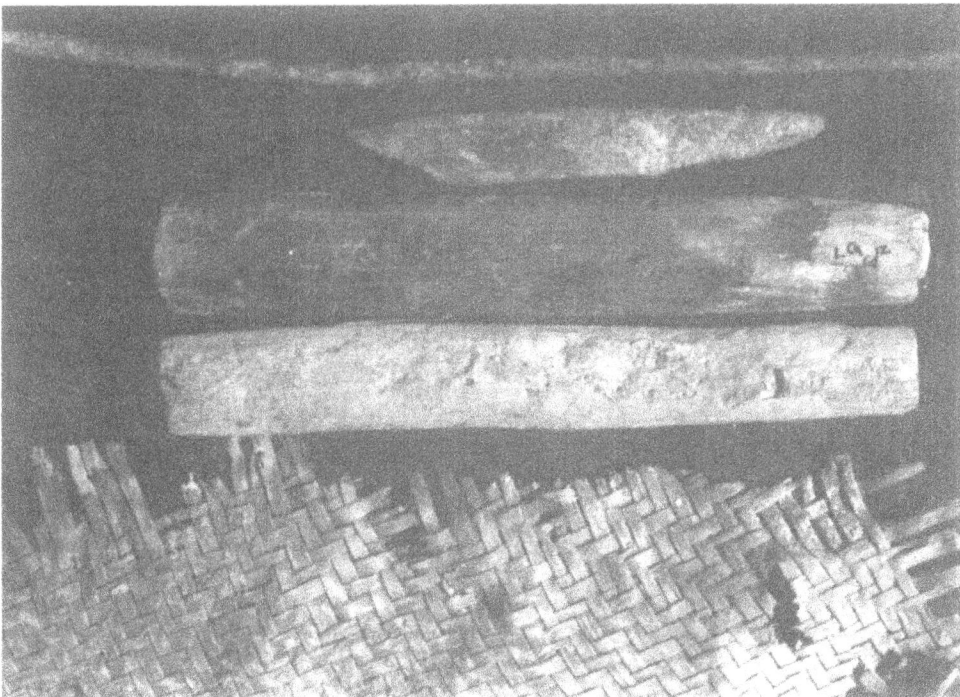

gada. The only knife is a fragment of a fine gray slate-like stone beveled on both sides by grinding and then sharpened by pressure flaking (Figs. 88, 89*n*). It was found in the surface level in Sector G-12 and should thus belong to the Initial Period.

The ground stone artifacts suggest a rapidly growing understanding of the working of stone. A mortar in F-12:B-2 (Fig. 89*a*) was made by grinding a shallow cup into a natural waterworn stone, selected for its appropriate size and shape but otherwise unworked. Its pestle (Fig. 89*b*) was shaped and ground smooth, but given the supply of waterworn stone, the natural shape was probably not greatly modified. All of the later mortars represent a much higher standard of craft, and it may be that the F-12:B-2 mortar was already an ancient heirloom when it was entombed, or perhaps it was intentionally primitive in technique. If it represents the best workmanship at the time it was entombed, then stonecarving made tremendous and rapid progress during the next century or two.

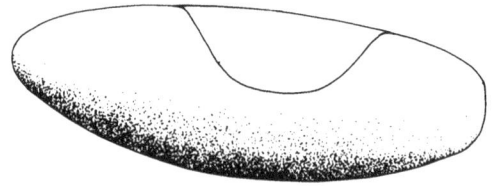

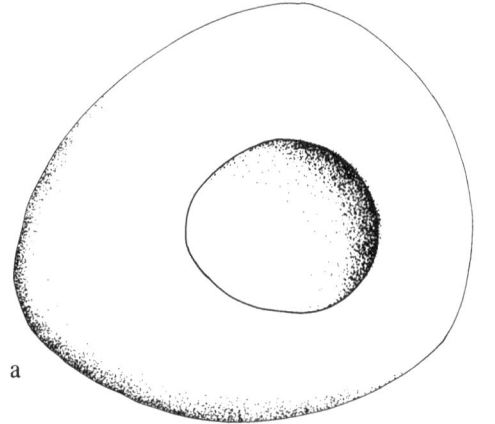

a

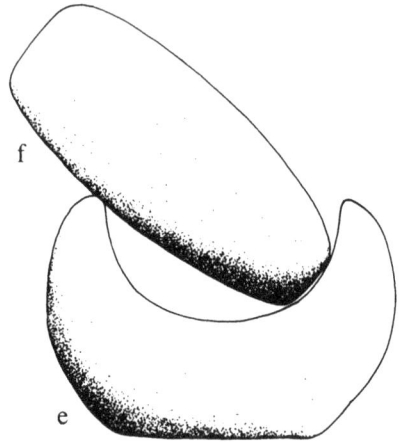

f

e

0   5   10 cm

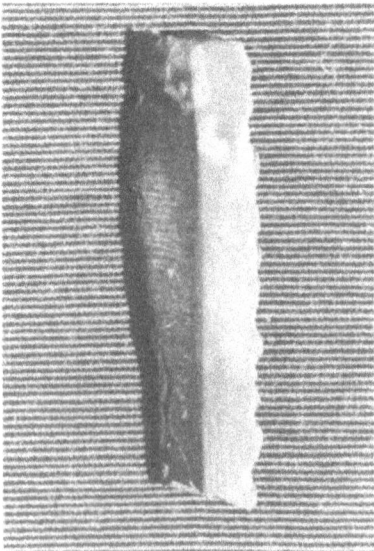

88. Gray slate knife fragment from G-12 surface.

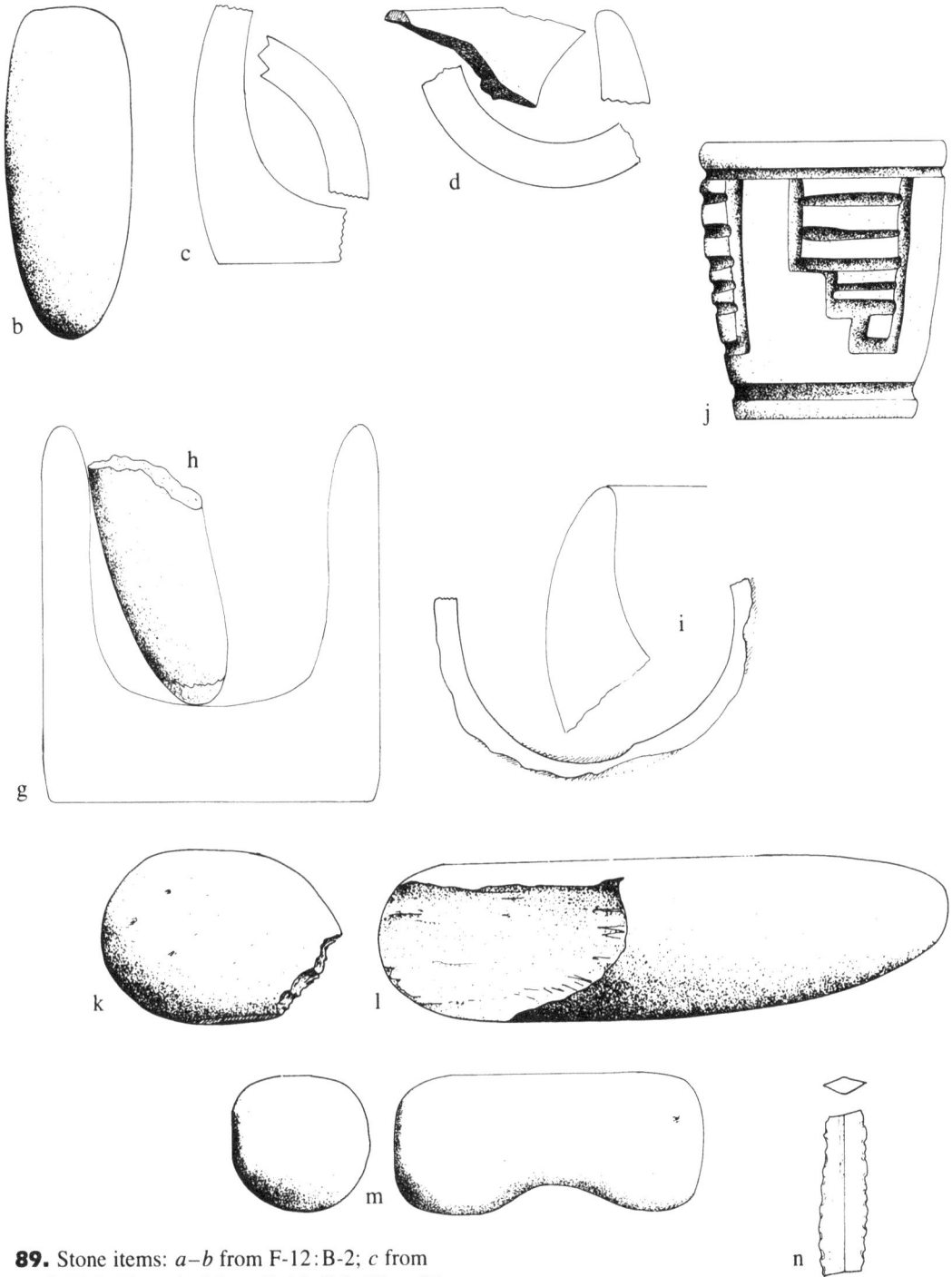

89. Stone items: *a–b* from F-12:B-2; *c* from
E-12:H-2, Floor 6; *d* from D-11:C-3, Floor 24;
e–f from C-10:E-10; *g–h* from C-10:G-10,
Floor 21; *i* from C-10:I-10; *j* from C-12:D-1;
k–l from H-11:FG-10, Floor 15; *m* from F-11
surface; *n* from G-12 surface.

90. Mortar and pestle from C-10:E-10.

92. Stone cup from C-12:D-1.

91. Green metamorphic stone mortar and pestle
in situ, C-10:I-10.

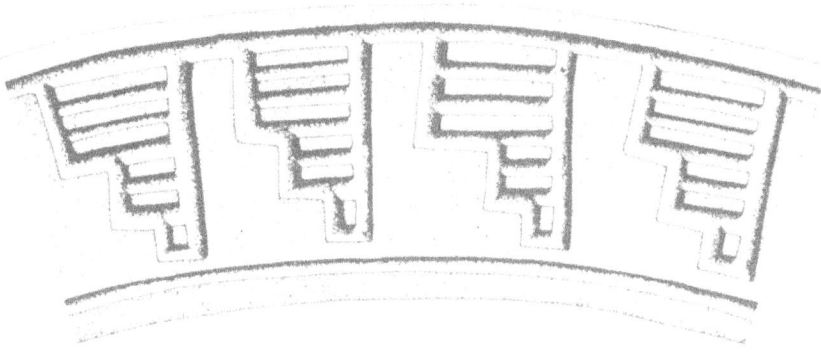

93. Roll-out drawing of stone cup from
C-12:D-1.

There are five mortars represented—three
of them fragments—in later tombs and
floors, all made from dense fine-grained
stone (Figs. 89c, d, e, g, 90, 91). Three are
green stone, two black, and two accompany-
ing pestles are gray and black. All the mortars are between 8.5 and 14.6 cm high, with
diameters in the 7.8–13.5-cm range. The
three intact bases are flat. Variation is found
in the shape of the vessel wall, three examples curving in, one vertical, and one
curving out. The top edge of the wall is
round in all cases, and the wall thickens
gradually as it descends to the thick base.
All these were very smooth, no flaws or
traces of tool marks remaining on the stone.
Perhaps that explains why a broken fragment
of a mortar was included as a burial offering
in D-11:C-3, Floor 24 (Fig. 89d), the fragment still carrying the prestige of fine
workmanship.

The stone cup from C-12:D-1 (Figs. 89j,
92, 93) is in an entirely different style from
the mortars. Even the stone is different, a
grainy gray sandstone. Like the mortars, the
cup has a thick base, but the flat rim and flat
floor are different. A step design composed
of abraded grooves decorates the exterior
wall, and there is a groove at the base and
one at the rim, all of them bearing traces of

white pigment. This cup was surely an import, and its owner valued it enough to repair
a break by winding brown cotton thread
around the rim groove to hold the broken
chip in place. Although it is stone, stylistically it is more similar to Waira-jirca pottery of Kotosh, which has grooved ornaments
with post-fire pigment, than to the other
stone items at La Galgada.

The ashes in the Initial Period fireplace in
H-11:FG-10, Floor 15, in the center of the
North Mound courtyard contained two waterworn stones which must have served some
function. Figure 89k, which may have served
as a pestle, was broken before being put in
the fire. The other, Figure 89l, which is not
evenly worn as a two-handed pestle would
be, was apparently broken by the fire. There
are numerous waterworn stones such as these
which were obviously brought up from the
riverbed for some reason, but the functions
they served are not clear now.

Figure 89m, the stone from the surface
level of Sector F, is the latest, along with the
knife (89n). Again, the function served is
not clear, but this stone was ground smooth
on the ends, flattened on two sides, and hol-
lowed on another side.

Stone was the most abundant of the raw
materials available at the site, and its poten-

tial was exploited principally in building and in mortar-grinding. The development of the great stone sculpture associated with Cerro Sechín and Chavín de Huantar occurred after La Galgada was abandoned, and there is no anticipation of that development in the stone artifacts of La Galgada.

GOURD VESSELS

Gourd vessels were common at Galgada and seem to have served as the basic containers for liquids. Twelve examples of bowls and dippers, or handled cups, were found, all *Lagenaria siceraria*. Figures 94 and 95 represent three variations in the use of gourds. Offering 9 from C-10:E-10 (Figs. 94*b*, 95) is a handled cup or dipper with only the tip of the handle broken. The rim diameter is 6.8 cm. This is a common form, along with the plain bowl without a handle. This specimen is a little smaller than average.

Figure 94*a* is a unique item, the top of a gourd spout with a finished edge, pierced, with a cord laced through the holes. It narrows downward to the break. This was on the floor of the earliest tomb, F-12:B-2, and was broken before being dropped, there being no other parts.

Figure 94*c* is another unique specimen, a fragment of a gourd bowl with burnt decoration. It comes from the Initial Period tomb E-11:J-7. This is the only decorated piece of gourd from the site. No definable pattern can be seen in the small burn marks, though the even line making a border suggests that the maker had a definite idea, that it is not mere random marking. These marks were made with some tool which made a small burn and immediately cooled, which suggests that it was not a metal tool.

No example of excision of the type found at Huaca Prieta (Bird 1963:Fig. 1) has been found on gourds at La Galgada.

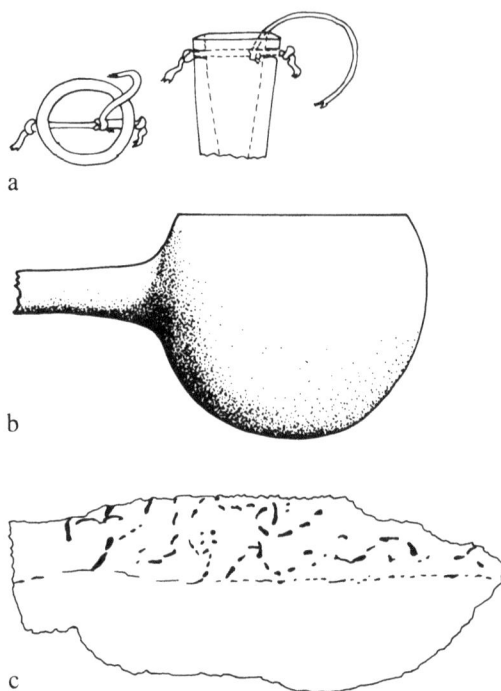

94. Selected examples of gourd vessels: *a*, spout from F-12:B-2; *b*, gourd cup from C-10:E-10, offering 9; *c*, fragment of gourd bowl with pyro-engraved design on outside, from E-11:J-7.

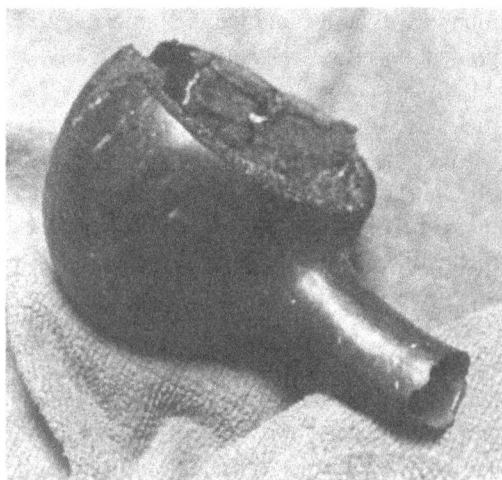

95. Gourd cup from C-10:E-10. It contained an unidentified liquid.

6. Skeletal Materials from La Galgada

ROBERT M. MALINA

Skeletal remains were recovered from nine tombs. All materials except those from tomb F-12: B-2 were examined and evaluated in Lima. The three individuals in F-12: B-2 were evaluated at La Galgada.

METHODS

Evaluation of sex and age at the time of death was based on the criteria presented by W. M. Krogman (1962), D. R. Brothwell (1963), and W. M. Bass (1971), as well as my own experiences. Sex and age determination depend, of course, upon the relative completeness of the skeleton available. Sex determination was based, in order of priority, on characteristics of the innominates, the skull, and long bones. Determining the sex of subadults, i.e., individuals under twenty years of age, is difficult prior to puberty, unless pelvic elements are present (Krogman 1962). When present, the pubic symphysis was used to estimate the age of adults. Todd's criteria (see Krogman 1962), based on ten phases of pubic symphyseal age, were used. Cranial suture closure (coronal, sagittal, lambdoidal) and dental attrition were used as corroborative indicators of age in the presence of pubic symphyses. The molar attrition criteria of Brothwell (1963) were used. These criteria place the molars into four broad age periods between seventeen and forty-five or more years of age.

Age of children and teenagers (subadults) was estimated from dental development and epiphyseal union. Diaphyseal lengths were also used to estimate age in very young children, especially infants. Reference data for diaphyseal lengths were the fetal dimensions reported by I. G. Fazekas and F. Kosa (1978) and the fetal and postnatal diaphyseal lengths of Amerindians reported by F. E. Johnston (1962) for the Archaic Indian Knoll population and by V. L. Merchant and D. H. Ubelaker (1977) for the Protohistoric Arikara.

Depending on the completeness of the materials, several craniofacial dimensions were measured:

1. Skull:
   a. Length—glabella to opisthocranion
   b. Breadth—euryon to euryon
   c. Height—basion to bregma
2. Face:
   a. Upper face height—nasion to prosthion
   b. Total facial height—nasion to gnathion
   c. Breadth—zygion to zygion
3. Mandible:
   a. Breadth—gonion to gonion.

Maximum morphological lengths were taken on all long bones. The formulae of S. Genoves (1967) for indigenous Mesoamericans were used to estimate "living" stature. Two estimates were made for individuals with reasonably complete skeletons. The first was derived from the table of expected maximum statures reported by Genoves (1967). If both sides of a bone were present, the longer of the two was used in the estimate. When several long bones for an individual were present the average of the expected maximum statures was used. The second estimate was based on tibial length (excluding the intercondylar eminences or spines as per Genoves' directions). Tibial length had a higher correlation with stature than femoral length, and the sex-specific equations using tibial length had smaller standard errors of estimate. The sex-specific formulae were as follows:

1. Males:
   Stature (cm) = 1.96 tibia length + 93.752 ± 2.812
2. Females:
   Stature (cm) = 2.72 tibia length + 63.781 ± 3.513

Since maximum morphological length of the tibia was measured 4 mm was subtracted to estimate the length required by Genoves' formulae. This value was based on the data of G. Olivier (1969) who reported heights of the intercondylar eminences to vary from 2 to 6 mm.

If the femur was the only bone available, it was used to estimate stature. Similarly, several femora from the looted tombs were also used to estimate stature with the formulae of Genoves (1967) as follows:

1. Males:
   Stature (cm) = 2.26 femur length + 66.379 ± 3.417
2. Females:
   Stature (cm) = 2.59 femur length + 49.742 ± 3.816

It should be noted that 2.5 cm was subtracted from the estimated statures to obtain an estimate of the "living" stature (Genoves 1967).

Although the degree of dental wear was used to provide an estimate of age, dental wear per se provides information about diet, cultural practices, and so on. Wear of the

molars was rated from 1 to 4 using the four broad stages of Brothwell (1963) and indicated in the descriptions as B1–B4. These stages were modified to provide an indication of attrition of the incisors, canines, and premolars as follows:

B1: slight wear, not into dentine
B2: wear into dentine
B3: wear deep into dentine, almost to root
B4: wear into root

A + after the stage, e.g., B2+, was used to indicate that wear was in the later part of a particular stage.

The following notations were used to indicate specific permanent teeth:

I1: central incisor
I2: lateral incisor
C: canine
P1: first premolar
P2: second premolar
M1: first molar
M2: second molar
M3: third molar

Thus, *RI2* refers to the right lateral incisor and *LM1* refers to the left first molar. Lowercase letters were used to indicate deciduous teeth.

C, T, and *L* were used to indicate the cervical, thoracic, and lumbar vertebrae respectively, and a number after the letter was used to indicate the specific vertebra involved; e.g., *T-11* refers to the eleventh thoracic vertebra. Skeletal and dental pathologies, as well as any other unique characteristics, were also noted.

Characteristics of the skeletal materials from each tomb are described in Appendix A. Demographic characteristics, craniofacial observations, stature estimates, and skeletal and dental pathologies in the La Galgada population are discussed below.

DEMOGRAPHIC CHARACTERISTICS

Two obvious and important questions must be considered in any skeletal series from an archaeological site: (1) how many individuals are represented, and (2) what age and sex categories are represented. The age and sex distribution of the skeletal sample from La Galgada by specific tombs and for the total sample are given in Tables 5 and 6 respectively. Tomb E-11:J-7 is the most recent of those at La Galgada and is also somewhat different from the others culturally. It also accounts for about 40 percent of the individuals represented in the site's skeletal series. Hence, a comparison of the sample of individuals in this tomb (N=27) with that for the other tombs (N=40) is warranted (Table 7). The individuals interred in E-11: J-7 are rather evenly distributed across all age groups, while those in the other tombs are concentrated in early childhood (birth to four years) and the older ages (over forty years). The sex distribution of adults is similar in both subsamples, i.e., only a slight excess of females (see Table 5). About 44 percent of the individuals in E-11:J-7 are subadults (under twenty years of age), and 25 percent of these subadults are less than five years of age. In the other tombs, only 25 percent are subadults, and 70 percent of these are less than five years of age. These figures may suggest greater mortality during infancy and early childhood in the older burials compared to the more recent burials (E-11:J-7). However, the rather even distribution of individuals across all ages in E-11:J-7 may indicate greater stress, perhaps disease and nutritional, in this subsample throughout the life cycle.

Although numbers are small, life expectancy in the two La Galgada subsamples was estimated after the procedures of D. H. Ubelaker (1978). Only data for individuals with reasonably accurate age estimates are included in the calculations. Estimated life expectancy in the two subsamples is shown in Graph A. The estimates are grouped into ten-year periods and have been smoothed to some degree by moving averages. The more recent and culturally different subsample from E-11:J-7 has lower estimated life expectancies, suggesting that these individuals may have been more stressed, probably by adverse nutritional and disease circumstances. The same is suggested in the stature estimates for this subsample (see below).

If the complete skeletal series at La Galgada is treated as a single sample, a total of sixty-seven individuals are represented. An age designation could be given to fifty-nine (88 percent). About one-third of the sample are subadult (33 percent), and of these almost one-half (45 percent) are less than five years of age. Among the adults, females are only slightly more represented (54 percent) than males. The sample of individuals recovered from several tombs at La Galgada may or may not be representative of the population who lived at the locality. This is true of most skeletal series from archaeological sites; such data must be used, however, in order to make inferences about the demographic characteristics of earlier populations.

Comparative data for Paloma, a coastal site from the Chilca Valley, Peru, are given in Table 8. Paloma spans several thousand years from approximately 4600 to 7000 B.P. Only the data from Level 200 of Paloma (4600–5200 B.P.) are included in this report, as it is closest in time to La Galgada (3400–3800 B.P. for the tombs, although the youngest and oldest dates for the site are approximately 3100 and 4100 B.P.). Three features are apparent in a comparison of the age and sex distributions of the two sites. First, the percentages of subadults and adults in the skeletal samples from the two sites are virtually identical, 33 percent and 32 percent for La Galgada and Paloma respectively. How-

Table 5. Estimated Number and Age and Sex Distribution of Individuals at La Galgada Grouped by Tomb

Age Group	F-12:B-2		I-11:D-5		D-11:C-3		C-10:E-10			C-11:F-5		
	M	F	M	F	M	F	M	F	?	M	F	?
B-1									1			1
1-4												2
5-9												1
10-14												
15-19												1
20-29			1							1	1	
30-39					1			1				
40-49					1			1		2		
50+	1	2			1	1		1		1		
? (adult)											2	1
(Tomb total)	(3)		(1)		(4)		(4)			(13)		

ᵃThis tomb also originally included skeletons of a woman and child, removed by looters before 1978 and not included in this analysis.

Table 6. Age and Sex Distribution of the Total Skeletal Sample at La Galgada

Age Group	Sex			Total	% of Total
	Male	Female	Uncertain		
B-1			6	6	9.0
1-4			4	4	6.0
5-9			3	3	4.5
10-14			4	4	6.0
15-19			5	5	7.5
20-29	3	3		6	9.0
30-39	2	3		5	7.5
40-49	7	4	1	12	17.9
50+	5	7	2	14	20.9
? (adult)	1	4	3	8	11.9
Total	18	21	28	67	100.2

C-10:I-10		C-12:D-1			C-11:E-8[a]		E-11:J-7		
M	F	M	F	?	M	F	M	F	?
				2					2
				1					1
									2
				1					3
									4
							1	2	
							1	2	
	2	1			1		2	1	1
		2	3						2
1	1							1	2
(4)		(10)			(1)		(27)		

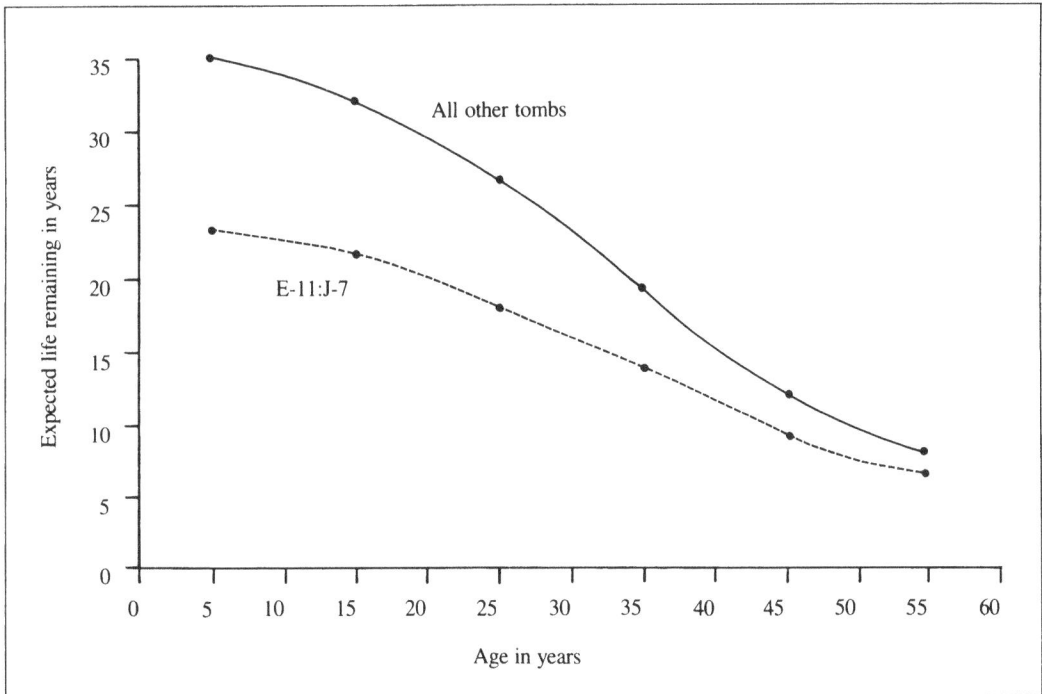

Graph A. Life expectancy at La Galgada: comparison of individuals in Tomb E-11:J-7 (approximately 3400 B.P.) with those in the other tombs (approximately 3700–3800 B.P.). Data are smoothed ten-year age intervals.

Table 7. Age Distribution of Individuals in Tomb E-11:J-7 (approx. 3400 B.P.) and All Other Tombs (approx. 3700–3800 B.P.) at La Galgada

Age Group	E-11:J-7 N	E-11:J-7 % of Total	All Others N	All Others % of Total
B–1	2	7.4	4	10.0
1–4	1	3.7	3	7.5
5–9	2	7.4	1	2.5
10–14	3	11.1	1	2.5
15–19	4	14.8	1	2.5
20–29	3	11.1	3	7.5
30–39	3	11.1	2	5.0
40–49	4	14.8	8	20.0
50+	2	7.4	12	30.0
? (adult)	3	11.1	5	12.5
Total	27	99.9	40	100.0

Table 8. Age and Sex Distribution of Individuals in Level 200 of Paloma (4600–5200 B.P.), Chilca Valley, Peru

Age Group	Sex Male	Sex Female	Sex Uncertain	Total	% of Total
B–4	1	1	6	8	21.6
5–9			2	2	5.4
10–14	1			1	2.7
15–19	1			1	2.7
20–29	5	1		6	16.2
30–39	3	6		9	24.3
40–49	2	2		4	10.8
50+	2	1	1	4	10.8
? (adult)	1	1	—	2	5.4
Total	16	12	9	37	99.9

Source: Adapted from Benfer 1984.

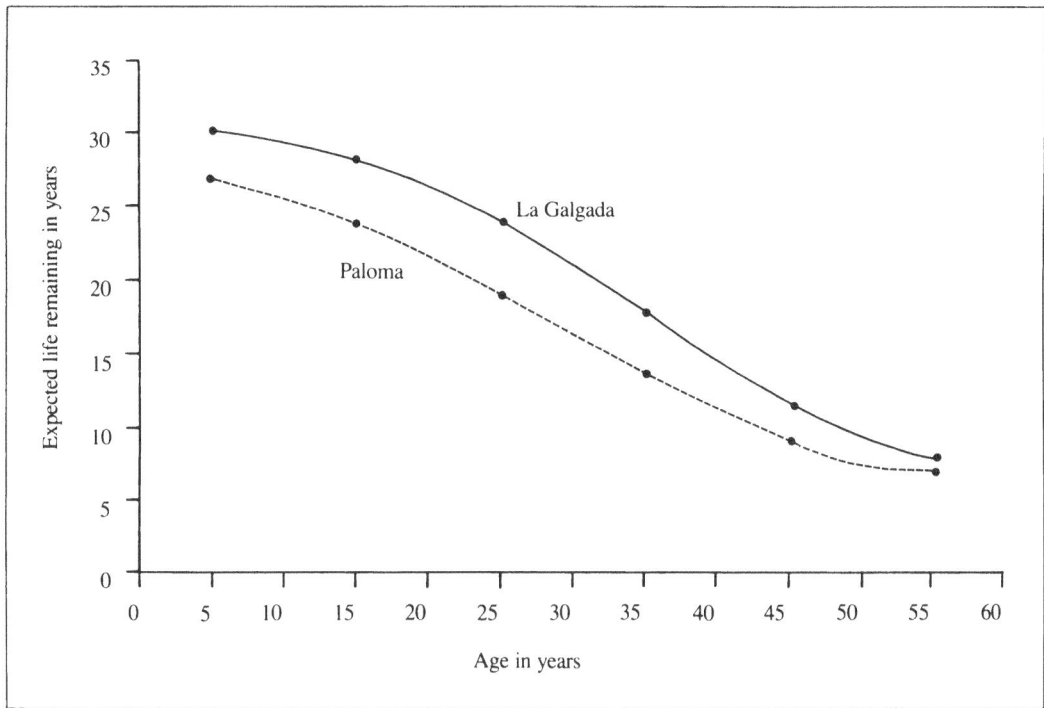

Graph B. Life expectancy at La Galgada and Level 200 at Paloma. Data are smoothed ten-year age intervals.

ever, 67 percent of the subadults at Paloma are less than five years of age in contrast to 45 percent at La Galgada. In this regard, it should be noted that death rates in preschool children (i.e., those between birth and five years of age) are generally viewed by public health officials as indicators of the overall health and nutritional status of present-day communities. If this generalization can be applied to La Galgada and to Paloma, it would suggest somewhat better health and nutritional circumstances in the former. Note, however, that samples are small and the application of this generalization to skeletal populations is complicated by the greater chance of disintegration of especially infant remains in the course of time due to detrimental soil conditions and perhaps by differential burial practices for young individuals.

Second, among the adults at the two sites, Paloma has a slight excess of males (54 per-

cent), while La Galgada has a slight excess of females. However, the sex distribution with age varies between the sites. At La Galgada, the sexes are rather evenly represented in the 20–29 and 30–39 age groups, while male mortality peaks in the 40–49 and female mortality in the 50–59 age group. In contrast, at Paloma, there are more males in the 20–29 and more females in the 30–39 age group, while the sexes are rather evenly distributed in the two older age groups. Both samples thus diverge from the pattern usually observed in skeletal series, i.e., higher female mortality in the twenties and higher male mortality in the thirties. The differences may reflect bias in assessing sex and age of the skeletal materials, although that is unlikely given the completeness of most materials. Differential recovery of skeletal remains is another factor that may be involved. Robert A. Benfer (1984) postulated that the sex difference at Paloma may reflect delayed marriage, and in turn a reduced risk of death during childbirth.

Third, there is a difference between La Galgada and Paloma skeletal samples in the age distribution of adults, using only samples for which age estimates are available. At La Galgada, the percentages of individuals in the 20–29 and 30–39 age groups are similar (10 percent and 9 percent respectively), and then increase in the 40–49 (20 percent) and in the 50+ age groups (24 percent). In contrast, the 30–39 age group has the highest percentage of individuals (26 percent) at Paloma, followed by the 20–29 age group (17 percent). Thus, Paloma has fewer older individuals than La Galgada.

The differences between the two Preceramic sites of approximately similar archaeological age may reflect the living conditions associated with the coast and the highlands. The former may have had a greater infectious disease load than the latter, and infectious disease is a prime contributor to mortality, especially mortality in early childhood. Coastal life may also have more risks for younger adult males, i.e, risks associated with fishing and swimming. On the other hand, the coast probably provided better access to high protein foods (fish) and thus to presumably better overall nutritional conditions.

Estimated life expectancies (after Ubelaker 1978) at La Galgada and Paloma are shown in Graph B. Only data for individuals with reasonably accurate age estimates (La Galgada, N=59; Paloma, N=35) are included in the calculations. The estimates are grouped by ten-year periods and have been smoothed to some degree by moving averages. Given the limited sample sizes in each age interval, and assuming that the samples are representative of the respective populations, it appears that estimated life expectancies are somewhat greater at La Galgada than at Paloma.

CRANIOFACIAL OBSERVATIONS AND DIMENSIONS

Twelve of the thirteen complete skulls have some degree of lambdoidal flattening. The flattening is slight or slight to moderate in the majority of these. It occurs high on the occipital bone at the junction of the parietals, i.e., at the junction of the sagittal and lambdoidal sutures. Only two individuals have extreme flattening (E-11:J-7 and C-12: D-1 [V]; see Fig. 172 in Appendix A), while the remainder have intermediate degrees of lambdoidal flattening (Figs. 96 and 97). According to Ubelaker (1978:68), "It is not clear whether it [lambdoidal flattening] is the intentional result of tying a flat object against the back of the head or the unintentional consequence of other behavior, such as use of a cradle-board." The presence of artificial flattening of the posterior part of the skull thus limits the utility of craniofacial measurements. Nevertheless, several dimensions and the estimated degree of lambdoidal deformation are given in Table 9. In addition, a depression at the junction of the lambdoidal and sagittal sutures is evident in six of the thirteen skulls. Most of the thirteen skulls have lambdoidal suture bones, while two have Inca bones.

LONG BONE LENGTHS AND ESTIMATED STATURES

Lengths of specific long bones and diameters of the femoral and humeral heads of the reasonably complete skeletons are given in Table 10. There do not appear to be any appreciable differences among individuals from the different tombs. Sexual dimorphism is consistent across all measurements. Males are about 1.1 to 1.2 times larger in lengths and diameters. Benfer (1984) reported a similar observation for Paloma adults. Males were about 1.1 times larger than females in average diameters of the femoral head.

Table 9. Characteristics of the Complete Skulls Recovered from La Galgada (measurements in mm)

Tomb	Burial	Cranial Length	Cranial Breadth	Cranial Height	Upper Facial Height
Males:					
F-12:B-2	I	168	148	147	63
D-11:C-3	I	175	141	136	62
	III	172	154	144	63
	IV	169	148	143	67
C-12:D-1	III	171	138	141	66
E-11:J-7		151	154	134	67.5
	Mean	171.0	145.8	142.2	64.2
	SD	2.5	5.7	3.7	1.9
Females:					
F-12:B-2	II	158	130	128	60
	III	166	140	130	56
D-11:C-3	II	164	151	138	
C-10:E-10	I	156	151	137	65
	II	161	150	132	59
	III	161	161	145	68
C-12:D-1	V	164	152	145	65
	Mean	161.0	147.2	135.0	61.6
	SD	3.4	9.8	5.7	4.3

Tomb	Burial	Bizygomatic Breadth	Bigonial Breadth	Lambdoidal Flattening
Males:				
F-12:B-2	I	147.5	99	Slight
D-11:C-3	I	129	96	Moderate
	III	147	101	Slight
	IV	139	94	Moderate
C-12:D-1	III	136	98	Slight
E-11:J-7		136		Considerable
	Mean	139.7	97.6	
	SD	7.0	2.7	
Females:				
F-12:B-2	II	122	86	None
	III	126	94	Slight/moderate
D-11:C-3	II	137	96	Moderate
C-10:E-10	I	128	89	Slight/moderate
	II	127		Slight
	III	133	95	Slight/moderate
C-12:D-1	V	144	98	Considerable
	Mean	128.8	92.0	
	SD	4.9	3.9	

Table 10. Maximum Morphological Lengths (mm) and Selected Diameters (mm) of the Long Bones from the Reasonably Complete Skeletons at La Galgada

Tomb	Burial	Lengths:							
		Humerus		Radius		Ulna		Femur	
		R	L	R	L	R	L	R	L
Males:									
F-12:B-2	I	322	322	232[a]	249	270	272	444	445
D-11:C-3	I	281	283	233	233	252	253	386	387
	III	312	313	248	240[a]	268	267	434	434
	IV	305	304		248		266		
C-11:E-8	I	290	288	220	220	233	236	393	399
C-12:D-1	I			247	246			411	
	III							409	
	Mean	302.0	302.0	237.0	239.2	255.7	258.8	412.8	416.3
	SD	14.8	14.7	11.5	11.2	14.9	13.0	20.6	23.9
Females:									
F-12:B-2	II	278	274	203	203	217	216	383	
	III	258	257	200	200	215	215	353	359
C-10:E-10	I	264	265	196	197	210	211	367	364
	II	254		202	193	219	213	350	352
	III	271	269	211	212	221	223	377	383
	Mean	265.0	266.3	202.4	201.0	216.4	215.6	366.0	364.5
	SD	8.7	6.2	4.9	6.4	3.8	4.1	12.9	11.5

[a] Healed fracture; length not used in calculating means and standard deviations.

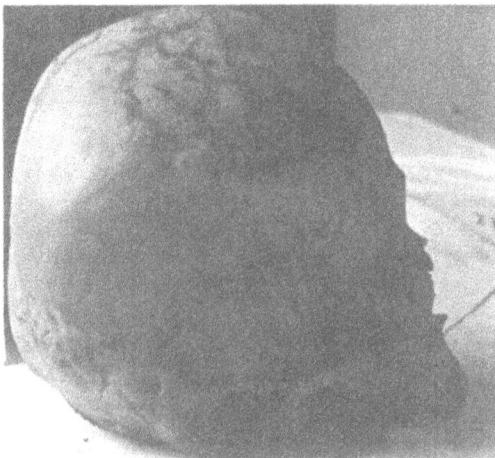

96. An example of artificial lambdoidal flattening with a slight indentation at the junction of the sagittal and lambdoidal sutures, C-10:E-10(I).

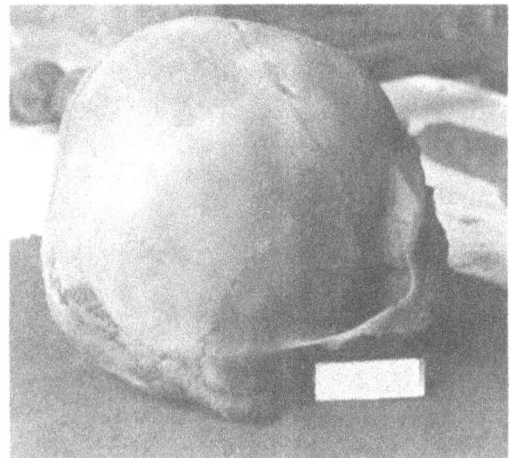

97. An example of artificial lambdoidal flattening with a slight depression at the junction of the sagittal and lambdoidal sutures, D-11:C-3(IV).

Tibia R	Tibia L	Fibula R	Fibula L	Diameters:	Humeral Head Vertical R	Humeral Head Vertical L	Transverse R	Transverse L	Femoral Head Vertical R	Femoral Head Vertical L
385	383	372	373		45	46	42	42	45.5	45.5
336	338	327			40.5	40	38	38.5	43	42
365	366				44.5	43.5	41	39	43.5	44
	365				45.5	46	40.5	41.5		
337	343		339		41.5	42	39.5	39.5	43	43
341	342								45	44
352.8	356.2				43.4	43.5	40.2	40.1	44.0	43.7
19.3	16.3				2.0	2.3	1.4	1.4	1.1	1.2
317	320	309	309		35.5	35	33.5	33	37	
312	313	306	303		33.5	33.5	32.5	33.5	34.5	35
308	309	296	297		35.5	35	34	34	37	37.5
	302				35		33		37	36
318	322	306			34	34.5	34	33	39	38.5
313.7	313.2	304.3	303.0		34.7	34.5	33.4	33.4	36.9	36.7
4.0	7.3	4.9	4.9		0.8	0.6	0.6	0.4	1.4	1.3

Lengths and diameters of the long bones from the looted tombs are given in Tables 11 and 12. The presence of several specimens with active epiphyseal union and lines of recent union would seem to suggest a younger sample than those in Table 10. However, average lengths and diameters do not differ significantly between the two series, especially in light of the small numbers represented.

Stature estimates at La Galgada are presented in Table 13. Among those individuals from tombs C-11:F-5 and E-11:J-7, the same individual may be represented among the femora and tibiae. Among those individuals with reasonably complete skeletons, there are negligible differences in estimated stature based on the tibia, i.e., the best predictor in Genoves' (1967) sample, and those based on the average of the expected maximum statures for all bones available (Table 14).

Within the La Galgada sample, the estimated statures of individuals from tomb E-11:J-7 are, on the average, shorter than those from the other, older tombs (Table 15). The difference is small between the subsamples of females (difference between means, 0.5 cm), but is considerable between the subsamples of males (3.5 cm). Thus, the estimated stature of the adult population represented in tomb E-11:J-7 at La Galgada is less than that of adults in the other tombs at the site. This trend is consistent with the age distribution of individuals (Table 7) and esti-

Table 11. Maximum Morphological Lengths (mm) of the Femur and Tibia, and Vertical Diameter (mm) of the Femoral Head for Materials from Looted Tombs C-11:F-5 and E-11:J-7

		Length		Diameter	
Tomb	Sex	R	L	R	L
Femora:					
C-11:F-5	M		442		
	M		406		
E-11:J-7	M	397*	398*	40*	41.5*
	M	391*	391*	39*	39.5*
	M	413			
	M	406		45.5	
	F	358*	359*		35
Tibiae:					
C-11:F-5	M	333*	333*		
	M		337		
E-11:J-7	M	335			
	M	351			
	M	332[a]			
	F	321			
	F	298[b]			
	F	317*	319		
	F	325			
	F		311[c]		

*Those on the same line represent a pair.

[a] Has a clear line of union distally.

[b] Has a line of recent union proximally and distally. An incomplete left tibia, lacking its malleolus, has a clear line of recent union proximally, and may be the mate of the complete bone.

[c] Has a line of recent union distally, but is farther along in the fusion process than the tibia above.

Table 12. Maximum Morphological Lengths (mm) of the Humerus, Radius, and Ulna, and Diameters (mm) of the Humeral Head for Materials from Looted Tombs C-11:F-5 and E-11:J-7

| | | Length | | Diameters Vertical | | Transverse | |
		R	L	R	L	R	L
Humeri:							
E-11:J-7	M		293		40		39
	M		285		38		35
	F		241		31.5		30
	F (?)		272		36		35
	F (?)		279		36.5		34
	F		256		36		33.5
	F	253*[a]	257*	36*	36*		34
	F	263[b]		36		35	
	F	235[c]		31		30	
Radii:							
C-11:F-5	M	251					
	M (?)		226				
E-11:J-7	M		228				
C-11:F-5	F		212				
	F (?)		219				
E-11:J-7	F	213*	213*				
	F	199					
	F		192[d]				
	F	203					
	F	195[e]					
	F		217				
	F		198				
Ulnae:							
C-11:F-5	M	246					
E-11:J-7	M	233*	234*				
	M		251				
E-11:J-7	F	213[f]					
	F		216				
	F (?)	229					

*Those on the same line represent a pair.

[a] Both bones show lines of recent union proximally, but the right is slightly farther along in the union process.

[b] Has a line of recent union proximally.

[c] Actively uniting proximally; the central part is fused, but laterally the epiphysis is still open.

[d] Has recently completed epiphyseal union distally, while the proximal head has a line of union that is beginning to disappear.

[e] The distal epiphysis is actively uniting; it is open on the periphery and is already capped medially and laterally.

[f] Union has occurred recently distally.

Table 13. Estimated Statures (cm) of Adults at La Galgada

Tomb	Burial	Average of All Bones Available	Tibia Only	Femur Only
Males:				
F-12:B-2	I	165.1	165.9	
D-11:C-3	I	156.8	156.7	
	III	163.1	162.2	
	IV	162.7	162.0	
C-11:F-5				163.8
				155.6
			155.7	
			156.5	
C-12:D-1	I	159.5	157.5	
	III			156.3
C-11:E-8	I	156.7	157.7	
E-11:J-7				153.6
				152.2
				157.2
				155.6
			156.1	
			159.3	
			155.5	
Females:				
F-12:B-2	II	145.7	147.2	
	III	143.2	145.3	
C-10:E-10	I	143.2	144.2	
	II	142.2	142.3	
	III	146.9	147.8	
E-11:J-7				140.2
			147.5	
			141.3	
			147.0	
			148.6	
			144.8	

Table 14. Comparison of Estimated Stature (cm) Based on All Bones Available for a Given Individual with That Based on the Tibia Only

	N	Average of All Bones Available		Tibia Only	
		Mean	*SD*	*Mean*	*SD*
Males	6	160.7	3.2	160.3	3.2
Females	5	144.2	1.8	145.4	2.0

Table 15. Estimated Statures (cm)[a] of Adults at La Galgada for the Total Sample, for Individuals in Looted Tomb E-11:J-7, and for Individuals in All Other Tombs, with Comparative Data for Individuals in Level 200 of Paloma, Chilca Valley, Peru

	Males			Females		
	N	Mean	SD	N	Mean	SD
La Galgada:						
Total sample	18	157.7	3.5	11	145.1	2.7
Tomb E-11:J-7	7	155.6	2.1	6	144.9	3.2
All other tombs	11	159.1	3.5	5	145.4	2.0
Paloma:[b]						
Level 200	6	168.9	4.0	3	156.9	3.1

[a] Based on tibia and/or femur lengths.
[b] Adapted from Benfer (1984).

mated life expectancy (Graph A), which suggest that the more recent sample in tomb E-11:J-7 was more stressed by adverse nutritional and disease circumstances than the earlier (older) sample elsewhere at La Galgada. Further, the larger difference between mean estimated statures for males than for females is consistent with the notion that males may be affected more than females by stressful environmental conditions (Stinson 1985).

Estimated statures for individuals from Level 200 at Paloma are also included in Table 15. The small sample of Paloma adults are, on the average, taller than those from La Galgada by about 11–12 cm. The sexual dimorphism in the two samples, however, is virtually identical. The differences between mean statures of males and females are 12.6 cm and 12.0 cm at La Galgada and Paloma respectively. Further, in both samples the average statures of males are about 1.1 times those of females. Thus, sexual dimorphism is similar in magnitude to that for specific long bone lengths and diameters.

Although samples are generally small, the comparison of estimated statures suggests

that the Paloma population was generally better-off in general nutritional and presumably health circumstances. In other words, the nutritional conditions of the coastal Palomans were probably better able to meet the nutrient needs of developing individuals, resulting in greater adult statures. This suggestion, however, is not consistent with the greater percentage of early childhood deaths at Paloma, which suggests greater nutritional and infectious disease stress. Given these contrasting indications, it is also possible that the populations of La Galgada and Paloma were genetically different. The former was probably a highland population. And, among present-day Peruvian populations, indigenous highland adults are, on the average, shorter than indigenous lowland adults (Frisancho 1976).

The utility of stature reconstruction from long bone lengths for earlier populations is questionable in light of the complexity of genetic and environmental factors capable of influencing growth of the long bones and other skeletal elements which contribute to stature. Population differences in bodily proportions and specifically the proportion of lower-extremity length to stature are also possibly confounding factors. In addition, prediction equations for stature are population- or sample-specific and have a built-in error component (see the standard error of estimate in the Methods section). Nevertheless, stature estimates provide an approximate indication of body size and should be accepted only as such.

Skeletal Pathology

Pathologies are limited indicators of the health status of skeletal populations since only those conditions affecting the skeleton are apparent. Some features such as arthritic lipping are labeled as pathologies, but probably represent to some extent the concomitants of normal aging processes, i.e., the normal wear-and-tear effects of daily activities over a long period of time on the skeleton. In addition, it is difficult to offer a comparative perspective for specific pathologies in skeletal populations, as there is considerable variation in the classification of such pathologies.

Pathologies of specific individuals in the La Galgada sample are indicated and at times illustrated in the descriptions of each tomb and its respective burials in Appendix A. A summary of the pathologies is presented here. All of the pathologies in the sample are limited to adults, as none of the subadults showed evidence of skeletal pathology.

Three of the twelve reasonably complete skeletons had healed fractures. One male over fifty years old, F-12:B-2(I), had multiple fractures involving primarily the left radius, ulna, and clavicle. In addition, the fracture sites also had osteomyelitis secondary to the fractures (Figs. 163 and 164 in Appendix A). The other fractures involved the left radius in a male over forty, D-11:C-3(III) (Fig. 166 in Appendix A), and the left clavicle in a female over fifty, C-10:

E-10(III). Among individuals from the two looted tombs, only one fracture was evident among the bones recovered. It was a healed fracture of the left fibular shaft with considerable overgrowth (E-11:J-7). Thus, four of the forty-five adults (9 percent) represented in the La Galgada sample showed healed fractures.

Six of the forty-five adults (13 percent) had evidence of inflammation of the skeleton excluding the vertebral column. Two—C-12:D-1(III), a male over fifty, and a male in his late forties from E-11:J-7—involved the surface of the skull and were characterized by many small holes and several larger lesions (Figs. 171 and 173 in Appendix A). Two other skulls—F-12:B-2(I), a male over fifty, and D-11:C-3(I), a male in his thirties—had a depression at the junction of the coronal and sagittal sutures with an associated overgrowth of bone and thus a rather irregular surface (Fig. 161 in Appendix A). The overall appearance was of some degree of osteitis. The other two inflammatory conditions were extensive periostitis with considerable exostoses of the right tibia and fibula of a female over fifty, F-12:B-2(III) (Fig. 165 in Appendix A), and a tumor-like exostosis on the mid-shaft of a fibula from an adult in the looted tombs (C-11:F-5).

Ear exostoses were not common in the La Galgada sample. Only two of the thirteen complete skulls (15 percent) had slight ear exostoses, one bilaterally and the other unilaterally.

Arthritis is a pathological condition which may be associated with infection, injury, unusual postural stresses and strains, and perhaps the normal wear and tear of daily activities over a considerable period of time. The vertebral column and the hip joints are among the more commonly affected areas of the skeleton. "Lipping" or osteophytosis is the primary characteristic of arthritis, although ankylosis (joint immobility of fusion) occa-

Table 16. Distribution of Arthritic Involvement by Joint Area of the Extremity Skeleton for 14 Adults, 30 Years of Age and Older

| | Degree of Arthritic Involvement | | |
| | None or Slight | Mild-to-Moderate[a] | Severe[a] |
Joint			
Shoulder		2	
Elbow		3	
Wrist			3
Hip		1	1
Knee		4	
Ankle		3	
All joints	9		

[a] Five of the individuals with mild-to-moderate or severe arthritic involvement had multiple joint involvement.

sionally occurs. Lipping is commonly characterized as being absent or slight, mild-to-moderate, or severe (Brothwell 1963).

The distribution of arthritic involvement by joint area of the extremity skeleton is shown in Table 16 for fourteen adults, thirty years of age and older, from the intact and collapsed tombs. Nine of the fourteen individuals (64 percent) showed only slight or no arthritic involvement at the joint surfaces. The five other individuals (36 percent) had multiple joint involvement. The mild-to-moderate arthritic changes occurred primarily in the knee, ankle, and elbow. The severe arthritic changes occurred in the hip and wrist of a male over forty years of age, D-11: C-3(III). The changes in the wrist apparently occurred subsequent to a healed Colles' fracture of the left radius, while the greater trochanters of both femora had considerable osteophytosis, especially the right (Figs. 166 and 167 in Appendix A). The two other severe arthritic changes in the wrist occurred in older individuals, a male over fifty, F-12: B-2(I) subsequent to a healed Colles' frac-

ture with associated secondary infection (Fig. 163 in Appendix A) and a female over fifty, C-12:D-1(IV). No evidence of a healed fracture was apparent in the latter individual.

Among the individuals in the two looted tombs (C-11:F-5 and E-11:J-7), arthritic involvement in the major long bones was slight to moderate in the majority. There was only one case of severe arthritic changes of the left femoral neck of an adult female. The degree of involvement was such that the joint may have been rendered immobile.

Arthritic involvement in the vertebral column was quite variable in expression and most likely involved infection, injury, and normal wear and tear singly or in combination in the La Galgada series. Two females—C-10:E-10(II), over fifty years, and C-10:E-10(III), forty-five to fifty—had severe angular kyphosis in the thoraco-lumbar region (see Figs. 169 and 170 and in Appendix A), with severe lipping, erosion, and collapsing (wedging) of one or more thoracic or lumbar vertebral bodies. The overall features are suggestive of spinal tuberculosis, which occurs most commonly in the lower thoracic and upper lumbar vertebrae (Brothwell 1963; El-Najjar 1981; Allison et al. 1981).

A male over fifty, F-12:B-2(I), also had severe angular kyphosis. T-11, T-12, and all lumbar vertebrae were involved. There was extensive osteophytosis and fusion of T-12 and L-1 (see Fig. 162 in Appendix A). The cervical and upper thoracic vertebrae also had moderate and severe lipping. The degree of arthritic involvement of the spinal column of this individual may be the long-term consequence of trauma. This individual also had healed Colles' fractures of both radii and a healed fracture of the left clavicle with evidence of subsequent infection (see Fig. 163 in Appendix A).

Five other individuals showed severe arthritic involvement of the lower thoracic and lumbar vertebrae. All were older individuals (probably over fifty years of age), and they included four females and one male. A brief description of each follows.

1. D-11:C-3(IV), older male, had one lumbar vertebra which was slightly compressed and another which was severely compressed anteriorly (i.e., wedging). The latter also had osteophytosis laterally. The cervical vertebrae were also severely lipped, and C-4 was somewhat flattened with severe erosion and pitting.

2. C-12:D-1(IV), older female, had one lumbar vertebra which was severely compressed and flattened anteriorly, and another which was severely lipped. T-11 and T-12 were also severely lipped, as was a single cervical vertebra (C-3 or C-4).

3. D-11:C-3(II), older female, had severe lipping of the lower thoracic and one lumbar vertebrae, while another lumbar vertebra had severe lipping and a partially compressed body.

4. F-12:B-2(III), female over fifty, had some severe lipping of T-10 through T-12,

with T-11 being the most severely lipped. T-11 also appeared wedged. T-12 and the lumbar vertebrae were not involved to the same extent as T-10 and T-11.

5. F-12:B-2(II), female over fifty, had severe lipping of T-11 and T-12. T-11 appeared as if it was beginning to be compressed or wedged anteriorly. In contrast, L-1 through L-3 appeared normal.

Thus, eight of the fourteen individuals (57 percent) represented by reasonably complete skeletons had relatively severe arthritic involvement of the lower thoracic and lumbar vertebrae. As a group they were old (probably over fifty years of age), and six of the eight were females. Although Brothwell (1963:136) notes that "vertebral deformity is by far the most reliable diagnostic feature" of tuberculosis, other factors are also involved in the compression of vertebral bodies, e.g., compression fractures or carrying heavy loads over a significant period of time. Osteoporosis associated with advanced age and/or inadequate calcium intake may be an additional contributing factor, especially in females.

The remaining six individuals with reasonably complete skeletons were younger. The two youngest individuals (one male and one female in the thirties) were free of arthritic involvement in the vertebral column. The other four (all males, three in the forties and one over fifty) had a degree of arthritic involvement of the vertebral column which ranged from mild to severe. Of the cervical vertebrae, C-3 through C-6 were most involved, and generally had moderate to severe lipping. One male in his forties had erosion of the body of C-3 with associated pitting. C-4 and the base of C-2 had lesser but related arthritic changes. The majority of thoracic vertebrae had slight involvement, while the lower thoracic and lumbar vertebrae had generally moderate arthritic lipping.

The vertebrae recovered from the looted

tombs presented a similar degree of arthritic involvement as noted for those recovered from the intact and collapsed tombs. That is, lipping ranged from slight to severe. Those for Tomb E-11:J-7 generally had lesser arthritic changes than those from Tomb C-11: F-5. None of the lower thoracic or lumbar vertebrae recovered from E-11:J-7 had compressed bodies. One individual from C-11: F-5 had severe lipping of the sacral promontory and of L-3 and L-4. The latter were fused on their spinal surfaces. Two lower thoracic vertebrae from another individual were severely lipped and quite compressed. The associated lumbar vertebrae had moderate to severe lipping. The overall features suggested an individual with angular kyphosis in the thoraco-lumbar region.

In summary, a relatively large number of adults from La Galgada had significant arthritic involvement especially in the thoraco-lumbar region of the vertebral column. At least ten adults had rather serious involvement in this region of the spinal column, and older females comprised the majority of these adults. The cervical vertebrae generally had a lesser degree of arthritic changes.

Comparative pathology data for other Peruvian skeletal samples of the same general time period are limited. Benfer (1984) reported relative occurrences of osteitis between 10 and 16 percent and of periostitis between 22 and 25 percent for the total Paloma sample. There were no differences in the relative frequencies between the stratigraphic levels represented at Paloma. These figures would seem to suggest a somewhat greater degree of inflammatory bone conditions in the Paloma sample than in the La Galgada sample. More specific pathological data are not yet reported for the Paloma skeletal population.

DENTAL ATTRITION AND PATHOLOGY

The analysis of dental attrition and pathology is limited largely to complete adult maxillae (fourteen) and mandibles (twenty-two), although incomplete maxillae (eight) and mandibles (twelve) provide some corroborative evidence. The age and sex distribution of dental pathology are given in Tables 17 and 18, while average tooth wear is given in Table 19. The most important feature in the dentition is tooth wear. As the wear progresses into the tooth, the exposed pulp surface hardens to dentine (Blumberg, Hylander, and Goepp 1971). In adults over forty years of age at La Galgada, most of the teeth present are worn to the neck or root. Samples are too small to evaluate sex differences in tooth wear.

The mandibular dentition in seven individuals presented rather uneven wear of the premolars and the first molar. In all cases, the degree of wear was rather sharply angulated (about 45 degrees) on one side. Of the seven cases, four were males and three were females; five of the seven teeth involved were from the right side; six of the seven involved only one tooth; and five of the seven individuals were over fifty years of age. The unusual pattern of wear may be related to altered chewing functions associated with the loss of other teeth.

The rapid rate of dental attrition affects other features of dental pathology. Attrition is related to tooth loss. Among individuals twenty to twenty-nine years of age represented by complete mandibles, only one of five had lost one or more teeth prior to death (Table 17). In contrast, all individuals thirty years of age and older had lost one or more mandibular teeth prior to death. Thus, on an overall basis, eighteen of twenty-two individuals (82 percent) twenty years of age and older had lost one or more mandibular teeth prior to death. Among individuals

Table 17. Age and Sex Distribution of Antemortem Tooth Loss and Dental Pathology of the Mandible

Age Group	Number M	Number F	Number ?	Completely Edentulous M	Completely Edentulous F	Mean Number of Teeth Lost M	Mean Number of Teeth Lost F
Complete (N = 22)							
20–29	2	3				2	0
30–39	1	2				1	3
40–49	4			2		12.7	
50+	3	7		—	4	11.0	13.0
	10	12		2	4		
Incomplete (N = 12)							
20–29	1						
30–39	1	1					
40–49	1	2	1				
50+	1						
? (adult)	1	2	1				
	5	5	2				

Table 18. Age and Sex Distribution of Antemortem Tooth Loss and Dental Pathology of the Maxilla

Age Group	Number M	Number F	Number ?	Completely Edentulous M	Completely Edentulous F	Mean Number of Teeth Lost M	Mean Number of Teeth Lost F
Complete (N = 14)							
20–29							
30–39	1	1				0	2
40–49	2	1			1	8.5	16
50+	3	6		2	3	15.7	13.8
	6	8		2	4		
Incomplete (N = 8)							
20–29							
30–39							
40–49		1					
50+		2					
? (adult)	2	1	2				
	2	4	2				

Number of Individuals with			
Cavities		Abscesses	
M	F	M	F
1	0	1	1
1	1	1	1
0		2	
1	1	3	4
3	2	7	6
1			
		1	
		2	
		1	1
1	0	4	1

Number of Individuals with				
Cavities		Abscesses		
M	F	M	F	?
0	1			
1		1	1	
1	1	1	2	
2	2	2	3	
			1	
		0	0	1
		0	1	1

thirty and older represented by complete maxillae, only one had not lost any teeth antemortem (Table 18). Thirteen of the fourteen individuals (93 percent) had lost one or more maxillary teeth prior to death.

Tooth loss increases with age, and the severity of tooth loss in the La Galgada sample is shown in the number of individuals who had lost all teeth prior to death. Among the twelve maxillae and fourteen mandibles of individuals forty years of age and older, 50 percent and 43 percent respectively were completely edentulous, i.e., had lost all teeth antemortem with considerable resorption. Complete loss of teeth antemortem was more common in females than in males, and two females over fifty years of age had lost all maxillary and mandibular teeth prior to death.

Dental attrition also contributes to more frequent abscesses. In the mandibles, thirteen of twenty-two individuals (59 percent) had evidence of an abscess, and three individuals had multiple abscesses. In the maxillae, five of the fourteen individuals (36 percent) had at least one abscess, and one individual had multiple maxillary abscesses. There was an increase in abscesses with age, but no significant sex difference. Observations of the incomplete mandibles and maxillae also indicated a rather high percentage of abscesses. Five of twelve (42 percent) and two of eight (25 percent) incomplete mandibles and maxillae respectively had evidence of abscesses. Abscesses frequently occur in association with pulp exposure by attrition (Greene, Ewing, and Armelagos 1967) and are often detectable after the tooth remnant is lost and alveolar healing has begun.

In contrast, dental caries are less common than abscesses and are not age correlated in the La Galgada sample. In the mandibular and maxillary dentitions respectively, five of twenty-two (23 percent) and four of fourteen (29 percent) have at least one cavity, and two

Table 19. Average Tooth Wear Based on Complete Maxillae and Mandibles[a]

Age Group	I1 N	I1 Mean	I2 N	I2 Mean	C N	C Mean	P1 N	P1 Mean
20–29							2	2.0
30–39	4	2.0	4	2.0	4	1.7	5	1.2
40–49							2	3.0
50+	7	3.3	9	3.7	9	3.6	8	3.4

Age Group	P2 N	P2 Mean	M1 N	M1 Mean	M2 N	M2 Mean	M3 N	M3 Mean
20–29	1	1.0	6	1.5	3	1.3	2	1.0
30–39	7	1.7	7	2.5	8	2.6	4	2.3
40–49	2	2.5	1	3.5	3	4.0		
50+	5	3.1	2	4.0	4	3.0		

[a] Tooth wear was rated on a scale from 1 through 4 (see Methods section); N = number of teeth.

of five mandibles and two of four maxillae have multiple caries. In the incomplete specimens, on the other hand, only one of twelve (8 percent) mandibles has at least one cavity and none of eight maxillae has caries. The percentages of caries for the complete specimens are rather high given the degree of dental wear in the sample. Presumably, extremely abrasive diets wear away the fissures where caries ordinarily begin (St. Hoyme and Koritzer 1976).

Comparative dental attrition data are available in Paloma, but a different scale of wear was used (Edwards 1984). Nevertheless, the evidence indicates a high degree of wear in the Paloma sample. Based on D. S. Edwards' observations, Benfer (1984:538) concluded that "Palomans were responding to stress with increased mastication of abrasive foods. Individuals over 40 years of age had to use roots or gums for mastication." Observations on the La Galgada sample are consistent with those for the Palomans. Data on caries and abscesses for the Paloma sample are not yet available.

Both Peruvian Preceramic samples thus have a degree of dental wear found only with extremely abrasive diets. The rate of caries at La Galgada is high enough to suggest substantial use of carbohydrates. However, it must be noted that variants in the chemical constituents of the enamel that react with soil minerals or solutes in the drinking water could contribute to both wear and caries (St. Hoyme and Koritzer 1976).

7. Floral Remains

C. EARLE SMITH, JR.

Along the banks of the Tablachaca River, expanses of broad, level land are very few. La Galgada occupies one of exceptional size, probably an ancient riverine terrace. A similar, lower terrace, about a kilometer upriver, currently serves as the farming area for the modern village of La Galgada, and that area too may have been under cultivation at the time the archaeological site was functioning. At an intermediate level in front of the archaeological site are other terraces which may have been under cultivation, as is indicated by the retaining walls erected to preserve terrace faces. Today these terraces are not watered, but they must have been in times past in order to grow crops. The lower terraces might also have been utilized as house sites.

At the present time no formal weather observations are made at La Galgada. Thus no recorded data exist for temperature or rainfall. However, the present inhabitants assure me that it only rains once a year for a few minutes. The youngsters tell me they take off their clothes and play in the rain. We have no reasons to believe that the climate of the region at the time the site was occupied was any different from the present climate. Unfortunately, the largest part of the plant remains recovered were from cultivated plants which were grown with irrigation, and these do not function as climatic indicators.

Excavation was limited to architectural features of the temple complex and a few of the surrounding houses. Plant remains were most abundant in the deeper levels of the temple complex, where the fill was so dry that plant parts were found in good condition as dried plant material complete with pubescence. Plant remains were found both buried in the fill and on the floors of burial chambers. From the amounts of plant material discarded, it is possible to postulate that these folks did not feel any shortage. Because the area is too dry for the natural growth of most of the plants represented at the site, it is obvious that they either were transported in or were grown nearby under irrigation. Considering the prodigal disposal of plant material, it is unlikely that any of the material had been transported very far. Thus, it appears that the greater part of the plant remains originated in the local area. When the one or two items are encountered that might have been carried in, they will be noted.

The plant remains will be considered in the order of the Engler and Prantl system of classification, rather than in usage categories. In the discussion, various uses will be considered. For the most part, the remains consist of food plants. Food has always remained a prime consideration for humans (and for other animals). Some of the plant fragments may represent medicinal or dye plants, but such uses are generally difficult to infer, particularly if the same plant has an edible portion.

GNETACEAE (EPHEDRA FAMILY)

Stems found in the site appear to be those of
Ephedra, a native Peruvian plant which has
long been used as a medicinal. In the Callejón de Huaylas, stems of *Ephedra* are
steeped to make a tea which is used to cure
stomach complaints. Since the species does
not grow under the extreme conditions found
in the Tablachaca Canyon, it is probable that
the material was brought in from a moister
area. (F-11, surface, Sample 30.)

GRAMINEAE (GRASS FAMILY)
Zea mays (Maize)

While maize is known from other South
American areas (Pearsall 1978) at this time
period, unfortunately it was not widely cultivated at this site. A single maize cob was
found in the upper portion of the site
(D-11:AD-4/7, Floor 3). The cob is entire,
cigar-shaped, and measures 68 mm long
and 15 mm in diameter at the widest part.
Cupule width is 2.9 mm, cupule height is
1.5 mm. The cob is ten-rowed, but the ar-
rangement of the kernels on the cob is spiral.
Cupules are completely pubescent. The con-
densation index for this cob is 6.6, a value
higher than we found for any of the maize
cobs from Guitarrero Cave (Smith 1980*b*) or
for any of the ancient, indigenous races of
maize of Peru. It is within the ranges of con-
densation demonstrated by Palomero Tolo-
queno and Arrocillo Amarillo, two of the
ancient, indigenous races of maize of Mexico. Unfortunately, no kernel was found associated with the cob. We feel that it is safe
to assume that the cob was grown elsewhere
and brought in to La Galgada as a single
example.

Other Grass Species

Parts of grass plants occur with other plant
debris under circumstances which suggest
that grass was consistently used. However,

the parts are insufficient to provide identification, even of genus, and the material gives
no hint of the uses to which it may have been
put. When basketry is analyzed, it is probable that grass will be recognized as a component in its construction. Unidentified grass
fragments are listed on page 127 (in chronological order from late to early).

The grasses represented by these samples
probably include several different species
which occurred as native grasses along the
flood plain of the river when it was low or as
weedy plants in areas of irrigation cultivation. The single sample of grass fiber indicates that at least a part of the grass material
was collected for the extraction of fiber.

TYPHACEAE (CATTAIL FAMILY)

Typha sp. Cattail leaf fragments are distributed through the site sparingly. Inasmuch
as cattail was and is a favorite raw material
for making mats, its use in La Galgada is not
surprising. Analysis of some of the mats recovered with burials will undoubtedly dis-
close cattail used in their construction. At
the present time, cattail grows in backchan-
nels on the Tablachaca floodplain. Fragments identified are listed on page 127.

PALMAE (PALM FAMILY)

The region along the Tablachaca River is too
dry for the native growth of palms, and it is
unlikely that they would have grown on the
floodplain, where they would have been sub-
jected to an annual inundation and the buf-
feting of flood waters. The single palm seed
fragment found (G-12:H-4, Floor 8, firepit,
Sample 23) must have been brought into the
site from an area of higher rainfall. Had
palms been cultivated nearby under irrigation, it would be reasonable to expect a
larger number of endocarp fragments. The
fragment found is too small to permit identi-

Unidentified Grasses	*Description*	*Provenience*	*Sample*
	Cane	G-12:H-4, Floor 8, firepit	23
	Stems	G-12, Floors 8–9	22
	Seed	H-11:B-9, below Floor 13	25
	Base	F-11, surface	30
	Stem	H-11:DF-6/8, Floor 20	40
	Sheath	D-11:C-3, Floor 24	28
	Fiber	H-11:EF-1/3, Floor 30, west portal	43
	Grass	H-11:E-2, Floor 30, offering	42
	Grass(?) stem	E-11:EF-4, Floor 4	20
	Seeds, stems, rhizome	F-12:B-2, surface	12

Typha sp. (Cattail)	*Description*	*Provenience*	*Sample*
	Leaf	H-11:E-9, Floor 30, firepit	24
	Leaf fragment	F-12:B-2, tomb antechamber	32
	Fragments	F-12:B-2, tomb floor	35
	Leaf fragments	F-12:B-2, floor	12

fication of genus and species, but it is in the correct size range for *Acrocomia* or *Guilielma*.

BROMELIACEAE (PINEAPPLE FAMILY)

At the present time, one of the few plants native to the area surrounding La Galgada is *Puya ferruginea*. The species occurs as patches on the site and on the slopes up and down the Tablachaca Canyon. *Tillandsia*, on the other hand, is much less prevalent. However, both genera are clearly represented in the plant remains from the site. It is probable that the bromeliad material was all being used for the extraction of fiber. Some quids seem to be *Tillandsia* leaves. The remains listed on page 129 occurred throughout the chronological sequence.

The bromeliaceous remains are found in all chronological levels. There is evidence that they were being utilized for fiber extrac-

tion, and *Tillandsia* and *Puya* may also have had other uses not shown by the condition of the remains. The single quid which appears to be *Tillandsia* may indicate a certain amount of usage as a medicine.

AMARYLLIDACEAE (AMARYLLIS FAMILY)

At La Galgada, the amaryllis family is represented by fragments of *Furcraea* which were being used as a source of fiber. The plants will not grow in the area without irrigation. Thus, the scanty record may indicate either that the supply of *Furcraea* used at La Galgada was brought in from a wetter area or that only a very few plants were cultivated in the region. The few remains are distributed throughout the chronological span of the site. The pieces identified are listed on page 129.

CANNACEAE (CANNA FAMILY)

At the present time, achira, or *Canna edulis,* is regularly grown at La Galgada, where the edible roots are a part of the carbohydrate base for the diet. Only a single specimen from the site could be identified as *Canna* leaves (E-12:H-12, Floor 6, Sample 15). If achira was extensively used in the past, it must have been prepared away from the ceremonial center. However, inasmuch as it does not appear in the burials, we suspect that it was not heavily used at La Galgada. The single specimen is from the oldest part of the site.

LAURACEAE (BAY FAMILY)

The only member of the Lauraceae discovered among the La Galgada plant remains is *Persea americana,* the avocado or *palta.* The material in Sample 23 represents four seeds, and we think that this implies a tree in the area growing with irrigation. The other seeds were from other levels indicating the early distribution of this Mesoamerican tree in Peru. All of the samples are cotyledons. Those found are listed on page 129.

The presence of this tree crop throughout the chronological breadth of the site imposes the question, if avocado was an early import into the area, why did not maize appear at the same time? However, it is fairly clear from several archaeological sites that most cultivated plants move as individual species. Even the maize-beans pair do not always appear together in introduction. Avocado probably provided a welcome vegetable oil source at La Galgada.

LEGUMINOSAE (BEAN FAMILY)

A number of representatives of the bean family are found among La Galgada plant remains. Most of these appear to have been cultivated in irrigated agriculture. A few

may have been gathered. All of the legume remains have been seen by Lawrence Kaplan, who has identified remains of *Canavalia, Erythrina*(?), *Inga,* and *Phaseolus.* The genera will be considered in alphabetical order.

Arachis sp.

A single fragment of peanut hull was found in Sample 23, which lies chronologically at the top of the deposit. A single item might well have been brought into the site from outside. Peanuts will only grow in the vicinity under irrigation. Inasmuch as M. A. Towle (1961) reports no earlier archaeological peanut remains than from the Cupisnique levels of Huaca Prieta (at the earliest, about 1000 B.C.), this hull constitutes the earliest evidence for the arrival of the peanut in Peru from its homeland east of the Andes. The provenience for the peanut hull is G-12:H-4, Floor 8, firepit.

Canavalia sp. (Jack Bean)

Jack bean was identified by Kaplan in many of the samples of plant remains from La Galgada. While the total volume of material is small, its persistent presence suggests that jack bean played an important part in La Galgada diet. Jack bean remains are listed on page 129.

Dry jack beans are reported to have 331 calories per 100 gm, 25.4 gm protein, 1.3 gm fat, 57.1 gm carbohydrates, 96 mg calcium, 343 mg phosphorus, 4.9 mg iron, 10 mcg vitamin A, 0.46 mg thiamine, 0.15 mg riboflavin, 2.1 mg niacin, and no ascorbic acid (Wu Leung and Flores 1961). With such an analysis for dry jack beans, it is apparent that they were an important part of the dietary intake throughout the Preceramic occupation of La Galgada.

Bromeliaceae	*Description*	*Provenience*	*Sample*
	Bromeliad stems	G-12:H-4, Floor 8, firepit	23
	Leaf fragments	G-12, Floors 8–9	22
	Tillandsia(?) quid	F-11, surface	30
	Leaf fragments and fiber	F-11, surface	30
	Leaf fragments	D-11:C-3, fill around tomb	31
	Tillandsia leaf	H-11:E-9, Floor 30, firepit	24
	Leaf fragments	E-11:EF-4, Floor 4	20
	Puya leaves (2)	E-12:I-2, Floor 6	19
	Leaf fragments	E-12:I-2, Floor 6	19
	Leaf fragments	E-12:H-2, Floor 6	17
	Tillandsia leaves	E-12:H-2, Floor 6	15
	Puya stem and leaves	E-12:H-2, Floor 6	15
	Puya fragments	F-12:B-2, tomb floor	35
	Leaf	F-12:B-2, tomb antechamber	32
	Leaf fragments	F-12:B-2, floor	14

Furcraea sp.	*Description*	*Provenience*	*Sample*
	Fragments	G-12, Floors 8–9	22
	Furcraea(?) fragments	H-11:DF-6/8, Floor 20	40
	Stalk	E-12:H-2, Floor 6	17
	Fragment	F-12:B-2, floor	14

Persea americana (Avocado)	Description	Provenience	Sample
	Cotyledons	G-12:H-4, Floor 8, firepit	23
	Cotyledon	D-11:C-3, Floor 25	2
	Cotyledon	E-12:H-2, Floor 6	15

Canavalia sp. (Jack Bean)	Description	Provenience	Sample
	Epidermis	D-11:C-3, Floor 24	28
	Bean	H-11:EF-1/3, Floor 30, west portal	43
	Seed	E-12:I-2, Floor 6	19
	Pods	E-12:H-2, Floor 6	17
	Hila	E-12:H-2, Floor 6	17
	Beans	E-12:H-2, Floor 6	15
	Pods	E-12:H-2, Floor 6	15
	Epidermis	F-12:B-2, tomb antechamber	32
	Pods	F-12:B-2, tomb antechamber	32
	Hila	F-12:B-2, floor	12

Erythrina sp. (Coral Bean)

While the genus *Erythrina* includes species with high chemical contents, some of the species bear edible seeds. Several seeds and pods from La Galgada were identified by Kaplan as possible *Erythrina* remains. See page 131.

Sample 40 is from the upper (later) portion of the ruin. The remainder are from early levels, where they are not abundant. It is conceivable that this species was only used for medical or ritual purposes because of its chemical content. On the other hand, it is also possible that this is an edible species. From the remains, it is impossible to make this determination.

Inga sp. (Pacay)

The tree legume, *pacay,* is valued for the sweet flesh around its seeds. The fragments recovered are listed on page 131.

In an area like La Galgada, *Inga* is a foreign tree, because of the lack of water supply except on the river flood plain. This seems to have been one of the early crops introduced into the irrigated farms which remained uniformly popular through time. A number of species from North and South America are in cultivation. The characteristics of La Galgada pods are not sufficiently distinct to allow them to be identified by species.

Phaseolus lunatus (Lima Bean)

The lima bean appears to have been a principal crop plant at La Galgada. See page 131 for remains identified by Kaplan.

Sample 28 included six intact lima beans. The measurements of these seeds provided L × W factors ranging from 154 to 216, and averaging 183.4. They are fully as large as later examples of lima beans from Peruvian sites.

All of the lima bean material was found in Preceramic contexts in La Galgada. Why it should not have been included in later fill is something of a mystery, as none of the other plant remains indicate a change in climatic conditions. The lima beans from the deposit are all clearly cultivated, including those from the lowest level in Sample 14.

Phaseolus vulgaris (Common Bean)

The common bean is well represented by pod material identified by Kaplan, as listed on page 131.

As with the remains of *P. lunatus, P. vulgaris* remains were found only in the Preceramic levels, where they were not uncommon. No seeds were found, which is unusual in view of the numbers of pods and the presence of food offerings in the burials. Apparently, beans were sufficiently highly regarded that they were always pursued when they were dropped.

Pithecellobium(?) sp.

Near the top of the chronological sequence were recovered pod fragments associated with circular, thin seeds which probably came from a species of *Pithecellobium*. The samples are from H-11:A-10, Floor 13 (Sample 5), H-11:A-9, Floor 13 (Sample 3), and H-11:B-9, below Floor 13 (Sample 25). Whether this material was once considered edible or whether it might have been utilized for another purpose is not discernible from the remains. Material with this identification was not reported by Towle (1961).

Measurements of Leguminous Samples

Relatively few of the remains of *Canavalia* (jack beans) were sufficiently intact to make measurements meaningful. A jack bean from Sample 43 measures 17 mm long, 11.9 mm

Erythrina sp.
(Coral Bean)

Description	Provenience	Sample
Pods	H-11:DF-6/8, Floor 20	40
Seed	E-12:I-2, Floor 6	19
Seed	E-12:H-2, Floor 6	17
Pods	F-12:B-2, tomb floor	35
Seeds (6)	F-12:B-2, floor	14

Inga sp. (Pacay)

Description	Provenience	Sample
Pods	H-11:B-9, below Floor 13	25
Pod	H-11:CF-7, Floor 20	44
Pods	D-11:C-3, Floor 24	31
Pod	D-11:C-3, Floor 25	27
Pod	E-12:I-2/3, Floor 6	18
Pod	F-12:B-2, tomb antechamber	32
Pods	F-12:B-2, floor	14

Phaseolus lunatus
(Lima Bean)

Description	Provenience	Sample
Pods	D-11:C-3, fill around tomb	31
P. lunatus pods	D-11:C-3, Floor 24	28
Lima beans	D-11:C-3, Floor 24	28
P. lunatus pods	D-11:C-3, Floor 25	27
P. lunatus pods	H-11:EF-1/3, Floor 30, west portal	43
P. lunatus pods	E-12:I-2, Floor 6	19
P. lunatus pods	E-12:I-2/3, Floor 6	18
P. lunatus fragments	E-12:H-2, Floor 6	17
P. lunatus pods	E-12:H-2, Floor 6	15
P. lunatus pods	F-12:B-2, tomb floor	35
P. lunatus pods	F-12:B-2, tomb antechamber	32
P. lunatus pods	F-12:B-2, floor	14
P. lunatus bean	F-12:B-2, floor	14

Phaseolus vulgaris
(Common Bean)

Description	Provenience	Sample
Pods	D-11:C-3, Floor 24	28
	E-12:I-2, Floor 6	19
	F-12:B-2, tomb floor	35
	F-12:B-2, floor	12

wide, and 9.1 mm thick. We have nothing with which to compare this among the remainder of the jack bean remnants.

Somewhat more of the possible *Erythrina* material could be measured. The following seeds were measured:

Sample	Length (mm)	Width (mm)	Thickness (mm)	L×W÷T
19	7.0	5.5	4.5	8.6
17	7.0	6.0	4.0	10.5
14	7.7	5.8	4.0	11.2
14	9.0	7.8	4.5	15.6
14	9.2	7.8	5.1	14.1
14	10.1	7.2	5.1	14.3

The variation denoted by the above measurements is probably normal for the species. All of these seeds are similar in color pattern, having a basic scarlet coat with orange in a band around the ends and bottom. In all, the hilum is at an angle to the long axis of the seed and there is no prominent caruncle. These characteristics remove the seeds from the genus *Phaseolus*. Lawrence Kaplan believes that they may belong to a species of *Erythrina,* but they are definitely not the edible *Erythrina* cultivated in the Callejón de Huaylas. Whether these were eaten could not be determined, nor could they be determined to be cultivated.

All of the seeds came from the earliest levels of the site. While the seed from Sample 17 is younger than the remainder (all of which are from the same level), it fits into the middle of the size range and shows no trend.

Measurements were made from two intact pods of *Inga* (*pacay*). These measurements are:

Sample	Length (mm)	Width (mm)
27	75	23
18	83	10.6

The measurements indicate that the *pacay* involved had surprisingly small pods, but these may have been collected from trees growing under subnormal conditions. *Inga* generally grows in much more mesic environments than the area around La Galgada. In spite of irrigation, the continuing dry air may have terminated pod growth at an early stage.

The only measurements made on *Phaseolus* remains have already been reported above. Inasmuch as all of the lima beans are from the same sample, there is nothing with which to compare them. No common beans were recovered. None of the *Phaseolus* bean pods were measured.

MALPIGHIACEAE

The malpigh family includes a number of plants which produce edible, fleshy fruits. At La Galgada, seeds or seed fragments of *Bunchosia* (*ciruelo del fraile*) were the only representatives found. These are listed on page 133.

Most of the specimens were found in Preceramic levels of La Galgada. From the material, it is impossible to tell if these were from cultivated trees or not. At the time of our visit, no wild *Bunchosia* trees were noted on the flood plain.

Measurements made of the whole seeds are as follows:

Sample	Length (mm)	Width (mm)	Thickness (mm)	L×W÷T
20	19.0	12.0	8.5	26.8
19	18.0	9.0	7.0	23.2
15	15.0	10.1	8.2	18.5
15	19.9	11.0	8.0	27.4
15	16.8	10.1	9.0	18.9
4	18.0	10.5		
4	18.0	7.5		

Malpighiaceae	*Description*	*Provenience*	*Sample*
	Bunchosia(?) seed fragments	H-11:DF-6/8, Floor 20	40
	Bunchosia seed	E-11:EF-4, Floor 4	20
	Bunchosia seed fragments (3)	E-12:I-2, Floor 6	19
	Bunchosia seeds	E-11:H-2, Floor 6	15
	Bunchosia seeds (6)	E-12:I-2, Floor 6	4
	Bunchosia	F-12:B-2(I), left shoulder	34

Although *ciruelo del fraile* is native to Peru, it has been in cultivation for a long period. The seeds found at La Galgada probably were from fruit harvested from trees grown under irrigation. The size of several of the seeds recovered argues for this; further, it is unknown as a native plant in this region of Peru where rainfall is virtually nonexistent. It seems to have been placed as an offering with a burial, indicating that *Bunchosia* was regarded as something of value to accompany the dead.

EUPHORBIACEAE (POINSETTIA FAMILY)

A single fragment of a Euphorbiaceous capsule was found at E-12:I-2, Floor 6, in La Galgada. We were unable to provide more accurate determination of the genus or species. Many of the members of this family are mildly to violently poisonous, and many have been used medicinally, while a few produce edible parts like chia and manioc.

SAPINDACEAE (SOAPBERRY FAMILY)

Several specimens of seeds from *Sapindus saponaria* were recovered from La Galgada. These fruits are still used in Latin America for the sapogenin in the fruit. It is preferred to soap by some women for washing hair and other tasks where they wish to avoid a soap film. The following were found:

Description	*Provenience*	*Sample*
Seed	E-12:I-2, Floor 6	19
Seed	E-12:I-2, below Floor 5	4
Seeds	F-12:B-2, floor	14

All of these came from early levels, but this is probably not significant, because the fruits are generally used away from domestic areas. The number of seeds recovered at La Galgada indicates a heavy usage, and that use probably did not stop in later times.

MALVACEAE (COTTON FAMILY)

La Galgada must have been a center for the production of cotton (*Gossypium*). From the top to the bottom, the site was strewn with fragments indicating use of cotton. Only Samples 33 and 13 (the earliest) were without any, and I suspect that, if a larger sampling of this level had been possible, cotton would have been recovered. The remains that were recovered are listed on page 134.

The cotton fiber seemed to be abandoned liberally, indicating that it was in good supply. In addition to the raw fiber, a number of yarns were recovered, many of which were spun from cotton. The cotton fiber ranged in color from white to tan. Inasmuch as it occurred in all parts of the site except the very earliest levels (Samples 13 and 33), it appears to have been one of the most important crops grown around La Galgada. It could

Description	Provenience	Sample	
Fiber	G-12:H-4, Floor 8, firepit	23	**Gossypium** (Cotton)
	G-12, Floors 8–9	22	
	H-11:D-10, below Floor 10	21	
	H-11:B-9, below Floor 13	25	
	F-11, surface	30	
	H-11:CF-7, Floor 20	44	
	H-11:DF-6/8, Floor 20	40	
	D-11:C-3, Floor 25	10	
	D-11:C-3, Floor 25	9	
	H-11:EF-1/3, Floor 30, west portal	43	
	H-11:E-9, Floor 30, firepit	24	
	E-12:I-2, Floor 6	19	
	E-12:I-2/3, Floor 6	18	
	E-12:H-2, Floor 6	17	
	E-12:H-2, Floor 6	15	
	F-12:F-2, tomb antechamber	32	
	F-12:B-2, floor	14	
	F-12:B-2, floor	12	
Cotton plug	G-12:H-4, Floor 8, firepit	23	
Seed fragments	D-11:C-3, fill around tomb	31	
	D-11:C-3, Floor 25	27	
	D-11:C-3, Floor 25	10	
	H-11:E-9, Floor 30, firepit	24	
	E-11:EF-4, Floor 4	20	
Seeds	E-12:I-2, Floor 6	19	
	E-12:I-2/3, Floor 6	18	
	E-12:H-2, Floor 6	17	
Seed fragments	E-12:H-2, Floor 6	15	
Seeds	F-12:B-2, tomb antechamber	36	
	F-12:B-2, tomb	35	
	F-12:B-2, floor	14	
	F-12:B-2, floor	12	
Boll segment	D-11:C-3, Floor 24	28	
Boll segments	D-11:C-3, Floor 25	27	
	E-12:I-2, Floor 6	19	
	E-12:H-2, Floor 6	17	
	E-12:H-2, Floor 6	15	
	F-12:B-2, tomb	35	
	F-12:B-2, tomb antechamber	32	
	F-12:B-2, floor	12	

have existed here only as a cultivated crop under irrigation. The abundance suggests that it may have been the base for an industry such as the production of nets for coastal fisheries.

Cottonseeds were abundant at La Galgada. Many of them were whole, enabling us to measure them, as shown below.

It is apparent that the older cottonseeds are larger than the most recent seeds, except that those from Sample 14, at the earliest level for which we have cottonseeds, measure smaller than all of the succeeding samples. This may be a function of the few seeds available for measurement rather than truly smaller seeds. The next chronological

Length (mm)	Width (mm)	L×W	Length (mm)	Width (mm)	L×W
			Sample 19		
8.0	5.0	40.0	9.0	5.5	49.5
12.0	7.0	84.0	8.0	5.5	44.0
9.0	5.0	45.0	9.0	7.5	67.5
8.5	5.0	42.5	8.0	5.0	40.0
8.5	6.0	51.0	7.0	5.1	35.7
7.5	5.0	37.5	8.0	5.2	41.6
7.5	5.5	41.3	7.9	5.3	41.9
7.2	5.0	36.0	8.5	4.8	40.8
8.0	4.8	38.4	9.5	4.3	50.4
8.7	5.1	44.4	8.7	5.5	47.9
7.0	4.5	31.5	7.0	5.0	35.0
7.3	4.5	32.9	7.7	5.4	41.6
8.7	5.0	43.5	7.2	5.1	36.7
7.2	4.8	34.6	8.1	5.8	47.0
7.0	4.5	31.5	7.7	4.1	31.6
		Average L×W=41.3			
			Sample 18		
7.0	5.0	35.0	9.0	5.2	46.8
7.8	4.7	36.7	7.9	5.0	39.5
8.5	5.0	42.5			
		Average L×W=40.1			
			Sample 17		
8.0	5.5	44.0	8.5	4.5	38.3
8.0	5.5	44.0	7.0	4.5	31.5
8.0	5.5	44.0	9.0	5.0	45.0
8.5	5.0	42.5	9.0	5.5	49.5
8.0	5.0	40.0	9.5	6.0	57.0
8.5	6.5	55.3	8.0	4.5	36.0
8.0	6.0	48.0	8.0	6.5	52.0
9.0	6.5	58.5	8.5	4.5	38.3

Length (mm)	Width (mm)	L×W	Length (mm)	Width (mm)	L×W
		Sample 17, continued			
9.0	7.0	63.0	8.5	5.0	42.5
8.0	4.0	32.0	9.0	5.0	45.0
9.0	5.5	55.0	10.0	5.5	55.0
7.5	5.5	41.3	8.5	5.0	42.5
8.5	6.0	51.0	8.0	5.5	44.0
8.0	5.0	40.0	7.0	5.5	38.5
9.5	5.5	52.3	8.0	6.0	48.0
		Average L×W=45.8			
		Sample 36			
9.6	6.2	57.4	9.0	5.9	53.1
8.0	5.0	40.0			
		Average L×W=50			
		Sample 12			
9.0	5.0	45.0	8.0	4.2	33.6
10.0	5.8	58.0	10.7	6.3	67.4
7.5	4.8	36.0	9.0	7.0	63.0
11.0	5.0	55.0			
		Average L×W=59.7			
		Sample 14			
7.0	5.0	35.0	8.0	5.0	40.0
8.0	4.5	36.0	7.0	4.0	28.0
		Average L×W=34.8			

level includes Sample 12, which has the largest cottonseeds of all those recovered.

Much of the cottonseed material is fragmentary. Some may have been broken by being walked on, and other seeds may well have been opened by rodents. However, a significant number of the broken cottonseeds have been split lengthwise, very unlike the pattern of opening displayed by seeds opened by animals or mechanically broken. It appears that much cottonseed material was purposely split lengthwise to extract the kernel for processing into oil or for direct human consumption.

A number of cotton boll segments were sufficiently intact that they were measurable, as recorded on page 137.

Much of the boll segment material was either broken or too curled to obtain measurements. Therefore, the averages for each sample are nearly meaningless. It does appear that the most recent boll material is smaller than earlier boll segments. This would be in line with seed size, which furnished a much better statistical sample.

If the larger size at earlier levels is real rather than apparent, it calls for speculation.

Sample	Length (mm)	Width (mm)	Beak Length (mm)	Septum Width (mm)
28	22.0	12.0	5.0	6.0
19	20.0	9.0	5.0	6.0
	21.0	12.5	broken	broken
	21.0	curled	broken	7.0
	22.0	15.0	broken	curled
	24.0	15.5	broken	curled
	28.0	broken	5.0	9.0
	26.0	curled	6.5	curled
	19.0	10.0 (est.)	broken	curled
	22.0	curled	broken	curled
	22.0	broken	6.0	curled
Average	22.5	12.4	5.6	7.3
17	20.0	broken	broken	7.0
	25.0	12.0	5.5	8.0
	24.0	14.0	broken	burled
	21.0	burled	broken	7.0
	22.0	burled	broken	7.0
	23.0	12.0	broken	8.0
	24.0	14.0	broken	7.0
	25.5	curled	broken	7.5
	23.5	curled	8.5	7.5
	broken	curled	7.0	7.0
	20.0	15.0	broken	7.0
	24.0	16.0	broken	8.5
	21.0	broken	none	broken
	21.0	curled	4.0	broken
	20.0	broken	none	broken
	broken	broken	broken	8.0
	22.5	16.5	broken	broken
	22.0	16.0	broken	9.0
	25.0	11.0	6.5	broken
	22.0	curled	6.5	7.0
	24.0	14.0	broken	broken
	24.0	16.5	broken	broken
	25.0	curled	7.0	broken
	broken	broken	broken	9.5
	25.5	12.5	broken	7.0
	25.0	curled	broken	7.0
Average	21.2	13.6	6.0	7.6
15	26.5	curled	5.1	7.2
	21.0	curled	broken	7.0
Average	23.8	—	—	7.1

Normally, at this chronological level, it is expected that the earliest samples will be smaller than later samples of cultivated plants. It is generally assumed that this is because of selection pressure under cultivation for larger units. At La Galgada, it appears that the situation is reversed. Another factor must be taken into consideration, however. La Galgada must have been built by persons supported by irrigation agriculture, because the local area is not suitable for flood-water farming and the climate is too dry to support any form of agriculture other than with irrigation. Considering this, the cotton found in the earliest levels of La Galgada must already have been in cultivation before it was introduced into the La Galgada area. We have no indication from where it may have come. It is supposed that all succeeding crops following the original introduction were grown from seed saved from the previous crop. If no additional strain of cotton was subsequently introduced, it is possible that the size of bolls and seeds in successive crops became gradually smaller and smaller. This is probably largely due to decreasing fertility of the soil (with irrigation agriculture, fields are reused continuously) because of the lack of application of organic material which would serve as fertilizer. Another factor is the salinity of the Tablachaca River, which, no matter how slight, is bound to be concentrated in irrigation ditches by evaporation, particularly in a climate as dry as that of La Galgada. Also, when crop plants are not exposed to fresh intermixing of germ plasm by hybridization with new genomes, it is possible for the genome to be gradually rearranged by selection so that variability is suppressed. Under such conditions, recessives may be activated which collectively result in decreased fruit and seed size. Any or all of these factors may have been operative at La Galgada.

The volume of cotton recovered at La Gal-

gada indicates that it must have been a crop produced for export. We assume that the fabrication of cotton into economically valuable artifacts was done at the site and that the finished products were traded either inland into the mountains, where cotton cannot be grown, or to the coast, which had a heavy demand for fish nets, string, and other such cotton products. It would have been illogical to have transported raw cotton very far because of its relatively low value, particularly to the coast, where cotton can be grown in the lower ends of the river valleys. At any rate, La Galgada obviously served as a major cotton-producing site from its founding about 2400 B.C. to its abandonment.

PASSIFLORACEAE (PASSION FLOWER FAMILY)

These herbaceous vines are naturally widespread in the Americas, and several of them bear edible fruits with a very fine flavor. Several species in South America are in cultivation and have been introduced into other tropical areas of the world. At La Galgada, fragments of seeds which are almost certainly *Passiflora* species appear at two levels. The most recent is a seed fragment which appears to be *Passiflora* recovered from H-11:B-9, below Floor 13 (Sample 25). A lot of 127 seeds was found in H-11:E-9, Floor 30, firepit (Sample 24). These are undoubtedly *Passiflora,* but they are not determined as to species. Fifty-one seed coats from Sample 24 were sufficiently intact to measure, as recorded at the top of page 139.

The average length times width for these seeds was calculated to be 8.4, but no other collection of measurable *Passiflora* seeds was available with which to compare these. The uniformity of the lot suggests that only a single variety of passion fruit was being grown. The paucity of material may indicate that the plant did not grow well in the desert atmosphere.

Length (mm)	Width (mm)	Length (mm)	Width (mm)	Length (mm)	Width (mm)
4.0	2.0	4.0	2.0	4.1	2.1
4.3	2.2	4.0	2.0	4.5	2.1
4.3	2.0	4.0	2.0	4.3	2.0
4.0	2.0	4.3	2.0	4.1	2.0
4.0	2.0	4.2	2.0	4.0	2.0
3.5	2.0	4.2	2.0	4.2	2.0
4.0	2.0	4.4	2.0	4.0	2.0
4.3	2.0	4.5	2.1	4.0	2.0
4.3	2.1	4.5	2.0	4.1	2.2
4.2	2.1	4.2	2.0	4.3	2.0
4.5	2.0	4.0	2.0	4.0	2.0
4.0	2.0	4.0	2.0	4.3	2.0
4.2	2.0	4.1	2.0	4.4	2.0
4.0	2.0	4.0	2.0	4.0	2.0
4.2	2.0	4.0	2.0	4.0	2.0
4.0	2.0	4.0	2.0	4.3	2.0
4.1	2.0	4.5	2.0	4.5	2.2

Cactaceae	Description	Provenience	Sample
	Spine	H-11:B-9, below Floor 13	25
	Seed (1)	H-11:FG-9, top firepit, Floor 20	37
	Seeds (2)	E-12:I-2, Floor 6	19
	Seeds (84)	E-12: H-2, Floor 6	17

CACTACEAE (CACTUS FAMILY)

The cactus family is represented by several species which are native to the La Galgada region. Cacti are everywhere used for food in America, and the spines are sometimes used for pins. The parts found are listed above.

The intact cactus seeds were not measured inasmuch as they all came from the same sample and thus could not be compared with other samples.

MYRTACEAE (MYRTLE FAMILY)

The myrtle family is frequently utilized in the tropics as a source of fruit or for the fragrant oils found in many of the members. Guava (*Psidium* sp.) is the only member of the family found at La Galgada. It is represented by three fruits and a number of seeds. The recovered specimens are:

Description	Provenience	Sample
Fruit	E-12:I-2, Floor 6	19
Seeds	E-12:H-2, Floor 6	17
Fruit	E-12:H-2, Floor 6	15
Fruit	F-12:B-2, Floor 6	14

A selection of seeds and the intact fruit were all measured:

Sample Description	Length (mm)	Diameter (mm)	L×D
17 Seeds	3.5	3.0	10.5
	3.0	2.5	7.5
	4.5	3.0	13.5
	3.0	2.5	7.5
	3.0	2.5	7.5
	4.5	3.0	13.5
	3.5 (est.)	2.5	8.8
Average			9.8
19 Fruit	7.0	1.0	
15 Fruit	12.8	12.0	
14 Fruit	14.0	13.0	

Guava seeds are sufficiently distinct that they are difficult to confuse with other genera. They appear to be bent in the middle, often acutely. Measurements are furnished so that these may be compared with future recoveries of guava seeds. The fruits are all small, but it must be remembered that they are completely dry and may have been immature fruit originally, which would account for their discard. Guava is not known as a native fruit in the La Galgada region and it is assumed that these remains came from trees under cultivation.

SAPOTACEAE (SAPOTE FAMILY)

Members of the sapote family have long been valued throughout the Americas for fruit which ranges from succulent to dry and from very sweet to subacid. Generally, fruits of the group are high in calcium and phosphorus, elements which are otherwise in short supply in the tropics because of low amounts of these elements in the soils. The only species recognized in the La Galgada remains is *lúcuma* (*Pouteria* sp.) which was recovered as fragments of seed coat. The remains are listed on page 141.

So far as we are aware, none of the sapotaceous fruits are native to the Tablachaca Canyon. The presence of these fragments in so many levels suggests that *lúcuma* was a very popular fruit from the earliest occupation of the site, and it must have been grown with irrigation.

SOLANACEAE (POTATO FAMILY)

The potato family is represented in La Galgada by a number of aji (*Capsicum* sp.) seeds. They were obviously popular throughout the chronological scale represented by the site as shown by the list on page 141.

The *Capsicum* seeds were measured when they were sufficiently intact. Measurements are given on page 142.

All of the *Capsicum* seeds recovered were ivory colored. While a few seeds were conspicuously larger than the remainder, the measurements indicate that intermediate sizes blend them into the measured population. From the seeds alone, the aji cannot be identified by species. It is evident that the largest number of seeds were recovered from

Sapotaceae	Description	Provenience	Sample
	Seed fragments	H-11:B-9, below Floor 13	25
		H-11:DF-6/8, Floor 20	40
		H-11:E-9, Floor 30, firepit	24
		E-12:I-2, Floor 6	19
		E-12:I-2/3, Floor 6	18
		E-12:H-2, Floor 6	15
		F-12:B-2, tomb floor	35
		F-12:B-2(I), left shoulder	34
		F-12:B-2, tomb antechamber	32
		F-12:B-2, floor	14

Capsicum sp. (Aji)	Description	Provenience	Sample
	Seeds	H-11:DF-6/8, Floor 20	40
		D-11:C-3, fill around tomb	31
		E-12: I-2, Floor 6	19
		E-12: H-2, Floor 6	17
		E-12: H-2, Floor 6	15
		F-12: B-2, floor	12

earlier levels, but this may be an artifact of the recovery procedures. The large number from Sample 17 were screened in the laboratory from a large flotation sample. We suspect that the aji seeds were missed in the upper levels of the site. Peppers are known to be high in vitamin A and must have performed a vital function in the diet of these desert people.

A single seed of a species of *Solanum* was found in H-11:E-9, Floor 30, firepit. It is 1.8 mm long and 1.5 mm wide. It might be from either a cultivated or a native species.

CUCURBITACEAE (SQUASH FAMILY)

Gourds and squashes are well represented at the La Galgada site. Containers fashioned from gourds were placed with the burials in addition to the scraps recovered from the remainder of the excavations. Gourd (*Lagenaria siceraria*) remains are enumerated on page 143.

Gourd seeds sufficiently entire were measured:

Sample	Length (mm)	Width (mm)	L×W
17	18.0	8.0	144.0
	17.5	9.0	157.5
	17.0	8.0	136.0
	Average L×W = 145.8		
12	10.8	broken	—
	16.0	7.0	112.0
	13.5	7.0	94.5
	16.0	7.2	115.2
	Average L×W = 107.2		

While the older lot of gourd seeds were smaller than the younger ones, no importance should be attached to the difference because of the few intact seeds available for measurement. All gourd fragments were identified by T. W. Whitaker.

Sample	Width (mm)	Width (mm)	Width (mm)	Width (mm)	Width (mm)	Width (mm)	Width (mm)
31	4.0						
19	3.5	4.0	3.0	3.5	3.2		
			Average 3.4				
17	3.5	3.8	3.4	3.3	4.5	3.5	4.4
	3.8	3.5	3.8	3.8	4.0	3.0	3.4
	2.5	3.0	3.5	3.9	3.8	4.0	3.8
	3.1	3.2	3.0	3.0	4.0	3.9	3.9
	3.2	3.7	3.1	4.0	3.8	4.0	4.0
	3.7	3.5	3.5	4.0	3.8	2.9	3.7
	4.0	3.2	4.0	3.3	3.0	3.2	3.8
	3.5	3.6	3.3	3.9	4.1	3.6	3.2
	3.1	3.9	3.6	3.0	3.1	4.0	3.5
	3.7	3.4	3.5	4.0	3.3	3.8	4.0
	2.4	3.2	3.7	3.4	3.5	3.6	3.6
	3.0	3.3	3.5	3.8	3.1	3.5	3.3
	3.0	4.0	3.8	4.0	3.4	3.4	3.1
	4.1	3.9	3.7	2.8	3.8	3.2	3.9
	3.9	3.5	3.2	3.4	3.0	3.8	3.0
	3.7	3.0	3.3	3.0	3.0	3.2	3.6
	3.2	3.4	3.5	3.7	3.4	3.3	3.8
	3.7	3.6	3.3	4.0	4.1	4.0	4.0
	3.4	3.7	3.5	3.4	3.5	4.1	3.3
	3.9	3.5	3.5	3.0	3.9	3.5	3.6
	3.5	3.5	3.9	3.0	3.7	3.8	3.2
	3.8	3.7	3.3	4.0	3.1	3.0	4.1
	3.8	3.5	3.0	3.2	3.3	3.8	3.5
	3.8	3.5	3.5	3.2	3.7	3.0	3.2
			Average 3.5				
15	3.0	3.2	3.8				
			Average 3.3				
12	4.0	3.2	3.8	3.3	3.5	3.4	4.0
	3.5	3.4	3.4	3.9	3.4	4.0	2.5
	3.0	3.5	4.0	3.0	3.5	3.7	3.9
	4.0	3.0	2.8	3.2	3.9	3.0	3.0
	3.0	2.9	3.5	3.1	3.0	3.5	3.1
	3.5	4.1					
			Average 3.4				

Capsicum sp.
(Ají)

Lagenaria siceraria (Gourd)	*Description*	*Provenience*	*Sample*
	Rind	H-11: A-9, Floor 13	3
	Neck (of gourd)	E-12: I-2/3, Floor 6	18
	Seed fragments	E-12: H-2, Floor 6	17
	Rind	E-12: H-2, Floor 6	15
	Rind	F-12: B-2, tomb floor	35
	Rind	F-12: B-2, floor	14
	Seeds	F-12: B-2, floor	12
	Rind	F-12: B-2, floor	12
	Seed	F-12: B-2, firepit	13

***Cucurbita* spp.** (Squash)	*Description*	*Provenience*	*Sample*
	Rind (wild)	H-11: A-9, Floor 13	3
	Seeds	H-11: DF-6/8, Floor 20	40
	Rind	H-11: EF-1/3, Floor 30, west portal	43
	Seeds (*C. moschata?*)	E-12: I-2, Floor 6	19
	Stem (*C. moschata*)	E-12: I-2/3, Floor 6	18
	Seed fragments	E-12: H-2, Floor 6	17
	Rind	E-12: H-2, Floor 6	17
	Stem (wild)	E-12: H-2, Floor 6	15
	Seeds (*C. maxima*)	F-12: B-2, tomb antechamber	36
	Seed (*C. moschata?*)	F-12: B-2, floor	14
	Seed (*C. moschata?*)	F-12: B-2, floor	12
	Seeds	F-12: B-2, firepit	13

Squash Fragments

A number of squash (*Cucurbita*) fragments were recovered from La Galgada site in addition to gourd fragments. All of these were also seen and identified by T. W. Whitaker. The recovered remains are listed above.

Seeds entire enough to be measured are these:

Sample	*Length (mm)*	*Width (mm)*	*L×W*
19	11.5	6.0	69.0
	11.5	5.5	63.3
	12.0	8.0	96.0
	13.0	8.0	104.0
	14.0	9.0	126.0
	Average L×W=91.7		
12	8.5	broken	

Little can be learned from the few measurements possible on the squash seeds. Both the South American squash, *Cucurbita maxima,* and the Central American squash, *C. moschata,* were identified. The identifiable remains are all in the same general chronological levels, which probably place them at about 2000 B.C. Inasmuch as these are fully cultivated, they are one more proof of the use of irrigation agriculture at the La Galgada site. It is uncertain where the wild cucurbit might have been gathered, but it was probably growing along the flood plain of the Tablachaca River in the algarroba-molle forest.

SIGNIFICANCE OF THE LA GALGADA PLANT MATERIAL

It is quite clear that the largest amount of the plant remains recovered from La Galgada are from the Preceramic portion of the excavation. Although most species are missing from the two earliest samples (numbers 13 and 33), these were small samples and it is probable that further sampling would have disclosed a larger array of the species which were found in levels above. At the Preceramic level, both cotton and gourds and squashes are present, indicating very clearly that irrigation agriculture was under way.

At this time, we have no evidence for the sophistication of the irrigation system. However, the Tablachaca River flows with sufficient velocity through this portion of the canyon that the flood plain is largely alluvium ranging in size from large cobbles to sand with very little area which could be profitably used for agriculture. Considering this, it is almost certain that all farming was done on agricultural terraces constructed on old river terraces high above the current water level. With the very meager precipitation in the canyon, farming is possible only with canal irrigation. The remains of agricultural terraces occupy the old river terrace

in front of the La Galgada ruins. These are probably the remains of terraces first used by the La Galgada people and probably reused by subsequent occupants of the valley. At the time of Inca occupation, the settlement was about 2 km upstream, but these La Galgada terraces might still have been in use.

No other form of cultivation is probable, and the natural resources of the area would appear to be too limited to provide long-term subsistence. The vegetation of the canyon sides above the river flood plain includes an occasional algarroba tree which has found an underground source of water, several species of cacti, and a species of *Puya* which furnishes fiber but little food. On the flood plain are occasional terraces which escape destruction for sufficiently long to permit the growth of a forest of *Acacia, Schinus, Prosopis,* and an assortment of composite shrubs and ferns. While the pods and seeds of algarroba are regularly used for human and animal food, the assortment of edible plant materials from this source is meager. We suspect that the Tablachaca Canyon was used for communication between the interior and the coast, but was unoccupied by settlements until irrigation agriculture was developed. It is doubtful that La Galgada is the earliest site along the Tablachaca River, but it is obviously of some importance if the amount of effort expended on the architecture is any criterion.

The placement of La Galgada indicates that it must have been an important way station on a line of communication. For this reason, the inhabitants must have always grown extra produce in the gardens to supply the travelers who stopped in at the settlement. In addition to the food supplies needed for the inhabitants and the transients, the amount of cotton suggests that La Galgada was growing extensive crops of fiber. In addition, other fiber plant materials appear to have been gathered from the local vegetation.

INDICATIONS ABOUT THE DIET OF LA GALGADA INHABITANTS

As with any archaeological site, the largest amount of plant remains recovered can always be assigned to the category "food plants." At La Galgada, it is obvious that food plant remains are predominant. However, it must be noted that the excavations were made primarily in the ceremonial structures rather than in the settlement, and a bias may have been introduced because many of the plant remains may have had ritual significance. With species which are not currently known as food plants, it is frequently impossible to know why they occur in an archaeological site. On the other hand, some plants not now used may well have been accounted as very edible and desirable in preconquest times.

As far as can be established from our excavations, the people of La Galgada did not leave behind any remains of a major carbohydrate resource. Only a single maize cob from a late level indicates that someone had an interest in maize. Tubers such as potato, sweet potato, and manioc are conspicuously lacking. None of the plant remains recovered at La Galgada can be interpreted as so abundant that they appear to have functioned as the primary carbohydrate source. The most persistent carbohydrate resource appears to have been *Cucurbita* (squash), which appears in both Preceramic and Early Initial chronological levels. The total amount of squash remains, however, does not indicate very heavy usage.

Other sources of carbohydrates recovered at La Galgada include lima beans (*Phaseolus lunatus*), recovered only in Preceramic levels, and achira (*Canna*) found in only a single Preceramic level. Sufficient lima bean pod material exists to indicate that it was important, but lack of this plant in the Early Initial levels suggests that it was not considered particularly important in later times. Jack bean (*Canavalia*), which has 57.1 percent carbohydrate as a dry bean (Wu Leung and Flores 1961), is also present only in Preceramic levels. Cottonseed (*Gossypium*) has been found split lengthwise in La Galgada. To the best of our knowledge, rodents open elongate seeds primarily by cutting off one end. We suspect that the cottonseeds were opened by human endeavor to secure the oil-rich contents. Whether these were then pressed for cottonseed oil or whether they might have been eaten, we cannot tell from the remains. Cottonseed meal is said to have 16.1 percent fat and 36.7 percent carbohydrates (Wu Leung and Flores 1961), so that it could have functioned effectively as the carbohydrate component in the diet, if the people of La Galgada did indeed eat cottonseed.

Cottonseed would also have functioned as a source of fat in an otherwise essentially fatless vegetable intake. Avocado (*Persea*) probably was being used throughout the occupation of the site, inasmuch as cotyledons were present in the Preceramic as well as at the upper level of the Early Initial period. A total of six avocados does not suggest very heavy use, though, and cottonseed oil appears to have been the only other source of vegetable oil among the species recognized in the plant remains. We feel that we must discount peanut because it is represented only by a single hull fragment in the uppermost chronological level.

Vegetable protein in the La Galgada diet seems to have been adequate. Leguminous plant remains were found in all levels. However, the recovery of *Phaseolus lunatus* and *P. vulgaris* remains only in Preceramic levels is unusual. When common beans appear in an archaeological site, they usually become more abundant through time. That this distribution is the same as that of jack bean (*Canavalia*) is doubly mysterious, inasmuch as abundant jack bean remains in later levels could have been interpreted as replacement of the species of *Phaseolus*. Remains of *Erythrina* were found in both Preceramic and Early Initial levels, but not in the abundance that we expect of a principal protein resource. *Pithecellobium* was found only in a single Early Initial level and may not have been eaten anyway.

The La Galgada diet appears to have been spiced primarily with aji (*Capsicum*). It was impossible to establish the species used from the seeds which were recovered, but they were found in both Preceramic and Early Initial levels. Wherever it is used, aji furnishes a particularly high level of vitamin A.

Fruits were obviously popular in the parched La Galgada region. *Bunchosia, Passiflora,* and *Pouteria* in the Preceramic and the Early Initial indicate a continuing use of fruit from plants which could have survived in the environs of La Galgada only as irrigated crops. Guava (*Psidium*) was recovered only from Preceramic levels. Generally, fruits fill in the diet with minerals and vitamins which are otherwise unattainable.

In summary, we find a mysterious lack of a primary carbohydrate resource among the La Galgada plant remains. None of the carbohydrate sources indicated by the fragments is present throughout the history of the site in sufficient quantity to function as the primary source. The protein-producing crops are primarily present in the Preceramic levels of the site. It is difficult to envision the leguminous species found in the Early Initial levels as being the principal sources of vegetable proteins. Only fruits were present in levels with sufficient time spread to suggest that they were in constant use around La Galgada. Aji also seems to have been used throughout the occupation. From expectations generated by modern nutrition studies, the diet in upper levels at La Galgada would seem to have been deficient.

We can postulate no logical hypothesis to account for this situation. Even had much of the food supply been transported in from the coastal sites or from the montane valleys, the debris occasioned by food preparation should still have been found at the site. It is possible that a great deal of food debris was burned to ash in the numerous firepits at La Galgada. However, samples for flotation were recovered from midden and from hearths. These did not have carbonized remains of plant debris other than wood charcoal and an occasional piece of cane. At other sites, in our experience, a substantial recovery of discarded plant parts which have been carbonized is the rule. Their lack at La Galgada indicates either that no substantial amount of plant waste was discarded in the hearths or that we did not discover the midden into which the hearths were emptied. The latter is more probable than the former. On the other hand, everything which was discarded in the excavation areas showed no signs of rotting in the dry climate. We feel sure that no other substantial amount of food processing occurred than that denoted by the plant remains recovered.

OTHER PLANT REMAINS

Among the La Galgada plant remains are a number which are obviously industrial raw materials. The most prominent of these is cotton, which appears in quantity throughout the site. The amount is sufficient to raise the question of export products which might have been made at La Galgada. While a number of bits of cotton yarns are included with the waste materials, nothing among the plant remains suggests which final product might have been La Galgada's specialty.

Other fiber plant remains include sufficient fragments of bromeliaceous origin to suggest that gathered material of *Puya* and *Tillandsia* was being processed for its fibers. Whether this is related to the large amount of cotton residue at the site is not known. Products made from bromeliad fibers might have been totally used up at the site. The few plant remains identified as *Furcraea* also must have been discarded from a fiber-extracting operation. The question arises, did this material arrive as raw material from the montane valleys (where it is native), or was *Furcraea* in cultivation at La Galgada? The material furnishes no clue.

A single fragment of capsule from a member of the Euphorbiaceae was found at the site. Many members of this family are poisonous, while others are edible or are used in medication. Hardly anyone needs an introduction to castor oil. Unfortunately, the fragment found is not further identifiable, nor is its use discernible from the fragment. It does not appear to be part of a manioc capsule.

Several seeds of soapberry (*Sapindus saponaria*) were recovered from the site. The fruits are used as a saponifying agent and we assume that the La Galgadians were using soapberry for this purpose. The tree may have been in cultivation along with a number of other trees.

A certain portion of the grass stem material may also have been raw material for the production of baskets or other textiles. Obviously, these people were skilled in the weaving of baskets, as the offerings with burials testify. Although we saw basketry and matting in the field, I had neither the time nor the equipment to make identifications of the plant raw materials from which the artifacts were fabricated.

The final fragment to be considered is the bit of scouring rush stem (*Equisetum*) from Sample 30. No indication is provided by the fragment of the use to which the material might have been put. Generally, the highly siliceous stems are utilized for scouring in many cultures. Also, material of scouring rush has been used as a folk medicine.

Towle (1961) does not mention the family in her treatment, so we assume that it has rarely been recovered in Peru. Smith and Roosevelt report a carbonized fragment which is probably *Equisetum* from the middle Orinoco sites in Venezuela.

LA GALGADA AND PERUVIAN COASTAL SITES

La Galgada is among the earlier sites along the South American coast from which plant remains have been reported. A survey of the literature indicated that plant remains have been identified from about thirty sites.

Generally, no matter where a site may be located around the world, plant remains usually provide evidence of a primary carbohydrate resource upon which the inhabitants of the site subsisted. Later levels of Peruvian coastal sites often have copious remains of maize (*Zea*), which almost surely was the primary carbohydrate in the diet of the inhabitants. However, some coastal sites have no maize, and no other plant remain found at these sites appears to be a primary carbohydrate. Two sites similar to La Galgada in chronology are the Alto Salaverry site (Pozorski and Pozorski 1979) and the Aspero site (Feldman 1980). At none of these three sites does maize appear in the Preceramic, nor is there a clearly demonstrable primary carbohydrate among the other plant remains. In a later level (Li-31) at Aspero, maize is a part of the food complex, but early maize material is scant and not clearly applicable to the stratum in which it was found. Like La Galgada, Alto Salaverry and Aspero had remains of *Cucurbita* and *Lagenaria*, but squash material was not present in sufficient abundance to be interpreted as the primary carbohydrate resource. At both sites, cotton was plentiful at early levels.

Maize appears to enter the deposits of South America at about 2500 B.C. (Pearsall 1978). During the 1970s, a number of reports confirmed early maize (Grobman and Ravines 1974; Grobman et al. 1977; Grobman and Bonavia 1978; Bonavia and Grobman 1978). At present, I am analyzing another large lot of beautifully preserved maize from the Casma Valley which will further confirm the presence of early maize. At the present time, the amount of maize recovered in Preceramic sites does not indicate that the use of maize burgeoned rapidly. Apparently, maize only became a major carbohydrate resource over a period of time.

Other recoveries of grass are largely fragments of cane which were probably gathered from wild plants. These imply raw materials for processing into baskets, mats, and other utilitarian wares, rather than edible grass material.

Other grass-like plants for which we have direct evidence on the Peruvian coast include the sedges, *Cyperus* and *Scirpus*. Both have leaves and stems which are valuable as a raw material. Further, both have species whose underground parts are edible and which are known to have been used in Peru. Finally, *Typha* (cattail), with its leaves so highly valued for matting and an underground edible rootstalk, has also been reported from the coastal valleys. Sedges and cattail fragments were found at La Galgada. It is impossible to distinguish cultivated material from gathered material in these species. It is reasonable to assume that the wild supply was so plentiful that such material was generally not cultivated.

In spite of the fact that a number of identifications of palm material were made at an early period (Towle 1961), more recent reports have not included palm identifications. The single palm fruit identified here confirms that palm material was occasionally making its way through the mountains to the desert area. Its single appearance indicates that it was not growing in the La Galgada area nor being imported in any significant amount.

Remains of bromeliaceous plants are not uncommon in Peruvian coastal sites. Members of the genera *Tillandsia* and *Puya* are often readily available. At La Galgada, the volume of this material suggests a fiber industry using bromeliad fiber. It was probably associated with the growing of cabuya (*Furcraea*) for fiber which seems to have been widespread in Peru (Smith 1980a).

Both Aspero and Alto Salaverry report an unusually large proportion of fiber plant material in relation to the remains of food plants, as at La Galgada. To the fiber plants, Shelia and Thomas Pozorski add the gourd, which is also abundant at all of the sites. They say, "First, the predominance of the industrial plants, cotton and gourd, relative to other cultigens, is suggestive of a prevailing coastal preceramic attitude toward plant cultivation (Pozorski, 1976)" (1979:378). They indicate that this bias toward raw materials for the fishing industry colored the coastal approach to plant cultivation. We cannot agree, inasmuch as the predominance of fiber plants and gourd also occurs at La Galgada so far inland that marine-oriented industry makes little sense. For the La Galgada people, the hypothesis makes even less sense when all of the cultivation must have been done with irrigation, indicating a major investment in time and labor.

The picture is less clear for many of the coastal sites excavated in earlier periods when the plant material reported is primarily food plant remains. It is unclear whether the excavator did not encounter any of the "industrial" plant remains or whether such remains were found but not saved and reported. Gourd, as a cultivated plant, is always reported, but bromeliad stems and leaves, which are generally assumed to be collected from the wild, are rarely listed. It is our suspicion that such material was neither noted nor collected and that many coastal sites may indicate employment with fiber industry. Obviously, this is advantageous for maritime people who employ large amounts of string and rope in procuring their subsistence. We cannot deny the evidence for fiber industry at La Galgada, but must insist that it was employed largely as a source of items to be traded in either direction, i.e., to the coast or to the highlands. That early Peruvians may have been heavily engaged in fiber fabrication is further suggested by the plant material found in the Guitarrero Cave deposit (Smith 1980a) where a similar interpretation is based on inordinately large amounts of fiber waste, including that from cabuya (*Furcraea*).

The major problem becomes, for what were manufactured fiber goods being traded? The inhabitants of La Galgada may have been bartering for marine resources from the coastal people at the mouth of the Santa River, but the fill processed in my laboratory contained only a small number of fish vertebrae (which could have come from the Tablachaca River inasmuch as I am unable to distinguish marine from fresh-water fish by their vertebrae) and no chitinous exoskeleton from marine Crustacea. Mollusc shells were found, but the small shells were probably from riverine and terrestrial forms. On the other hand, none of the plant materials clearly suggested trade with the interior highlands except a fragment of cabuya or with the far interior Amazon drainage except a single palm fruit fragment.

Were all of the artifacts manufactured from plant fiber being totally consumed at home? Some were. The array of matting and basketry found with burials at La Galgada indicates a conspicuous consumption of grass and bromeliad fiber in these goods. If all of the rooms of the massive La Galgada structure were used as tombs (only a small number were excavated), the total volume of fiber material consumed is large. It would not appear to account for the amount of

waste fiber material in relation to food-plant debris, though. If La Galgada were a station on the route from the coast to the interior, fiber products would not be needed in quantity for the inhabitants or the passers-by. A large amount of food debris from feeding guests would be more logical than masses of cotton and bromeliad debris. In the absence of other information, one can do little more than emphasize that the proportionally large amount of fiber-plant material must indicate an industry, for what end purpose we are not yet sure.

Achira (*Canna* spp.) has long been recognized as a cultivated tuber for human consumption in the Andean area. In later levels, it is not uncommon along the coastal valleys. Material at early levels of La Galgada consists of leaf fragments which give no indication that they might have been cultivated. However, achira does not ordinarily grow wild along flowing streams (*Canna* is at home in still water in marshes and along lake margins), and its presence at La Galgada therefore must indicate cultivation.

One of the surprises at early levels in coastal Peru is the presence of avocados. Present evidence suggests the *Persea americana* var. *drymifolia* is directly derived from populations of wild avocado growing historically in the montane evergreen forests of the eastern cordilleras of Mexico and perhaps Guatemala. Its presence in the early levels at La Galgada indicates an even earlier introduction from Mesoamerica. Avocado appears also in the upper levels of Aspero and among the plant remains of Alto Salaverry. Wherever it appears in the Peruvian desert region, avocado signifies a knowledge of irrigation. In coastal Peru, avocado is generally distributed fairly evenly through time following its early appearance at La Galgada. Incidentally, this species serves to strengthen the probability that La Galgada was a post along a route to the Pacific Ocean from the Amazon drainage, where avocado is very successful.

Another fruit, distributed equally through time along the coastal desert, is *lúcuma* (*Pouteria* cf. *lucuma*). This inhabitant of more mesic habitats always must have an assured water supply for growth in the desert valleys. The species appears in the Guitarrero deposit even earlier (Smith 1980a), but it may have been native along the Santa River in the Callejón de Huaylas. Its appearance alongside avocado is additional evidence that the La Galgada community was practicing irrigation.

In many of the desert valleys, leguminous crop plants were regularly grown. Prominent are *Canavalia, Phaseolus lunatus,* and *P. vulgaris.* Only the *Canavalia* (jack bean) may have been wild along the Pacific strand, but the cultivated species, *C. ensiformis* and *C. plagiosperma,* are not known to be directly derived from *C. maritima,* the highly specialized tropical strand plant (Sauer 1964). Neither of the *Phaseolus* species is native to the desert of Peru; both must be grown with irrigation like the jack bean. Both *Phaseolus* beans and jack beans were absent from the earliest levels of Aspero, although they are plentiful at other coastal sites. *Canavalia* beans were absent from the plant remains at Alto Salaverry, but both *Phaseolus lunatus* and *P. vulgaris* were present. Obviously, the beans and jack beans were valuable protein sources in the Peruvian coastal diets. The one mystery about their distribution is the absence of *Phaseolus* species from the upper levels of La Galgada. Many other cultivated plants are represented throughout the occupation.

Cotton is another plant which is generally distributed through time once it appears in Peruvian coastal deposits. It is in the early levels of La Galgada in sufficient quantity to suggest that it was a principal crop. It has been reported on the central coast sites

at ca. 2500 B.C. in the Ancon-Chillon area (Stephens and Moseley 1973). Here it appears to show some characteristics indicating that it is between wild cotton and fully domesticated cotton. All of the Peruvian material appears to be *Gossypium barbadense,* although such critical identification could not be made for the La Galgada material because of lack of peduncles with their attendant glands. Characteristics of the boll segments are clearly those of *G. barbadense.* The Peruvian coastal area had a substantial cotton textile industry originally perhaps devoted largely to nets and lines, but later to manufacturing fabrics.

Another crop group which appears in the early level of La Galgada and which is generally present in sites representing all time periods is the squash group. *Cucurbita moschata,* another species which probably came into cultivation in Mesoamerica, appears in the earliest level of La Galgada. It is thereafter represented at most of the Peruvian coastal and desert valley sites. At later levels, *C. maxima* appears and, at times, seems to replace *C. moschata.* However, the reverse has been noted for the Virú Valley where *C. maxima* appears about 1800 B.C. and is replaced by *C. moschata* at about A.D. 600 (West and Whitaker 1980).

A number of other species are represented in many of the Peruvian desert sites throughout a long period of time, but have somewhat less significance, because they represent local species. Guava (*Psidium guayava*) apparently originated in South America and came into cultivation there. La Galgada included guava at an early level and it appears in many other sites through time. Both Aspero and Alto Salaverry report guava at all levels. Pepper seeds are in Alto Salaverry, but they were not recovered in the earlier deposits at Aspero. Similarly, seeds of *Capsicum* (aji) were abundant at La Galgada and they are frequent at many sites at later time levels. Often, the species cannot be identified, but they probably all represent species brought into cultivation in South America.

Throughout the Peruvian coastal area, once it arrived, maize became the primary carbohydrate resource. It was in many of the valleys by 2000 B.C. However, La Galgada somehow missed maize or maize missed La Galgada. A single cob near the top of the deposit is the single representative. Kernels could not have been overlooked when sample recoveries of pepper and passion fruit seeds were made from all levels. This leaves La Galgada without a clearly identifiable primary carbohydrate resource.

La Galgada, Aspero, and Alto Salaverry display a number of similarities in the composition of the plant resources used at the sites. None has a clearly defined primary carbohydrate resource. If there was a tuberous resource, all trace has vanished from all of the sites. Inasmuch as potato and manioc have been recovered on occasion from later sites (particularly those like Ancon and Paracas with large amounts of plant remains), they should have left a single fragment, at least. If pushed to speculate, we would suppose that squashes (*Cucurbita* spp.) may have served in this capacity in all of these sites, but the volume of squash material recovered makes this difficult to argue.

All of the sites have a leguminous protein resource at some level. La Galgada has a surprising shift from *Phaseolus* to jack beans, if the plant remains are to be credited. Alto Salaverry lacked *Canavalia*, while Aspero had them only at the later level. Inasmuch as *Phaseolus* beans appear at about 8000 B.C. at Guitarrero Cave, their appearance in the coastal sites and La Galgada is not remarkably early. The Mexican-based avocado appears early in the sites and the presence of *lúcuma,* as well, clearly indicates an understanding of the role of water in the growth of the tree crops. Avocado may have been particularly valued at all of the sites for its high oil content. The lack of *Capsicum* in early levels at Aspero is notable. Its early appearance in the highlands in Guitarrero Cave allows sufficient time for it to have become widespread by 3000 B.C.

A common denominator for La Galgada, Aspero, and Alto Salaverry is cotton (*Gossypium*). While the importance of the fiber in local industry at all sites is not doubted, we suggest that for the La Galgada people, cotton may have had dietary importance. A portion of seed testa split lengthwise suggests human opening to extract the kernel, which may have been directly consumed or may have been extracted for oil. In light of the lack of a prominent starch resource, the high caloric content of the cottonseed may have supplied a need.

8. Fiber Arts

TERENCE GRIEDER

All specimens of fiber arts encountered in the excavations were collected and studied. The final sample presented here consists of 209 specimens which represent the whole range of fiber arts practiced or used at La Galgada. (See Appendix C.)

TECHNICAL ANALYSIS

The sample consists of the following techniques, with the number of specimens of each one. (Only representative examples of categories 1–5 and 11 are included; categories 6–10 include all examples found.)

1. Matting—oblique twill interlacing of totora, or junco fiber twined with cotton string or achupalla fiber: 4.

2. Baskets of oblique 2 × 2 twill interlaced totora fibers: 9.

3. Vegetal, or bast, fiber thread, string, cord, or rope: 8.

4. Vegetal, or bast, fiber and/or cotton netting made by looping or linking: 22.

5. Cotton thread, cord, string, or yarn: 13.

6. Twined cotton textiles, mostly mantles: 36.

7. Looped cotton textiles, some flat cloth but mostly bags: 39.

8. Linked cotton textile bags, and perhaps some flat cloth: 20.

9. Interlaced cotton belts: 13.

10. Cotton cloth presumed to have been woven on a harness loom: 37.

11. Other techniques: one each of a vegetal fiber sandal (Fig. 98) made by interlacing; a vegetal fiber pad of compacted loose random fibers; a wrapping of cotton thread and bast thread on a small wooden loop; a folded and sewn barkcloth purse(?); a twined maguey fiber flat piece; a cord of cotton and vegetal fiber twined together; a twined and woven totora basket; and an interlaced cotton and totora flat piece.

The study collection has been selected from the larger set of examples found on the basis of two criteria. First, all examples of cloth were studied to determine how many items were originally present, and each item was counted once. Particularly in the case of burial offerings which had been disrupted in ancient times (e.g., C-10:I-10) or modern times (e.g., C-11:F-5, Floor 23), most of the individual items had been torn into several pieces. In the case of some other arts, such as ceramics, it is sometimes difficult to tell how many items were originally present because the items were very similar in the details of their fiber. In the textiles, and especially in the hand-manipulated textiles of the Preceramic Period, each item is so individual in its thread, construction, and decoration that one can be reasonably sure about the number of items. Thus the sample describes complete original pieces, as far as that can be done, without reference to the number of fragments they may be in now.

The sample includes every item of cloth, but only representative examples of the less variable techniques of matting (Fig. 99), basketry (Fig. 100), thread, cord, and rope. The only fiber art not represented in the cata-

98. Sandal toe with tie of vegetal fiber (T.S. 187). Initial Period level of H-12:A-6/7, Floor 15.

99. Totora mat of oblique interlacing (T.S. 5) which was laid over bodies II and III in F-12:B-2.

100. Basket of oblique interlaced totora (T.S. 18) from F-12:B-2, offering 8.

log is beaten barkcloth (Figs. 69, 101).
There are numerous examples, some inter-
grading with the quids and pads of fibers.
Like the vegetal or bast fibers, they have
been examined by a botanist, but their
sources remain unidentified. The sample is
thus skewed toward the finest products of the
fiber arts. Since the excavations focused on
the ceremonial areas rather than on houses
and workshops, the entire sample must be
considered to be skewed toward high quality
and elite ceremonial concerns.

The textile and fiber sample is interesting
on two counts: it shows the development of
techniques of clothmaking over a period of
several centuries which included the introduction of the harness loom with heddles,
and it provides evidence of designs and symbols in use during that period. Those two
aspects are closely linked, since the early
techniques gave opportunities for the introduction of designs which later techniques did
not provide. Since the expression depended
on the technique, the techniques are examined first.

The sample falls into three groups. The
earliest set, composed of specimens 1–40,
comes from tomb F-12:B-2, its antechamber (E-11:J-10), and the slightly later chamber just south of it, E-12:I-2, Floor 6. Two
radiocarbon tests accompany this material,
TX-4449 and 4450, giving radiocarbon ages
of 3790 ± 70 B.P. and 3820 ± 100 B.P.,
which suggest that these specimens represent
an absolute period between 2625 and 1980
B.C. This group is set apart by its early position archaeologically and the presence of
three undisturbed burials which contain no
examples of rectilinear interlacing or harness-loom weaving. Those related techniques are the basis for the definition of the
other two groups.

The weaving of mats did not change during these periods, and it has changed very
little to the present day. Two types are found

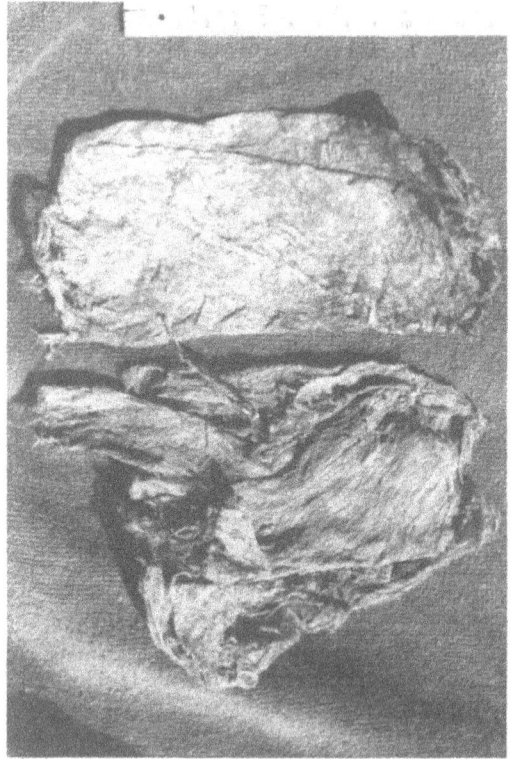

101. Barkcloth from C-11 surface debris related
to destroyed areas of C-11:E-8 or C-12:D-1.
Plant source is unidentified.

in this early group: stiff mats of totora reed
strips (Fig. 99) about 1 cm wide in oblique
twill interlacing, usually 2 × 2, and soft
mats of straw-like junco reed in bundles
twined with cotton string. Totora strips were
also used for baskets (Fig. 100) carefully
made by oblique 2 × 2 twill interlacing and
finished with a doubled flat rim. Baskets always had a flat bottom and slightly flared
walls, with a typical height-to-width ratio
from 3:4 to 3:6. These earliest burials (Fig.
68) contained the largest sample of barkcloth
found, but barkcloth also appears in later
levels, presumably pounded out from the un-
derbark of some unidentified species of the
fig or mulberry family. The artisans of the
early group were expert spinners of coarse or

fine filaments of both cotton and other stiffer vegetal, or bast, fibers. A range of local plants, including *Puya, Tillandsia,* and *Furcraea,* were used for fiber. These fibers were sometimes spun to thread a half-millimeter in diameter. Cotton was available in natural colors of white and light brown, and it was dyed other colors: bright yellow, dark brown, black, red, and in rare cases blue and pale purple. (Dyes are discussed under "Color" at the end of this chapter.) No evidence has been found for the use of animal fibers or human hair. The absence of camelid fibers agrees with the evidence from Huaca Prieta (Bird, Hyslop, and Skinner 1985:101–102), but camelid fibers do make an appearance at Los Gavilanes (Bonavia 1982:132).

Three techniques were used to make cloth: looping, linking, and twining. Each of these techniques had a particular range of uses to which it was most easily adapted. Linking and looping had the most varied uses, but the uses can be divided by fiber. Looping (Fig. 102) and linking (Fig. 103) made of cotton always produced dense solid cloth, usually circular bags (e.g., Fig. 104), but rarely pieces of flat cloth. With bast fiber those techniques always were used for openwork which has the appearance of a net (Figs. 105–107). There are no examples known at La Galgada of the technique of knotted netting; the term "net" always refers to an openwork cloth made of bast fiber by looping or linking, with the single exception of one small openwork textile (T.S. 20) made of cotton in simple linking. No doubt the stiffer bast fibers were preferred because they gave a firmer structure for nets, which were often used as an outer wrapping for the body in burials (Fig. 107). Nets were also ordinarily shaped as bags rather than as flat cloth.

Twining, in contrast, was usually done in cotton and was used for flat cloth, most often for mantles and shawls made by weft-

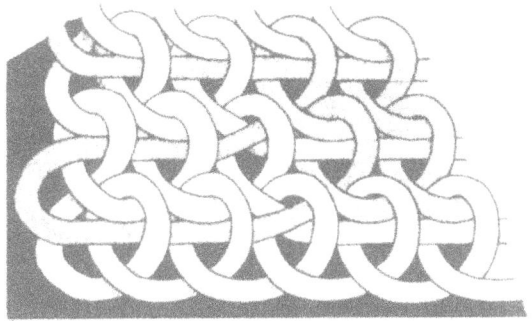

102. Looping on a foundation element. Note that the two threads exchange places, giving an opportunity for color changes.

103. Linking.

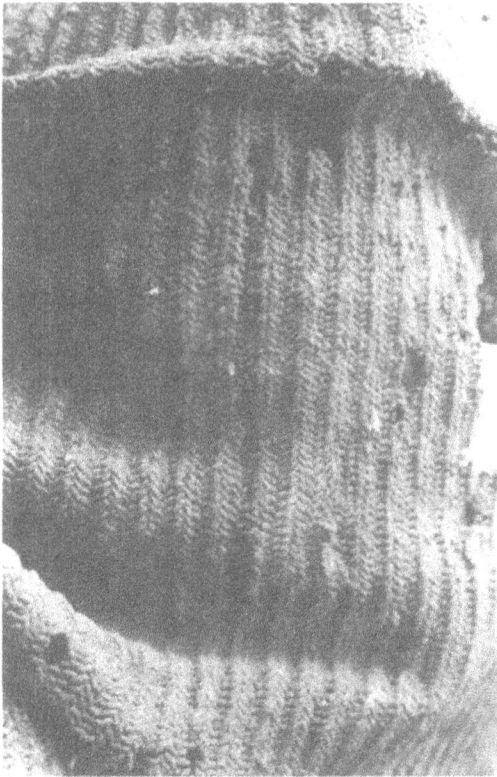

104. Linked cotton bag-hat (T.S. 3) from F-12:B-2(I).

twining pairs of warp threads (Figs. 108, 109). Such cloth was commonly made by using from three to ten pairs of warp threads per centimeter, twined every 5–10 mm with pairs of the same two-ply thread. In fine decorated pieces wefts are as close together as 2.5 mm (T.S. 86) and in coarse pieces spaced as much as 15 (T.S. 68) or 17 (T.S. 37) mm apart. Warp pairs moved in every possible variation: parallel pairs, alternate pairs, and transposed (Fig. 110). Alternate pairs was the basic technique for plain weft-twined flat mantles and blankets, and there is no evident change in this technique over the period it was in use. In the Initial Period it was superseded by weaving on the harness loom.

The first group includes the only mantle made by looping (T.S. 10), an undecorated cloth made by simple looping without a foundation element. It appears that the use of plain looping for flat cloth was already obsolete and was being replaced by twining,

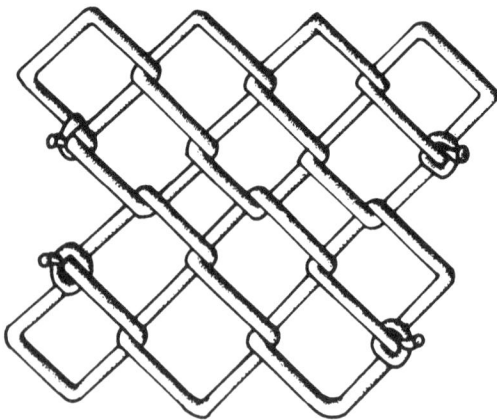

105. Openwork net of vegetal fibers made by looping.

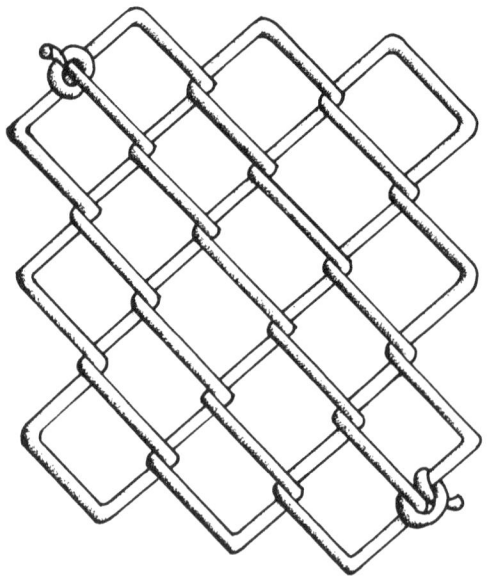

106. Openwork net of vegetal fibers made by linking.

which is a much more efficient way to produce flat cloth. In the same tomb, along with a twined mantle, were eight bags made by looping on a foundation element which permitted decorative designs to be worked into the fabric by using different colors for the loop and its hidden foundation, the colors exchanging roles as the design required (see Fig. 102). Bags made by looping always remained a common decorative form.

Linking as it was practiced at La Galgada is a particularly interesting technique, one which has not been accurately described, although it has been found before (Engel 1963: Figs. 64, 65). It is constructed with a single needle and thread in a pattern of *over-two, under-two, turn back,* making a circular cloth which was probably always used for bags. Its distinctive feature is ribbing perpendicular to the thread, both sides being identical in appearance. The turn-back forms a crossing of the threads, a notable feature of the cloth which may have survived as a design motif in Initial Period art after the textile technique had become obsolete (Fig. 111). Cotton linking appears in the earliest group as a bag (T.S. 31), a small net (T.S. 20), and two caps, for a man and a woman (T.S. 3, 8), but it is possible that both the caps were intended as bags. In the later groups cotton linking is found only as bags, and the technique seems to have gone out of use in the Initial Period. Although linking could be constructed in colored designs, most of the bags are plain. Compared with looping on a foundation, linking is harder to decorate, and consequently the decorated linked pieces have relatively simple designs, such as the stepped mountains on the man's cap (T.S. 3; Fig. 122) and a bag from C-11: F-5 (T.S. 94; Fig. 124).

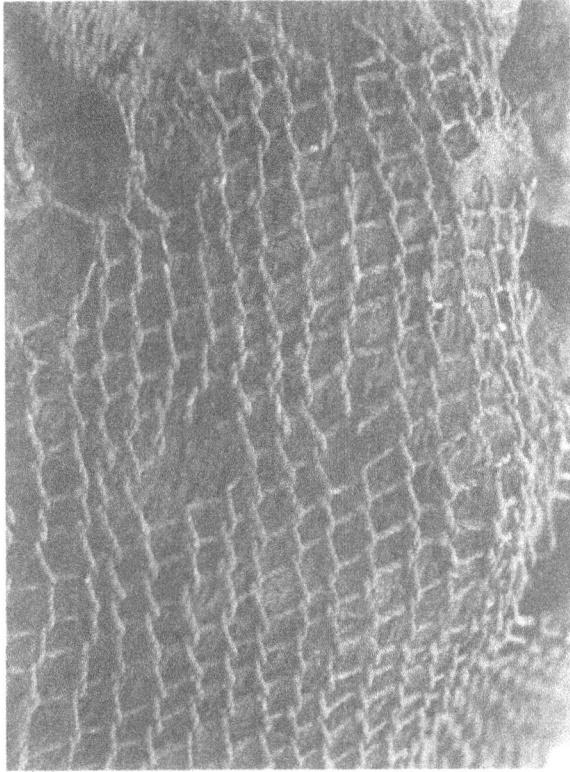

107. Vegetal fiber net of linking (T.S. 1) wrapping Burial I in F-12:B-2. Note weft-twined mantle (T.S. 2); warp is alternate pairs.

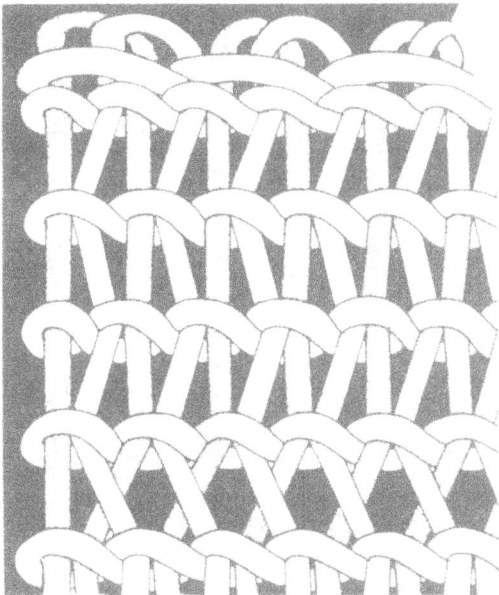

108. Weft-twining with alternate pairs, showing two selvages. Warps split in first and second wefts, then cross between third and fourth.

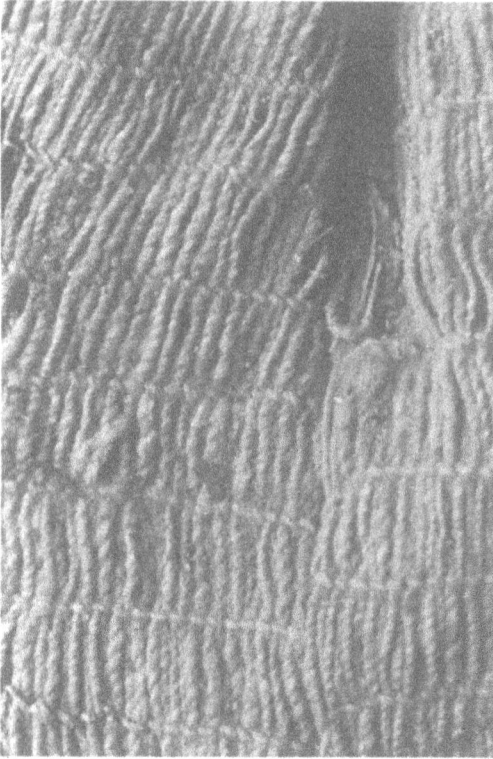

109. Weft-twining with alternate pairs: mantle (T.S. 68) from C-10:E-10(II). Wefts are spaced 1.5 cm apart.

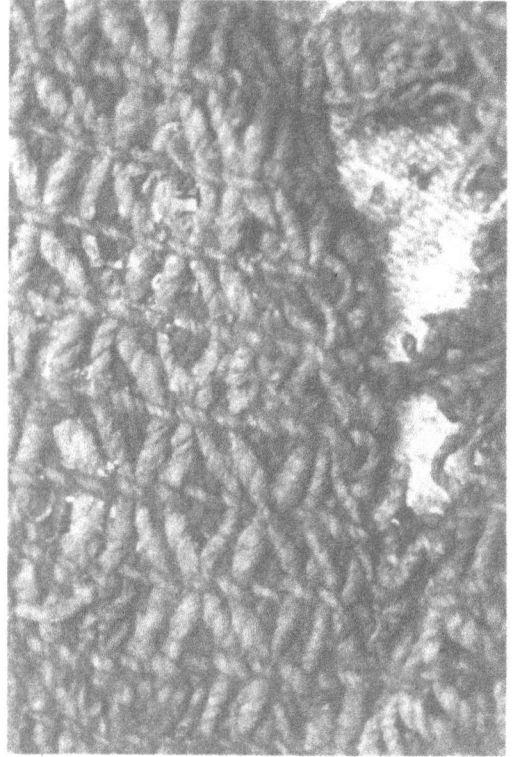

110. Weft-twining with transposed pairs: mantle fragment (T.S. 84) from C-11:F-5.

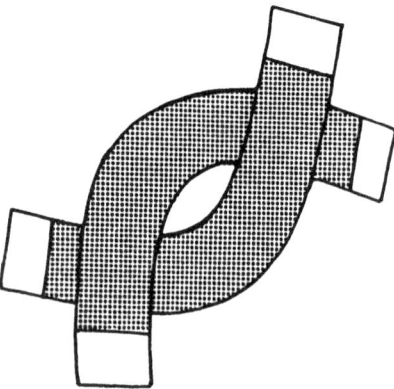

111. Turn-back motif from a mud relief at Moxeke, Casma Valley, after Tello 1956:Fig. 28.

The second group of textile specimens includes seventy-six items, T.S. 41–116, from six sources: D-11:C-3 fill, which seems to represent an old burial broken up by later construction; D-11:C-3, Floor 25, seven items on the floor of a firepit chamber, which may also be a disrupted burial offering; C-10:I-10, Floor 21, a set of burials which had been disrupted and burned in ancient times; C-10:E-10, Floor 26, an intact tomb; C-11:F-5, Floor 23, a tomb which had been looted during roadwork in 1975 but which still provided a large sample; and D-11:C-3, Floor 24, bodies I and II, the earlier burials in an undisturbed tomb.

This second group cannot be set off from the first by radiocarbon dating, since it includes material from D-11:C-3, Floor 25, whose firepit gave an age of 3820 ± 60 B.P. It is the presence of rectilinear interlacing in that set of material which places it in the second group, which is defined by that technique. The only other technique present in the second group that was absent in the first is net made by figure-eight looping (T.S. 132–133), a technique which was probably very old and only accidentally absent from the earlier group. Interlacing, which played a critical part in the development of textiles at La Galgada, is another matter. Oblique interlacing had a long history in mat-making but rectilinear interlacing—hereafter called simply "interlacing"—was used at La Galgada for narrow warp-faced belts, with one exception, the earliest example (T.S. 51; Fig. 112), which has a twined selvage and a pattern made by weft floats in the interlace.

The interlaced belts form such a consistent group in themselves and grade so smoothly into weaving, which defines the third group, that their absence from the first group gives the appearance of historical fact: that is, that interlacing was in rare use in the earlier period for flat cloth, and that it was these belts which introduced the technical changes which led to weaving on the harness loom.

Thirteen warp-face interlaced belts from the second and third groups can be set in an approximate developmental order (Table 20). All of them range from 2.0 to 7.5 cm in width.

All of the belts are warp-face with the weft turning back at the selvages. From Table 20 it is evident that the belts can be separated into groups on the basis of plied (two-ply) or unplied (one-ply) thread, the number of colors, and the use of supplementary warps. Features that go together are narrow width, fewer warps, unpaired warps, all

112. Interlaced mantle with twined selvage and weft floats (T.S. 51) from D-11:C-3, Floor 25.

Table 20. Warp-face Interlaced Belts

T.S.	Width (cm)	No. of Warps	Warp Pairs	All 2-Ply	1-Ply Weft	Mono-chrome	Bi- or Poly-chrome	Suppl. Warp	Figure
Earlier group									
98	2.0	19	No	X		X			
97	1 selvage >2.5		No	X		X			113
100	1 selvage		No	X		X			
206	2.0	23	No	X		X			
46	3.6	39	No	X			X		
55	2.8	48	No	X		X			
Later group									
209	4.2	39	No		X	X			114
62	1 selvage		Yes		X		X		
99	3.0		No		X	X			
116	No selvage		No		X	X			
143	1 selvage		No		X		X		115, 151
142	7.5	64	Yes		X		X	X	116
108	7.5	56	Yes		X		X	X	117

two-ply thread, and monochrome, and in a second group, wider width, more warps and warp pairs, a one-ply weft, more colors, and supplementary warps. The next step is represented by specimen 180, which is counted with the woven cloth: it is a cotton belt 9 cm wide, all one-ply thread, with single warps and weft pairs, and no decoration. The earliest group of textiles are characterized by all two-ply thread and unpaired threads except in twining. One-ply thread and pairing of either the warp or weft threads are characteristics of Initial Period textiles. Thus we see in the interlaced belts transitions in a wide range of traits from earlier to later characteristics. (See Figs. 113–117.)

It appears that the structural warp threads in the belts were manipulated in groups. The significant example is T.S. 46, with thirty-nine warp threads in a brown, red, and white alternation. The pattern was a chance outcome made by raising alternately half the warp threads. That is an indication that a batten was separating the warps into two sheds, probably a system like a modern inkle loom, and the warps were manipulated in groups, but probably not using heddles since the groups were small. In the later belts three traits appear which were to lead on toward the Initial Period textiles. First, the warp threads were not only divided into sheds by alternation, but also into design groups which were treated differently, with one group in the middle in which warps were paired opposed to a group on each selvage in which the warps were single. Second, thinner, one-ply thread began to be used for the wefts, since they were not meant to show. Third, it began to be evident to the artisans that interlacing provided few opportunities for decora-

115. Interlaced belt scrap (T.S. 143) from C-12:D-1(III). Scale in millimeters.

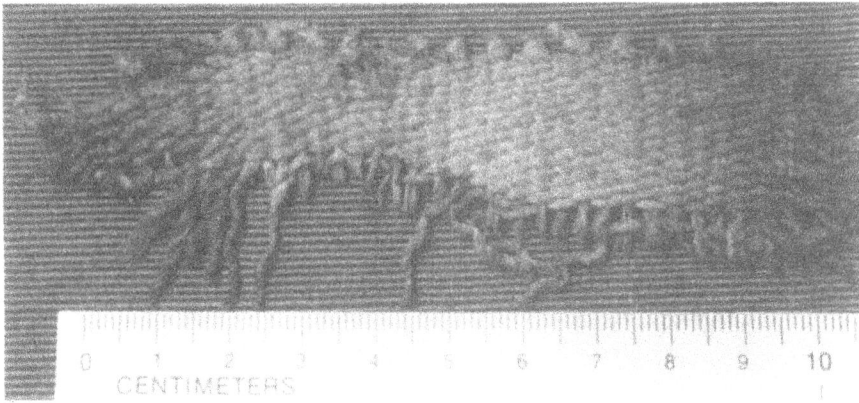

113. Interlaced belt (T.S. 97) from C-11:F-5.

114. Interlaced belt (T.S. 209) from C-11 surface.

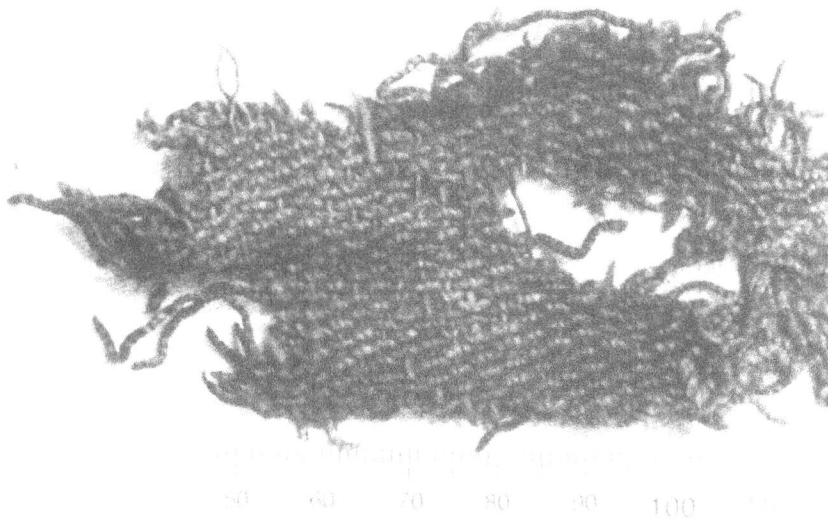

116. Interlaced belt (T.S. 142) from C-12:D-1(I).

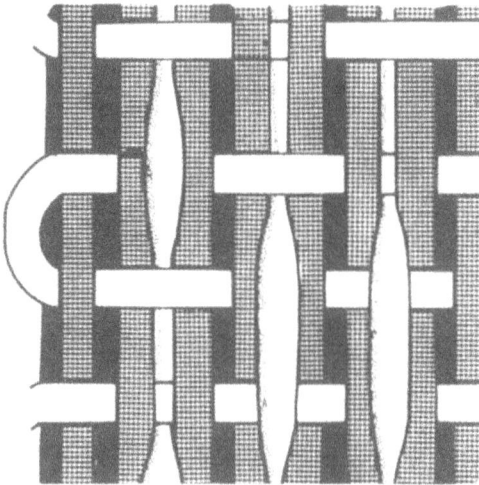

117. Interlaced belt with supplementary warps making floated designs, as in textile specimens 108 and 142.

tion in its structure, so supplementary warps were introduced to provide more color. They represent the first nonstructural decorations (Fig. 117).

These technical developments might suggest that La Galgada artisans invented each of these features independently, but the same general sequence of development is found in all the Peruvian centers which have been studied. It would surely be more correct to consider the La Galgada artisans as participants in a development which encompassed a wide region.

The third group of textiles includes ninety-three examples (T.S. 117–209) from various locations: D-11:C-3, Floor 24, bodies III and IV; C-12:D-1, Floor 18; D-11:D-1, Floor 21; H-12:I-2; C-11, Floor 17 and above; H-11/12, Floor 20 and above; the surface levels in sectors F-11, G-11, and C-12; and one example each from C-10: HJ-10, below Floor 20; C-10:E-7; and D-12. The technique which unites the group is weaving on the harness loom, with heddles to raise the warp threads, and the consequent elimination of twining.

Table 20 is divided into an earlier and a later group on the basis of thread types, the presence of two-ply thread indicating an earlier stage, the use of only one-ply thread marking the later stage. Certainly there was overlap between the two groups, but the trend was in that direction. Separating the interlaced belts from the narrower pieces of weaving in the third group of textiles is arbitrary, there being no reliable evidence of the use of heddles in place of finger manipulation to raise the warps. The separation is made on two criteria: specimens defined as interlacing are found in burial sets which include twining, while those defined as weaving are from burial sets which do not include any twining, and the "woven" group are all wider. The narrowest members of the group defined as woven are 9 and 10 cm wide, and they accompany still wider pieces of cloth. There is a width—about 8 cm at La Galgada—at which efficiency dictated the use of twining rather than interlacing in hand-manipulation. Beyond that width interlacing was inefficient and led to the use of heddles on a harness when they were available. The difference between interlacing and weaving cannot be defined with certainty by examining particular pieces of cloth, but it can be defined by examining all the cloth in a particular burial. Between the extended burials in D-11:C-3, Floor 24, which used twining and interlaced belts, and the flexed burials placed on top of them wrapped in woven shrouds, that border between interlacing and weaving was passed.

Table 21 is also divided into two parts on the same criterion as Table 20: an earlier group in which two-ply thread was used for either the warp or weft, or both, and a later group in which only one-ply thread was used. The archaeological levels strongly support this division.

Another feature of the later group of woven textiles is the shift to Z-spinning for cotton thread. Z-spinning had always been used for non-cotton fibers (see T.S. 1, 6, 40, 82, 117), which were ordinarily used as one-ply thread. Z-spinning began to be used for cotton at the time the harness loom came into use.

Even though the earlier group is too poorly preserved to show more than two complete loom widths, it is pretty clear that the trend was toward wider looms. One of the early group is 10 cm wide, the other 25.5 cm. In the later group, despite the presence of several narrow pieces, the average width is 22.5 cm, and one piece reached 35 cm.

The thirty-seven examples of harness-loom weaving at La Galgada provide a graphic illustration of the processes of cultural change in action. Threads were changing from S-spun Z-plied (S-2Z) to Z-spun unplied (Z), from two-ply thread to one-ply, from single-thread wefts to pairs, and from plain, undecorated woven cloth toward decorative stripes. Of the earlier sixteen, only four have sufficient selvage to show which was warp and which weft, but those four all show different variations of plying and pairing (T.S. 130, 140, 161, 176; Fig. 118). That is an indication of a surprising instability in patterns of work. Twelve of the sixteen use one-ply thread for either the warp or the weft, following the new manner, but the one-ply thread is still always S-spun as cotton thread always had been in the past. In the later group one-ply thread was always used for both the warp and the weft, but the new work patterns stabilized with paired wefts, one spun S, the other Z, and the warp spun Z (Figs. 119–121). The consistent patterns of work found in the later group show the artisans settling into a new set of accepted habits after a transition period marked by disorder.

Table 21. Cotton Cloth Woven on the Harness Loom

T.S.	Item	Spin[a]	One-Ply Weft	One-Ply Warp	Both Two-Ply	Weft Pairs[b]	Warp Pairs[b]	Bi- or Polychrome	Selvage	Loom Width (cm)	Figure
Earlier group											
121	Mantle	S, S/Z	X or X			X or X					
129	Mantle	S, S/Z	X or X			X or X					
130	Mantle	S, Z	X			X			X		
139	Mantle	S, S/Z	X or X			X or X					
140	Mantle	S, S/Z	X				X		X		118
141	Mantle	S, S-S	X	X		X					
159	Flat piece	S, S/Z	X or X			X or X					
160	Flat piece	S, S/Z	X or X			X or X		Stripes in non-pairs			
161	Flat piece	S/Z			X					25.5	
168	Mantle	S, S/Z	X or X			X or X					
169	Flat piece	S/Z			X						
170	Flat piece	S, S/Z	X or X			X or X					
171	Flat piece	S, S/Z		X		X					
176	Flat piece	S/Z			X	X				10	
177	Flat piece					X		Plaid			
208	Flat piece	S/Z			X						
Later group											
178	Flat piece	Z, S-Z	X	X		X				24	
179	Flat piece	Z, S-Z	X	X		X				28	
180	Belt	Z	X	X		X				9	
181	Flat piece	Z	X	X		X		Plaid		13	
182	Flat piece	Z	X	X		X				17	
183	Flat piece	Z	X	X		X				>18	
184	Flat piece	Z, S-Z	X	X		X				28	
188	Flat piece	Z	X	X		X					
189	Flat piece	Z	X	X		X					
191	Flat piece	Z, S-Z	X			X					
192	Flat piece	S, S-Z	X	X		X				20, 23, 23.5	
193	Flat piece	S, S/Z	X			X					
194	Flat piece	Z, S-Z	X	X		X				20	
195	Flat piece	Z, S-Z	X	X		X					120
197	Flat piece	Z, S-Z	X	X		X				20	
198	Flat piece	Z, S-Z	X	X		X				27	121
199	Flat piece	Z, S-Z	X	X		X		Weft stripes		27	
200	Flat piece	Z, S-Z	X	X		X				35	
201	Flat piece	Z, S-Z	X	X		X					
202	Flat piece	Z, S-Z	X	X		X		Weft stripes		26.5	
204	Flat piece	Z, S-Z	X	X		X		Weft stripes			

[a] S/Z indicates spin/ply of one thread; S-Z indicates spin-spin of a pair of single-ply threads.
[b] In the cases in which the warp or weft is one-ply and one or the other is paired, it is always the one-plies which are paired.

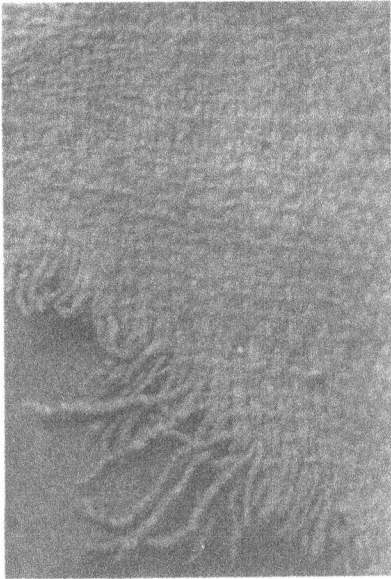

118. Mantle (T.S. 140) from C-12:D-1. This cloth is unusual for its paired warps. It is transitional in its two-ply warp, one-ply weft.

119. Woven cloth of early Initial Period with paired wefts, single warps; note header cord at top of warp.

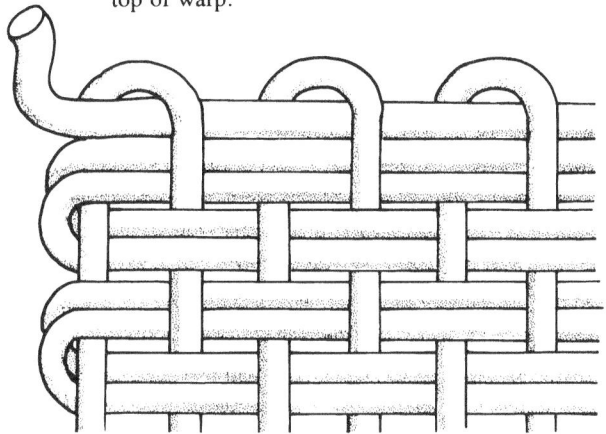

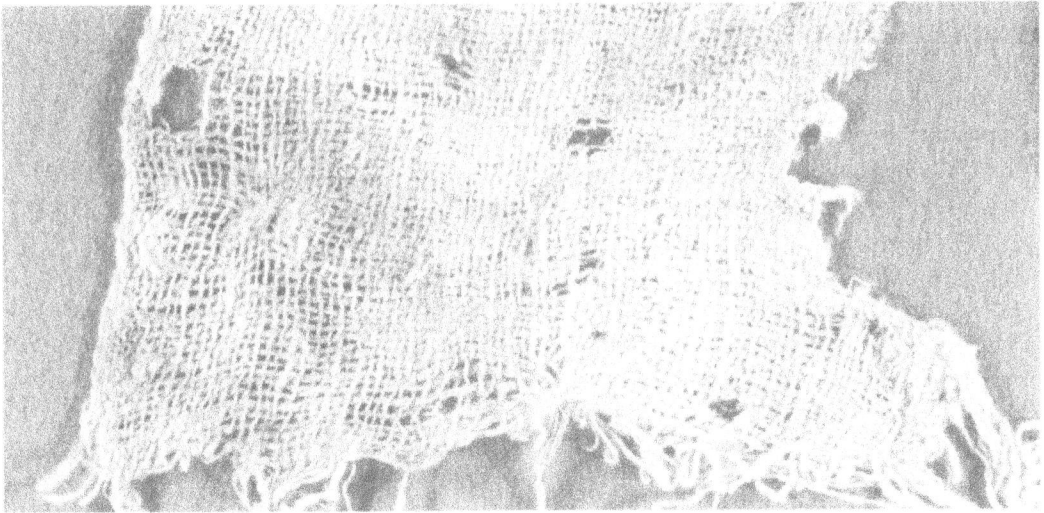

120. Coarse cloth (T.S. 195) attached to shell disks in Initial Period cache in H-11:G-10; dated on radiocarbon scale to 3320 ± 270 B.P. (TX-5606).

121. Loom-woven cloth (T.S. 198) from H-11: A-9, 27 cm wide, with weft pairs spun S and Z.

Decorations

The textile sample at La Galgada is especially interesting for the large number of decorated items. Twenty-eight examples are sufficiently preserved that a decorative design can be recorded, and long-term study could probably increase this number slightly. That is about the same size as the sample of decorated cloth from Huaca Prieta, despite the much larger size of the Huaca Prieta sample as a whole (Bird, Hyslop, and Skinner 1985: 92–214). The nature of the sites and La Galgada's high percentage of burial offerings explain that difference. Other differences, such as the predominance of looping in decoration at La Galgada, as opposed to twining at Huaca Prieta, will be discussed later (Chapter 12).

It is convenient to divide the decorated textiles into tomb groups and deal with them in approximate chronological order.

F-12:B-2

Of the thirty-two fiber specimens in this tomb, nine of the cloth specimens are important for their decorative designs. Seven of the nine are looping, the other two linking. Linked decoration is rather rare and can be disposed of here. Of the twenty pieces of linking in the total sample, ten show no sign of decoration, five have unreconstructable decorations, and five have recorded decorations. The two in this tomb were a registered step design on the man's cap (T.S. 3; Fig. 122) and yellow geometric shapes on red-brown on a bag (T.S. 31; Fig. 123). In other tombs there are a black bag with a pattern of yellow circles (T.S. 77; Fig. 141) and a white bag with a red stripe (T.S. 148). But especially interesting is a second composition of registered steps on a bag in C-11:F-5 (T.S. 94; Fig. 124). The step designs on two of these linked items interlock dark and light stepped pyramids, the earlier example being the more elaborate in its changes in the pyramids in each register and its subtler color. This kind of design was common in later Pre-Columbian art—in Inca art (Bennett 1954: Fig. 119), for example, and in Mixtec art of Mexico. In some places it seems to have represented a cosmic mountain, rising in steps to the heavens and descending in steps to the underworld (Holland 1964:302, 305), and it may have had that kind of meaning at La Galgada.

The looped cloths in F-12:B-2 are especially rich in decoration, no doubt because decorative designs are easier to make in looping than in any other technique known to the people of La Galgada. The nine examples of looping in this tomb include one plain mantle, a plain bag, and seven decorated bags. Two of the seven are abstract—yellow diamonds on black (T.S. 24; Figs. 125–126) and a series of red ladder-like triangles on white (T.S. 32; Fig. 127). The

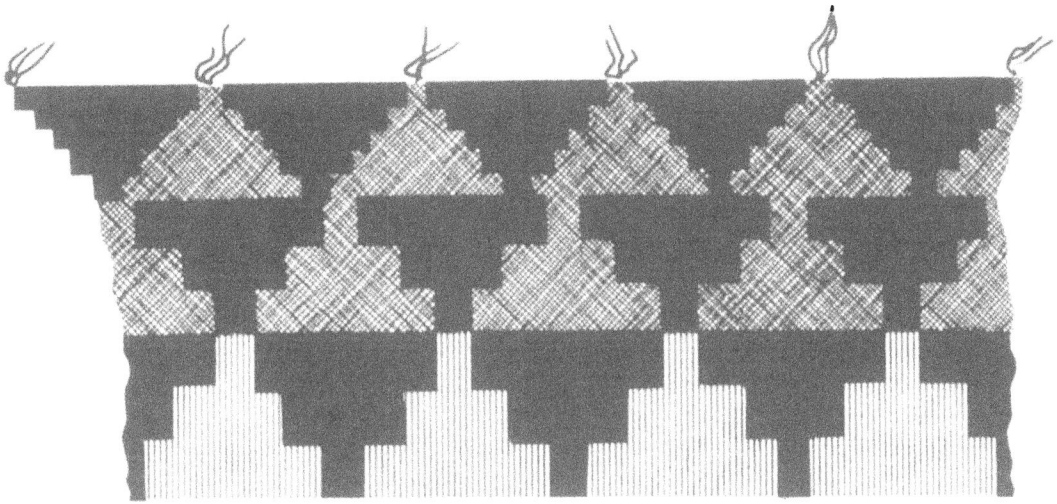

122. Linked bag (T.S. 3) used as cap on F-12: B-2(I); black and two shades of tan.

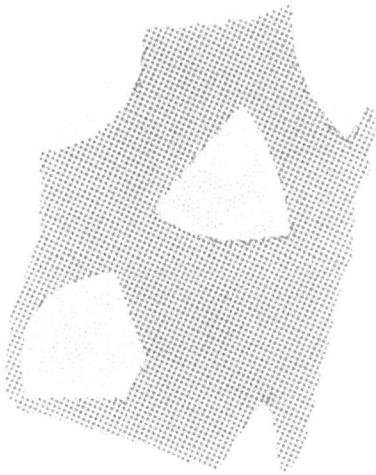

123. Linked bag in yellow on red-brown (T.S. 31) from F-12:B-2.

124. Linked bag with black and white stepped-mountain design (T.S. 94) from C-11:F-5.

125. Looped bag with yellow diamonds on black
(T.S. 24) from F-12:B-2.

other five give more scope for interpretation:

T.S. 14. Black serpents on yellow (Figs.
128–129).

T.S. 15. Black double-headed raptorial
birds with smiling serpent masks on yellow
(Fig. 130).

T.S. 17. Black serpents and a border of
steps on yellow (Fig. 131).

T.S. 27. Black raptorial birds, step frets in
wings, and serpent border on red (Fig. 132).

T.S. 29. Black birds and possible small
quadruped on yellow (Fig. 133).

These are among the most elaborately
decorated textiles at La Galgada and among
the earliest. The designs are intricate both in
technique and in concept, a matter we will
return to in Chapter 12. The artisans never
hesitated to make curving lines in their textile decorations, especially in looping, but
the design on T.S. 27 is remarkable for its
curvilinearity. That design also seems to an-
ticipate the step-fret design, which came into
common use only much later. Serpents and

126. Design of T.S. 24.

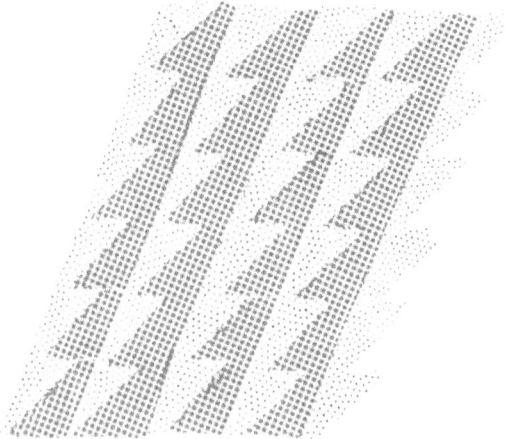

127. Looped bag with red ladder on white
(T.S. 32) from F-12:B-2.

128. Looped bag with black serpents on yellow
(T.S. 14) from F-12:B-2.

129. Serpent design from T.S. 14.

130. Looped bag with double-headed birds and serpent faces in black on yellow (T.S. 15) from F-12:B-2.

birds are the principal subjects, sometimes alone, sometimes together. The artists make it clear that they belong together; for example, inside the square of the large serpent on T.S. 14 is a small bird with a raptor's curved beak, and on T.S. 27 a serpent forms a border for the birds. Aside from the small possible quadruped (right margin) on T.S. 29, no felines or other mammals, and no human figures, are found in this group.

D-11:C-3, Floor 24

Of at least six textiles in this tomb which were decorated, only T.S. 123, a looped bag with a black bird on a yellow ground (Fig. 134) has a representational subject which can be identified. The dark dye, probably tannin, usually weakened or destroyed the cloth, and in this case the dark areas were largely missing. Although a straight-beaked bird was one element, the others cannot be identified. An interlaced belt (T.S. 108) has an abstract design of diamonds.

131. Looped bag with black serpents and a border of steps on yellow (T.S. 17) from F-12:B-2.

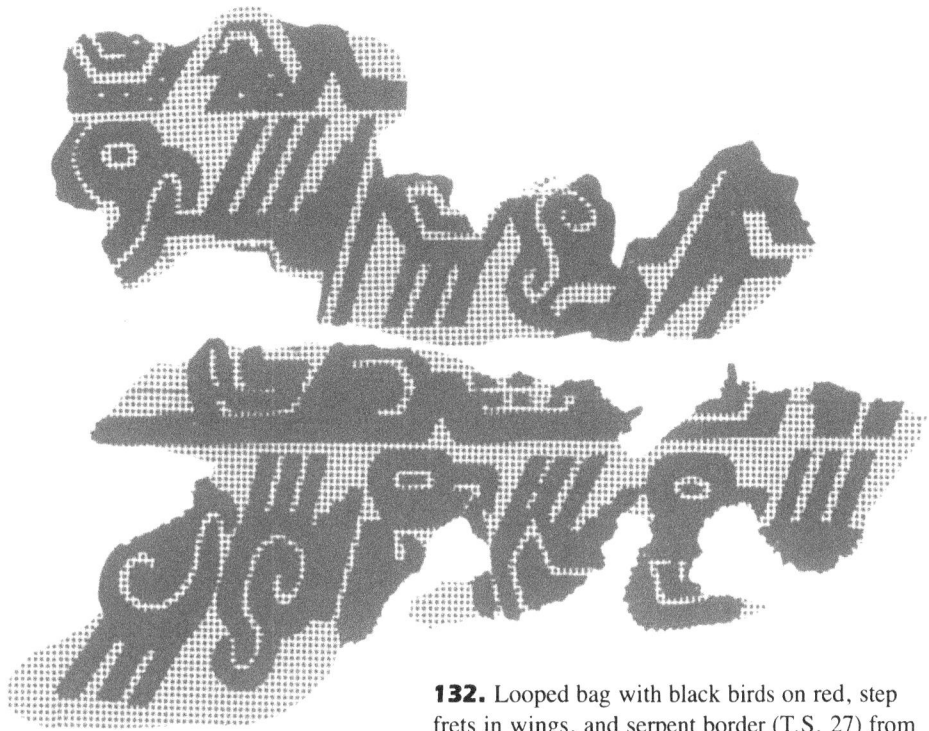

132. Looped bag with black birds on red, step frets in wings, and serpent border (T.S. 27) from F-12:B-2.

C-11:F-5, Floor 23

Although this tomb had been looted, it still produced a rich set of decorated textiles, though all of them had been reduced to small scraps. Twining, linking, and looping appear in decorated examples, of which eight designs can be reconstructed. A linked step design was shown earlier (Fig. 124). The remainder are one weft-twined cloth (T.S. 86) and six looped bags (T.S. 87–92).

The weft-twined cloth, T.S. 86 (found in four fragments; Fig. 135) is bordered differently—in tightly twined green on all four selvages apparently—from any of the mantles and does not appear to have been clothing. It has 18 warp threads per centimeter, weft-twined in transposed pairs with a fine .5-mm diameter thread every 2.5 mm. Narrow red stripes in the warp every 8.8 cm make a module into which angular linear designs in brown and white (probably natural cotton colors) were fitted. Only two of the designs

can be named: an S-design, and, in the marginal strip of one piece, a frontal smiling face in a trapezoidal shape, probably with a twin mirroring it. From the surviving pieces, it appears possible that each modular strip had a different design, all of them complex and surely significant to the maker and audience, though no longer interpretable. This textile is the most similar of the La Galgada sample to the decorated twined cloths at Huaca Prieta.

Four of the looped bags have bird subjects, all highly conventionalized, but all different. T.S. 87 (Fig. 136) is the simplest: horizontal registers of red-brown frontal birds with straight beaks. Variations in the spacing of the registers keeps the pattern irregular, surely intentionally, since the duplication of the birds is very exact. The irregular spacing results in a more casual, less rigorous feeling in the design. T.S. 88, of which we have only the triangle border and some geometric elements which include a

133. Looped bag with black birds and possible small quadruped on yellow (T.S. 29) from F-12:B-2.

134. Looped bag with black bird on yellow (T.S. 123) from D-11:C-3, Floor 24.

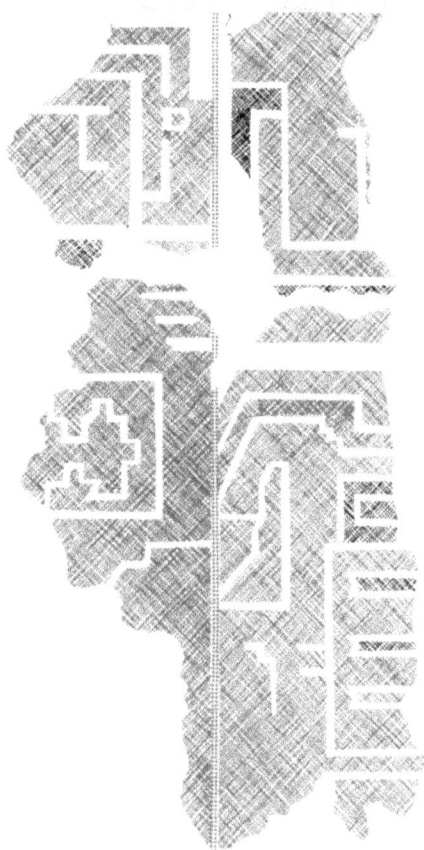

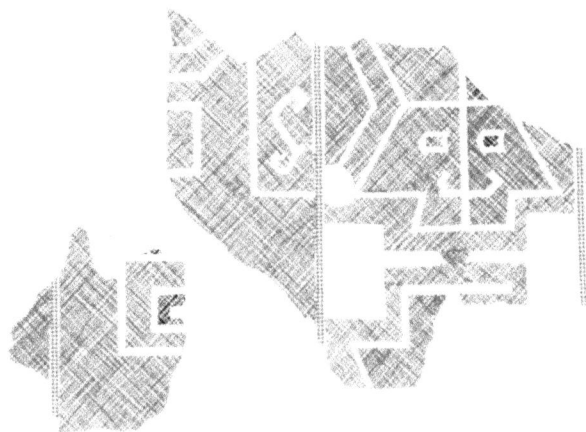

135. Weft-twined cloth with modular designs in brown and white, with red stripe and green borders (T.S. 86), from C-11:F-5.

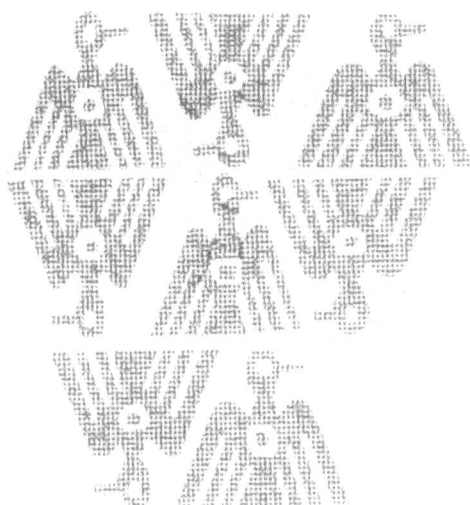

136. Looped bag with red-brown birds on tan (T.S. 87) from C-11:F-5.

137. Looped bag with triangle border and wings in red-brown on tan (T.S. 88) from C-11:F-5.

wing, was a more disciplined design (Fig. 137). T.S. 92 (Fig. 138) could be part of the same bag, though that remains uncertain. It has a similarly rigorous design with a series of vertical bands of irregular width incorporating bird wings into the designs. T.S. 90 (Fig. 139), of which a large segment survives, had a double border of small triangles at the base of the circular bag and at least four registers of double raptorial birds in red on tan. Note the small serpent interpolated into the design.

One of the most interesting bags, T.S. 91 (Fig. 140), represented by four pieces, was decorated with at least two registers of frontal human-like figures. Only after the drawing was made were the faces recognized, and no changes were made in the figure to show what should be on the faded scraps of cloth. Thus the head at right must have had eyes, but they are no longer visible, and the center head must have had a body, and the diamond at the left of the left

head must have been part of a form that extended beyond the edge of that scrap. The feet of the upper range of figures are visible above the right and left heads. (See C-11: E-8 section below for further discussion of these designs.)

The destruction and dispersal of the textiles in C-11:F-5 was a major loss for the history of Peruvian art. We are fortunate to have these remaining traces.

C-10:E-10

This intact tomb contained a set of baskets and bags among the offerings. Four of the bags had recordable decorations, three in looping, one in linking.

Although a large area of the linked bag, T.S. 77 (Fig. 141), remains, it is in poor condition. Separate yellow threads were inserted to make the small areas of design in the ribbed pattern of the cloth. The unique design might be taken as suggestive of snakeskin or the night sky, but its delicate

138. Looped bag with bird designs (?) in red on tan (T.S. 92) from C-11:F-5.

139. Looped bag with double birds, triangle border at base (T.S. 90) from C-11:F-5.

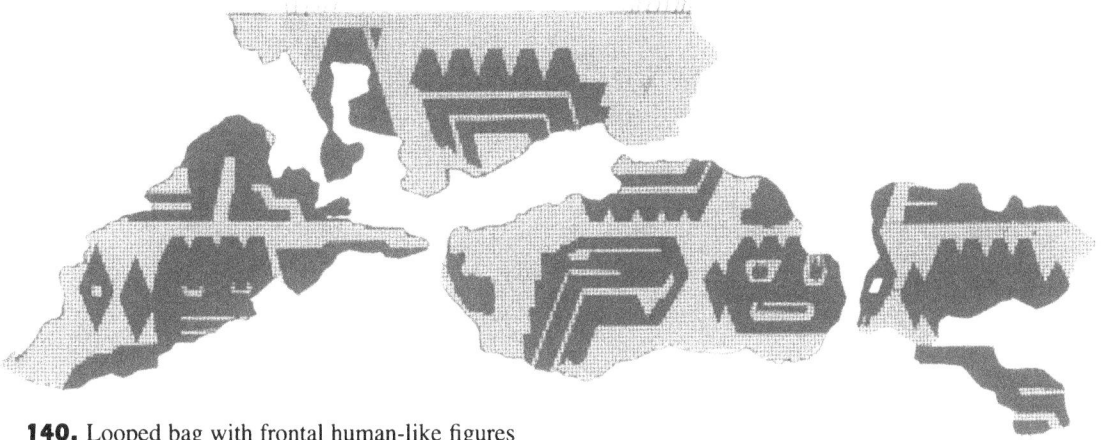

140. Looped bag with frontal human-like figures in brown on tan (T.S. 91) from C-11:F-5.

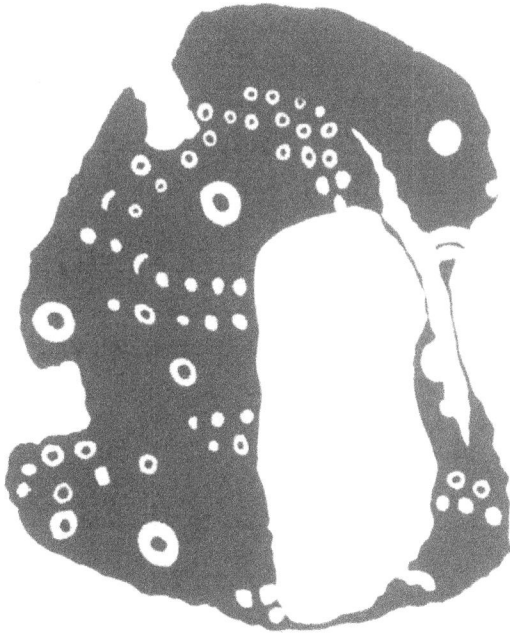

141. Linked bag with yellow shapes on black (T.S. 77) from C-10:E-10.

condition does not permit a confident interpretation.

The three looped designs, T.S. 66, 74, and 80, were all on bags in stacked basket offerings such as that shown in Figure 142. T.S. 80 (Fig. 143) lay folded in the lowest basket of a stack, and only a narrow strip was revealed. The remaining traces of the design are amazingly curvilinear yellow shapes on black. It appears to have been representational, but not enough remains for an interpretation. The other two are both serpent subjects. T.S. 74 (Fig. 144) shows a small S-shaped double-headed spotted serpent in black on a red ground. Much more impressive are the angular, smiling, spotted serpents on T.S. 66 (Figs. 145–146). A small shape beside the body of one of the serpents on T.S. 66 appears to be a wing, which suggests that these may be winged or feathered serpents.

C-12:D-1

Figures 147 and 148 show the lowest register of a looped bag, T.S. 146. Although two adjoining designs are similar, the other design elements are all different and suggest that the whole design was made up of a variety of strong, geometric forms in red on tan. Traces

142. Offering of baskets and textiles in tomb C-10:E-10.

143. Looped bag with yellow shapes on black (T.S. 80) from C-10:E-10.

144. Looped bag with black double-headed snake on red (T.S. 74) from C-10:E-10.

145. Looped bag with black winged, spotted serpents on yellow (T.S. 66) from C-10:E-10.

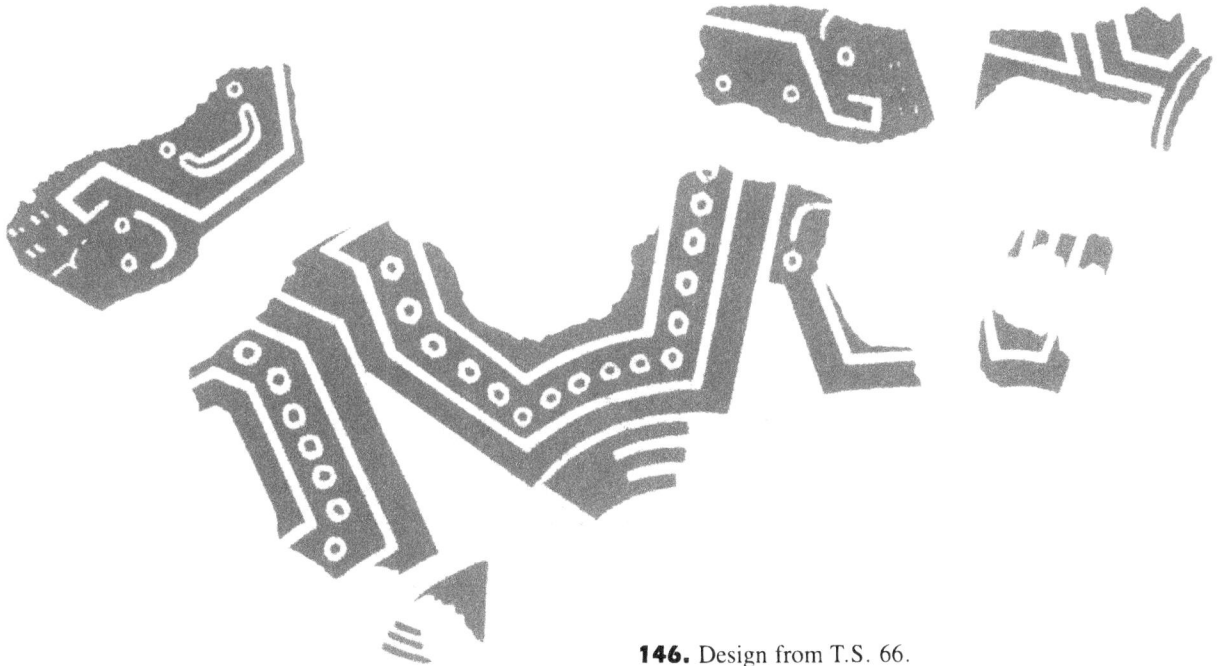

146. Design from T.S. 66.

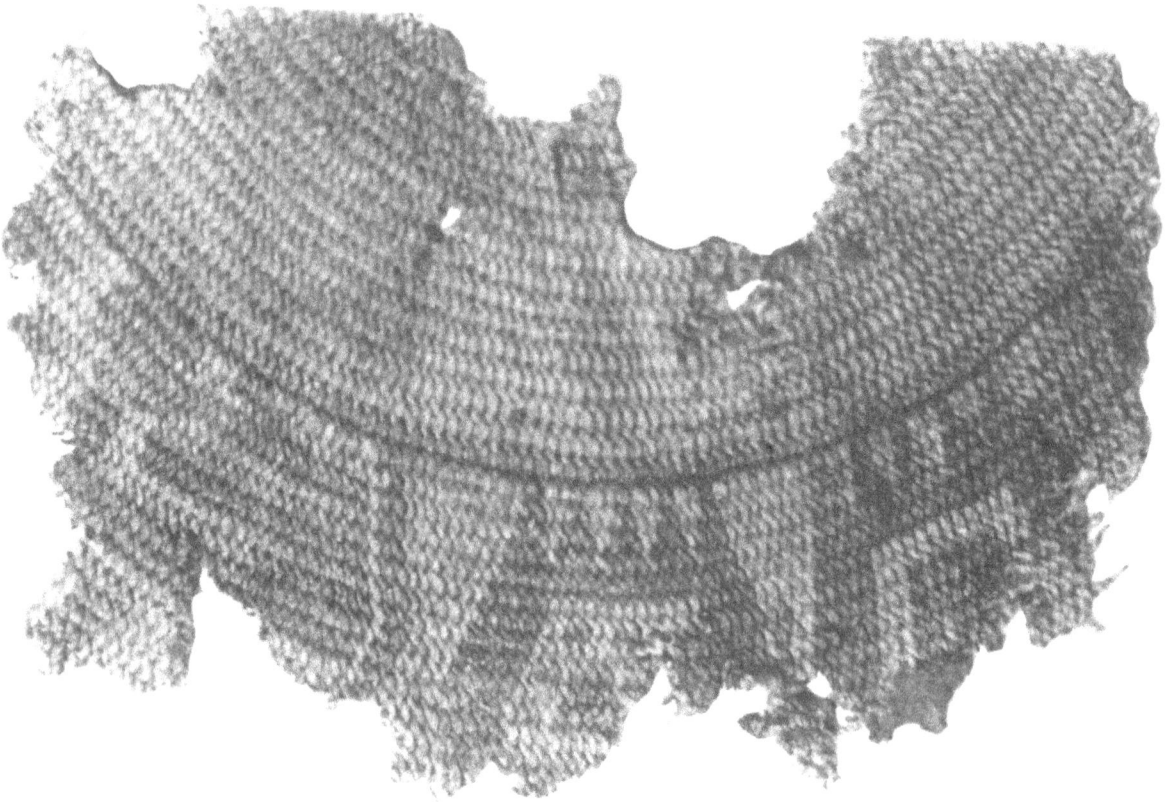

147. Looped bag with red designs on tan (T.S. 146) from C-12:D-1.

of decoration are found in other techniques: an angular floated design possibly representing bird wings in an interlaced belt (T.S. 143; Fig. 151), and stripes in a linked bag (T.S. 148) and a twined mantle (T.S. 138).

C-11:E-8

The only decorated textile found in C-11: E-8 is T.S. 173 (Fig. 149), a looped cotton bag under and to the left of a man's head. The design is in registers with alternating red and yellow backgrounds. Parts of the motifs in two registers remain, the upper showing two legs with two-toed feet, the lower part of the body, and one wide band pendent from the body and curving up. The elements in the lower register can be identified, by comparison with T.S. 91 (Fig. 140), as the top

148. Design from T.S. 146.

of a head and ear and the top of the same pendent band on the design above it.

Comparison of the designs on T.S. 91 and 173, both of which show frontal anthropomorphic figures, suggests that they represent the same motif. By combining the two versions it is possible to reconstruct the whole motif with considerable confidence (Fig. 150). Although there is no place one can be absolutely certain about the middle of the figure, the breadth of what appear to be the hips in the later version (T.S. 173) and the small horizontal red lines at the bottom of the right-hand fragment of the earlier piece, which seem to be continuations of the red stripes in the pendent flanking elements, lead to the conclusion that the flanking elements take the place of arms. It appears that the points at which the red stripes in the flanking elements turn back toward the figure mark the midpoint of the height of the design.

The result is similar to many later designs especially associated with the Chavín culture, but it also participates in a long tradition of deity images running down to the fifteenth century A.D. In the later versions the pendent elements hang from the belt and additional attributes are held in the arms or hands. Those seem to be later elaborations of this motif, which appears here in its oldest, Preceramic form.

The latest type of decorative motif, except for stripes and plaids, is found on a pair of interlaced belts from C-12:D-1. T.S. 142 (Fig. 116), which has both side selvages, was 7.5 cm wide, woven of brown cotton with one-ply wefts. The structural warp is two-ply brown cotton with single strands on the selvages and paired strands in the middle in a pattern of sixteen singles, thirty-three pairs, and fifteen singles. The decoration was added as black two-ply thread floating from side to side between the paired warps. The motif seems to have been simple triangles.

149. Looped bag with black figures on red and yellow (T.S. 173) from C-11:E-8.

150. Reconstruction of the motif on T.S. 91 and 173.

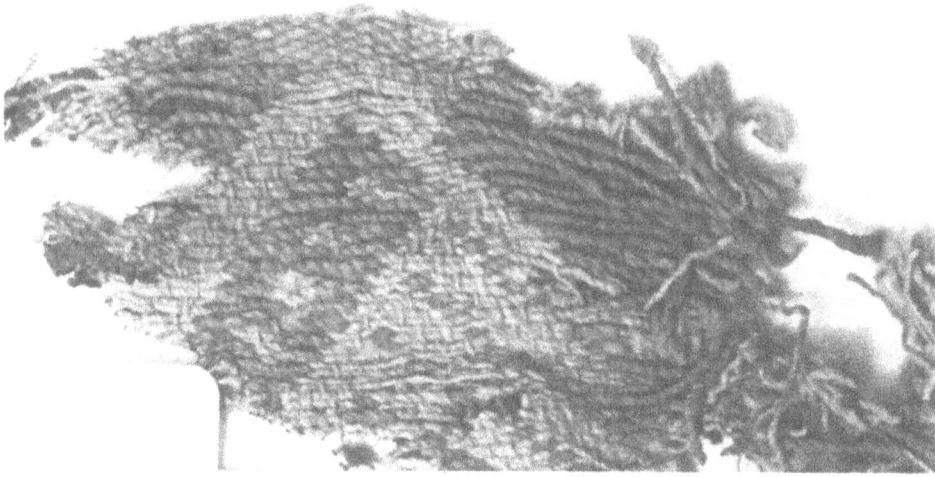

151. Interlaced belt in brown and white warp floats (T.S. 143) from C-12:D-1 (photo and design reconstruction).

T.S. 143 (Fig. 151), from the same tomb, has white structural warps and wefts, one-ply wefts and two-ply warps. Eight warp pairs on each selvage are plain, but the center area has dark brown two-ply thread floating to make the design. The rectangular area with small squares, for example, is composed of eighteen threads floating over the structural fabric. The design, with its narrow bands, is reminiscent of older designs of bird wings, but not enough remains to be sure.

These belts with designs made by warp floats which are not a structural part of the fabric mark the end of the Preceramic style of textile art. Initial Period textiles are woven, and the weavers could make only stripes, crossing warp and weft stripes to make plaids. To make the elaborate designs found in Preceramic cloth they would have

had to sacrifice the principal advantage of the loom, which was that it gave the artisans the power to produce much more cloth in the same time. The result of the shift to the harness loom was much more cloth, but almost all of it plain.

COLOR

Another aspect of decoration is color. Throughout the Preceramic Period three colors appear and are dominant: a range of yellow-tan-cream, most of which is probably natural undyed cotton; a brownish black which was mildly acidic and in many cases eventually destroyed the fiber; and a red or brick red, which fades toward tan or brown. A sample of red cotton thread from C-11: F-5 was submitted to Max Saltzman for analysis of the dye. The red in that specimen was *Relbunium* with alum as the mordant. The dye comes from the root of the common, but rather inconspicuous, American relative of the European madder family, which is found in tropical and temperate climates from Mexico to Argentina. In Peru the species *Relbunium nitidum* is that commonly identified as the source of red dye (Towle 1961:89). The cotton thread was soaked in an alum solution before immersion in the red dye. To judge by colored textiles, the use of *Relbunium* with an alum mordant was already established when our earliest textile examples were made. That technique remained in use until it was superseded by cochineal in the Early Intermediate Period (Dwyer 1979:75 n. 2).

The history of ancient technology is still so poorly documented that this specimen from La Galgada is currently the oldest tested sample of ancient dyeing with madder dyes. R. J. Forbes (1964:4:107) writes: "It has been claimed that samples of cotton from Mohenjo Daro dating to the third millennium B.C. were dyed with madder, but we have no knowledge of its introduction and use in Mesopotamia. In ancient Egypt it was used quite frequently." The cultivation of madder and its use in dyeing spread westward from Asia Minor to Rome in Classical times and to western Europe around Paris by the seventh century A.D. (ibid.: 108).

The brownish black, which also remained a basic dye color in Preceramic cloth at La Galgada, may have been tannin, according to Max Saltzman, but no test has been made.

Thread samples from the later Preceramic levels have not been tested chemically, but they suggest an expansion of the range of colors available. Yellow was in common use. Very small thread scraps testify to rare use of a blue which looks as if it might have been an indigo, which also requires a complicated dyeing process, and there are rather mysterious bits of thread clinging to other textiles which show a bright blue and a brilliant emerald green. It appears that a considerable range of dye colors was known at La Galgada and its trading connections before 2000 B.C. The only additions to the range of colors made in the Initial Period that are evident in our specimens are a related set of purple, lavender, and rose or pink which may represent new dye sources or mixing and fading of dyes known earlier. (See Chapter 11 for intersite comparisons.)

9. Petroglyphs

ALBERTO BUENO MENDOZA and TERENCE GRIEDER

Two green metamorphic boulders about 150 m north of the North Mound have petroglyphs on their upper surfaces. Both boulders are oxidized to a leather-like brown, and the designs are nearly invisible (Fig. 152). On Rock 2 they can be seen only as dull marks when the smooth surface of the stone reflects the bright sun.

Two styles are present, both made by pecking. In neither style are the lines deeply cut, but merely roughened. When the marks were new they stood out against the brown surface of the stone as a brilliant green. These particular stones, the only ones we could find with petroglyphs, were surely chosen for their color contrasts between the green glyphs and the brown weathered surface.

The styles can be attributed to the Preceramic and Initial Periods. The smiling

152. Petroglyphs on Rock 1.

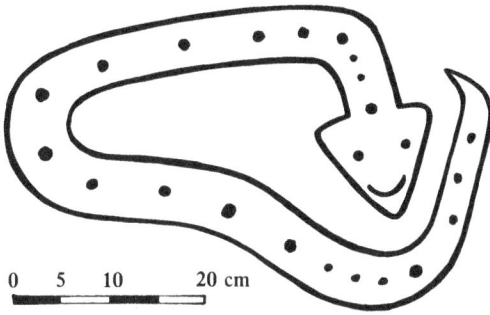

153. Petroglyph of spotted snake. This appears in the center of Figure 152.

serpent on Rock 1 (Fig. 153) and the large-beaked bird on Rock 2 (Fig. 155) share subjects with the Preceramic textile designs. Those, along with the clusters of S and other curved designs, are all composed of single elements; that is, in each design there seems to be one thing represented and it is made up of a few closely related shapes.

The other designs, one large complex design on each boulder and a fragment of another on Rock 1 (Figs. 154, 155) are composed of several elements which attach to each other and fit together. These designs are not only impossible to name, they are unlike any identified style. But their unity, complexity, and the use of related bands and stripes connect them with the modular designs of the Chavín style. These are thus attributed to the time period in which the shell ornaments (Figs. 83, 84) were imported. The petroglyphs show the naturalization of the style at La Galgada, and also the local variant of it.

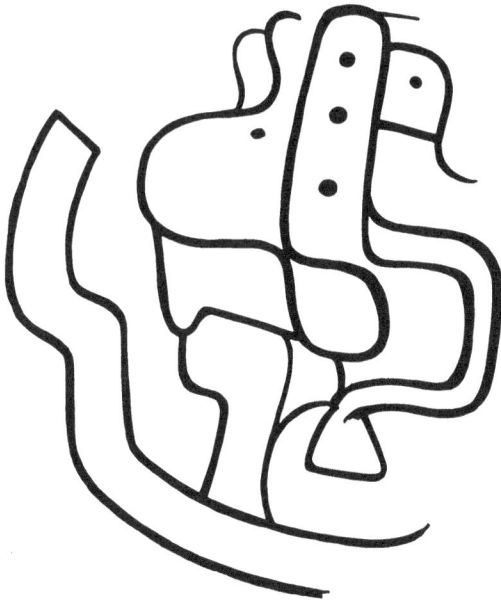

154. Petroglyphs. These designs flank the snake, appearing at left in Figure 152 and on the right-hand point of the boulder.

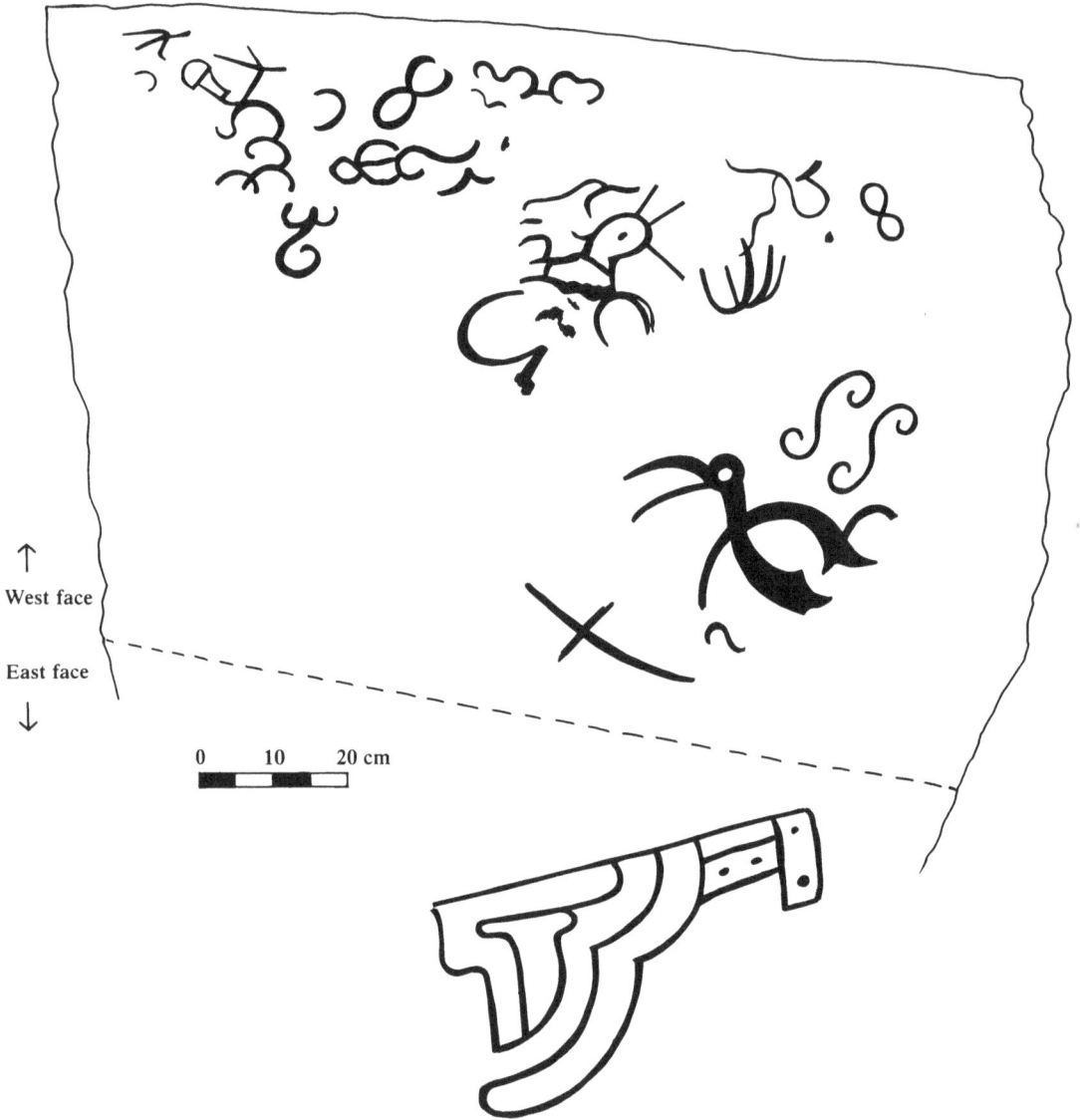

155. Petroglyphs from boulder below road,
Rock 2.

10. Ceramics

TERENCE GRIEDER

Our excavations have yielded a total of 181 specimens of pottery, including 1 whole vessel, 1 whole lid, 30 rim sherds, and 149 body sherds. (See Table 22 for locations of specimens.) The scarcity of ceramics might suggest that very little was made at the site, but ritual areas were kept very clean (Burger 1985:506) and the ceremonial buildings could not be expected to produce refuse. Most of the potsherds were found in the upper levels of G-12 and the mound slope below it (EF-13), which is an indication that those areas lost ritual importance in the Initial Period.

The preceramic and ceramic levels of the two mounds are clearly separated by floors, Floor 19 in the North Mound and, coincidentally, the unconnected Floor 19 in the South Mound. Only tombs, such as those on Floors 21 and 24 in the South Mound, reached by shafts from higher levels, show pottery at deeper levels. The radiocarbon tests bracket the appearance of ceramics as having occurred between 3660 ± 80 B.P. (TX-3166) and 3670 ± 70 B.P. (TX-4447); or alternatively, shortly after 3590 ± 75 B.P. (UGa-4583). On the uncorrected radiocarbon scale that would date the introduction of ceramics between 1790 and 1565 B.C.; on a calibrated scale between 2295 and 1705 B.C. These dates might be compared with the date of 3580 ± 130 B.P. (GaK-607) for the introduction of ceramics to the coastal site of Las Haldas (Tokyo Daigaku 1960:518), or between 2325 and 1665 B.C. The midpoint of both of those calibrations happens to be 1995 B.C. The dates for La Galgada are in general agreement with those of other Peruvian sites (cf. Lumbreras 1974: Fig. 11).

The ceramics can be divided into three groups based on vessel and rim forms, firing, and color, with a pair of isolated items which belong to a style not otherwise represented at La Galgada.

The first group is the oldest, both by its stratigraphic level and by comparison with related styles. It is represented exclusively by neckless jars with round bases. Fourteen rims belong to this group (Fig. 156a–n). The type is defined by rims which were sealed under Initial Period floors, Floor 9 in G-11:G-9 and Floor 10 in H-11. Rims are sometimes thin and smoothly rounded (Fig. 156a–d), but more often they are reinforced by folding the rim under (Fig. 156g–i; Fig. 157a), sometimes smoothing it into the body of the wall (Fig. 156e,f,m), or buckling it to make a ridge both inside and outside the rim (Fig. 156j–l). Only a few of the rims are large enough to give a reliable idea of the size of the vessel's mouth, which varies from 14 to 16.5 cm in diameter, a range that appears to be typical of the group. Body sherds are very thin, typically about 4 mm thick, with a gray or black core. All this group was fired at a low temperature in an unoxidizing atmosphere (Shepard 1965:103–107, 216–222), that is, with the fire muffled to keep out oxygen, thus producing black or dark gray pots. This group of pottery is sand-

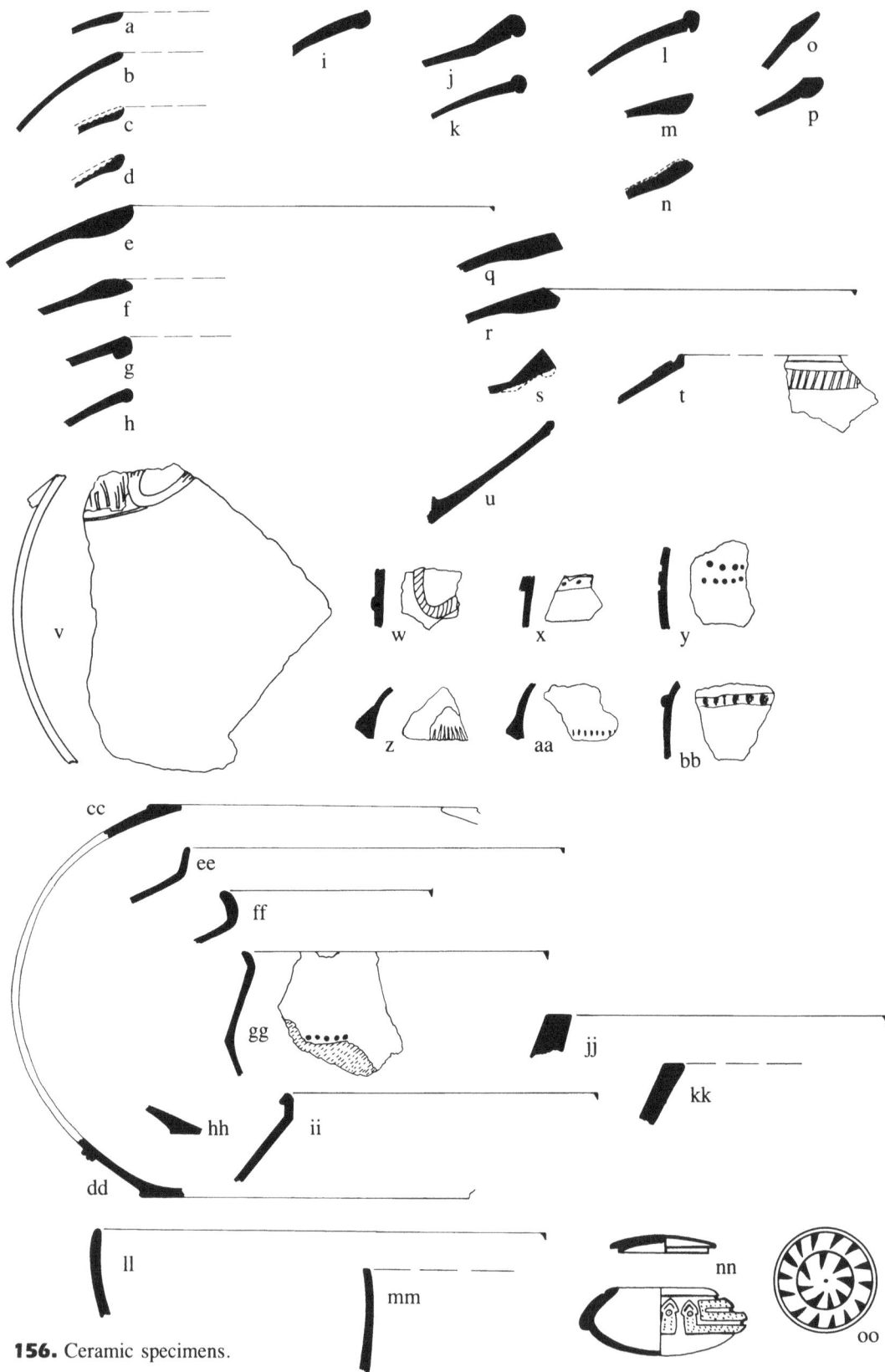

156. Ceramic specimens.

tempered, unslipped, unburnished, and heavily carbonized on the exterior, presumably showing use in cooking.

No decorations can be definitely associated with the first group, but neither can they be defined as absent since rims of the first-group type come from the surface levels of G-12, from E-12:I-1 above Floor 3, and from EF-15. That could mean that punching, incised or punched fillets, lugs with incisions, or even a possible figurative subject made of fillets (Fig. 156v–bb) could belong to this earliest group. But the evidence is stronger for all of those decorations belonging with the second group, in which there is an incised fillet on a rim sherd (Fig. 156t).

The second group was made of the same sandy, unoxidized paste into neckless jars with round bases, but the group is set apart from the first by beveled rims (Fig. 156o–t). All of these neckless jars had the top or inner edge of the rim trimmed and flattened, an extra effort with no utilitarian advantage but a noticeable stylistic difference. The seven rim sherds in this group come from the southeast corner of the North Mound from a trench excavated by Alberto Bueno in 1980 (EF-13) and from the surface level on the adjoining sector of the mound top (G-12), and one from the disturbed levels of the west front of the mound (H-10). On the basis of archaeological strata the beveled rims can be set apart as later than the round rims since none come from sealed early Initial Period levels represented by four of the rim sherds in the first group.

One of the rim sherds in this second group (Fig. 156t) is decorated with a wide stick-incised fillet just below the rim, and on that basis the decorated body sherds (Fig. 156v–bb) in the ware characteristic of these first two groups are assumed to belong mainly with the second group. All of them come from strata at the higher levels where the second group of rims were found. The deco-

rations are all plastic: stick-punching, filleting with stick punching or incising, filleting with finger-punching, and a lug with stick-incising. One (Fig. 156v) might represent part of the body and arm of a human figure.

A third group (Fig. 156cc–ii) can be defined by color and firing, all examples having been fired at a higher temperature in an oxidizing atmosphere which produced a lighter brown, tan, or orange paste. One of the rim sherds (Fig. 156gg) has post-fire red paint, but more significant is a body sherd with a good polished red slip inside and out. All of these six rims and two bases come from higher strata in G-11:FG-6/9 above Floor 9, E-12:I-1 above Floor 3, and the trench in EF-13, and they are considered to represent a later period than the groups previously defined. The beveled-rim neckless jar has grown a little more elaborate—Figure 156cc–dd has a flat base to match the rim, a rough "brushed" brown unslipped surface, and an incised fillet ornament above the base. The other rims all show incipient necks on the rim (Fig. 156ee–ii).

Up to this point there is no rim or base which shows the presence of a form other than the globular jar. Other forms are rare, and four rims (Fig. 156jj–mm) of bowls or open basins, all distinguishable in some way from the other groups, can be set aside as a fourth and final group. The two bowls (Fig. 156ll,mm) both have a polished black slip on a well-fired oxidized paste. The rims of two basins (Fig. 156jj,kk), one from the trench at the southeast corner of the North Mound and the other from the excavated houses nearby, are both thick-walled with flattened rims.

The whole vessel and lid (Fig. 156nn,oo; Figs. 158, 159) are unique in the site in many respects and deserve a separate discussion. Although they were found in different places, they fit together in size and style. The pot was found beside the head of a man, extended on his back to the west, in C-11:

Table 22. Archaeological Provenience of Ceramic Sample

Sector and Floor	Total Sherds	Rims	Traits
C-11:E-8, on Floor 17	1 whole vessel		
C-10:I-10, on Floor 21	1 whole lid		
C-11/12, above Floor 5	12	0	7 black, 4 orange, 1 red slip
D-11:D-2, entrance to tomb, on Floor 24	11 (1 vessel)	1	thin black
E-12:I-1, above Floor 3	4	1	
EF-13	10	7	jar, stick punch on shoulder
EF-15, house area	16	3	1 filleted dec.
G-11:FG-6/9, below Floor 9	3	2	
G-11:FG-6/9 above Floor 9	5	2	bowl, red, polished black
G-12, above Floor 8	101	11	
G-10, west front, North Mound	4	1	
H-11, below Floor 10	4	2	
I-11:J-12, above Floor 13	9	0	
Totals	181	30	

157. Examples of potsherds: *a,* interior of rolled rim of neckless jar (Fig. 156*g*); *b,* fillet with punch (Fig. 156*x*); *c,* fillet with grooves (Fig. 156*t*).

E-8 on Floor 17 in the South Mound. The lid was found in the burnt deposit on Floor 21 in C-10:I-10. Those constructions are of approximately the same time at the very beginning of the Initial Period, and it may be that the pot and lid were a set but were divided to provide offerings for separate burials. The lid is now black from the fire which blackened everything in the disturbed tomb, but it presumably matched the gray-brown oxidized paste of the pot originally. The pot was well fired, with some fire clouding on one side.

The pot is very small—7.5 cm in diameter and 3.0 cm high—but sturdy and thick walled. The upper surface of the flattened globular form has a heavy appliqué, clearly visible as appliqué viewed from the base, which has been carved with wooden tools into two symmetrical designs of pairs of snakes. Each snake has a "smiling" mouth, a round eye with a center dot, and an angular spiral body. The snakes stand out in relief from an excised background, their bodies nicked with a sharp point after the clay had dried.

The lid exactly fits the 4.0-cm opening of the pot and overlaps the opening, to a total diameter of 4.8 cm. It curves slightly on the inside and out and is obviously not an experiment, but rather a perfected form. A small pit marks the center of both the inside and the outside. The outside has a pattern of two concentric incised circles which are animated by excised triangles, fourteen on the outer circle and eight on the inner. Like the pot, the upper surface of the relief is bur-

nished. The angle of the excised triangles gives the design a pronounced spin. This design is an interesting anticipation of similar designs carved on stone and painted on pottery at the nearby center of Pashash more than two millennia later (Grieder 1978: 179–180).

Assuming that the pot and lid were imported to La Galgada as a set, it is impossible at this time to assign them to a source. The slightly carinate form, the firing and paste color, and especially the decoration remind one of Valdivia pottery, particularly

158. Pottery jar from C-11:E-8 and lid from C-10:I-10.

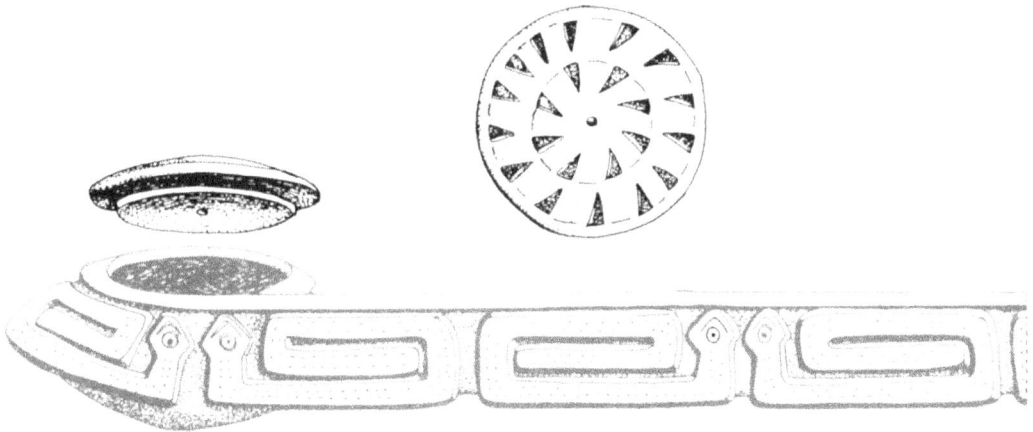

159. Roll-out of design on jar from C-11:E-8.

Valdivia Broad-line Incised, Excised, or Carved (Meggers, Evans, and Estrada 1965:47–54, 58–60, Plates 39, 47, 59), but the form with its lid, the particular motif, and the nicking and details incised on the dry clay are not found in the Valdivia style.

The set also bears comparison with the carved gourds found at Huaca Prieta (Bird 1963; Bird, Hyslop, and Skinner 1985:70–74), which are just slightly smaller but very similar in vessel and lid form (particularly the flange), as well as sharing the plano-relief technique and the angular design. One of the gourd lids bears a double bird head (probably male condors according to Bird), somewhat like designs found at La Galgada. The fact that the Huaca Prieta carved gourds were the only ones of their type among 10,770 gourd fragments in the same pit suggests that they, like the La Galgada pot lid, may have originated elsewhere at some still undiscovered art center.

Despite its small size, the ceramic sample offers the possibility of interesting comparisons. Among the Initial Period ceramic styles the significant comparisons seem to be with Guañape pottery from the coast of the Virú Valley, with pottery from Las Haldas on the coast near Casma, and Toril style pottery from Huaricoto in the Callejón de Huaylas. Given the apparent architectural relationships with Kotosh, it is noteworthy that there is no similarity in the earliest pottery of the two sites, nor with the other early ceramic styles from the eastern slope of the Andes (Lathrap 1970:84–107). The other three pottery centers are the closest ones which have produced specimens of Initial Period pottery, and each of them shares certain traits with the specimens from La Galgada.

The headwaters of the Virú Valley are just west, over the mountains, from La Galgada. The earliest pottery types, of the Guañape Period, are close in style to the La Galgada

sample, especially Guañape Black Plain and the decorated types, Guañape Finger-pressed Rib, Incised, Modeled, and Punctate (Strong and Evans 1952:253–254, 277–284). But these types include a slightly different range of rim forms and perhaps greater use of oxidizing firings and red slip than is found at La Galgada. Greatest similarities are found in the basic neckless jar forms, in the thin walls, and in the plastic ornaments. Beveled rims, which begin to play a major part in La Galgada pottery very early, are absent from the Guañape types.

The Toril style at Huaricoto (Burger 1985) contains vessels very similar to La Galgada neckless jars (especially Burger's Neckless Olla 2) and has similar decoration of incised fillets. But the Toril style also includes a much wider variety of vessel forms and surface finishes, including bowls and an incipient neck, than are found in the first two groups of La Galgada pottery. "Trimming" of jar rims described by Burger does not seem to have produced such pronounced rim bevels as are found at La Galgada until the succeeding Huaricoto Period, which belongs to the later part of the Initial Period and shows a style more advanced than any found in La Galgada pottery. Oxidizing firing and red slip also appear in the Toril style. Those traits suggest that the entire ceramic sample from La Galgada, not just one or two groups, should be compared with Huaricoto's Toril style. There were more than six times as many Toril sherds (1,133, with 60 rims), but the total La Galgada sample contains many more variations in form and decoration than Toril, while having little in common with the succeeding Huaricoto style. For example, Toril shows only incised fillets as a decorative addition, but this is just one of the decorations found at La Galgada.

The pottery of Las Haldas, although poorly published, includes several features found at La Galgada, in particular the shift from round rims on neckless jars to folded-under and then to beveled rims (Grieder 1975). Las Haldas pottery also includes punching and incising, filleting, modeling, and the use of post-fire paint among its early decorations, but its pottery sample has not been finely enough divided to distinguish phases in the development of the Initial Period style. Zoned punching especially differentiates Las Haldas pottery from that of La Galgada, and Las Haldas pottery shares that feature with the early pottery of Chavín de Huantar and Kotosh.

The best stratigraphic information on the ceramics of Chavín de Huantar shows the earliest phase, Urabarriu, still retaining neckless jars with round or beveled rims, but filleting had been largely replaced by grooving and zoned punching (Burger 1984: Figs. 54–138). This phase is clearly later than the latest pottery at La Galgada and is contemporary with the Old Temple and the Lanzón at Chavín de Huantar, with the Kotosh Kotosh Period, and Larco Hoyle's Cupisnique style (ibid.: 78–80, 229–230).

The small ceramic sample from La Galgada is interesting because enough is known about Initial Period pottery that comparisons can be made. The separation of the groups at La Galgada, imperfect as it is, suggests historical phases in the development of pottery that may apply in a general way to other sites. It also suggests that there is a general western-slope style definable by the common features of Guañape, Toril, Las Haldas, and La Galgada.

11. La Galgada in the World of Its Time

TERENCE GRIEDER, ALBERTO BUENO MENDOZA, C. EARLE SMITH, JR., and ROBERT M. MALINA

On the banks of the principal tributary of the largest river on Peru's west coast, equidistant from the Pacific Ocean and the Marañón River, La Galgada was central for a large region during a period of rapid cultural development. In its deep, warm canyon, surrounded by the highland plateaus and mountain ranges, it was a knot in a net of related centers, where regional interests connected. Four thousand years later it is at first hard to see in the isolated and desolate ruins of La Galgada the intense life that once was lived there. But with growing familiarity the observer begins to note not only the ruins of numerous stone buildings, but massive earth platforms and mounds, the terracing of fields, and the horizontal lines of irrigation canals. Although nature has reasserted dominance over this environment in the relative absence of human population, in the region around La Galgada virtually the whole canyon floor is a cultural artifact.

ARCHITECTURE, IRRIGATION, AND THE SOCIAL ORDER

The stratified buildings and the radiocarbon series make it possible to describe the history of this site with considerable precision. It is noteworthy that the site must have begun with a resident population engaged in agriculture, as the plant remains indicate. Although our excavations did not reach the earliest levels of the North Mound, which was the main focus of ceremonial life, the radiocarbon measurements on the mound

and the early structures around its periphery suggest that the ceremonial area may have begun to take shape by about 3000 B.C. The earliest samples of plants include a range of cultivated plants which could not have been grown without irrigation, including most abundantly cotton, but also squash, gourds, guava, *lúcuma*, lima beans, and avocado. Rainfall agriculture preceded irrigation agriculture, as Karl A. Wittfogel has pointed out (1957:12), so it is clear that the earliest plant materials recovered from La Galgada are far from the beginnings of agriculture. Two possibilities suggest themselves: that the early agricultural settlers along the river arrived from a highland region where rainfall agriculture was possible, or that they moved into the Tablachaca Canyon from some other region where they had already developed irrigation. In either case a long period of prior development is indicated. Ester Boserup (1965) has pointed out that irrigation agriculture is less efficient per worker-hour than rainfall agriculture, although more efficient per unit of land. Irrigation systems and the intensive agriculture they produce will only be found, she argues, where the population is dense enough to force people to put more work into the system because the amount of land is limited. The intense occupation of the canyon floor evident in Bueno's survey shows two things: that the more easily farmed adjacent highland areas were already fully utilized and that the excess population was sufficient to make the construction of canal systems economical. Once in place, the labor requirements of the irrigation system necessitated, and the yield would have permitted, a denser population than could have been typical for the surrounding highlands. Yet irrigable land in the immediate vicinity is and always was extremely limited and put a limit on the size of the population.

The houses clustered around the temples and packed close above the irrigation canals indicate a resident population whose size could probably be determined by further work. The abundance and variety of irrigated plant remains in the earliest levels show that the people were well aware of the value of irrigation, but built their canals to curve tight against the west wall of the circular court, which must antedate the canals. This strongly suggests, but does not prove, that the extant canals are not just later than the circular court, but also not the first to be built on the site.

To accurately assess the effects of irrigation on the history of the site we would need to know the relative histories of the immediate neighbors in the valley and whether all of the sites were occupied at once. At higher elevations along the canyon both irrigated crops and those watered only by rainfall are possible, and the people of those districts may also have looked to La Galgada as their ritual center.

This early development of irrigation agriculture is interesting for the light it throws on social development. Barbara J. Price (1971:47) remarks that "the ultimate solution to the problem [of a shortage of arable land]—the development of artificial irrigation on an initially small and progressively expanded scale—was undoubtedly preceded by considerable conflict." That is not evident at La Galgada, which provides evidence of egalitarian attitudes throughout the Preceramic. If that period succeeded one of "considerable conflict," in which groups

struggled for dominance, one would expect to find expressions of dominance in the art and architecture. Such expressions only slowly begin to appear during the Preceramic and come to the fore only at its end.

The system of canal irrigation was used by a group of people living in scattered clusters of small houses, carrying out ceremonies in various small chambers which permitted seating only around a circle with a fire at the center, and constructing cloth of a single element. All these things show habits of mind and behavior in which there is minimum opportunity for expression of dominance or submission. As far as we can tell, families built their houses wherever they liked and lived in them as they wished. In ceremonies the fire occupied the center, the only unique position, and all the human participants' positions were eccentric and equal. Perhaps the position on axis opposite the door had prestige, but there is no evidence of that in the architecture. So far as we can tell, everyone in the ritual chambers had an equal position around the circle. Perhaps the failure of the rectangular chamber, which gives just a hint of dominance to the axial position, reflects the distaste of the local population for any hint of inequality in the ritual. The older forms of clothmaking (looping and linking) used only one thread going around and around. If a colored design was made it was produced by the equal interaction of threads which each played the same role, following the same path but exchanging places at the proper intervals. Twining, in which two large sets of threads play different roles and move in contrary ways, and in which only one set plays much part in decoration, shows the beginning of consideration of dominant and submissive roles.

Canal construction and maintenance must have resulted from a cooperative system of shared authority and shared labor. Modern models of such systems can still be found in the Andes in such events as the Yarqa Aspiy, the annual ritual of canal cleaning carried out by crews composed of one male from each household under supervision of community officeholders (Isbell 1978:138–145).

The history of La Galgada can be described conveniently in terms of Richard N. Adams' theory of social power (1975). Adams proposes an interdependence among several factors, of which the particularly relevant are control of environmental resources, the amount and kind of energy used, and the size of the population and its social complexity. If there is a first cause among these it is the ability to draw energy from the environment. An increase in energy flow permits population growth and requires the development of power relationships within the society based on differential control over the flow of energy. As energy use increases, the society enters a growth sequence from *identity* to *coordination* to *centralization,* a sequence which is repeated on a larger scale each time the energy flow rises to a level sufficient to support the higher complexity. Conversely, as energy flow declines, social power likewise diminishes and the society falls back to lower levels of integration.

Wittfogel's comments (1957:12) on irrigation agriculture providing the opportunity, but not the necessity, for the growth of despotic patterns of government are a point of departure for consideration of the later history of La Galgada. The ceremonial architecture of the North Mound, especially, supports the idea that the people of La Galgada centralized, eventually choosing one individual to occupy the central position in a symmetrical plan. Even though it took several centuries for the result to become evident in building, can we attribute this change to the introduction of canal irrigation? We will examine below evidence of trade in luxury or ritual items which may reflect compe-

tition and coordination with other societies as causes of change, but energy flow during the Preceramic Period was principally a factor of irrigation agriculture. "Large enterprises of water control will create no hydraulic [political] order if they are part of a wider nonhydraulic nexus," Wittfogel writes (ibid.). The change in La Galgada's ceremonial architecture suggests that the site may have changed partners, from being part of a nonhydraulic network to membership in a hydraulic order. That would seem to imply that the Preceramic network was based in the highlands, where a true hydraulic despotism never emerged, and the Initial Period network was predominantly centered on the coast, where large-scale irrigation was the basic factor in agriculture. Evidence from the excavations supports conflicting conclusions. Trade items, particularly marine shells, seem to support the idea that coastal influence increased over time; burial positions, in which highland-style seated flexed burial in gallery tombs becomes dominant in the later period, may be taken to suggest continued highland dominance. While there can be no doubt that the basic source of energy for life at La Galgada was the permanently flowing river, the use of canal irrigation was just one factor in several which contributed to centralization of the society.

THE HISTORY OF ART AND ARCHITECTURE AT LA GALGADA

Although the history of the settlement at La Galgada falls neatly into two periods—a Preceramic and an Initial (Ceramic) Period—the most interesting feature of that history is the slow change that led from one to the other. We naturally tend to think simplistically of historical periods as static, but the sampling of La Galgada immediately forces us to recognize the constant process of change. The changes were not arbitrary nor the result of natural forces in the environment, but were products of the desires and intentions of the people. Tracing the patterns of change, we can follow the intellectual history of the period.

The Preceramic Period is most conveniently described in terms of two phases, of which the earlier was already in existence in our oldest excavations. Houses and canals were present; the circular court and the temple mound were in place, using waterworn stone from the river as building materials. The ritual buildings, at least, were painted white or black (one case) and polished. The temple chambers showed variations which suggest an older development. Although the subcircular plan with a central firepit, with a vent under the doorway and niches in the wall, was universal, there was a variation between chambers with flat floors and those with a low bench level and between those with flat walls and those with a dado setback at the base of the niches.

The chambers also varied in orientation between west and north, but both were very close to exact cardinal directions according to the modern magnetic compass. Since the North Star is not visible from the site and there is no obvious sighting point, it appears that a compass of some sort must have been in use to establish the orientation of the north-facing chambers. One could face west and extend the right arm and get a good approximation of north if one had the concept clearly in mind, but the concept comes first and would seem to be dependent on the idea of direction as measurable. The dominant orientation was west, which seems to be a different matter. Those chambers face due west across the Tablachaca River toward the point of Cerro Pajillas, which forms the breast of a natural earth form of a woman. This can be interpreted as a Mother Earth image, properly in the west, direction of women and the powers of the earth, death, and immortality. Although movements of the celestial bodies would make the definition of west easy, its measurement may have been superfluous in this case, since the temple center is the only place where a clear view of the terreform can be obtained. Orientation remains an interesting problem at La Galgada.

Architecture serves as the best gauge of the processes of social growth described by Adams (1975). These buildings, which an ethnological interviewer might regard as mute, are objective witnesses that neither lie nor provide a merely private viewpoint. The architectural series is unusual in its completeness, and its language, whose content is the placement of people during sacred ceremonies, is very clear. A series of independent individuals or families (or larger social units) take the first step in this sequence when they recognize that they have something in common. This process of self-identification produces an identity unit, and "if these fragmented units could directly interact and coordinate—then we would be witnessing a process whereby individuals and units were using their common identification as a basis for granting each other rights to make decisions for them, or decisions in common. They would be coordinating their activities" (Adams 1975:60). A coordinated unit centralizes—allocates power to a minority of its members—in response to pressure, "and in human societies the only continuing pressure is that exerted by other societies" (ibid.: 211). As the society centralizes at home, it will ordinarily be coordinating with other similar units outside.

The scattered placement of the early chambers (H-10:F-4; F-12:B-2; D-11:C-3, Floor 25; C-11:F-5) and their variety of colors and orientations suggest complex sources which had not been entirely integrated and that those chambers are the oldest components, probably older than the circular plaza. Each chamber expresses an early centralization at a low level of energy use, when individuals identified themselves as followers of the same cult and merged their ritual fires in one pit. These individuals would have been what Adams (1975:62) calls a consensus unit, each able to withdraw at his or her own discretion. These early chambers are so small they could have accommodated only ten or fifteen people, which sounds like a family group. Given the burial of men, women, and children equally in the chambers, it is hard to imagine that admission to the ceremonies was restricted by age or sex (as in most kiva ceremonies in the U.S. Southwest, for example). Thus, there were other bases of consensus besides the cult, since each chamber was probably occupied by no more than a parental generation, their married children, and their grandchildren. When the parents died they were buried in the chamber, with any children or grandchildren who had died within the same period of years. In some cases (D-11:C-3, Floor 24; C-12:D-1), there is no doubt that burials were added later than the first ones. But there is no evidence of bringing in burials which had been in storage elsewhere, nor of the practice of secondary burial. There is, on the other hand, considerable evidence of the disruption of burials by new construction of tombs and chambers. Older burials were obviously not venerated by all the later builders, which suggests that they had importance for certain restricted groups, those which took the trouble to build the tombs, perform the burial rites, and leave the offerings. It seems most plausible to imagine that those groups had a basis in kinship and that the chambers were built and used by groups of kin, and the bodies in the tombs were members of that kin group.

That makes it more difficult to estimate whether all, many, or only a few of the inhabitants were buried in tombs in the ceremonial area. If the tombs served as family crypts, we have no way to tell with the available evidence whether all the local families are represented, or only a few. If each tomb contains related people, then F-12:B-2 may contain a man and his two wives and C-11: E-8 may have contained a husband, wife, and their child. Since it is unlikely that whole families ordinarily died all at once, the tombs must have remained accessible through the shafts for long enough to place all the relevant bodies in them. The only category that appears strongly under-represented in the tombs is infants, who would typically be expected to be about half the bodies. The bodies of most, but not all, of the infants must have been disposed of in some other place. Their relative absence implies an important ceremony in childhood or at puberty which would define the child as having reached fully human status, with a soul, having become a potential ancestor and a candidate for burial in the chamber tomb. Why the bodies of some infants were placed in the tombs we do not know, but it appears to have become more common in the Initial Period, which suggests a breakdown of an earlier traditional ceremony.

The earlier period had an elaborate burial ritual. The hair of the dead was cut in short locks and the shorn head was covered with any handy cover, a basket or a bag. The bits of hair were placed next to the body as it was flexed and bundled in bark cloth, usually a cotton mantle, and a net. These practices, along with tying the body into its flexed position, were soon to go out of style. Cutting the hair and placing it around the body, although unique in detail, conforms to beliefs about the sacredness of the hair of the head found throughout native American societies. For example, Yaytrunbiá, a Secoya Indian from the Amazonian region of Peru, drew and described a region in the lower heavens where the dead have their hair washed and where their earthly hair falls out and new hair grows (Ortiz Rescanière 1975:

52). This practice at La Galgada broadens our understanding of the contemporary figurines from the Valdivia culture of Ecuador, in which the naked female figurines have large, elaborate hairdos, but wear no clothing. The Valdivia figurines probably accurately represent the people of La Galgada, who were equally concerned about their hair and also wore only a mantle or shawl and carried a fancy purse or bag, but had no other clothing or footwear.

Although cutting the hair of the dead went out of style, the later Preceramic people were vain about their hair, as numerous bone pins show. In only one case, C-12:D-1(V), were the pins found in place in the hair on the head, but the small-headed pins were always found near the head. Jewelry clearly played an important role in dressing and self-presentation. Throughout the later phase of the Preceramic it was the main focus of importation, so far as we can tell. Burial rites shifted in the later phase from emphasis on the preparation of the body to provision of offerings in the form of jewelry, clothing, bags, baskets, gourds, and stone vessels. The change accompanies other evidence of the growth of status distinctions, for everyone had hair to be cut, and cord and bark cloth were probably available equally to everyone, but the things which accompany the later burials were unique or rare, represented much more labor, and not everyone had equal amounts or equal quality.

Although the Preceramic community remained egalitarian and fragmented in its ceremonial organization, there is abundant evidence of the growing awareness of social integration. The early construction of the circular plaza and the North Mound represent a much higher level of integration, even though the mound continued to hold several separate chambers for a long time. This union of chambers on the mound formalized the long-held agreement to build ceremonial buildings in this place, but made coordination much stronger and presumably brought the separate chamber groups together in the building and use of the circular plaza and the mound. The rapid pace of building on the North Mound is evidence of the growing commitment of the larger part of the population to increasing centralization.

As the North Mound grew higher with each layer of construction, the wall supporting the platform became more essential, but nowhere at La Galgada do we have evidence of the building of a platform for its own sake. Mounds were built by filling rooms, and the resulting platform was coincidental, a practice found also at Aspero (Feldman 1985:73), which is contrary to Central Coast pyramid building of the same period (Patterson 1985:59; Williams 1985:229). Although Aspero and La Galgada mounds appear similar to the Central Coast pyramids, they represent a different building tradition from one in which the platform is envisioned from the start. At La Galgada the mound never really looked like a pyramid, since its massiveness was mitigated by the curve of the walls and by their ornamentation. In successive rebuildings the wall grew higher, and corbel tables and a frieze of niches were added to at least two successive walls. The higher the wall, the more important the central staircase became. It seems always to have been on axis perpendicular to the front of the mound, which might seem obvious except that in Early Intermediate Period buildings in this region stairways were usually parallel to the walls they ascended (Grieder 1978:Figs. 13, 15).

Not everyone was part of that coordinated group, for there remained isolated chambers to the south which were later united inside encircling walls. The separation of the South Mound is manifested also in the appearance there of a series of rectangular ritual chambers, a plan so far unknown on the North

Mound, and the use of two cases of polished yellow clay as a finish coat on the interiors of chambers. Yellow paint is found only on the Square Chamber (C-11:I-3, Floor 22) and on its remodeled neighbor (D-11:C-3, Floor 24), whose floor and walls were raised to match those of the Square Chamber. Rectangular plans and yellow interior paint are typical of the ritual chambers at Kotosh, 250 km away by air, and finding those two features together is an indication of contact with Kotosh. Yellow walls had a very brief popularity at La Galgada, for those two buildings were both repainted the standard pearly white before they were converted to tombs. The rectangular plan lasted longer, since Floors 15 and 17 in the South Mound both held rectangular chambers, although later chambers all returned to the subcircular plan. The Square Chamber is evidence that some important member of the South Mound group was from Kotosh or had recently been there and brought back the determination to adopt Kotosh-style rectangular plans and yellow interiors. The rectangular plan was carried on for several later generations of construction in the South Mound, probably by the descendants of that person.

Everyone, even outside the North Mound group, was designing chambers with more levels of elements, literally, with the walls divided into two levels with a setback at the base of the niches, or three levels with another projection in the wall above the niches (C-11:I-3; G-12:I-2). A shift from round river cobbles to flat-sided quarrystone facilitated the articulation of the wall surfaces, which was clearly a subject of interest and experiment. For example, we find one case (H-11:A-8) in which the dado rises vertically to frame the door. The bench level also grew higher during this period, and we find the first expression of the masonry pattern alternating standing blocks and courses of smaller stones which became common in

later periods. The design of the walls surrounding the North and South mounds in the later part of the Preceramic was of interest to the whole community since the walls were common property of all the chamber groups on each mound. These encircling walls were elaborated with setbacks, projections, and bands of ornament, either corbels or niches. All these architectural details articulated the basic form. Adams (1975:75) writes of levels of social articulation in which "two adjacent levels are marked out wherever there is a continuing superordinate-subordinate relationship. Thus, within some domestic units, parents and children comprise two levels." Parents and children could not have been the only social groups the inhabitants of La Galgada recognized by this time, for the North and South mounds were obviously distinct and the superordinate position of the North Mound was being continually enhanced. The articulation of the architecture shows the builders playing with the concept of articulation, forcing the elements of the buildings to "negotiate," adapt, and conform to a dominant plan.

If the South Mound suggests the dominance of a kin group with connections to Kotosh, the North Mound also shows evidence of the dominance of one group with a local background. On Floor 30 the large central chamber is flanked on the north by two chambers with independent entrances on the west, parallel to the central chamber, and on the south by two chambers which open into the central chamber. None of the surrounding chambers could have rivaled the central chamber in importance, but the two on the south are clearly satellites of the central chamber. They represent generations of building: G-12:I-2 was converted to a tomb and buried, and its entrance shaft opens onto the bench of the central chamber, while H-11:A-8 replaced the burial chamber. That satellite had a satellite of its own—the Log-

Roofed Tomb (G-11:I-5)—though one with its own entrance from the court. The dominance and generational aspects of this complex of buildings which occupied most of the top of the North Mound at the end of the Preceramic are strong indications that a hereditary upper class was emerging. It is unfortunate that the looting of every tomb of this period on the North Mound has deprived us of more knowledge of these people. We are in the surprising position of knowing more about those outside this central group, whose tombs were in the South Mound. Their distinctions were probably a shadow of those belonging to the central group.

Cloth is the most abundant offering in tombs throughout the Preceramic Period, and it seems to have been the principal manufactured product of the village. Two forms were made at first, mantles and bags, and the most popular techniques required only a single thread. Those techniques, looping and linking, were decorated by the addition of a second color, and additional colors entered as the Preceramic Period progressed. The earliest examples show natural white or tan cotton with a brownish-black (probably tannin) and a rare *Relbunium* red, made from a local root using alum as a mordant. Yellow dye may also be present, as it surely is later. Those remained the basic colors, the red becoming ever more common, but traces of other colors appear: a blue that looks like indigo, but also another blue that is a brilliant aquamarine and a similarly brilliant emerald green, both found only in thread samples, and finally a soft purple or pinkish lavender. All these colors would seem to have been available also to the Initial Period weavers, but we have little evidence of their use in that period.

Cloth made by the interaction of two threads appeared in the earliest burial group, and it gradually grew to dominate clothmaking. It appeared in flat cloth as twining and

in belts as interlacing. Twined mantles and shawls were the basic items of clothing in the later phase of the Preceramic, accompanied by looped or linked bags, which were the main vehicles for individualized decoration. Technical progress in clothmaking, in which interlaced belts grew wider and began to be made on a harness loom, eliminated the elaborate decorations which could only be done by hand-manipulation of individual threads. Many centuries later cloth with elaborate decorations built into the structure of the fabric regained its importance in Andean art, but hand manipulation of individual threads was still required.

At the end of the Preceramic, textiles changed more rapidly, and perhaps even more drastically, than any other element of the culture. It is no doubt in cloth that we can witness the confusion people felt as they struggled to find their way in new circumstances. The changes reached the basic level of spin direction of thread, changing from S to Z, and in the use of one-ply (or unplied) thread instead of the two-ply S-Z thread traditional at La Galgada. It was not a matter of learning new techniques, since La Galgada clothmakers had traditionally used Z spinning and one-ply thread for non-cotton vegetal fibers used mainly for nets. The change was the elimination of one traditional practice and its replacement by another. The introduction of the harness loom was so gradual as to be imperceptible, giving an impression that it was a local invention—surely a false impression, since the same change occurred at all the other known sites in Peru at about the same time. Los Gavilanes on the coast near Huarmey, for example, shows the same change and the same confusion (Bonavia 1982:118–119). Since all the features which were new at La Galgada at this time—Z spinning, single-ply thread, and the harness loom—were probably or certainly in use in the Valdivia culture of the Ecuadorian coast by about 2700 B.C., there can be little doubt that northern Peru or Ecuador was the source of the stimulus for these changes in textiles at La Galgada and the other Peruvian sites (Marcos 1979:23–25; note that the calibration table for radiocarbon dates gives ages several centuries older than that used in this report).

The use of a harness with heddles, which raise a set of threads simultaneously with one movement, had two important effects on clothmaking. One was that it could be done much faster, permitting a great increase in production. The other was that the invention was useful only for weaving plain cloth, with decoration limited to stripes and plaids. Much of the resulting cloth is very loosely woven and suggests that quantity production was foremost in the weaver's mind (T.S. 130, 192, 195, 200), but other pieces (T.S. 188) are fine, even fabrics with a machine-like regularity.

The later phase of the Preceramic saw ever widening contacts. Old connections with highland districts were presumably increased, the greater availability of finished turquoise beads perhaps showing such contacts. In the oldest burial (F-12:B-2) there is just one turquoise bead; its uniqueness and its finish indicate it is not a local experiment, but an import. The source of turquoise beads was presumably the highlands, but beyond La Galgada's own region of dominance. The turquoise beads, which are numerous in the later tombs, provide good evidence that they were manufactured outside La Galgada and imported there. The fact that they all have drilled perforations, even when they were glued onto the tops of bone pins where the hole serves no purpose and actually mars the appearance of the stone, shows that the beads were imported already finished. That contrasts with the bone pins to which they were attached, which were most likely local products. Bone hairpins may have been one of La

Galgada's export products and, if so, Kotosh may have been one of its customers, for bone hairpins are so rare at that site as to appear to have been imports (Yamamoto 1972:262; photo 64, nos. 2, 3, 11).

Connections with the Pacific coast of Peru are indicated by marine shells in the tomb offerings, both as natural shells and as beads, necklace pendants, and ear pendants. The scallop and mussel shells which are common in the later Preceramic tombs originated in the cold waters of the Humboldt Current, which follows the Peruvian coast as far north as Lambayeque. *Spondylus* shells, probably from the warm waters of the Gulf of Guayaquil, make a single appearance in the Preceramic as the central pendants of two necklaces on women's bodies in C-10:E-10. *Spondylus* does not appear again until the Chavinoid disks of the Initial Period. That earlier case seems to represent the first identifiable penetration of this area by materials from Ecuador or the far north coast of Peru, and it helps us understand the Valdivia-like decoration of the first pottery pieces, the jar and lid divided between C-11:E-8 and C-10:I-10. *Spondylus* shells and pottery, along with the harness loom, are markers of the end of the Preceramic which testify to a much larger area of interaction.

The Amazon basin is the region with which contact is least in evidence. Colored feathers are the most likely imports, but they have not been identified by species. Orange feather down was found on the floor of I-12:C-5, a late Preceramic chamber on the North Mound, and it is the best candidate for an Amazonian import. Perhaps they are parrot feathers or from the red-orange cock-of-the-rock (*Rupicola peruviana*). White feather down was found in Floor 25 of D-11:C-3 and a small green feather on the floor of C-11:I-3, but both those colors would have been easily available from birds found on the Pacific slope of the highlands.

Throughout the Preceramic Period there is a consistent set of design themes dominated by birds, snakes, and a group of conventional designs. They were made mainly on looped bags, but there are also a few designs in petroglyphs. The beaks of birds are mostly hooked (though there are exceptions such as on Petroglyph Rock 2 and T.S. 87), which tells us that a hawk or eagle is represented. They were subject to a conceptualizing design process which resulted in a set of bars standing for wing and tail feathers, concentric circles for the head and eye, and a maze or spiral for the body. Such a conventional design is easily manipulated into interlocking and doubled designs. The variations on bird themes are very rich; perhaps the concept was sacred but no particular design was. One of these variations, T.S. 15 from the earliest tomb, merges bird and snake themes. They belong together conceptually, even if, perhaps, as a polar dyad.

The heads of birds were always shown in profile, that being the distinctive view, and snakes always frontally, or perhaps from above, with a smiling mouth. The most natural snake is that on Petroglyph Rock 1, but it follows the conventions in having a smile and spots on its body. On textiles snakes usually take an S shape, with one head (T.S. 66) or a head on each end (T.S. 74). The S designs on Petroglyph Rock 2 may stand for snakes, or they may be the earliest examples of the *pawsa* design representing feminine fertility of the earth or of women (Isbell 1978:143). One of these snakes on a textile (T.S. 66) looks as if it was meant to have a wing, which would again bring snakes and birds together. The frontal snake head may have prepared the way for the human and monster faces that begin to appear at the end of the Preceramic and become characteristic of Initial Period art.

Compositions in modular banding are basic to Preceramic design from the begin-

ning. The tightly compressed squares and rectangles of bird and snake designs were laid in rows in the earlier examples. Later there is greater awareness of the row as a unit, forming a strip or band of design (T.S. 86 and 92, both from C-11:F-5). Modular banding is an important feature of the Chavín style later, so it is interesting to find the idea growing in Preceramic art.

The conventional designs are various. A few, such as the stepped mountain (T.S. 3, 94) and perhaps the ladder-like design (T.S. 32), may be interpretable as world-mountain or heaven-ascent symbols, but many are more obscure, though almost certainly meaningful to the audience of that period. Wavy bands (T.S. 80), for example, may have snake significance, and concentric circles and dots (T.S. 77) may refer to celestial bodies, but without more evidence we cannot tell.

The later phase of the Preceramic shows the same kinds of technical progress in several arts. The changes in architecture are especially evident. Firepit chambers grew slowly larger as successive levels of chambers were converted to tombs and new temples built on top. Construction with massive unworked boulders and slabs of stone was practiced in tomb-building within the old chambers, and the builders grew expert at the construction of rough columns and narrow stone-roofed galleries. The tombs are apparently intended to look like natural caves, so the dead returned to the womb of the earth, perhaps recalling more ancient burials in natural caves. This distinctive way of building tombs remained in use at La Galgada in the Initial Period on a larger scale.

Although there are at least ten good examples of rough stone ceilings on tombs, none of the ritual chambers appear to have had that kind of roof when they were in use for ceremonies. The doorway of I-11:B-8 still has a lintel of wooden beams, and the small tomb G-11:I-5 still has a ceiling of logs. The presence of log-printed mud lumps in the South Mound road cut debris and fill, and the presence of similar material at Kotosh, where it was given the same interpretation as roofing, suggest that the ritual chambers were originally roofed with logs and mud.

Another feature of which we have only a little evidence is the stairway on the west front of the North Mound, which seems always to have been on axis perpendicular to the front of the mound. That impressive feature must have accentuated the orientation of the mound, whose curving walls alone would have de-emphasized it.

By the end of the Preceramic Period the observer below in the village or the fields probably could not see any of the chambers, for they must have been hidden by the encircling walls. The temples by this time were two high, dense blocks, the unity of the design compromised only by the presence of the smaller mound beside its massive neighbor.

The Initial Period came into existence slowly at La Galgada, and it is hard to tell that pottery, which ordinarily defines the period, was ever a common local product. The abundant scatter of potsherds usual on later sites is absent even among the houses, where there is ash but very scant evidence of broken cooking pots. It is in other features that the new period discloses itself, mainly in architecture and weaving, but also in the introduction of new designs.

The firepit chamber quickly went out of style, and the proliferation of small chambers was replaced by one single chamber on top of each mound. Even two mounds may have been considered too many after a short time, for the traces of building on top of the smaller South Mound do not form parts of a U-shaped temple, as those on the North Mound do. The buildings on the South Mound were small, rectangular structures.

Their orientation, which was 5 to 11 degrees east of north, was also quite different from that of the Preceramic buildings, which were aligned with the cardinal points. The North Mound was converted step by step into one large, symmetrical U-shaped temple. The firepits of the separate chambers were first consolidated into one large central firepit. The kind of ceremonies practiced in the widespread U-shaped temples of the Initial Period and Early Horizon is unknown, but a fire does not seem to have been an essential element. There are traces of fires at several places in the levels associated with the U-shaped temple, but only one (G-12:H-4) has a horizontal vent from a firepit (see radiocarbon sample TX-4446). One possible interpretation of that very late firepit is that the ancient fire ceremony may have been revived at La Galgada by a few surviving adherents of the cult after the site had been abandoned by the people of the U-shaped temple. We know the fire cult, or Kotosh Religious Tradition, survived the disappearance of Preceramic culture, for at Huaricoto firepit chambers remained in use into the Early Horizon (Burger and Salazar Burger 1980).

During the Preceramic most of the tombs had been built into buried firepit chambers, but with the large open area of the U-shaped temple a new form of tomb was also required. E-11:J-7 was the result, an independent structure, though set against previous structures on two sides. The cyclopean style of earlier tombs was only slightly modified, the large stones being only slightly worked, and the interior chambers were multiplied.

At this time we begin to find indications of external contacts of such a variety and character that there can be no doubt of the pressure they applied to the local population, the introduction of pottery and the harness loom being the most noticeable. At this time one can only speculate about the form that pressure took, but the ways La Galgada tried to confront it are evident. Both mounds were centralized, with single large firepit chambers covering the whole top of each mound. Textile production increased, with emphasis on quantity production of plain woven cloth rather than the decorated twined and looped cloth of earlier times. It would seem likely that the second irrigation ditch, slightly lower but also slightly wider, was built at this time to help increase the production of cotton. Greater labor was required to support the energy demands of centralization, the labor apparently going into the growing of cotton and the fabrication of large amounts of plain woven cloth. The cloth could only have served the purposes of energy flow if a large part of it was for external trade.

Successful confrontation demanded that the people of La Galgada become more like the opposition and attempt to coordinate with them, so we can also learn something about the other group by examining the changes at La Galgada. The outsiders had a different ceremonial cult in which fire was not sacred, but had been harnessed to technology, the production of pottery. Although birds and snakes may have played minor parts in this religion, the central place belonged to an anthropomorphic being who was represented frontally and who later developed the fangs of a jaguar. The *Spondylus* shell played an important part in this religion, and may have been the food of that frontal supernatural (Davidson 1981). The cultivated plants of the outsiders included maize, which was unknown at La Galgada in Preceramic times and apparently was never a local product during the period this site was occupied.

The designs new to La Galgada in the Initial Period consisted of a pair of similar compositions in petroglyphs whose significance is unknown, the frontal human-like figure which first appeared in textiles of the end of the Preceramic but seems to belong to the later period, a set of bird, human, or monster heads on shell disks, and a pair of designs on pottery, with fragments of half a dozen others. After the Preceramic concentration on birds, snakes, and conventional designs, on single-element designs raised in complexity by interlocking or doubling, the Initial Period designs are striking in their intensity and complexity. Although the petroglyphs are impossible to date with precision, it appears likely that the mysterious and complex designs pecked on boulders are not the first manifestation of the new style. That was more likely the two looped bags showing frontal figures (T.S. 91 and 173), one of which (T.S. 173) was accompanied in its tomb by a small pottery jar.

The last couple of centuries during which La Galgada was occupied give an impression of a period of intense adaptation to outside pressure. The firepit temples were buried, and the South Mound may have disappeared under secular buildings. The North Mound was converted into a U-shaped temple, one of several known in the canyon. Perhaps the pressure was exerted by colonies of outsiders who actually settled within La Galgada's domain and began to compete with it, building their own U-shaped temples. Ultimately the ancient site was abandoned and not inhabited again until about A.D. 500, when a couple of families lived for a while in the fields beside the ancient irrigation canals.

12. Art as Communication at La Galgada

TERENCE GRIEDER

Art in the Preceramic was a more comprehensive category than it is for us, encompassing all the recorded symbols which were consciously manipulated with the intention to communicate. Architecture, which for us is principally functional, was then unequivocally a form of symbolic art. Between the Preceramic and the Initial periods symbolism changed from a widely held conventional system, which we find in the earlier material, to a unique and more complex system in the later period. With this change in symbolism came a change in style. The styles were basic to the expressions of their periods and, once learned, became the unconscious vehicles of cultural assumptions. While symbolism was always consciously manipulated, style was controlled automatically to "look right." The style and symbolism of art and architecture are the surviving communication mediums of the ancient people.

ART AND MYTH IN THE PRECERAMIC PERIOD

Art, including architecture, is by nature symbolic, a material form with a semantic character. The visual arts, which are the only kind of art preserved in archaeological sites, differ from music, storytelling, theater, and dance in being simultaneous rather than sequential. The visual arts tend to present what we may call *emblems* as opposed to narratives. Emblems are synchronic rather than diachronic, suggesting timelessness or cyclical repetition as opposed to the historical

particularity of narratives. Art shares those features especially with the literary form we call myth, and sometimes with poetry.

The myths of the Preceramic Period seem irrecoverable, along with their other performance arts, except as we can find reflections of them in the visual arts. In "Genesis as Myth," Edmund Leach (1967:3–4) argued that (1) "Binary oppositions are intrinsic to the process of human thought"; (2) "In every myth system we will find a persistent sequence of binary discriminations as between human/superhuman, mortal/immortal, male/female, legitimate/illegitimate, good/bad . . . followed by a 'mediation' of the paired categories thus distinguished. . . . This middle ground is abnormal, non-natural, holy. It is typically the focus of all taboo and ritual observance"; (3) "This pattern is built into the structure of every mythical system; the myth first discriminates between gods and men and then becomes preoccupied with the relations and intermediaries which link men and gods together."

Leach gives us a way to initiate an interpretation of the art of La Galgada. Art and myth not only share a sense of timelessness or cyclical repetition, they also both derive from a system of binary discriminations "intrinsic to the process of human thought." The categorization of a stimulus into one of a binary set, such as dangerous/benign, is the second of a series of psychological processes which we unite under the name perception, which is preceded only by the simple registration of the stimulus by the central nervous system (D'Aquili, Laughlin, and McManus 1979:164–169). That moment when the stimulus has been received but not yet categorized has (as yet) less significance in its own right than as a theoretical expression of primordial unity, before categorization has eliminated forever half of the possibilities of meaning. The mediating category of myth, which bridges the two terms of the binary set, returns us to that instant of unity before the stimulus has been categorized. Since binary categories are largely cultural, rather than natural (with the notable exceptions pointed out by Leach of alive/dead and male/female), categorization is largely a learned cultural process. The mediating category not only returns us to a precategorization condition, but is also precultural in the sense and to the degree that the particular cultural values attached to one member of the dyad are suppressed. The mediating category is thus "dead but also alive," "male but also female," and so on. That is quite obviously the realm of myth. It is also, but perhaps less obviously to us, who have inherited cultural attitudes that art is "pictures of things," the realm of art. The emblematic character of art, including architecture, lends itself to the unifying and ambiguous nature of the mediating category. If, as Leach maintains, this system "is built into the structure of every mythical system," then it was built into the mythical system of La Galgada. Although its myths cannot be recovered, its art can be, in some measure, and it is clearly an art which was not pictorial in our sense, but rather symbolic and mythic.

Art at La Galgada may be summarized as a set of designs, materials, colors, and techniques, each of which had a semantic character. The unity of time and place in which they are found testifies that they are related parts of a general expression and that an in-

dividual part—a material or a color, for example—can be placed in a new context in which its meaning changes the meaning of the context, as a word changes the meaning of a sentence. That is evident from the repetition of these elements in varied contexts. The square-in-circle design of the ritual chamber, for example, is repeated on the base of a basket (Fig. 160), and the green of a tomb vault is the preferred color for stones set on hairpins. La Galgada's Preceramic art forms an unusually cohesive and interconnected set of elements encouraging the idea that it can be interpreted as a kind of visual code. It was a code played out in the drama of sacred ceremony as it gave form to daily life, and we can read much of its meaning simply by describing the order and placement of works of art.

The ritual chamber came first, with its central firepit. The standard plan at La Galgada was circular with a square floor in the center around the firepit. The rare departures from that plan may reflect nonlocal ideas. The roofed chambers were a place where a small group of people, probably blood relatives, sat closely grouped around the central fire into which offerings, probably mostly of food, were placed. Fire is the most rapid and obvious form of interaction between material, earthly things, and the air, and it has always been understood as the epitome of all transformations. In the chambers the fire was nourished by a subfloor vent from the outside which kept the fire supplied with oxygen. At night in the white interiors the fire provided the only illumination, and there was no decoration on the walls to compete for the attention of the participants. That means the fire was not utilitarian, for heating or cooking, but the focus of attention, for meditation on its nature and significance.

To enter the chambers typically required the participant to climb a short distance upward and step down to enter the chamber.

160. Base of basket from F-12:B-2 with mandala-like design.

This variation in levels was surely part of the program. The interior space was separated from the natural world by its white color, encircling wall, precision of design, and finally by the climbing and descending at the entrance, as if penetrating a barrier. Since the chambers were converted to tombs, the participants were surely aware of the chamber as a potential tomb, its fire to be quenched by a massive stone column, its roof to be converted to stone, the white walls to be partially replaced by dark stone, and the places of the living participants to be taken by the dead, most likely themselves transformed. The chamber door would be sealed with stone, and the entrance to the tomb would be through a narrow shaft capped with a round, flat stone. It is hard to escape the thought of the tombs as cave-like or, by extension, womb-like, with the wrapped bodies of the dead, accompanied by offerings, waiting seed-like to be reborn. The orientation of the majority of the chambers to the silhouette of a colossal feminine form on the western horizon enhances this interpretation. The treatment of the bodies of the dead—their placement in a subterranean shelter, carefully wrapped, accompanied by selected objects—shows that they were considered to be dead but alive, which is to say that they belonged to the realm of myth.

The preparation of the bodies for entombment further supports the idea that they were prepared for rebirth, not oblivion. Particularly those tied into a fetal position appear to be prepared for rebirth. The lost vitality of the body was replenished with things which seemed especially full of life: the hair of the head, cloth made from the bark of a tree. Those two materials are well known ethnologically among South American Indian people as symbols of vitality. The "forest ogres" who are the spirits of natural vitality among the Amazonian peoples are described as especially hairy (Roe 1982:223), and trees, whose skin is barkcloth, are their allies (Goldman 1963:225). The apparent durability of these symbols over several thousand years is less surprising than it might seem at first. These are not arbitrary symbols like an alphabet in which any handy mark can stand for a sound, as long as we all agree on it. Hair, bark, fire, and many of the other things used in La Galgada ceremonial life were symbolic only in the sense that they were used in ways in which it appears they were meant to transfer their natural character to another substance, as the regenerative power and growth of hair and bark might be transferred to the dead body simply by contact, or used in contexts in which some notable characteristic such as color was meant to bring to mind some other object of a similar color. These might be called natural symbols as opposed to conventional or arbitrary symbols, and it is surely that naturalness which accounts for their continual or repeated use in similar ways.

The Preceramic design vocabulary of birds, snakes, and combinations of the two, and of steps up and down, may have taken on many arbitrary, conventional meanings, but fundamentally it is also made up of natural symbols. Birds are distinguishable for their ability to move among the levels of the cosmos, from the ground to the sky, and even to dive beneath the water. Snakes have nearly equal powers to cross cosmic zones, from being at home in the water or in burrows in the earth to resting or hunting in the treetops. The shedding and renewal of a snake's skin may also have been significant. A simple description of the nature of the creature suffices to suggest the kind of ideas these images were meant to convey. They also suggest that spiritual power was equated with or compared to the ability to move from one cosmic level to another, from the underworld to the earth's surface and into the sky. That vertical model for the world is also abundantly recorded by modern ethnology. An interesting example is in the drawings of Yaytrunbiá, a Peruvian Secoya Indian, who shows the terrestrial surface with five levels below and five above, with at the top level of the heavens both a mountain and a tree, in which sits Tatatau, the supreme god, in the form of a bird (Ortiz Rescanière 1975:54).

The stepped-mountain and ladder-like designs from the looped bags share with the bird and snake designs the idea of going up and down. The remodeling of ritual chambers into tombs and the construction of new chambers on top may have had no particular implications to begin with, but in time the vertical relationships must have taken on significance. The great effort to make a green stone vault on C-11:F-5 suggests that the color had meaning, probably in the context of verticality and probably as the color of the sky. That way the subterranean level would share a feature with the heavens, which might be compared with the power attributed to spirits to move bird-like or snake-like between the universal levels.

The iconography of Preceramic art at La Galgada is far from unique. It is similar to a widely shared ancient iconographic system (see Grieder 1982, especially pp. 100–128), so similar that the question of relationship arises. That question is much too large to deal with here, where our focus is on La Galgada itself, but the question reminds us again that contact, not isolation, was basic in La Galgada life.

Although a system of symbols was in widespread use, there was no particular style associated with it. It appeared in a great variety of local and regional styles. Where we find similar styles we must consider the possibilities of contact. It may be true that similar conditions will result in similar styles, though it cannot be satisfactorily demonstrated. But given the natural human propensity to learn from each other and to imitate, contact is by far the most economical explanation for similarities in style. The following discussion will first define the local style of La Galgada as it found expression in textiles. Then some comparisons with other art styles will be made and some conclusions suggested.

THE PRECERAMIC STYLE

Of the various aspects of art, style is the most difficult to analyze because it is complex, multivalent, and deeply embedded in a particular culture. To members of a culture, their style appears entirely natural, the constant elements becoming unnoticed (Arnheim 1964:92–95), though to an outsider they are obvious. "As far as the artists themselves are concerned," Arnheim writes (ibid.), "there seems to be little doubt that they see in their works nothing but the exact equivalent of the object. Their utterances make it quite clear that they think of 'style' simply as a means for obtaining this result." Those constant elements that define a style are taken for granted by the members of the culture and are expressions of attitudes that are also taken for granted. Thus a style reveals a culture's assumptions, though it may be difficult to put them into words, even, or especially, for a member of the culture.

Style is emphasis on particular principles of composition (unity, balance, rhythm, etc.) and on particular elements of art (line, shape, mass, color, etc.). Style is inevitably influenced by the technology in which it is expressed, some materials and techniques having potential for color, or mass, etc., not possible in others. La Galgada's Preceramic art found its most varied expression in textiles, which offered a limited range of possibilities in size, mass, colors, textures, and precision of detail. One of the notable features of the Preceramic textiles is that decorations are always built into the structure of the cloth. That means that decorative units must be planned ahead, not created spontaneously as the work proceeds. The number of threads in a particular color must be counted as they are placed, and that number must be matched or varied to control the design. Counting had to be done in two directions since cloth-construction proceeds across and down (or up). Thus the technology lent itself to a modular style with emphasis on parallel lines, repetitive measurements, and the repetition of design elements. Those features of style would have reduced the number of counts the clothmaker would have had to keep track of. The various techniques suggested different kinds of compositions, looping, for example, encouraging parallel lines horizontally or at a slight angle from the vertical and twining lending itself to larger color fields with vertical extension. The feature of the textile medium which the artists found most resistant to their manipulation was precision of detail, which depended on the fineness of the thread in relation to the size of the motif. They sought greater precision—or to put it in current photographic terminology, finer grain—by using finer thread or increasing the size of the

motif. The constructive nature of the medium thus encouraged a unified, modular style with many parallel lines, serial repetitions, and a tendency toward diagonal symmetry (since construction proceeded across and down) as in the double birds of Figure 139.

If we discount those features which can be attributed to the nature of the medium, what remains is a surprising amount of variety and freedom. Despite the textile structure, the designs are full of curving lines and shapes. They are not mere angular approximations, but truly appear curved, and the cursive quality of shapes is found in many examples (Figs. 123, 132, 141, 143) and was clearly a feature sought by the artists. Considering that fact, it is interesting that there is no art preserved which permitted a freely cursive style, such as drawing or painting on cloth or on walls, both of which came into use in later periods.

The Preceramic style is composed mainly of isolated motifs like vignettes which may repeat but are in essence complete units in themselves. No surviving motif uses more than two colors, although there are examples of the use of more than two colors on individual textiles (T.S. 43, 46, 64, 69, 74, 79, 86, 106). That means that motifs are composed of positive/negative shapes and all transitions are eliminated, as in a silhouette. Unlike more recent silhouettes, there are no implications of mass or space, of overlapping or perspective, and the result is more like a modern logotype. But there are several ways of combining motifs and it appears that composition was the focus of artistic concern, in much the way articulation of the wall masses was in architecture. Figure 126 shows simple repetition of a diamond to make a tight pattern; the stepped-mountain pattern of Figure 124 is similar except the design is reversible in terms both of top and bottom and of figure and ground. The red double birds of Figure 139 repeat an identical motif, but a small serpent, perhaps double-headed, is interpolated into the design. That kind of interpolation of small extra motifs is found also in the elaborate snake design of Figures 128–129. The extras, two of which appear to be birds, were added in different spots in the larger design, giving liveliness and spontaneity to the more regular general pattern. Figure 136 shows another way to vary a repetitive pattern: the birds are all identical, and each register is an identical row of birds alternately upright and inverted, but the spacing varies slightly to break the head-to-head, tail-to-tail pattern. It is clear that the artists could achieve exact repetitions when they wanted to, but that they usually chose to disrupt the regularity of their patterns. Figure 130 shows more variation: the top register is made up of at least two different versions of a design of double birds and a variant adding a serpent head. In the next two registers only three motifs are preserved, but all three are slightly different. This is an unusual example of a design which appears to have been done visually rather than by counting rows and stitches; that would account for the kinds of variations in the motifs, which the artist wanted to look similar and fit tightly together on the textile, but positively did not want to be identical. Another design (Fig. 131) is too incomplete to permit confident discussion, but appears to offer several variations of the serpent subject, with stepped bands added.

A very different kind of design is found in a few later Preceramic textiles which show modular bands. One (T.S. 86, in Fig. 135) was made by weft-twining, a technique which would favor modular design, since showing one warp thread of a particular color at regular intervals would define the module. But another in a similar style was made by looping (T.S. 92, Fig. 138). Modular patterning shows the dominance of com-

position over motif. The individual motif now must fit within the firmly expressed grid of the module, not merely within an implicit composition of registers. In the earlier examples the grid was formed by an agreement of the individual motifs and was an outcome, not a precondition, as it became in the later works. Perhaps there are social implications in that change.

The most remarkable compositions seem to be two poorly preserved fragments from C-10:E-10, Figures 141 and 143, both looped bags with circular and curvilinear designs, the former suggestive of constellations of stars. They hint that there was a Late Preceramic Period in art when that cursive preference noted earlier achieved full expression, based on the technique of looping on a foundation element, the most variable textile technique in use at La Galgada.

COMPARABLE STYLES

There are decorated textile specimens of the same period as La Galgada from Huaca Prieta (Bird 1963; Bird, Hyslop, and Skinner 1985) and from Asia I in the Omas Valley (Engel 1963). The former group is by far the more extensive and offers the more illuminating comparisons, but the main example from Asia I is important.

The most elaborate design found at the Asia I site is a double-headed serpent in a natural brown and white weft-twined cloth (Engel 1963; best reproduction is in Kajitani 1982:10). The motif is about 70 cm long and appears twice on the cloth, which originally measured 78 by 109 cm. The motif is the same as the black-on-red double-headed serpent design on a looped bag at La Galgada, although it has greater detail since it is about ten times larger than the La Galgada example. Color is preserved in the example from Asia I.

The Huaca Prieta textile sample was very large—"4,256 fabrics and pieces of fabrics of all types" (Bird, Hyslop, and Skinner 1985:101), not counting small fragments and scraps. As at La Galgada, only cotton and bast were used, and though a similar range of techniques was known, decorated cloth was apparently almost always made by weft-twining, the only published exception being a double bird made by warp floats in a woven cloth (ibid.: Fig. 139). Twenty representational designs have been published, along with a few geometric decorations. By the standards of La Galgada, the Huaca Prieta artists were advanced: there is a greater variety of motifs, many of them are more complex than any found at La Galgada, and five of the specimens include two or more motifs on the same cloth. At La Galgada one can speak of variations in a motif, or of interpolation of minor elements, but in all cases a single motif dominates each design. Although twining and looping cannot be definitively separated chronologically at La Galgada, a looped blanket and a twined blanket appear in the earliest tomb (F-12: B-2), and in later tombs only twining was used for flat cloth, to be superseded by weaving. That appears to be the sequence at Huaca Prieta (Bird, Hyslop, and Skinner 1985:113, Table 10, 248) and no doubt contributed to Junius Bird's impression that looping was "among mankind's first products using twisted fibers" (ibid.:203). The absence of knotted netting at La Galgada, the dominance of looping for all categories of cloth in the earliest phase, and the appearance of elaborate modular designs in twining only in the last phase of the Preceramic at La Galgada suggest that the decorated looped bags at La Galgada represent an earlier or more primitive stage of art than is known at Huaca Prieta. Given the fact that the radiocarbon series at Huaca Prieta (Bird, Hyslop, and Skinner 1985:53) is older than that at La Galgada, it appears that La Galgada retained the older looping techniques longer than

Huaca Prieta and was much more interested in decoration in looping than the coastal people at Huaca Prieta. La Galgada was slower to develop twining and was late in using the kind of elaborate designs on twined flat cloth so characteristic of Huaca Prieta.

Nevertheless, there are great similarities in style between the textile arts of the two sites, even though the La Galgada examples are looped and the Huaca Prieta ones are twined. Individual motifs are isolated flat color areas vignetted against a plain ground. The diagonal symmetry popular at La Galgada was also common at Huaca Prieta (Bird, Hyslop, and Skinner 1985: Fig. 120), but motifs could break up into their elements at Huaca Prieta to form intricate abstract patterns (ibid.: Fig. 121). In composition Huaca Prieta produced much more complex designs because it brought together several different motifs, found at La Galgada only in the latest Preceramic weft-twined textiles (Fig. 135). But similar compositional rules were accepted. Found in both sets are simple repetition (Bird, Hyslop, and Skinner 1985: Figs. 116, 124), repetition reversed or inverted (ibid.: Fig. 117), and interpolated elements (ibid.: Figs. 119, 131). Different spacing of repeated motifs in registers is not found at Huaca Prieta, where registers of the same motif are spaced the same (ibid.: Fig. 125).

The Preceramic style found in textiles at La Galgada, Huaca Prieta, and Asia I can be considered a single style on the basis of the similarities in the design of motifs, the ways in which they were combined in compositions, and some repetitions of particular motifs, with La Galgada representing an earlier stage of the style and Huaca Prieta (and probably Asia I) a later stage. But specific motifs repeat only in part. The double-headed serpent is definite at Asia I and La Galgada, but uncertain and in very small scale at Huaca Prieta (Bird, Hyslop, and

Skinner 1985: Fig. 101 center stripe, 123). A single-headed snake attached to a rock crab at Huaca Prieta (ibid.: Fig. 131) is like the La Galgada examples. Hooked-beaked birds in profile are common at both sites, and frontal birds with spread wings are found at both, although the motif is actually somewhat different (cf. ibid.: Fig. 111 and this volume, Fig. 136). Doubled birds in diagonal symmetry are duplicated at the two sites, including an angular spiral inside the body and four bars for wings. The Huaca Prieta birds have been called parrots and condors (which have indications of a caruncle which is absent from the more generalized La Galgada birds). Both sites have frontal standing human-like figures, but at La Galgada all the fragmentary figures on the two textiles seem to be alike, whereas at Huaca Prieta there are three different figures on the two textiles, none of them very much like the La Galgada figure type. Both sites have frontal human face or mask designs, although they are different in detail.

La Galgada has spotted (Fig. 141), ladder, and stepped-mountain designs which are not comparable to any Huaca Prieta design. On the other hand, Huaca Prieta has "cats," rock crabs, and shrimp, not found at La Galgada. Since La Galgada is surrounded by mountains and Huaca Prieta is on the ocean beach, these differences may be in part attributable to the influence of local environments. But Huaca Prieta also shows the introduction of new iconography in which monstrous long-haired frontal humans and felines are joined in a single composition (Bird, Hyslop, and Skinner 1985: Fig. 130).

The Preceramic pictorial style found in textiles at La Galgada, Huaca Prieta, and Asia I used serial designs—i.e., designs in which a motif is repeated without axial symmetry—representing mythical subjects—i.e., subjects which bridge natural categories and are thus non-natural. Natural-appearing birds and snakes, in the context of the whole body of work, may be taken as allegorical. Motifs are simple shapes in one flat color, often diagonally symmetrical outward from the center to make double birds or snakes. Technical requirements often dictated geometric shapes, but the style was always as curvilinear and free as the medium (and the simplicity of the style) allowed, often interpolating minor elements or variations in the motifs to enhance freedom. The Preceramic style expresses the equality of varying units and their independence within an accepted order.

THE INITIAL PERIOD STYLE

If there is a consensus about the description of the general style associated with the end of the Preceramic Period, in spite of local variations, the same cannot be said of the Initial Period, which is currently under investigation from various points of view. Although the Initial Period material at La Galgada is not abundant, it contributes to our understanding of the beginning of that period. Currently the main problem is the uncertain relationship between the Initial Period and the Chavín style which has been taken as the virtual definition of the succeeding Early Horizon. That uncertainty leaves the whole period, approximately 2000–200 B.C., in confusion.

Art does not represent a pre-existing set of ideas, but every work of art makes a contribution to a constantly expanding body of ideas. That is especially true in non-literate societies, in which works of pictorial art may be the only permanent material expression of an idea or a theology. A notable example of an ideology whose material expression was in a constantly growing and changing body of art and architecture is the Chavín tradition.

Although there may be natural laws governing the invention and spread of cultural

traits (Grieder 1982), they do not extend pre-
dictability to the nature of the inventions or
the survival and spread of particular traits. If
such laws exist they are still obscured by the
complexity of historical situations. The period 2000–200 B.C. in Peru is represented
by an abundant body of material, most of it
accumulated in recent years, which is only
slowly yielding to our desire for historical
understanding. Studies of the development
of art styles, especially, have revealed that
they are contingent parts of general cultural
history which can be rediscovered by archaeology, but not apprehended by recourse to
logic or natural law. Only archaeological
study has revealed, for example, the early
place of Cerro Sechín (Bischof 1984; Samaniego, Vergara, and Bischof 1985). Archaeological evidence is the basis on which
theoretical constructions rest.

INITIAL PERIOD ART FROM
LA GALGADA

By far the most important Initial Period art is
in the architecture of the temple mounds, especially the North Mound, and the large gallery tombs. Although the ritual setting
changed from small separate units to a unified communal space, and from circular
chambers to rectangular blocks, the outer
walls of the temples remained nearly circular. Comparisons might be made with the
temples of Moxeke and Cerro Sechín in the
Casma Valley, both of which show rounded
corners (Tello 1956:57, 250; Samaniego,
Vergara, and Bischof 1985:167). The general pattern of Moxeke recalls La Galgada,
though Moxeke is larger, is built of conical
adobes, and has architectural relief sculpture
which is entirely absent at La Galgada. The
oldest structure (also of conical adobes) at
Cerro Sechín, which measured about 34 m
square (Samaniego, Vergara, and Bischof
1985:173), was close to the size of the North
Mound and shared its symmetrical plan and

rounded corners. The latest constructions at
La Galgada appear to connect especially to
the sequence of building in the Casma Valley, though they lack the important mural
paintings and reliefs found on the coastal
buildings.

These Initial Period buildings share design
features which distinguish them sharply from
the Preceramic chambers on a mound. Most
important is the unity of the design. In the
Preceramic buildings the separate parts were
the important thing and it was much less significant that they were placed near each
other. It appears that Preceramic chambers
might have been in different positions without seriously affecting their usefulness. In
these Initial Period buildings the parts are
significant only as members of a larger unit
and it is inconceivable that a wing might be
placed in a different position.

Another important feature of the new designs was their symmetry. A design can be
unified but asymmetrical (implying a toler-
ance for variety or multiple centers of authority), but La Galgada, Moxeke, Cerro
Sechín, and many other complexes of this
and later periods show an axially symmetrical U-shaped plan. While the central position in a Preceramic chamber was occupied
by the fire and humans could occupy only
eccentric positions, in the Initial Period
buildings the center could be occupied by a
human, with all non-central positions doubled symmetrically. A person could occupy
the position at the top of the central stairs at
La Galgada and hold the only unique and
unrivaled place, a position of authority which
had no antecedent in Preceramic design.

These features of symmetrical unity are an
aspect of the general centralization of Initial
Period design. It was not incidental that the
Initial Period and Early Horizon produced
some of the most powerful and thorough designs ever achieved. Advanced study during
that period was concerned with how parts re-

late to larger units. There is good reason to think that the basic discoveries were made very early and that many centuries were devoted to working out the implications of those discoveries and perfecting their presentation. The U-shaped temple is a good example, for we see its basic form emerge over a short period at the very outset of the Initial Period at La Galgada. This is not to say that it was invented there, but that the plan was already current and that the basic elements of El Castillo at Chavín de Huantar already existed in prototype.

In other Initial Period work at La Galgada we can see other aspects of the emerging preoccupation with design. The introduction of ceramics defines the period, but that is little more than an archaeological convenience, since ceramics played a minor role in the earlier phases of Initial Period design. There is, for example, no comparison in design quality or expressiveness between the carved shell, to be discussed below, and the pottery. It appears that the soft surface of the clay did not seem at first to offer the precision La Galgada artists and their audience sought and they preferred more resistant materials. In a short time, however, potters began to finish the drying clay with sharp edges where surfaces met and to build more complex forms which allowed the expression of the idea of unified parts. The small jar and lid (Fig. 158), which are still very close to the Preceramic in design, already show the beginnings of Initial Period unification and symmetry. The serpents are spotted and in an angular spiral not unlike Preceramic examples (cf. Fig. 153), but symmetry in Preceramic serpents would require two heads on a single body, forming one motif. In the Initial Period it is typical to use two separate motifs which make parts of a unified design, with separate bodies and their heads facing. Whereas in Preceramic design parts are merged into a single unsegmented form, in

the Initial Period the segments are separate and dominated by a design. The same principles rule the design of the lid, which has separate concentric bands of triangles. The two lids of Preceramic gourd bowls found at Huaca Prieta (Bird 1963:Pl. II) make the difference clear: one has double bird heads, the other a cross, both tightly unified symmetrical motifs, but neither indicates the center; the emphasis remains on the periphery, as in the seating in a firepit chamber.

The ideological unity of the Chavín tradition is manifest in the later history of pottery in which stamped designs appear. Stamping eliminated the variations of incised designs and achieved unprecedented unity of design. Absent at La Galgada, it is found on the sherds scattered on the later Castillo de Cocabal (see map, Fig. 5) and is one of the traits which define the Janabarriu Phase of pottery at Chavín de Huantar, contemporary with John Howland Rowe's Phase D in sculpture (Burger 1984:139–141, 245). Phases in the Chavín style can be defined most successfully on the basis of the tightening of design unity, rather than on the introduction of motifs. It is surely unity rather than efficiency which motivated the use of stamps on pottery instead of freehand incision, since the gain of time would seem inconsiderable.

That conclusion is probably transferable to textiles, where the use of the harness loom may have appealed to Initial Period thinkers primarily as a way to produce cloth which was consistently uniform and unvarying. That it increased efficiency may have been a welcome but incidental outcome. Textiles, like pottery and architecture, developed over a long period traits we associate with the Chavín style. Among seven features identified by William J. Conklin (1978) as textile inventions of the Early Horizon are several which are now known to have come into use earlier. (The Early Horizon, as defined by Rowe [1962b:49] based on the entrance of

Chavín style into the Ica Valley, encompasses only the later phases [D, EF] of the history of Chavín de Huantar.) For example, the use of *Furcraea* fiber and the introduction of heddles are found at La Galgada in the Preceramic and Initial periods, respectively. The Initial Period also produced standard loom widths equal to the Chavín cloths Conklin describes. The situation in textiles correlates exactly with that of the architecture which Conklin adduces, Garagay and Huaca de los Reyes, which show a similar gradual accumulation of architectural forms and decorations over a long period, all of them sharing a strong centralized style and varied monster motifs.

The shell carvings at La Galgada are especially revealing of the rapid transformation of style which appears to us now as a turning point in history. Surely it must have seemed at least equally revolutionary to those who lived through it. None of the technical confusion which is apparent in the textiles can be seen in the shell carvings, which show a confident step-by-step development of a new style. We are fortunate to have good examples of each stage, from both the Preceramic and Initial periods. The small rabbit pendant (Fig. 77) which was found at the neck of the woman extended in D-11:C-3, Floor 24, belongs to the Preceramic Period, while the shell disks, mosaic, beads, and cloth found together at H-11:G-10, Floor 11, are of the Initial Period (Fig. 83).

The rabbit, presumably a pendant though the manner in which it was suspended is not clear, is in a simple, naturalistic style. It was carved from a thick slab of shell by sawing, scraping, and drilling, leaving fairly equal bands in relief to form ears and legs. By the standards of later art, it is under-designed and looks simple and raw. But it is colorful, with a green inlay for the eye and an oblong inlay of pink shell in the back.

Varicolored inlays are shared by two of the shell disks in the Initial Period cache. The smallest (about 2.5 cm in diameter) has four bird heads with alternating pink and green inlaid eyes. The idea of birds in relation to the circle is the message, but they are treated simply, with the circle of the head large enough to hold the inlay, and the beak indicated by a bulge with two saw cuts. The design makes a minimal contribution to the meaning of the work; the beauty of the materials (inlays and a clear white shell circle) becomes important as a statement of the importance of the circle and bird, since the design does not tell the observer that they are important. Among the Preceramic arts which have survived, the textiles show the strongest consciousness of design, and it may be that the progressively stronger design quality of Initial Period and Chavín art shows the adaptation of a design theory worked out first in textiles. The linear and modular character of later styles would support that idea.

The other three shell disks represent later stages of design. One is a plain disk, but the other two represent successive designs of profile heads: one of raptorial birds, the other of fanged monsters. The three ornamented disks all have four profile heads around the rim of the circle, with circular eyes and the mouth indicated. They differ so strongly in style that at first it is easy to overestimate the span of time they represent. Although heads around a disk is a common motif in Chavín-related art (e.g., Rowe 1962a:Figs. 19–21), the relationships among these disks are so close as to suggest a single workshop learning a new style over a period of a few years. The second bird disk (Fig. 83, upper left; Fig. 84, no. 7) differs from the earlier design mainly in its tightly knit structure of bands. The circular pits for the eyes (which follow Preceramic precedents) may have been inlaid originally with red pigment, of which some traces remain. Between the bird heads are divided bands similar to those on a Chavín-related stone cup (ibid.: Fig. 39a).

On the third of the decorated disks (Fig. 83, lower center; Fig. 84, no. 8) at least one of the round eyes was inlaid with a green stone and two others were filled with the same red paste which fills the third modular band. While that feature could be considered to ally the disk with its Preceramic antecedents, the mouth design with two points might be considered to place the design in Phase D, or the middle, of the Chavín style sequence (Rowe 1962: 12). The modular banding in the two later designs aligns them with the Chavín style as originally defined by Rowe, the slight variations in band width placing them early in that style's development (ibid.: 14).

Those two designs are very similar in their basic elements: a complete inner band as margin of the hole, a second band which becomes part of the heads, a third which is filled with red paste and is interrupted by the heads, and a fourth which forms the outer margin and is broken by a division. It is hard to believe that they were not the products of a single workshop, or at least that the design of one was not dependent on the other.

Also present in that cache were two other items, a slate disk 3.37 cm in diameter at widest which seems originally to have had a white shell mosaic frontal monster face glued to it, of which eight of the mosaic pieces survive (Fig. 83, upper right; Fig. 84, nos. 9–10), and a fragmentary figurine of a brown resinous paste, not over 3.0 cm high, with white shell and turquoise inlays to form a monster with U-shaped eyes of white shell. (This item has not been reconstructed.) The stylistically significant element of these two designs is the U-shaped eye, which also sets them apart from the shell disks. That was an especially long-lived feature, found both at Cerro Sechín and in many stone sculptures at Chavín de Huantar. In other words, within

this single cache we find closely related items characteristic of the late Preceramic style, an early Chavín-like style, and a mid-Chavín style. Accepted dating for the Chavín style is 1200–300 B.C. (Rowe 1967: 73). The radiocarbon sample TX-5606, from cloth tied to the carved shells, gave an uncalibrated date range of 1640–1100 B.C., calibrated 2310–910 B.C. The center of those date ranges, 1370 B.C. on the radiocarbon scale and 1610 B.C. on the absolute scale, are more plausible datings than the extremes of the ranges. The close relationship of the three disks implies a much more rapid development of the Chavín style than has been envisioned. One might argue, on the other hand, that the cache is intrusive and represents work of a much later period, early in the first millennium B.C., when the Chavín style was at its climax. Aside from the difficulty of explaining the archaeology, there remains the difficulty of explaining the style of the two disks with bird heads, which would be described as archaistic in that context. Copying a very old style is an easy explanation, but the group of three disks together would oblige us to imagine an artist recreating not a single work in an old style, but a whole historical sequence.

Ancient Peruvian art shows the recurring revival of two opposed traditions: a tradition emphasizing serial designs which has its roots in the Preceramic and a centralized style, usually focusing on anthropomorphic or animal figures, which emerged in the Initial Period. It is hard to distinguish phases and revivals of those Peruvian traditions. The shapes of body parts and other handy clues to a style's period not only are easy for us to learn, but were always easy to learn and imitate, and were subject to several important local variations. The serial style and the centralized style remained in use or were revived over several millennia, as long as an audience accepted their implications as valid.

The U-shaped eye has little value as a phase marker, but it helps explain the underlying motivation of the Initial Period style. It sets certain human, animal, and monster figures apart as belonging to the realm of myth. One La Galgada textile shows frontal faces with U-shaped eyes, which I take to be variations on the same symbol whether angular (as in the shell mosaic) or rounded (as in the textile). (The same range from rounded to angular is common in the sculpture of Chavín de Huantar, what Burger [1986:103] calls an "eccentric eye [i.e., eyes with the irises off-center].") The frontal figure which first appears in Preceramic serial designs at both La Galgada and Huaca Prieta became the focal point of Initial Period centralized designs; the Lanzón at Chavín de Huantar is the premier example. The ultimate center of centralized design, for whom all humans who occupied central positions must have been mere surrogates, appears to have been this supernatural being, who appears in various guises. One of the Huaca Prieta textiles shows figures (the only ones whose heads survive) with large eyes (not yet U-shaped), teeth, and double rows of long hair on the top and sides of the head (Bird, Hyslop, and Skinner 1985:Fig. 130), which should be compared with a stone relief from Chavín de Huantar (Rowe 1962a:Fig. 11). U-shaped eyes are found on the warriors in procession at Cerro Sechín, suggesting that they were mythic beings. Although animals often were represented with U-shaped eyes, human dead and trophy heads, such as we see at Cerro Sechín, never were.

The unifying feature of the new art which appeared around 2000 B.C. was supernaturally sanctioned centralization, with firmly bordered segmentation. The subtext in every design, whether architectural, ceramic, or pictorial, was the new order. Particular iconographic schemes seem to have appeared, been widely copied, gone out of style, and been revived depending on historical circumstances, but there is no mistaking the general trend toward wider and tighter order.

We often feel that life has speeded up in our times, that the pace of change has so quickened that the human consciousness can barely stand the shock. The history of La Galgada suggests that its inhabitants may also have felt that shock of rapid change. Their art and architecture especially show changes at a continually increasing pace, with building going on constantly and the patterns of such basic rituals as burial undergoing constant change. Contacts with outsiders were continuous and expanding and seem to have affected social patterns as much as they affected art. The architectural changes evident at the beginning of the Initial Period show that the imposition and rationalization of a new order occurred over a fairly short period. To judge by the art and architecture, the changes introduced a way of life based on principles which were diametrically opposed to the traditions of the local population. Yet we can see the roots of this revolutionary change throughout the Preceramic history of La Galgada. It is the multifaceted, interlocking surge of changes in which the people of La Galgada participated which we see expressed, dramatized, and insofar as possible, controlled in their architecture, art, and design.

Description of Skeletal Material by Tomb

ROBERT M. MALINA

F-12:B-2

This tomb contained three relatively complete skeletons, one male and two females.

Burial I was a male most likely over fifty years of age. Both right and left pubic symphyses were in Todd phase X (50+ years).

The skull had rather slight flattening in the area of the junction of the sagittal and lambdoidal sutures. Several suture bones were apparent bilaterally in the lateral parts of the lambdoidal suture. The junction of the coronal and sagittal sutures had a slight depression with some overgrowth of bone in the area, and thus a very irregular surface (Fig. 161).

All maxillary teeth were lost antemortem except LM1. There was considerable resorption so that the tooth sockets were not evident. LM1 was worn unevenly well into the dentine (B4+) and had a large cavity.

In the mandibular dentition, the molars on the left side were lost antemortem and there was considerable resorption. LP2 was worn into the dentine, but the wear pattern was uneven, angling toward the distal part of the tooth. LP1 was not worn much, but had a large cavity distally. LC was worn flat like a peg, and LI2 was worn into its root. LI1 and RI2 were lost antemortem and there was much resorption in the area. RC and RP1 were worn well into the dentine, almost to the root. RP2 was also worn deep into the dentine and had only a very thin rim of enamel. RM1 and RM3 were lost ante-

mortem and the area beneath each resorbed. RM2 was present and was worn into the dentine (B3). Although it was assumed that the mandibular third molars were lost antemortem, the molar area appeared rather crowded, perhaps having little room for either M3.

The postcranial skeleton had extensive pathological involvement. The vertebral column is shown in Figure 162. A sixth lumbar vertebra was present. The entire column had angular kyphosis with extensive involvement of T-11, T-12, and all the lumbar vertebrae. T-12 and L-1 were fused. T-11, T-12, L-1, L-2, and L-4 had extensive osteophytosis, while L-3, L-5, and L-6 had osteophytosis of a lesser degree. In contrast, the sacrum was not involved. T-8, T-9, and T-10 had only slight lipping, while C-2 through C-7 and T-1 and T-2 had moderate to severe arthritic involvement.

The left radius and ulna had healed fractures distally with complete bony overgrowth of the ulna styloid process and distal part of the radius (Fig. 163). The right radius and ulna also had severe joint involvement distally, the former more so than the latter. The right radius also had a healed fracture. The right and left radii and ulnae, on the other hand, had no joint involvement proximally, and the two humeri were not involved proximally or distally. The overall appearance of both radii is that of healed Colles' fractures, due to a fall on the hands, the left hand apparently taking the brunt of the trauma.

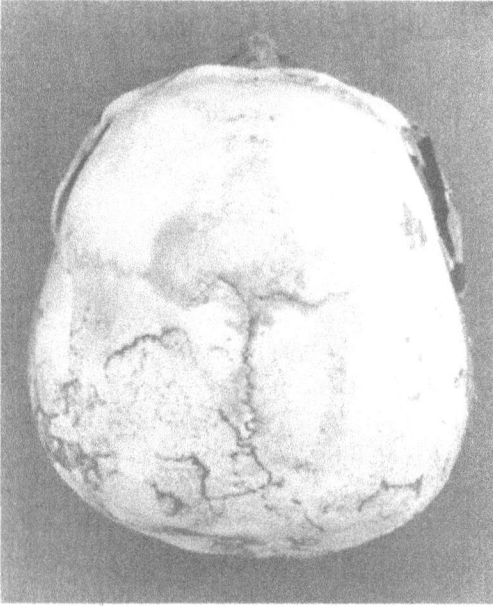

161. Slight depression at the junction of the coronal and sagittal sutures with some overgrowth of bone in this area, F-12: B-2(I). Note also the slight flattening at the junction of the sagittal and lambdoidal sutures.

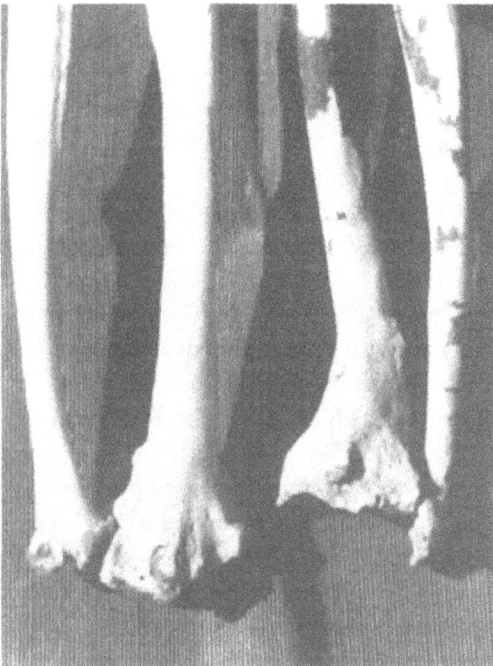

162. Extensive pathological involvement of the vertebral column, F-12: B-2(I). The entire column has angular kyphosis with extensive involvement of thoracic vertebrae T-11 and T-12 and all lumbar vertebrae. Note fusion of T-12 and L-1, and extensive osteophytosis of T-11, T-12, L-1, L-2, and L-4. A sixth lumbar vertebra is present in this individual. The cervical and upper thoracic vertebrae also had moderate to severe arthritic lipping.

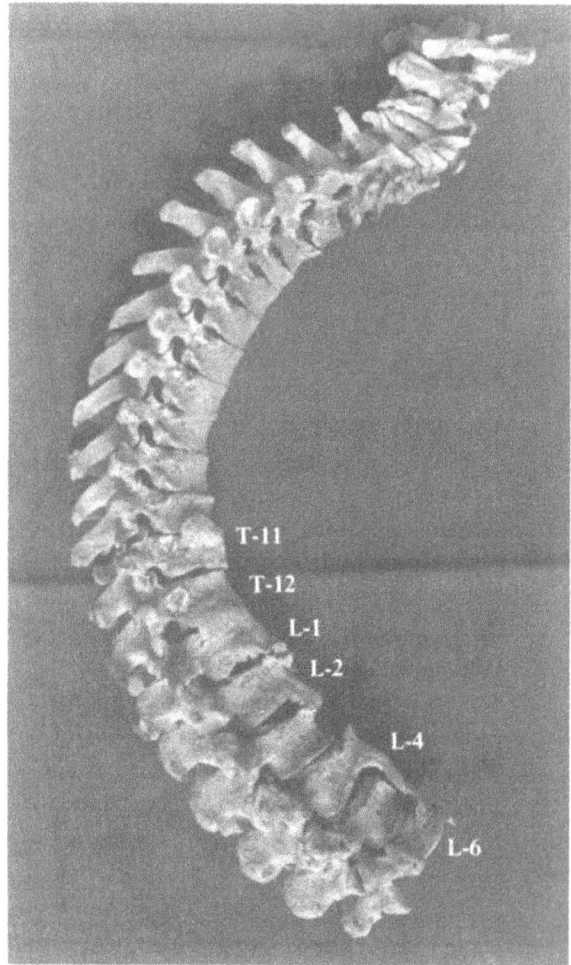

163. Healed Colles' fractures of left radius and ulna with complete bony overgrowth of the ulna styloid process and distal radius, and of the right radius with severe joint involvement, F-12: B-2(I).

The left clavicle also had a healed fracture at its sternal end with considerable bony overgrowth and irregular healing. The left side of the manubrium had involvement in the clavicular notch (Fig. 164). The fracture of the left clavicle would suggest that the trauma of the fall radiated up the left arm, thus involving the left clavicle.

Both the left radius and the left clavicle had lesions at the site of the fractures. This would appear to be indicative of osteomyelitis secondary to the fractures.

The scapulae were not involved with the pathology of the arms and left clavicle. Both did have slight lipping in the glenoid area, and the right scapula had a rather large, elevated bony spur on its costal surface while the left did not. In addition, the inferior angle of the right scapula had a slight downward arthritic growth.

In contrast to the upper extremities, the lower extremities of this male showed little arthritic involvement, except for slight lipping at the knee and ankle. However, the proximal femora had joint involvement with associated changes in the innominate, but the degree of arthritic involvement was less than that in the lower vertebrae.

Burial II was an older female with an estimated age over fifty years. Both pubic symphyseal faces were in Todd phase X.

The skull had no artificial flattening like that of the male in Burial I. The lambdoidal suture had a single, small suture bone bilaterally. All maxillary teeth were lost antemortem except for LI2 and LC. Both were worn deep into their respective roots. The sockets of LP1 and LP2 were not completely resorbed, while extreme resorption occurred in all other areas, more so on the right side than the left. There was evidence of an abscess above RC and RP1.

In the mandibular dentition, LM2, LM1, LP2, RP2, and RM1 were lost antemortem and had their sockets completely resorbed. The mandible was small, so that it does not appear as if there was enough room for M3 on either side. RM2 was not worn so much

164. Healed fracture at the sternal end of the left clavicle, F-12:B-2(I).

(B3+ to B4), but had a large cavity on the buccal side near the gum line. The other remaining teeth were all worn rather evenly into the roots, except for LP1, which was worn unevenly into its dentine and root at a sharp angle. LI1 had an abscess, while RI2 had what appears to be a small cavity.

The postcranial skeleton was delicate and quite porotic. The various joint surfaces had slight arthritic involvement, likely reflecting the normal wear and tear of age. The vertebral column had mild to moderate arthritic involvement. Moderate lipping was evident on the superior and inferior surfaces of C-4, the inferior surface of C-3, and the superior surface of C-5. T-7 through T-9 had slight lipping, while T-1 through T-6 had little if any lipping. T-10 had moderate lipping, while T-11 and T-12 had more lipping. T-11 was most severely involved and appeared as if it was beginning to be compressed on the anterior aspect of the vertebral body, which would suggest an incipient kyphosis. In contrast, L-1, L-2, and L-3 appeared normal, while L-4 and L-5 had only mild lipping. The lipping was most prominent on the superior and inferior surfaces of L-5. The sacrum also showed similar mild arthritic involvement at the junction of L-5.

Burial III was also an older female with an estimated age over fifty years. Both pubic symphyses were in Todd phase X.

The skull showed some flattening in the area of the sagittal and lambdoidal sutures, more so than the other two burials in this tomb. The lambdoidal suture had several small suture bones bilaterally, with a medium-sized Inca bone at the junction with the sagittal suture.

The maxillary dentition was lost antemortem. Resorption was almost complete, more so on the right than on the left side. All the mandibular teeth were lost antemortem with the exception of RI1 and RC. Both were worn into the dentine. There was

an abscess in the area of LC.

The upper-extremity skeleton showed little arthritic involvement. The humeri were quite robust for a female, especially at the deltoid insertion area. Both humeri also appeared somewhat rotated at the area of the deltoid insertion.

The right tibia and fibula had periostitis throughout the length of the bones (Fig. 165). The tibia had two raised lesions (exostoses) on its anterior/medial surface in the distal half of the bone. The distal fibula had extensive periostitis with rather sharp raised lesions. The proximal portions of both bones were not as extensively involved as the distal portions. The knee and ankle had minimal arthritic involvement, although the lateral condyles of the femora had small bony spurs.

The cervical vertebrae had only slight lipping, except C-5 and C-6 which had moderate to severe lipping. Most of the thoracic vertebrae had slight lipping, except for T-10 through T-12. T-11 had more severe lipping and looked slightly compressed. The lower surface of T-10 also had moderately severe lipping. T-12 and the lumbar vertebrae were not involved to the same extent as T-10 and T-11. L-5 did have some moderate lipping on both the superior and inferior surfaces of its body.

I-11:D-5

An isolated mandible was recovered from the fill of this chamber. The symphyseal portion was broken, but the right and left portions of the body were reasonably robust with large teeth (probably male?). RM1, RP2, and RP1 were lost postmortem, while LM1 was lost antemortem. The right and left second molars were just worn into the dentine (B2), while both third molars had enamel polishing (B1). This wear pattern suggested an individual in the twenties. LM3 had a pinhole-sized cavity.

D-11:C-3, FLOOR 24

This tomb contained the remains of four adults, three males and one female, and the probable disintegrated skeleton of an infant.

Burial I was a relatively complete skeleton of an adult male in the mid-thirties. Both pubic symphyses were in Todd phases VI–VII (30–39 years).

The skull was flattened at the junction of the lambdoidal and sagittal sutures, but with no associated depression as observed in several other skulls. The junction of the coronal and sagittal sutures had a depression with some associated overgrowth of bone in the area. The lambdoid suture had several small suture bones.

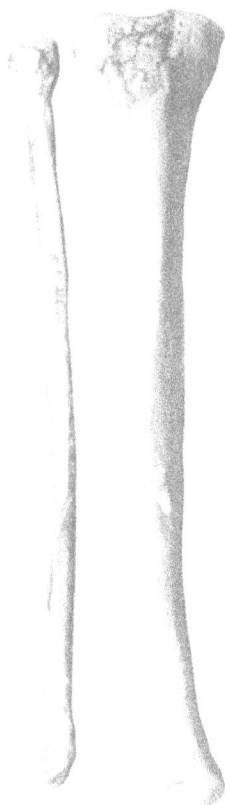

165. Extensive periostitis of the tibia and fibula with raised lesions on the distal portions, F-12: B-2(III).

None of the maxillary dentition was lost antemortem, but LM3, LP2, LP1, both canines, and all incisors were lost postmortem. Maxillary LM2 had a Carabelli's cusp. Of the mandibular dentition only RP1 was lost antemortem. LP1 and the four incisors were lost postmortem. Mandibular LM2 had a deep cavity, while LI2 had a slight abscess. The wear patterns of maxillary molars were consistent with the criteria for the age range thirty-five to forty-five years (B3+). Mandibular M1 and M2 were slightly less worn than the corresponding maxillary molars, but in the same age range. Mandibular M3's were worn the least (B2). The overall pattern of molar wear thus was consistent with the age estimated on the basis of the pubic symphyses.

The postcranial skeleton was that of a reasonably robust individual. The sternal epiphyses of the clavicles were fused, with no evidence of recent union. This was consistent with the age estimate given above. Except for the ulnae, which showed some slight lipping at the olecranon margins, the other long bones had little, if any, arthritic involvement. Of the vertebrae, only L-1 and L-2 showed the beginning of slight arthritic changes, while the others had none.

Burial II was a very fragmentary, incomplete, and porotic skeleton. The postcranial skeleton was that of a rather delicate, older individual, probably a female. This indication was consistent with the skull and mandible, which showed feminine features, i.e., small parietal bossing, weak development of the ridges over the orbits, rather sharp margins of the orbits, moderate mastoids, etc. The skull was flattened and had a depression in the posterior one-third of the sagittal suture as it approached the lambdoidal suture. The coronal suture was not completely closed endocranially and ectocranially. However, the parietal bones were slightly elevated over the suture, especially near its midpoint, indicating overgrowth of the parietals. The sagittal suture was virtually closed over its distal two-thirds, while the lambdoidal suture was open throughout. The latter had a few small suture bones.

The maxillary and mandibular dentition had been lost antemortem and there was severe resorption throughout. The resorption of the maxilla almost reached the base of the nasal aperture. The extreme resorption of the mandible resulted in a thickness of only 8 and 7.5 mm in the right and left molar areas respectively. The right premolar area had a moderate-size abscess. The state of the dentition would seem to suggest an older individual.

None of the long bones were complete, but all were rather delicately constructed. The available joint surfaces showed nothing unusual other than normal wear. The vertebrae were also small and delicate, and incomplete. C-3 and C-4 had moderate to severe lipping, while the lower thoracic and one lumbar vertebrae had severe lipping. Another lumbar vertebra had extremely severe lipping and a partially compressed body. The preceding was a condition similar to that observed in several other individuals in this skeletal series.

Burial III was a reasonably complete skeleton, including the complete innominates, of an adult male. Both pubic symphyses were in Todd phase IX (45–50 years).

The skull had only slight flattening and no depression at the sagittal-lambdoidal junction. The lambdoidal suture had many suture bones, and both auditory meatus had slight exostoses.

The maxillary dentition was lost antemortem, with the exception of RP2. There was considerable resorption on the left side, while several root sockets were still apparent on the right. There was a moderately large abscess in the area of RC and RP1 and a

small abscess above LC. RP2 was worn well into its dentine and almost into the root.

The mandibular dentition was represented by C, P1, P2, and M1 on the right side. All other teeth were lost antemortem with complete resorption in the molar areas. RC was worn to its root, while RP1 and RP2 were worn deep into the dentine. RM1 was worn unevenly into the dentine on the buccal side. There was a large abscess below the incisors and canines on the left side.

The postcranial skeleton was robust with good muscular definition. With the exception of the left radius and proximal femora, the joint surfaces of the long bones had only slight arthritic changes, the type associated with the normal wear of age. The left radius had a healed fracture distally (Fig. 166). It appeared to be a Colles' fracture, the type associated with a fall on the hand. The greater trochanters of both femora had considerable osteophytosis, especially on the right (Fig. 167). All lumbar vertebrae and T-11 and T-12 showed moderate lipping, while the remaining thoracic vertebrae had only minimal involvement. C-3 through C-6 had moderate to severe lipping.

Burial IV was an almost complete, but rather fragmented skeleton of an older male. The innominates were broken, but the sciatic notch and a lack of a deep pre-auricular sulcus indicated that the individual was probably a male. The skull was generally robust, with robust mastoids, moderate supraorbital ridges, rounded orbits with blunt margins, etc., characteristics consistent with the male designation. There were no pubic symphyses present, but the coronal, sagittal, and lambdoidal sutures were closed endocranially and almost closed ectocranially. Along with the dentition (see below), these features suggested an older male, probably fifty years or older.

The skull had moderate flattening with slight depression at the junction of the sagit-

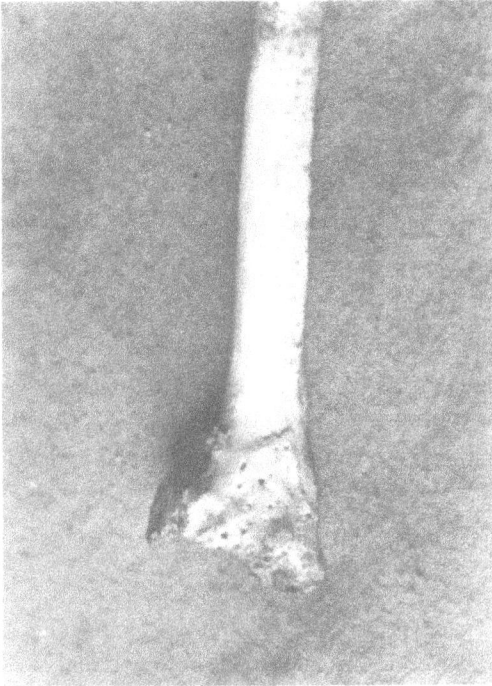

166. Healed Colles' fracture of the left radius, D-11:C-3(III).

tal and lambdoidal sutures (see Fig. 97). The latter had several suture bones, and the left auditory meatus had a slight exostosis which was not present on the right.

The maxillary dentition was lost antemortem with resorption of the sockets being well along. The mandibular dentition was also lost antemortem with the exception of RM1. The latter was worn unevenly well into its dentine. RM2 was lost recently before death. The left molar area was already completely resorbed. The area below RI2, RC, and RP1 had a deep abscess, while that below LI2 and LC had a small abscess.

The postcranial skeleton was largely broken with the exception of several complete long bones. The bones, however, were quite robust. The joint surfaces of the knee had moderate arthritic wear, while the ankle had less. Slight to moderate lipping was evident in the glenoid fossae, distal humeri, and proximal ulnae. These changes most likely represent the normal wear and tear associated with age.

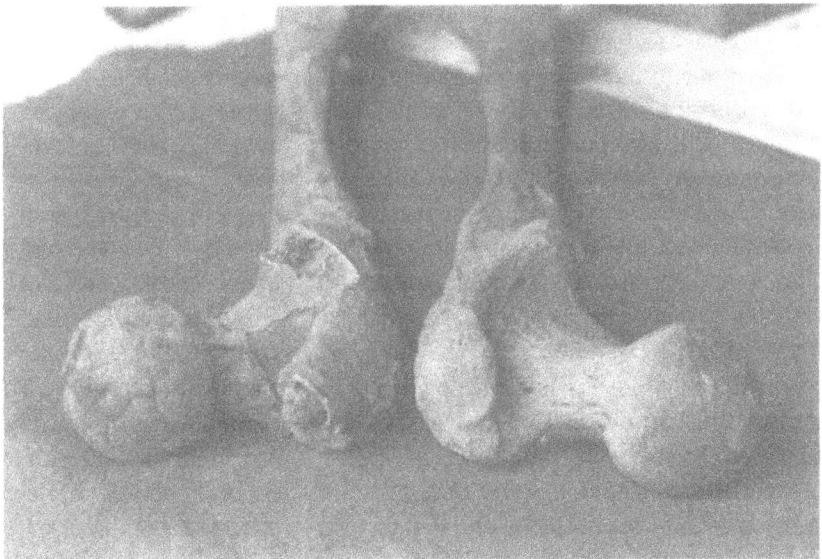

167. Osteophytosis of the greater trochanters of the femora, D-11:C-3(III).

The vertebrae were all rather fragmentary. The sacrum was porotic. Several of the cervical vertebrae were severely lipped; C-4 was somewhat flattened and had severe erosion and pitting. The thoracic vertebrae were all lipped, though not as severely as the lumbar vertebrae. The latter showed severe arthritic changes. One of the lumbar vertebrae was severely compressed. The general features suggest an angular kyphosis as noted in several other individuals, but with more severe lipping.

C-10:E-10

Three relatively complete skeletons of females were found in this tomb.

Burial I was probably in her early thirties. Both right and left pubic symphyseal faces were in Todd phase VI (30–35 years), and the medial epiphyses of both clavicles showed evidence of relatively recent union.

The skull showed artificial flattening with a slight indentation at the junction of the sagittal and lambdoidal sutures (see Fig. 96). The latter had eleven or twelve suture bones.

Of the dentition, maxillary LP2 and LM2 and mandibular RM1 were lost antemortem. The maxillary and mandibular incisors were shoveled, the former more so than the latter. All incisors were worn rather evenly into the dentine, while the three available canines were worn just into the dentine (i.e., the dentine was just visible). All of the premolars showed little wear, while the molars showed uneven wear. Those on the left side (B2, B2+) were worn more than those on the right (B1, B1+).

Maxillary LM3 was peg-shaped with a wrinkled surface, while RM3 appeared to be impacted. Its side was visible in the socket along with a curved root. There was no evidence indicating the presence of the mandibular third molars. Maxillary RP2 was crowded to the lingual side of RM1 and was slightly rotated (Fig. 168).

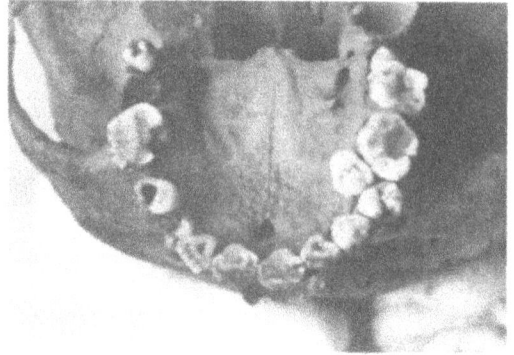

168. Examples of variation in dental morphology, C-10:E-10(I): peg-shaped third molar on the left side, and crowding and rotation of the second premolar to the lingual side of the first molar on the right side.

Cavities were present in both maxillary and mandibular teeth. Among the former, LM1 and LP1 had deep cavities, while among the latter, RM2 had a large cavity into its root.

In contrast to the dentition, the postcranial skeleton was free of pathology. However, a rather complete infant skeleton was found in the vicinity of the pelvis of Burial I. Diaphyseal lengths of the long bones of the upper and lower extremities are shown in Table 23. They had the size of an infant at or near term. Estimated length of the infant, based on the average of estimates using bone-specific equations for each of the long bones (Fazekas and Kosa 1978), was 51.3 cm. It may be postulated, perhaps, that this rather young female and her child died in childbirth.

Burial II was probably over fifty years of age. Both the right and left pubic symphyseal faces showed rarefaction, erosion, and pitting, Todd phase X (50+ years).

The skull showed artificial flattening with a slight depression at the junction of the sagittal and lambdoidal sutures. An Inca bone

Table 23. Diaphyseal Lengths (mm) of the Infant Found in Association with C-10:E-10 (I), with Comparative Data

| Diaphysis | Right | Left | Mean Lengths | | |
			Fetal[a]	B−0.5[b]	B−0.5[c]
Humerus	63.5	63	64.9	67.7	70.5
Radius	50.5	51	51.8	55.1	57.4
Ulna	59	59	59.3	63.7	66.1
Femur	73.5	73	74.3	78.8	82.2
Tibia	64.5	64.5	65.1	69.3	71.6
Fibula	61.5	62	62.3	65.4	68.9

[a] Mean lengths for 10 fetuses, age 10 lunar months (280 days) (Fazeka and Kosa 1978).
[b] Mean lengths for archaic Indian Knoll infants with ages estimated between birth and one-half year. Number of individuals varies with each bone, 37 to 71 (Johnston 1962).
[c] Mean lengths for protohistoric Arikara infants with ages estimated between birth and one-half year. Number of individuals varies with each bone, 37 to 51 (Merchant and Ubelaker 1977).

and several small suture bones were also present.

Both maxillary and mandibular dentition were lost antemortem. All sockets were resorbed. There appeared to be a vestige of a small abscess in the left mandibular premolar area.

The postcranial skeleton was very light and osteoporotic. Arthritic lipping was quite minimal at the hip and knee, slight at the elbow (right ulna more than the left), and slight at the wrist (right radius more than the left). In contrast to the long bones, the thoracic and lumbar vertebrae showed extreme porosity and collapsing of several bodies (Fig. 169). T-10 and T-11 were virtually flat on the anterior aspect, while T-12 was only slightly compressed. L-1 was virtually eroded away and L-2 was slightly compressed. The net result was an angular kyphosis in the thoracolumbar area. The remaining vertebrae were fragmentary and porotic with considerable lipping.

Burial III was about fifty years of age or older. The right pubic symphysis was in Todd phase X (50+ years) while the left was

in Todd phase IX (45–50 years). The skull had some artificial occipital flattening with an indentation at the junction of the sagittal and lambdoidal sutures. The latter had several small suture bones.

The maxillary dentition showed antemortem loss of C, P2, M1, M2, and M3 on the left side with resorption of the sockets. LP1 and LI2 were worn to the root, while LI1 was worn unevenly deep into the dentine. On the right side, C, P2, M1, and M3 were lost antemortem and I2 was lost postmortem. I1 was worn unevenly into the dentine, while P1 was worn to its root. M2 was worn into the dentine (B3), and had a large cavity on its mesial surface adjacent to the area of M1.

The mandibular dentition was represented by all teeth except LM3, LM1, RP1, RM1, RM2, and RM3, which were lost antemortem. There was considerable resorption in the right molar area with no evidence of the sockets remaining. The incisors, canines, and premolars were all worn into the dentine, with more uneven wear on RC and RP2. The uneven wear was characterized by more wear on the lingual surface. The single remaining molar, LM2, was also worn into the dentine (B3).

The postcranial skeleton showed mild arthritic involvement in the distal femora and proximal ulnae and radii. With the exception of T-11 through L-3, the vertebrae showed little if any lipping. T-11 had mild lipping, while T-12 had severe lipping, especially on the lower part of its body. The latter corresponded to the collapsed body of L-1, which also had severe lipping on its upper and lower surfaces. L-2 and L-3 also had severe lipping on the upper part of their bodies. The spinous processes of T-12, L-1, L-2, and L-3 also showed osteophytic involvement. The net result was an angular kyphosis in the area of T-11 through L-3 (Fig. 170), similar to that noted in Burial II (Fig. 169). In addition, the left clavicle had a healed fracture on its lateral end in the area opposite the conoid tubercle. The left scapula had some arthritic lipping in the glenoid cavity, while the acromial process had an arthritic overgrowth. The latter is suggestive of trauma, perhaps related to the fracture on the lateral end of the clavicle.

C-11:F-5

The tomb was accidentally opened by a road crew and subsequently looted in 1975. The skeletal materials were considerably broken and mixed. A minimum estimate suggested the presence of thirteen individuals, eight adults and five subadults. The estimated age and sex distribution is given in Table 24. An inventory of the recovered skeletal materials is presented first for the adults and then for the subadults.

Adults

1. Innominates. Two fragments of adult innominates were recovered. Based on the shape of the sciatic notch, one was a male and the other a female. In addition, two iso-

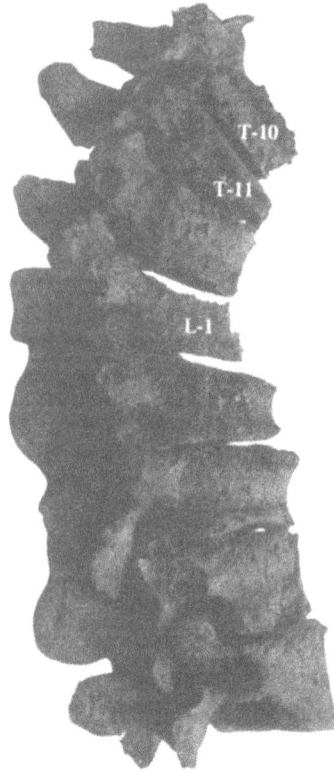

169. Extreme porosity and collapsing of lower thoracic and upper lumbar vertebral bodies resulting in angular kyphosis in this area, C-10: E-10(II). T-10 and T-11 are quite compressed, while L-1 is extremely eroded.

lated fragments of the pubic bone were recovered. They were from different individuals, both apparently adult.

2. Sacra. The sacra of six individuals were represented. Three were rather large and curled under at the coccyx, and were probably males:

a. The first had an associated set of lumbar vertebrae. The sacrum had severe arthritic lipping on its promontory, and the associated vertebrae were also severely lipped. L-3 and L-4 were fused on their spinal surfaces.

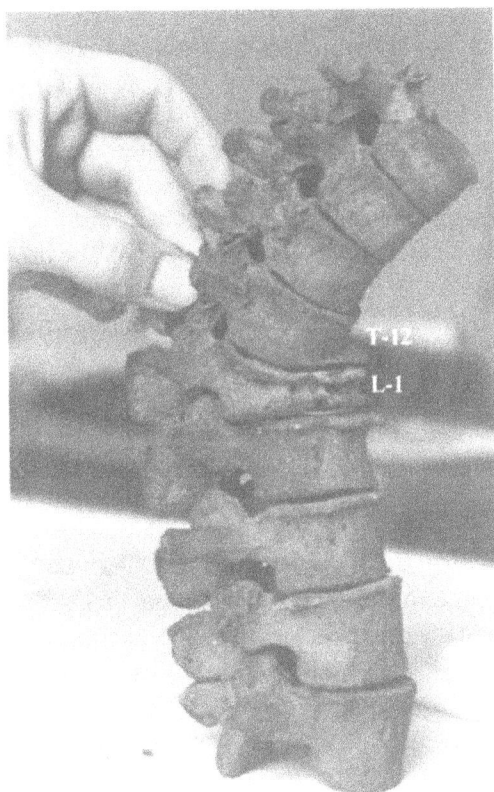

170. Angular kyphosis in the thoracolumbar region, C-10:E-10(III). Severe lipping on the lower aspect of T-12 which corresponds to the collapsed body of L-1.

b. The second was also associated with several lumbar vertebrae. The sacrum and L-5 and L-4 presented nothing unusual, but L-3 had slight to moderate lipping.

c. The third sacrum had no unusual features save for some slight lipping at the junction of L-5.

The remaining three sacra were fragmentary, but adult.

3. Vertebrae. Several vertebrae have already been described above. At recovery, the other vertebrae were sacked by type, making reconstruction difficult.

a. The lumbar vertebrae of at least five adults were present. Four had moderate to severe arthritic lipping, while the fifth had very severe arthritic involvement.

b. The thoracic vertebrae of four individuals were present. Several showed slight to moderate lipping. Two lower thoracic vertebrae, which had matching lumbar vertebrae with moderate to severe lipping, were quite compressed and severely lipped, suggesting perhaps an individual with angular kyphosis.

c. The cervical vertebrae of four individuals were recovered. A dens and atlas from the same individual had severe arthritic involvement. The others had generally slight to moderate lipping.

4. Femora. Two complete left femora and two fragmentary femora, representing four individuals, were recovered. Dimensions of the complete femora as well as other long bones from the looted tomb are given in Chapter 6, Tables 11 and 12. One of the complete femora was quite robust (probable male), while the other had moderate robusticity (probable male).

Table 24. Estimated Number and Age and Sex Distribution of Individuals in Looted Tomb C-11:F-5

Age Group	Sex			
	Male	Female	Uncertain	Total
B–1			1	1
1–4			2	2
5–9			1	1
10–14				0
15–19			1	1
20–29	1	1		2
30–39				0
40–49	2			2
50+	1			1
? (adult)	—	2	1	3
Total	4	3	6	13

5. Tibiae. One pair of complete tibiae, a broken pair, a left tibial shaft, and a fragment of a tibial shaft were recovered and suggested four adults. Both pairs were rather robust and most likely males.

6. Fibulae. Four adults were represented, but only one right fibula was complete and moderately robust (probable male). One of the broken fibulae had a tumor-like exostosis at mid-shaft, 13 mm long, 7 mm wide, and about 5 mm high.

7. Humeri. One robust pair (probable male) and three broken bones were recovered. Of the latter, one fragment was delicate (probable female), while the other two were difficult to place.

8. Radii. The radii of five individuals were clearly present, two males and two females, with one too fragmentary to evaluate. Fragments of the shafts of another two or three individuals were also recovered.

9. Ulnae. The ulnae of four individuals were clearly present. Only one was complete. Fragments of two or three other individuals were also recovered.

Arthritic involvement of the long bones was minimal. One femur had moderate lipping distally, while the single complete ulna had some lipping at the olecranon process.

10. Clavicles. Five pairs of clavicles and three isolated clavicles were recovered. These would indicate the presence of at least eight individuals. Based on overall robustness of development, the clavicles represented three males, three females, and two whose sex could not be ascertained. The medial (sternal) epiphyses of all clavicles were fused, which would place the individuals beyond the mid-to-late-twenties.

11. Scapulae. Three complete scapulae, two left and one right, one robust and two small, from different individuals were recovered. In addition, there were a pair of broken scapulae and a fragment with the glenoid cavity.

12. Calcanei. Twelve adult calcanei, five left and seven right, were recovered. Three clear pairs were apparent.

13. Crania. The cranial materials were extremely fragmentary. At least three adults were represented, but the sex of only one (probable male) could be estimated from a moderately robust mastoid process. The material also included a complete maxilla. All teeth were lost antemortem and the sockets completely resorbed. The area over the right premolars had an abscess.

14. Mandibles. Three adult mandibles, two complete and one almost complete, were included.

a. The first was robust with a square symphysis. Its bigonial diameter was 105 mm (probable male). The central incisors and the right and left premolars and molars were lost antemortem. There was near complete resorption of the root sockets in these areas. All this would suggest an older individual. There were abscesses under the roots of the canines and lateral incisors on each side.

b. The second was moderately robust with a rounded symphysis (probable female). It was broken at the gonial areas. The premolars, except for RP1, canines, and incisors were lost postmortem. RP1 and the right and left M1 and M2 were worn just into the dentine (B2), suggesting an individual in the age range twenty-five to thirty-five years. There was no sign of M3 on either side nor did there appear to be sufficient room for them.

c. The third was robust with a square symphysis and bigonial diameter of 103 mm (probable male). All teeth except LM1 and LP1 were lost postmortem. The roots of M3 on both sides were shallow. M1 was worn unevenly into the dentine (B2). Overall, these features suggest an individual between twenty-five and thirty-five years of age.

Subadults

The subadult skeletal materials were apparently recovered and stored in separate containers, sometimes as specific individuals, but more often as individual specimens.

1. A more or less complete long bone skeleton of a young child. Only one diaphysis, however, was complete, right radius, 75 mm. Using the criteria indicated in Chapter 6, the child falls into the age range 0.5–1.5 years.

2. Broken diaphyses of a humerus, ulna, femur, and tibia of a young child, most likely older than the child described above, i.e., probably under five years of age.

3. Two immature innominates, including each of the separate elements. Maximum widths across the ilia were 72 mm and 101 mm, corresponding to youngsters 2.5–3.5 years and 6.5–7.5 years of age respectively. A third innominate was represented by a part of an ilium. It was smaller than the others and probably represents an infant.

4. An immature pair of scapular bodies and an immature left scapular body.

5. A loose ephiphysis of a humeral head. The three ephiphyses of the proximal end of the humerus usually coalesce into a single center by about the sixth year, which does not fuse with the shaft until the late teens.

6. A pair of ulnae and a broken radius from the same individual. The ulnae had evidence of recent but incomplete union distally. The radius was broken distally, but the head was already united. These features would place the individual in the late teens.

7. A tibial diaphysis, 155 mm in length. This length corresponds to that of a child 2.5–3.5 years old, using the criteria of Merchant and Ubelaker (1977) or 3.5–4.5 years old, using the criteria of Johnston (1962).

8. A broken tibial diaphysis and a broken right femur from different young individuals. The circumferences, texture, and size would suggest children under ten years of age.

9. Diaphyseal fragments, apparently from a late fetus or a newborn infant.

10. Immature vertebrae from at least three individuals.

11. A calcaneus with a line of recent union at its epiphysis, which would suggest an individual in the late teens.

12. Fragments of the parietal and frontal bones of an infant skull.

13. Fragments of broken skulls of at least three individuals. One occipital bone had its lateral parts already fused to the basilar portion of the occipital bone, while a second did not. The third individual was represented by an isolated basilar part of the occipital. It was smaller than the two above, and the lateral parts were not yet united to the basilar portion. The lateral portions of the occipital unite with the basilar portion after the fourth or fifth year. This would place one child above five or six years, and the other two below that age.

14. Four mandibles were recovered.

a. A complete mandible with lm2, lm1, and rm1. All other teeth were lost postmortem. lm1 was not yet erupted, but it could be seen in its crypt. The permanent central incisors were visible in their crypts. These features suggest a child under six years of age, probably closer to five.

b. A partial mandible (left side broken off) with all deciduous teeth lost postmortem: rm1 was visible in its crypt and had a well-formed crown. The crown of rm2 was also formed, but not as far along as rm1. These features would suggest a child between three and four years of age.

c. A front end of the mandible with the deciduous incisors and canines lost postmortem. The crowns of the permanent central incisors were visible in the crypts, placing this child probably under two years of age.

d. The right side of a mandible with no teeth. It probably represents an infant.

C-10:I-10

This tomb contained the burned remains of four individuals.

1. The first was represented by skull fragments with a more or less complete upper face (orbits and frontal bone), the right and left temporal bones, a section of the occipital, the maxilla, and a fragment of the body of the mandible. Overall, the architecture suggested an adult female, i.e., slight orbital ridges, small mastoids, small size, and general lack of robustness. The few sutures present indicated closure endocranially and a fine line of suture activity ectocranially.

The associated long bones (broken right humerus, tibial shaft) were likewise not robust in development. The vertical and transverse diameters of the head of the right humerus were 35.5 and 33.5 mm respectively. Both values were well within the female range of this series (see Chapter 6, Tables 10 and 12).

The maxillary dentition was lost antemortem and most of the tooth sockets were resorbed. There was an abscess over the left premolar area. Among the mandibular dentition, there were small root sockets and some resorption for LP1 and the four incisors, indicating antemortem loss. There was an abscess below the right incisors. LC and LP2 were lost postmortem and were not recovered. The left mandibular molars were lost antemortem and the area showed much resorption.

2. The second individual was represented by the completely fragmented skull of an adult female. The bones were generally thin and badly broken. The mastoid process of a broken temporal was small and clearly not robust in development. The few sutures available indicated complete closure endocranially. Ectocranially, there was a fine line of suture activity at the junction of coronal and sagittal sutures, and there was some

obliteration of the sagittal suture as the lambdoidal junction was approached. The cranial fragments suggested some flattening in this area with a slight depression at the suture junction.

The left part of the maxilla included the sockets of the incisors, the canine, and the first premolar, all of which were lost postmortem. P2 and M1 were lost antemortem and the area was extensively resorbed. A fragment of the right side of the mandible included the sockets of P2, M1, and M3, all of which were lost postmortem. M2 was lost antemortem and the area was healed (resorbed). A fragment of the left side of the mandible included the socket for P2, which was lost postmortem. M1 through M3 were lost antemortem and the area was completely resorbed.

3. The third individual was represented by the front end of a mandible. The fragment was rather robust and rather square, possibly suggesting an adult male. LI1, RI1, RI2, RC, RP1, and RP2 were lost antemortem, but the sockets were still present. The area leading to RM1, though broken, suggested that it was lost antemortem and the socket resorbed. There was a small abscess below LI1.

4. The fourth individual was represented by a small section of the symphyseal area of a mandible. It was rounded and very delicate, suggesting an adult female. The area of the right incisors and canine had considerable resorption, and a depression beneath the incisors appeared to be the vestige of a deep abscess.

C-12:D-1

This was a collapsed tomb. Some of the skeletal material was mixed in situ and some was not recovered. Nevertheless, the materials indicated the presence of six or seven adults and four or five children. The estimate was based primarily on the number of skulls with corroborating evidence from innominates and long bones, and on the archaeologist's field of notes.

Burial I was a severely fragmented skull, a robust mandible, and a variety of postcranial elements. The innominates, though broken, had male features. The general characteristics of the cranial bones, the mandible, and the long bones were consistent with the male designation. One of the pubic symphyses, though broken, appeared to be in Todd phase VIII (39–44 years).

The maxilla was not present. Mandibular dentition indicated the following: The left and right molars with the exception of RM2 were lost antemortem and the sockets were resorbed. The four premolars were worn into the dentine. The canines and lateral incisors were lost postmortem and not recovered. The central incisors were lost antemortem. RM2 was well worn into its dentine (B4).

The long bones showed little or only slight lipping at the joint surfaces. However, the lumbar and lower thoracic vertebrae had severe lipping. No cervical vertebrae were

The long bones showed little or only slight lipping at the joint surfaces. However, the lumbar and lower thoracic vertebrae had severe lipping, and no cervical vertebrae were recovered.

Burial II was a badly broken cranium, mandible, and several postcranial bones from an older female. Both mastoid processes were small. There was a moderate ridge over the nasal area, and the orbits, though broken, seemed to be small. The overall lack of robusticity would seem to suggest an adult female. An innominate fragment found with the skull also appeared to be that of a female (sciatic notch).

Although the cranial bones were broken, the coronal, sagittal, and lambdoidal sutures of the right parietal were closed endocranially. Ectocranially, they were not completely closed. Several suture bones were

evident in the lambdoidal suture.

The front half of the maxilla was completely edentulous with extensive resorption. There were abscesses over the left C/P1 area and the right I2/C area. The mandible was completely edentulous, also with considerable resorption. The mandibular body was reasonably robust, for a female, but this feature appeared consistent with the moderate development of the ridge over the nasal area.

Burial III included a complete skull and mandible and a badly broken postcranial skeleton of a male. The skull had moderate supraorbital ridges, a robust occiput, and very robust mastoid processes (Fig. 171). The postcranial materials associated with this skull included a broken right innominate and a robust femur (see Fig. 73). The shape of the sciatic notch was characteristically male. All other long bones were broken and rather robust. The cervical and thoracic vertebrae had mild lipping, and of the two lumbar vertebrae recovered, one had moderate lipping while the other did not.

The skull had slight flattening but no depression as noted in several others. The sutures were closed endocranially, while they were actively closing ectocranially. The lambdoidal suture had large suture bones bilaterally. The area of the junction of the sagittal and lambdoidal sutures appeared porous with many tiny, pinpoint-like holes and some lesions. These features would seem to suggest an inflammatory condition.

All the maxillary teeth were lost antemortem with considerable resorption in the molar areas. There was an abscess above RC and RP1. Only the roots of LI2, RI2, and RC and an unevenly worn RP2 were present in the mandibular dentition. The latter was worn deep into the dentine. All other mandibular teeth were lost antemortem with extensive resorption in the molar and central incisor areas. There was an abscess under LC and LP1. The overall state of the denti-

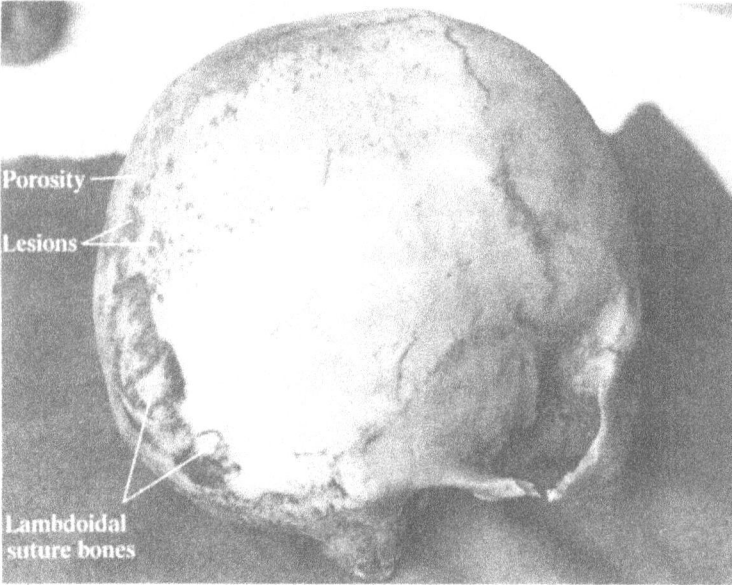

171. Skull of a male with extremely robust mastoid processes, C-12:D-1(III). Slight lambdoidal flattening with relatively large bones in the lambdoidal suture. Extreme porosity in the area of the junction of the sagittal and lambdoidal sutures with several lesions suggestive of an inflammatory condition.

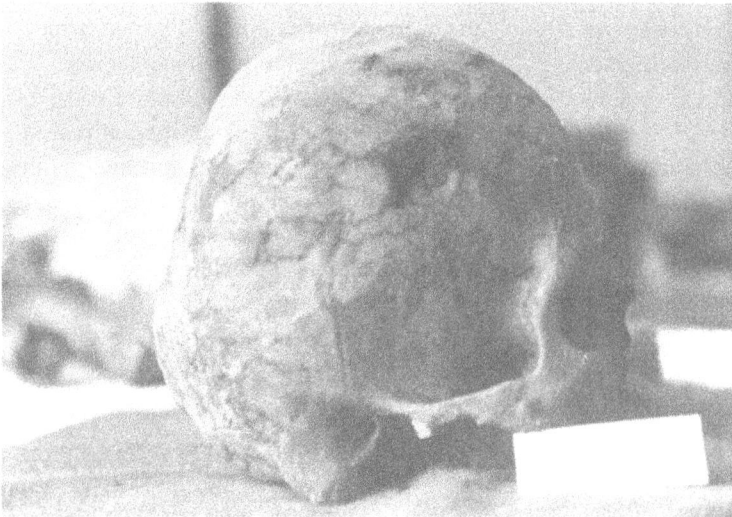

172. A moderately robust female with considerable lambdoidal flattening, but without any depression at the junction of the sagittal and lambdoidal sutures, C-12:D-1(V).

tion would seem to suggest an individual fifty years or more of age.

Burial IV included a very fragmented skull of an adult female. The frontal bone had rather small rounded orbits. The other bones were quite broken, but generally not robust, thus suggesting a female. All teeth were lost from the broken left maxilla. The area of the incisors, canine, and premolars was completely resorbed. The socket of M1 was almost completely resorbed, while only two root sockets of M2 remained.

The postcranial bones associated with the fragmented skull included a pair of broken innominates. The right innominate had a wide sciatic notch, which would indicate a female, and thus corroborate the cranial features. The other bones generally lacked robustness. Only two measurements were possible. The vertical diameter of the left femoral head was 37.5 mm, while a broken right femoral head was 39 mm. Both values were in the female range for this skeletal series (see Chapter 6, Tables 10 and 11). The broken right humerus had a medium-sized perforated septum.

The distal part of the radius (side ?) had considerable arthritic changes, while the left femoral head had mild lipping. The vertebrae were really fragmentary and porotic, and included only one complete cervical, one complete thoracic, and two complete lumbar vertebrae. The cervical vertebra was either C-3 or C-4, and was severely lipped. The thoracic vertebra was T-11 or T-12 and also was severely lipped. One of the lumbar vertebra was severely lipped, while the other was severely compressed and flattened. The general condition of the vertebrae, especially the thoracic and lumbar, was indicative of pathological involvement similar to the angular kyphoses noted in other burials. Overall, the skeleton appeared to be that of an older female.

Burial V was represented by only a complete skull and mandible. The general features of the skull (Fig. 172) were those of a female, though moderately robust: rounded orbits with sharp margins, slight development of the supraorbital ridges, moderate mastoids and occipital, some parietal bossing, and posterior parts of the zygomatic processes that just reach the external auditory meatus. The dimensions of the skull (see Chapter 6, Table 9) were generally large compared to other females in this skeletal series, but were consistent with a moderately robust female. The cultural artifacts found in association with the skull (see Fig. 75) were also consistent with the sex designation. The skull had considerable flattening, but no depression at the junction of the sagittal and lambdoidal suture. The coronal, sagittal, and lambdoidal sutures were largely obliterated.

The maxillary dentition was represented by only RC and LP1, which were both worn into the dentine. LC and LP2 were lost postmortem. The four incisors, all molars, RP1, and RP2 were lost antemortem. The right molar area and the incisor area were extensively resorbed. The left molar area was also completely resorbed except for a single root socket of LM1. There was evidence of an abscess in the buccal aspects of LM1.

The mandible was moderately robust. It was completely edentulous, with considerable resorption. The LM1, LM3, and RC areas had large abscesses.

Burial VI represented the badly broken remains of an adult male (sciatic notch). A single pubic symphysis was in Todd phase X (50+ years). The vertical diameters of the right and left femoral heads were each 43 mm., within the male range for this skeletal series (see Chapter 6, Tables 10 and 11). The greater trochanter was also reasonably robust, and the right humerus had a small perforated septum.

Burial VII was also a badly fragmented postcranial skeleton. The long bones were generally not robust, and all were incomplete. The vertical diameter of a loose femoral head was 32 mm, which is in the female range. The vertical diameter of the right humeral head was 37 mm, which is on the large side of the female range in this skeletal series. The fragments of long bones represented in this burial suggest an adult female; it is likely that they belong to one or more of the females already described above.

In addition to the adult materials, the remains of four or five children were recovered from the collapsed tomb.

A. The first child was represented by a reasonably complete young skeleton, including the skull fragments but no complete bones, a section of the right mandible with no teeth yet erupted, several diaphyses, a scapula, an ilium, and many epiphyses. Diaphyseal lengths are given in Table 25. They appear to be those of an infant from birth to six months, probably closer to birth.

B. The second child was represented by a temporal bone, the right mandibular body with no teeth erupted, an ilium, and a part of a femoral diaphysis. They appeared to be the remains of a very young infant.

C. A pair of isolated humeri may represent another child. One was complete and had a length of 70.5 mm. This length would place the infant in the birth-to-six-months age range (see Table 25). It is likely that the humeri may be associated with child B described above.

D. Another child was represented by a section of the right mandibular body: rm1 was lost postmortem, while rc was represented only by its root, as the crown was broken off postmortem; rm2 was visible in its crypt, perhaps approaching eruption since its bone covering was worn away. These features would place the child at about eighteen months of age.

Table 25. Diaphyseal Lengths (mm) of an Infant Recovered from Tomb C-12:D-1

Diaphysis	*Right*	*Left*
Humerus	67	67
Radius	53	54
Ulna		61
Femur		79.5
Tibia	69	69
Fibula	64.5	

Note: See Table 23 for comparative data.

E. The last child was represented by a rather small, delicate right mandibular fragment. C, P1, P2, M1, and M2 were lost postmortem. It appeared that M2 may have been only recently erupted. If this is so, the child was probably between ten and fourteen years of age.

C-11:E-8

This tomb contained an adult male about forty years of age. (A woman and child present in 1976 were missing in 1978 and are not included in this skeletal analysis.) The skeleton was complete except for the skull. The pubic symphyses were in Todd phases VII (35–39) to VIII (39–44). The long bones were reasonably robust with good muscular definition. There was no evidence of arthritic lipping at the joint surfaces of the shoulder, knee, and ankle, and only slight changes in the elbow. The lumbar vertebrae showed no arthritic lipping, and only the lower thoracic vertebrae (T-10, T-11, T-12) had moderate lipping. T-1, T-2, C-5, C-6, and C-7 had mild to moderate arthritic involvement. C-3 had erosion of the body with pitting and some severe lipping, while C-4 and the base of C-2 (axis) had some similar involvement.

The mandible associated with the skeleton was generally squarish in appearance, with a bigonial breadth of 91 mm. All teeth were lost antemortem, and there was an extreme degree of resorption, especially in the left molar area.

E-11:J-7

This tomb was looted in 1978 and the skeletal materials were quite mixed. It was a large tomb with three chambers. A minimum estimate suggested the presence of twenty-seven individuals, twelve subadults and fifteen adults. The estimated age and sex distribution is given in Table 26. An inventory of the recovered skeletal materials is presented first for the adults (including young adults) and then for the subadults.

Adults

1. Innominates. All of the innominates were broken. There were nine right (six female, three male) and five left (four female, one male) innominates. Only two partial pubic symphyseal faces were recovered, and both were in Todd phase X (50+ years). Only one pair could be clearly matched (female).

2. Femora. There were fifteen right (five complete) and fifteen left (three complete) femora. Estimated sex was based on overall robusticity and muscular definition. Selected dimensions of the bones that could be measured are given in Chapter 6, Table 11. The remaining femora (broken) included one delicate, very porotic pair which had severe arthritic involvement of the femoral neck (probably female); eight right femora, seven of which were not really robust or broad-shafted; ten left femora, three of which were robust while the other seven were clearly not robust; and two rather delicate femoral heads, having vertical diameters of 36 and 34 mm respectively (well within the female range for this skeletal series; see Chapter 6, Table 11). Note that the isolated femoral heads are most likely associated with the fragmentary

femoral shafts. With the exception of the female with arthritic involvement in the femoral neck (above), the remaining femora had no pathologies and little if any arthritic lipping.

3. Tibiae. There were eleven right tibiae (seven complete) and nine left tibiae (two complete). Estimated sex and maximal morphological lengths of the completed bones are given in Chapter 6, Table 11. The four remaining right tibial shafts included three that were rather delicate and one that was too fragmentary to evaluate. Of the remaining seven left tibiae, three were clearly delicately built, three were somewhat robust, and the seventh is described in Table 11, note *b*. None of the tibiae showed significant arthritic changes either proximally or distally.

4. Fibulae. Six right and eight left fibulae and seven fragmentary shafts for which the side could not be ascertained were recovered. However, only two were complete, a right (322 mm maximum length) and a left (319 mm). A distal portion of a right fibula had a line of recent union. Given the frag-

Table 26. Estimated Number and Age and Sex Distribution of Individuals in Looted Tomb E-11:J-7

Age Group	Sex			
	Male	Female	Uncertain	Total
B–1			2	2
1–4			1	1
5–9			2	2
10–14			3	3
15–19			4	4
20–29	1	2		3
30–39	1	2		3
40–49	2	1	1	4
50+			2	2
? (adult)	—	1	2	3
Total	4	6	17	27

mentary nature of the materials, no effort was made to estimate the sex of the individuals. One left fibula had a healed fracture distally; it also had considerable overgrowth of bone at the fracture site. Two left fibulae also had slight arthritic involvement distally. Otherwise, the remaining bones showed no pathologies.

5. Humeri. There were eight right (three complete) and fifteen left (seven complete) humeri. Estimated sex and dimensions of the complete bones are given in Chapter 6, Table 12. Sex estimation was based on overall robusticity, especially at the deltoid insertion. Of the remaining right humeri, two were robust, two were too incomplete to evaluate, and one was represented only by the head. The latter had vertical and transverse diameters of 36 and 35 mm respectively. Of the remaining eight left humeri, four were robust and four were delicate. Two of the more robust left humeri had some arthritic lipping distally, while the others showed no arthritic or pathological involvement. Two of twelve left distal sections and one of nine right distal sections had perforated septa.

eight left (five complete) radii were recovered. The maximum lengths of the complete bones are given in Chapter 6, Table 12. Two complete radii, which had recently united distally, had a corresponding member among the incomplete bones. An additional broken radius had a line of recent union distally. As a rule, neither the complete nor the broken radii were clearly robust, so that assessment of sex was difficult. There were no pathologies, and only one radius had some arthritic lipping proximally.

7. Ulnae. There were ten right (three complete) and five left (three complete) ulnae. Lengths of the complete bones are given in Table 12 in Chapter 6. In addition, there was an ulnar fragment whose side could not be assessed. One of the ulnae was clearly ro-

bust, while the others were moderately robust to delicate, making assessment of sex difficult. The three complete left ulnae had slight lipping at the olecranon margins, while five of the nine ulnae which included the olecranon processes had only slight to moderate lipping at the olecranon margins. Otherwise, there were no other pathologies.

8. Scapulae. Seven right and five left scapulae, all of which were broken to some extent, were recovered. Three rights and lefts matched closely and probably represented three individuals. One of the pairs was large and quite robust (probably male), while the other two pairs were rather small and delicate (probably females). One of the delicate pairs was that of a young adult. The ephiphyses of the acromial process and the inferior angle were lacking, while the glenoid cavity and coracoid process were already adult. Of the remaining scapular fragments, one right was robust (male?) and two (a right and a left) were rather delicate (females?). The others were intermediate in development or too incomplete to evaluate. No pathologies were evident.

9. Clavicles. Ten clavicles were recovered, three complete left, one complete right, three broken right, and three shaft fragments. The available sternal ends had complete union of the sternal epiphysis. Two of the complete clavicles were quite robust (probably males), while the others were rather slender and delicate (probably females). The others were intermediate in development or too fragmentary to evaluate.

10. Vertebrae. The vertebrae were quite mixed and many were broken during recovery from the looted tomb. Hence, it was difficult to estimate the number of individuals. The vertebrae showed patterns of wear generally consistent with the long bones, i.e., little or mild arthritic lipping. Nevertheless, several showed moderate and/or severe arthritic involvement. These were primarily

the lower thoracic and lumbar vertebrae, and occasionally a cervical vertebra. None of the vertebrae had compressed bodies as observed in several of the more complete burials.

11. Crania. One complete skull and parts of six crania were recovered.

a. The complete skull was probably that of a male. Dimensions are given in Chapter 6, Table 9. It had moderate supraorbital ridges, semiblunt orbital margins, robust mastoids, and clear muscular definition on the occipital. It had considerable flattening, a slight depression at the junction of the sagittal and lambdoidal sutures, and some asymmetry. The sutures were closed endocranially and largely closed ectocranially. Most of the maxillary dentition was lost postmortem. Only the right and left third molars were lost antemortem. RM2 was worn deep into the dentine (B4), almost reaching the root. This degree of wear would suggest an individual in the late forties or early fifties. LM2 was somewhat more worn (B4+), and had a deep cavity into its root. RP1 also had a cavity.

The top of the skull had numerous small, porous holes in the area from the coronal to the lambdoidal sutures (Fig. 173). In addition, there were four relatively large lesions on the parietal and frontal bones, suggesting an inflammatory condition.

b. A broken skull, including both parietals, the frontal, and the occipital bones of an adult, were recovered. Sex of the individual was not clear from the bones available. However, the estimated cranial length (142 mm) was rather small compared to that of other adults in this skeletal series. The skull had considerable flattening of the occipital. Ectocranially, the coronal suture was closed over most of its length, the sagittal suture was almost closed except for its central portion, and the lambdoidal suture was actively closing, though not yet completed. Endocranially, all sutures were closed.

c. A fragmentary skull, including the frontal and temporal bones, appeared to be that of an adult male. There was a moderate ridge especially over nasion, one complete orbit with more rounded/blunt margins, and a moderate mastoid process. The associated left maxilla had no teeth. It appeared that the coronal suture was actively closing ectocranially, but was not that far along in the process.

d. Another individual was represented by a fragment of another left maxilla. No teeth were present and there was considerable resorption of the molar area. The area above P2 had an abscess. The degree of resorption suggests an older individual.

e. Another individual was represented by a more or less complete maxilla. Only one tooth (RM2) was lost antemortem. LM1 was represented by its roots; RM1 and LP1 had their crowns broken off; all others were lost postmortem.

f. Other cranial elements included a parietal and an occipital from an adult and fragments of two other adult parietals.

12. Mandibles. There were five complete and eight broken mandibles. When molars were present, molar wear was used to estimate age of the individual. The complete mandibles are described first.

a. A rather robust body and square front suggest a probable male. Bigonial breadth was 103 mm, well within the male range for this skeletal series (see Chapter 6, Table 9). The incisors, canines, and premolars, except for RP2, were lost postmortem. LM2 and the three right molars were lost antemortem. The sockets of the right molar area were completely resorbed. The wear of LM3, LM1, and RP2 was relatively slight, not yet into the dentine (B1). This would suggest a relatively young adult in the twenties. However, the loss and resorption of the other molars may possibly indicate an older individual. LM3 had a small, pinhead-sized cavity,

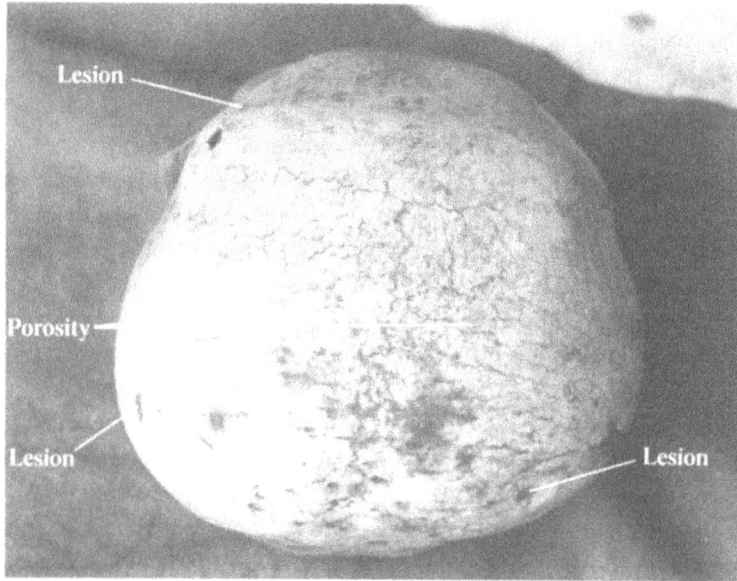

173. A male with considerable lambdoidal flattening, slight depression at the junction of the sagittal and lambdoidal sutures, and asymmetrical shape, from E-11:J-7. Extreme porosity in the area from the coronal to the lambdoidal sutures, with four relatively large lesions on the parietal and frontal bones suggesting an inflammatory condition.

while LM2 had a large abscess.

b. A moderately robust body but somewhat rounded symphyseal region (almost blunt, semipointed in shape) characterize this mandible. Bigonial breadth was 96 mm. These features suggest a possible female. LM1, LM3, and RM1 through RM3 were lost antemortem. All other teeth except LC and RP2 were lost postmortem. The former was broken and the latter was worn to its roots. The right molar area had considerable resorption, though not yet complete elimination of the sockets. LM3 had a large abscess on its lingual side. The overall pattern of tooth loss and wear suggests an older individual than that described above, probably in the thirties or forties.

c. A small mandible with a rounded chin suggests a female. Bigonial breadth was 82 mm. All teeth were lost postmortem except LM3, LM1, and RM3. LM3 had a deep abscess, while LM1 and RM3 had a degree of wear characteristic of a young adult in the early to mid-twenties (B1).

d. A small, delicate mandible with a rounded symphyseal region indicates another female. Bigonial breadth was 78 mm. All teeth were lost postmortem except LM1, RM1, and RM2. The wear pattern of RM1 was uneven and its degree of wear was greater than that of LM1 and RM2 (B2 in contrast to B1). This would suggest an individual in her mid- to late-twenties. LM3 had a deep root socket. There was no evidence of RM3.

e. A rather robust and square mandible suggests a young adult male. Bigonial breadth was 93 mm. All teeth were present and had little wear. The incisors had slight shoveling. Right and left M1 and M2 had the wear pattern of a late teenager, while RM3 was in the process of erupting but not yet completely erupted. LM3 was also erupting, but it was not as far along as RM3. The overall pattern of wear and eruption suggests an individual in the late teens.

The broken and/or incomplete mandibles included the following:

a. A fairly rounded symphysis from an adult represents a possible female. Of the teeth present, the canines, lateral incisors, and RP1 had their crowns broken off and were represented only by their roots. The central incisors, RP2, and RM1 were lost antemortem. LP2 and LP1 were worn into the dentine. RM2 was apparently lost postmortem as the mandible was broken across its socket.

b. A section of the left mandibular body with part of the ramus represents another adult (sex uncertain). M2 was worn completely into the dentine (B4+), suggesting an older individual (45+ years). M3 was apparently lost antemortem and the socket resorbed.

c. Two sections of a seemingly robust mandible, broken at the incisor area, represent a young adult (probable male). The canine and incisor area was broken, and all teeth were cracked to their roots. RC, RP1, and RP2 were lost postmortem. LP2 and LP1 had little wear. M1 and M2 on both sides had the wear pattern of a young adult, probably in the late teens (B1), and both M3's were just erupting.

d. An incomplete mandible with part of the left body and ramus missing represents an older adult, possibly a female. The symphysis was rather rounded with somewhat of a point. All teeth were lost antemortem except the root of RC. There was an extensive resorption throughout the mandibular body in the right premolar and molar areas and ex-

treme resorption into the anterior portion of the body on the left side.

e. A mandible with the right molar area and ramus missing represents a probable male. The body was somewhat robust and the symphysis generally square. All teeth were lost antemortem, and there was extreme resorption throughout, except for the root socket of RC. These features would suggest an older individual. The left canine and premolar area had the vestige of a large abscess.

f. A broken mandible with the right side from L1 onward and the ramus missing represents a probable male, based on overall morphology and robusticity. LM2 and RP1 were lost antemortem. All other teeth were lost postmortem, although the shallow root sockets of the incisors and canines may possibly suggest antemortem loss. There was no sign of LM3. LP1 had a small abscess at the base of its root, while RP1 had what appears to be the vestige of a small abscess.

g. The small, delicate fragment of left mandibular premolar and molar area suggests an adult female. P2, M1, and M3 were lost postmortem. M3 had an abscess and may have been lost antemortem.

h. A fragment of the left side of a mandible with only the root of LM3 represents another adult of undetermined age and sex.

Subadults

1. Innominates. Three juvenile innominates or component parts were recovered:

a. A complete left ilium. There was no evidence of union with the ischium, which would place the individual at about ten to twelve years of age. The sciatic notch was not sufficiently developed for sex to be estimated.

b. A small, complete right innominate with a characteristically female sciatic notch. The epiphysis of the iliac crest was in the process of union, but not yet completed.

There was a clear line of active union at the epiphysis of the ischial tuberosity. These features would place the individual in the late teens (18–19 years).

c. A complete left innominate with a characteristically male sciatic notch. The epiphysis of the iliac crest was actively uniting with the ilium. Union was evident centrally, but the epiphysis was open laterally. A clear line of union was apparent at the junction of the ischium and the ilium. These features would place the individual in the mid-teens (15–17).

2. Femora.

a. A broken pair of femoral shafts (right and left) lacking the epiphyses of the head and greater trochanter. The epiphyses of the femoral head and greater trochanter usually unite between fourteen and eighteen years, which would place this individual at perhaps eleven to thirteen years of age.

b. A pair of femoral diaphyses having lengths of 186 mm (right) and 187 mm (left). Using the criteria indicated in Chapter 6, these diaphyseal lengths would place the individual in the age range 2.5–4.5 years.

c. A moderately robust and clearly not delicate left femur. The distal epiphysis was separate but the femoral head was fused. These features would place the individual, a probable male, in the late teens (17–19 years).

d. A delicate, broken femur (female?). The distal epiphysis had a clear and recent line of union on its anterior and posterior surfaces. Assuming the individual is a female, this feature would place her in the mid-teens (14–17 years).

3. Tibiae.

a. An isolated distal tibial epiphysis with a well-developed malleolus. The distal tibial epiphysis generally unites with its diaphysis between fourteen and eighteen years of age.

b. Two broken tibial diaphyses, upper and distal sections respectively. These are clearly juvenile diaphyses, and may or may not be from the same individual.

4. Fibulae. Three broken diaphyses were recovered. One was almost complete and had an estimated length of 254 mm. Using the criteria indicated in Chapter 6, this individual would fall into the age range between 7.5 and 10.5 years (although the numbers in the reference sample were quite small at these ages).

5. Humeri.

a. A pair of incomplete diaphyses. No evidence of union was apparent. Length could not be measured.

b. A pair of incomplete diaphyses. The left diaphysis was almost complete and had a length of 198 mm. This would place the individual in the estimated age range of 6.5–7.5 years.

6. Radii.

a. A right diaphysis. There was no evidence of union distally or proximally.

b. A small right radius. There was no evidence of union distally, but the proximal epiphysis was just beginning to unite with the diaphysis. Assuming the small length (178 mm, including the proximal epiphysis) represents a female, the individual may be approximately thirteen years of age.

7. Ulnae. Only a right diaphysis with no evidence of union proximally or distally was recovered.

8. Scapulae. One pair of scapulae represented by only the body of each was recovered. This would place the individual under fourteen years of age.

9. Mandibles. Two complete mandibles were recovered.

a. One had a bigonial breadth of 78 mm. All teeth were lost postmortem except for LM1. The sockets for right and left M2 indicated that eruption of the second molars was completed. The bone over right and left M3 was just beginning to open, suggesting that eruption of the third molars may have been imminent. If so, these features would place the individual in the mid- to late teens (15–18 years).

b. The other mandible retained all its deciduous teeth, although the central incisors and the right lateral incisor and canine were lost postmortem. Both permanent first molars were fully erupted and both permanent second molars were visible in their crypts, perhaps nearing eruption. The status of the permanent molars suggests a child of about ten years of age. The deciduous molars were worn just barely into the dentine.

In addition to the mixed collection of bones described above, the long bones of a juvenile skeleton were recovered more or less as a unit. All bones were fragmentary and delicate, so that diaphyseal measurements could not be made. The heads of the right and left femora appeared to be in the process of union, but were somewhat eroded. The distal epiphyses were loose. Both right and left tibial epiphyses were fusing with their respective diaphyses distally, but not proximally. In contrast, the distal humeri, proximal left radius, and left ulna had no evidence of epiphyseal union activity. The small size and delicate nature of the bones suggest a young female, probably in her mid-teens.

The remains of two very young individuals were also recovered:

1. The right and left tibiae, a left fibula, a broken right femur, and a loose pubic bone from a single individual. The lengths of the tibial diaphyses were 72 and 72.5 mm respectively, which would place the child in the birth-to-six-months age range, using the criteria indicated in Chapter 6. The length of the fibula was 76 mm, which is at the upper range of values for the birth-to-six-months age group.

2. Right and left femora, a left humerus, and a scapula from another infant. The length of the right femur was 72 mm, and that of the left humerus was 62 mm. Both lengths suggested a child at or near term. When the lengths were inserted into the fetal equations provided by Fazekas and Kosa (1978), the estimated fetal length was approximately 46.5 cm, which is well within the range of lengths of children at birth.

Catalog of Tomb Contents

TERENCE GRIEDER

Tomb F-12:B-2

This set of three burials was undisturbed when it was opened June 12, 1981. A radiocarbon test (TX-4450) on the contents of the firepit gave a reading of 3820 ± 100 B.P., which agrees with the archaeology in placing this as the oldest of the tombs.

Body I, on the west nearest the entrance, was a man over fifty, tightly flexed and lying on his left side. Like the other two bodies, this one tended to roll onto its back as it decayed. After death the naked body was tightly flexed and wrapped in strips of barkcloth, now dark brown and most abundant around the hips and legs. Next the body was tied with 49 loops of Z-spun unplied cotton string of 1.3 mm diameter into the flexed position with the knees tightly against the chest, the arms flexed inside the knees. Perhaps at this point the body was laid on a cotton mantle (Textile Specimen 2), a yellow and brown striped weft-twined blanket that covered the whole body. Before the blanket was wrapped, tufts of human hair were tucked around the body. This may have been the man's own hair, since very little hair was found around the skull. The mantle was then wrapped tightly around the body, with voluminous folds around the shoulders. On the head a cotton bag or cap (T.S. 3) made of linking with a stepped-mountain design was pulled down over the eyes. It is impossible to be sure whether this was originally made as a cap or was a bag adapted to this use when the hair was cut at burial. All three bodies in this tomb had head coverings and hair around their bodies, the head coverings being items which could have had other uses.

Finally, the wrapped body was enclosed in a net made of bast fiber and was laid on a totora reed mat on the floor of the tomb. The offerings were already in place when the bodies were put in, and this body, being nearest the door, was probably the last to be placed. All three bodies appear to have been placed at about the same time.

Body II was a woman over fifty lying on her left side, tied into a tightly flexed position. There was no barkcloth on this body, but it was tied with twenty-five loops of cotton string (T.S. 7). Human hair tufts were abundantly tucked around the body, but there was no blanket or other item of clothing on the body. On the head, which shows no evidence of hair, was a plain cotton cap of fine linking, again perhaps a bag adapted to this use. The body, naked except for the string tying it in position, the tufts of hair placed around it, and the cap pulled down over the upper part of the face, was wrapped in a bast fiber net (T.S. 6). In the neck area were several items: four bone pins, four small pieces of anthracite, two halves of a white stone bead, two chips of rock crystal, of which one has a tiny retouched blade on one edge, and four small, heavy black natural mineral globes, probably of magnetite (diameters in cm: 2.0, 1.5, 1.4, and 1.0), unpierced and apparently simply laid on the body.

Bodies II and III were laid together on a soft mat of twined junco fiber (T.S. 4), and a totora mat of 2 × 2 basketweave was laid over them both. The offerings were in place around the wall before the junco mat was laid.

Body III was a woman over fifty, tightly flexed and lying on her left side. There were tufts of hair tucked around the body, which was then wrapped in barkcloth strips, but fewer than were placed on Body I. Then a yellow cotton mantle (T.S. 10) of plain looping was wrapped around the body, the material bunched around the neck and shoulders. Outside the mantle about twenty loops of cotton string (T.S. 11) bound the body into its flexed position. Her hair seems to have been cut, since there was none around the skull, but a bast fiber in a loose hair-like bunch had been placed next to the skull; it must have been brown originally but has faded to yellow. Over this fiber a basket was placed as a hat (T.S. 12). No necklaces were found with any of these burials, but one drilled bead, 3.0 mm in its largest dimension, of a fine-grained bright green stone was under the head. A curl (1.5 cm long) of salt crystal was also under the head.

The offerings were laid around the heads and are listed in order beginning with those nearest the entrance, probably the reverse of the order in which they were deposited.

1. A fragment (about half) of a totora basket woven 2 × 2, 16 cm in diameter. It contained one Solenidae shell, a piece of gourd 6 cm long, and a bundle of fine bast fiber thread (T.S. 13).

2. Cotton bag of looping on a foundation which once contained a basket (lost by decay). The bag has black serpents on yellow as the decoration (T.S. 14).

3. A gourd set in no. 2 above.

4. A cotton bag of looping on a foundation decorated with double-headed birds in black on yellow (T.S. 15).

5. A plain yellow cotton bag of looping over a decayed basket (T.S. 16).

6. A cotton bag of looping on a foundation with a black serpent design on yellow, with a decayed basket inside (T.S. 17).

7. A gourd bowl, part of the top broken.

8. A totora basket 8.5 cm high; part of the rim lost (T.S. 18).

9. A gourd dipper.

10. A gourd dipper.

11. A totora basket 10 cm high (T.S. 19), containing a fine cotton linked net (T.S. 20).

12. A totora basket 11.5 cm high (T.S. 21) containing a twined cotton plain cloth (T.S. 22).

13. A stone mortar 6.0 cm high, 17 cm maximum width; a pestle 13.0 cm long.

14. A looped cotton bag, plain yellow (T.S. 23), enclosed in a decayed basket.

15. A set of two nested baskets with looped cotton bags. On the bottom was a 2 × 2 totora basket (T.S. 25) with a double rim. It is enclosed by a bag with yellow diamonds on a black background (T.S. 24). Nested in the lower basket was another totora basket (T.S. 26), now half missing. Folded in the basket was a looped cotton cloth, probably a bag, with a black design of birds and serpents on a red ground (T.S. 27).

16. A totora basket, 2 × 2 weave, 10 cm high, 17.5 × 20 cm across (T.S. 28), which held a cotton looped bag (T.S. 29) decorated with black birds on a yellow ground.

17. A totora basket (T.S. 30) of 2 × 2 interlacing 6 cm high, 20 cm diameter, the rim lost. It held a cotton bag (T.S. 31) of linking decorated with yellow circles on a red-brown ground.

18. A totora basket in 2 × 2 weave containing a looped cotton bag (T.S. 32) decorated with diagonal bands of red triangles on white. Inside the bag was a roll of bast fiber thread, a marine clam shell, and a small gourd containing four shell beads and one green turquoise bead.

Cleaning of the sunken area of the floor around the firepit produced two fragments of mussel shell (probably from the same shell), three pieces of crustacean antennae (perhaps all parts of one), and three scraps from one feather which measured 4 cm from rib to edge.

TOMB C-10:E-10

This late Preceramic tomb chamber was especially built and was never part of another construction. It contained three women's bodies, extended on their backs, their heads to the south.

Body I, on the left, was a young adult woman who was pregnant at the time of her death. The bones of the fetus were in the pelvic area. She lay on a totora mat, and a junco mat had been placed over the body. The top mat was made of thin junco reeds twined with cotton wefts every 4 cm, the reeds running the length of the body. Around her legs and ankles was a loose rope (T.S. 65) 28 cm long made of two plied cords, one of nine strands and the other of four, of brown and white natural cotton plied together. Around the upper body was a weft-twined cotton mantle (T.S. 64), the warps of red and yellow stripes, the wefts dark brown and spaced 5 mm apart. A totora reed mat was placed over Body I, on top of the junco mat.

She wore two necklaces looped in multiple strands around her neck. One was of white shell beads 9–11 mm in diameter by 7–9 mm thick. The other was of alternating groups of small dark brown stone beads (1–2 mm thick by 3–4 mm diameter) with pink or white shell beads, in groups about 10 cm long. There are several other longer (about 16 mm) beads of stone and bone which seem to have been mixed into these necklaces, and both of them had pendants, one of stone and one of *Spondylus* shell.

By the head and upper arms were six bone pins, one of them plain, three with blue-green turquoise beads glued on with resin adhesive, and four with flat trapezoidal heads, two plain and two with incised designs. From their position it is hard to be sure whether these fastened the hair or clothing.

Body II, in the middle, was a woman over fifty years old with spinal curvature probably caused by tuberculosis. Her skull was flattened on the back. Her body was extended on a totora mat, but no mat was laid over her. Although some hair remained by her skull, there were also hair tufts 7–8 cm long placed next to the skin inside her blankets. A quid (2 × 6.5 cm) of an unidentified fiber, perhaps barkcloth, had been placed between her thighs. The body was wrapped in two cotton textiles, a mantle (T.S. 68) and a shawl (T.S. 69). The mantle is weft-twined with brown every 15 mm, the warps being natural brown and white cotton plied together to give a yellow-tan color. The shawl was around the shoulders and has red and yellow stripes in a brown background and brown twined wefts.

Around her neck were multiple loops of a long necklace of small black and white beads alternating for about thirty beads, then one long white shell bead. One plain bone pin was still in the hair beside the skull.

Body III was an old woman lying against the right wall on a totora mat with a totora mat similar to that on Body I spread over her. Her body was wrapped in a cotton mantle (T.S. 70) with warps of natural brown and white cotton plied together and brown wefts Z-twined every 12 mm. It covered the whole body and was bunched around the neck. She had a necklace of black and white beads similar to that of II, with a double-drilled *Spondylus* shell at the center. Her hair was still around the skull, and in the head area were four bone pins with trapezoidal heads, two incised and two with shell beads attached, which may have been in the hair, or possibly fastened clothing.

A set of offerings were placed around the bodies, numbered clockwise beginning at the feet of III, nearest the entrance.

1. A stone mortar, 8.4 cm high, 13.6 cm diameter, and pestle, 13.2 cm long and 6.0 cm maximum diameter.

2. A totora basket in 2 × 2 weave. Inside it is a white cotton looped bag (T.S. 72), with unidentified leaves inside.

3. A plain cotton bag made by linking (T.S. 73).

4. A wooden spindle with yellow cotton thread wound onto it (T.S. 67).

5. A set of three totora baskets, the top and bottom of 2 × 2 weave, the middle twined. The top basket is covered by a looped cotton bag with black double-headed snakes on a red ground (T.S. 74). A handful of unspun cotton lay in the top basket. The edge of a looped cotton bag (T.S. 80) is visible on the bottom basket with yellow shapes on black.

6. A 2 × 2 woven totora basket about 15 cm in diameter containing a yellow linked cotton bag (T.S. 5) on which were set three small packets of leaves and herbs, presumably medicine.

7. A 2 × 2 woven totora basket 9.7 cm high, oval 18.5 × 13 cm. It contains a linked cotton bag (T.S. 77) decorated with yellow circles on black. This offering is in the southeast corner beside the right shoulder of Body I.

8. A 2 × 2 woven totora basket 9.5 cm high, oval 14 × 19.5 cm. It contains a looped cotton bag (T.S. 78) with a design of brown zigzag lines on yellow.

9. A 2 × 2 woven totora basket preserved up to 15 cm height, oval 15 × 19 cm. It contains a looped cotton bag (T.S. 79) with a brown bird-wing design on yellow-tan, and some raw cotton fiber.

10. A soft interlaced mat of junco reed

bundles and cotton and bast string about 30 × 12 cm. Selvage on one end has seven rows of interlace, three of cotton, four of bast, closely interlaced. On body of mat interlaces are spaced 1 cm. Offering 11 was set on this mat.

11. A 2 × 2 woven totora basket now 11 cm high, 15 × 21 cm. One end and top edge missing. Contains only some leaves and one round fruit or nut 3 × 6 cm.

12. A gourd cup 6.4 cm high, 11.4 cm long with handle, 8.0 cm wide. No decoration. Beside the head of Body II, between I and II.

13. A set of two baskets and, on top, a plain gourd bowl. The bottom basket is enclosed in a looped cotton bag (T.S. 66) with black snakes on a yellow ground. This offering was laid at the head of Body II.

Unspun cotton and human hair made a mixed pile by the head of Body I, probably an accidental mixture when the skull fell back, and bast fiber was laid irregularly along the east wall.

TOMB D-11:C-3, FLOOR 24

The tomb contained four adult burials and the probable disintegrated skeleton of an infant, in two groups. The two extended adult burials, a man (I) and older woman (II), and the infant (unnumbered) were placed first, and later the two male bundle burials, III and IV.

Body I was a man lying extended, head to the south, on a wooden litter which was covered with a woven totora mat. Three weft-twined mantles were over his body (T.S. 101, 102, 103), and two decorated looped bags (T.S. 104, 105) beside his head, as well as a fragment of a linked bag (T.S. 106) and a hank of cotton yarn (T.S. 107). A 7.5-cm-wide interlaced belt (T.S. 108) with warp-float decoration was also worn by this man. Around his neck he wore a necklace of four long red diatomite beads, their flat front faces inlaid with small circles of green turquoise. Just above his left shoulder were two scallop shells filled with red powdered pigment laid face to face with the valves at opposite sides, and above each shoulder was a razor clam shell. A small broken bone pin of the type probably used as hairpins was found near his head, along with four flat blue-green turquoise beads of the type found on bone pin heads in other burials.

Body II was the extended body of an old woman lying, head to the south, on a totora mat. Two plain twined mantles (T.S. 109, 110) were over her body and one to three looped bags (T.S. 111–113) and a plain linked bag (T.S. 115), plus the center of a looped bag base (T.S. 114) were beside her head. There is part of an interlaced belt (T.S. 116) 2 cm wide. Around her neck she wore a necklace of white beads with a shell pendant of a rabbit. A scallop shell lay by her right shoulder. A fragment of a black granite mortar, possibly belonging to Body IV, lay between her knees. The two razor clam shells by her left foot and one near her right leg may also belong to Body IV.

Two later bundle burials of the beginning of the Initial Period were set on the hips and feet of Body II. These are Bodies III and IV, both men.

Body III was set in the northeast corner of the tomb. The body was tightly flexed, but not tied, and wrapped in a plain white or tan cotton woven mantle or shroud (T.S. 121) and set on a small totora mat. A bast net (T.S. 117) was wrapped around the outside of the shrouded body. Before it was closed several items were put in with the body: three smaller bast nets (T.S. 118–120), one or two decorated looped bags (T.S. 122, 123), two linked bags (T.S. 124, 125), some cotton yarn and bast fiber thread (T.S. 126, 127), and a razor clam shell.

Body IV was set on the hips of the earlier burial, Body II. The body had been flexed

and tied into position with a bast rope (T.S. 131) 64 cm long, which may have been on the outside of the bundle. The body was wrapped in two plain woven cotton shrouds or mantles (T.S. 129, 130) and then in a coarse bast net (T.S. 128).

TOMB C-11:E-8, FLOOR 17

This tomb in the South Mound was opened by the road crew in 1975 and was disturbed, but was partly intact in 1976 when Bueno and I examined it. It was walled up in 1976, but was looted again before 1978, when the remaining material was studied and removed. There were originally three skeletons lying extended on their backs with heads to the west. They are numbered from north to south, only Body I remaining in 1978, then with the skull missing. Body I was an adult male; in 1976 it was our impression that Body III was an adult female, with a child, Body II, between them.

Body I lay on a totora mat woven in a tight 1×1 pattern. The body was wrapped in a plain woven mantle (T.S. 168). A looped cotton bag (T.S. 173) with a frontal figure was placed at the left of his head, along with the small whole pottery jar with relief serpents (Fig. 158). Probably associated with this body was a necklace of seventeen flat rectangular shell beads, fifteen drilled laterally twice, two drilled once. The shells are pink and white. It appears that the center of this necklace was a complete shell of a razor clam, with a drill hole in the middle of one side. Bunches of unspun cotton were placed around the body.

Several other pieces of textile were found in this tomb, probably originally associated with the other skeletons; see Appendix C, T.S. 163–170, 173–174.

TOMB C-12:D-1

Although this partly destroyed tomb contained fragmentary remains of seven adults and four or five children, clothing and jewelry can be associated with only three of the adults (I, III, V) and two of the children (A, B). It appears that all the burials were seated flexed bundle burials which had fallen over.

Body I, a male, had a woven shroud or mantle (T.S. 139) which may have been fastened with an interlaced belt (T.S. 142). The shrouded body was probably enclosed in a bast net (T.S. 132). Two plain bone pins, of a type probably used to fasten the hair, were found with this body. Two shell ear pendants—circular disks 5 cm in diameter—belonged with this body, or with III, also a man. A stone cup which had been broken and repaired with brown cotton thread lay between I and III. It contained one cervical vertebra, which presumably fell into it when the body collapsed.

Body II was a damaged skull from a destroyed burial, without associated offerings.

Body III was an old man's body originally seated facing east wrapped in a plain weft-twined cotton mantle (T.S. 136), and a second twined mantle (T.S. 137) may have belonged with this body, as well as an interlaced belt (T.S. 143). A plain white looped bag (T.S. 144) was at his left shoulder. The most unusual feature was a tight net cap covered with small, thin, square white shell beads pierced in the centers.

Body V was a destroyed burial represented only by the skull and mandible of a woman, the flesh decayed but the hair still largely present. The hair was drawn up and held in place by four bone pins with blue-green turquoise beads attached to their heads with resin. A natural cactus spine about 12 cm long was also used to pin the hair.

A child's burial, A, against the south wall was accompanied by a woven mantle (T.S. 141), a fine-textured looped bag (T.S. 147), and a fine bast net (T.S. 134), which probably enclosed the flexed body in its wrappings. Another child, B, was wrapped in a

twined mantle (T.S. 138) decorated with a striped design in brown and yellow.

TOMB C-10:I-10, FLOOR 21: THE BURNED BURIAL

This tomb, which held four adult bodies, probably three women and a man, had been disrupted and burned when Floor 19 and the upper levels of the South Mound were built.

Two weft-twined plain mantles (T.S. 57, 58) would suggest that at least some of these burials were Preceramic, despite the ceramic lid (listed below) among the offerings. A looped bag (T.S. 59), two linked bags (T.S. 60, 61), and a 1-cm-wide interlaced belt (T.S. 62) with zigzag yellow and brown warp stripes would also be likely Preceramic items. Only fragments of such combustible materials survived burning. Ten other items or sets survived:

1. Stone mortar of a green metamorphic stone 14.6 cm high, 13.5 cm maximum rim diameter, 10.5–11.0 cm interior diameter, 10.8 cm deep.

2. Black stone pestle (inside mortar no. 1) 10.2 cm long, 4.3 cm diameter.

3. Fragment of a black stone mortar (two fitting pieces), making up half the rim and about half the height, 9.5 cm high, 10.5 cm inside diameter. Wall is 4.4 cm maximum thickness.

4. Pottery lid, 4.6 cm diameter. Exterior has a whirl design of two concentric bands of excised triangles. Polished. Burnt black in the fire. This lid fits the small jar found in the C-11:E-8 tomb.

5. Fragments representing seven bone pins.

6. Stone plaque 2.5 × 2.45 × 0.2 cm. Very smooth, almost perfect rectangle. Two small channels were cut in one side, and something is caked or burnt on the other, perhaps paint or glue.

7. Amber pendant with a biconical perforation, 3.5 cm long, 2.3 cm wide, 1.8 cm

thick. It is shaped like a slightly flattened plumb bob, but it does not hang straight.

8. Fragment of a circular mat or low basket 12.5 × 12.0 cm. Twined totora reed with an ornamental border.

9. Seven small smooth pebbles. The largest is 1.7 × 1.3 cm, the smallest 0.8 cm diameter. Two of them appear to be petrified seeds or small fruits, but are probably natural hematite.

10. A piece of reniform hematite, of shiny metallic mineral, 5.8 × 4.9 × 3.5 cm.

La Galgada Textile Specimens

TERENCE GRIEDER

Sector, Square	Specimen	Floor	Body/ Offering	Function	Fiber: Cotton, Vegetal	Spin Angle		Ply Angle		Thread Diameter (mm)
						S	Z	S	Z	
F-12:B-2	1		I	Body net	V		40			2
"	2		"	Mantle	C	30			55	1
"	3		"	Bag-hat	C	20			60	.7
"	4		II–III	Mat	V, C					
"	5		"	Mat	V					
"	6		II	Body net	V		30			2
"	7		"	String	C	40			50	2
"	8		"	Bag-hat	C	30			65	.7
"	9		III	Body net	V	30			55	1.5
"	10		"	Mantle	C	30			50	1
"	11		"	String	C	30			60	1–2
"	12		"	Basket-hat	V					
"	13		1	String	V	30			35	1
"	14		2	Bag	C	30			40	.7–1
"	15		4	Bag	C	40–50			60	1
"	16		5	Bag	C	20			65	1.2
"	17		6	Bag	C	30			50	1
"	18		8	Basket	V					
F-12:B-2	19		11a	Basket	V					
"	20		11b	Net	C	X				
"	21		12a	Basket	V					
"	22		12b	Flat cloth	C	30			40	1.3
"	23		14b	Bag	C	50			45	.8

Structure	Color: Red, Yellow, Black, White, BRown, Tan	Motif or Design	Remarks	Specimen
Linking				1
Twining	Y, BR	Warp stripes 1.5 cm wide; wefts alt. Y, B	10 warps/cm, paired; wefts 7 mm apart	2
Linking	T, B	3 registers of stepped mountains	20 cm diameter, 22 cm deep; 8.5 threads/cm; ribs 6 mm apart	3
Twining	BR		Junco in bundles, 5 mm diameter, twined with BR cotton 6 cm apart	4
Oblique interlacing			Totora reed 2 × 2 interlacing; over bodies	5
Linking			5-mm openings	6
Spinning	Y		25 loops tie body in flexure	7
Linking			Ribs 5 mm apart	8
Linking			9-mm openings	9
Looping	Y		No foundation; 5 loops/cm; 2 rows/cm; string tie on selvage	10
Spinning	Y		About 20 loops tie body in flexure	11
Oblique interlacing			Totora basket 2 × 2 interlacing used as hat	12
Spinning			Fine string in basket	13
Looping	B, Y	B serpents on Y	Contained decayed basket	14
Looping	B, Y	Double-headed birds with serpent masks, B on Y	7 loops/cm; 5 rows/cm; top half of bag	15
Looping	Y		8 loops/cm; 1 row/cm; contained decayed basket	16
Looping	B, Y	B serpents and steps on Y	8 loops/cm; 5 rows/cm; contained decayed basket 6 cm high, 10 cm base	17
Oblique interlacing			Totora reed 2 × 2 interlacing; double rim; 8.5 cm high, 12.5 cm base, 13 cm rim diameter	18
Oblique interlacing			Totora reed 2 × 2 interlacing; double rim; 10 cm high, 16 cm rim diameter	19
Linking			Barely visible folded in basket; 3 mm openings	20
Oblique interlacing			Totora reed 2 × 2 interlacing; 11.5 cm high; double rim 16 cm diameter	21
Twining			Wefts one-ply S, twined Z, 6 mm apart; warp selvage has 5 mm fringe	22
Looping	Y		In basket; 30–36 cm high, 16–19 cm wide; 7 loops/cm; 2 rows/cm; ties on edge	23

Sector, Square	Specimen	Floor	Body/ Offering	Function	Fiber: Cotton, Vegetal	Spin Angle		Ply Angle		Thread Diameter (mm)
						S	Z	S	Z	
"	24		15b	Bag	C	X			X	
"	25		15a	Basket	V					
"	26		15c	Basket	V					
"	27		15d	Bag	C					
"	28		16a	Basket	V					
"	29		16b	Bag	C	30			50	1
"	30		17a	Basket	V					
"	31		17b	Bag	C	10–20			30	1
"	32		18	Bag	C	40			60	.8
E-11:J-10 (antechamber)	33			Cord	C	40			50	1.5
"	34			Flat piece, 8 × 4 cm.	C	40			20	1
E-12:I-2	35	6		Flat pieces	C	40			50	1–1.25
"	36	"		Flat piece	C	40			65	1
E-12:I-2	37	6		Flat piece	C	50			70	1
"	38	"		Basket	V					
"	39	"		Flat piece	C	30			40–55	1
"	40	"		Wrapping	⎡ C	30			50	.6 ⎤
					⎣ V		25			.7 ⎦
D-11:C-3	41	25		Net	V	40			50	1.4
"	42	"		Net	V	30			35	1.5
"	43	"		Mantle	⎡ C	20 (wefts)			35	1
					⎣ C	40 (warps)			40	1.4

Structure	Color: Red, Yellow, Black, White, BRown, Tan	Motif or Design	Remarks	Specimen
Looping	Y,B	Y diamonds on B	7 or 8 loops/cm; contains basket, T.S. 25	24
Oblique interlacing			Totora reed 2 × 2 interlacing; double rim	25
Oblique interlacing			Totora reed 2 × 2 interlacing; only one side extant; in T.S. 25	26
Looping	B, R	B birds and serpents on R	In T.S. 26	27
Oblique interlacing			Totora reed 2 × 2 interlacing; rim 17.5 × 20 cm across, doubled outward; 10 cm high	28
Looping	B,Y	B birds on Y; possible quadruped	8 loops/cm; 4 rows/cm; rim ties Y wound with B; in T.S. 28	29
Oblique interlacing			Totora reed 2 × 2 interlacing; 6 cm high (rim lost); 20 cm diameter; contains T.S. 31	30
Linking	R-BR, Y	Y circular shapes on R-BR	Vertical ribs 2/cm	31
Looping	R, W	R triangles in ladder effect on W	7 loops/cm; 5 rows/cm; ties on rim selvage	32
Spinning			2 pieces 5.15 m, 50 cm; hung from cover into tomb; 16 strands	33
Twining			Parallel warps; wefts 5 mm apart; selvage triple-twined	34
Twining			Wefts twined 8 mm apart; selvage with 4 rows of twining	35
Twining			9 warps/cm in pairs; wefts twined 6 mm apart	36
Twining		Burnt	Single warps; wefts twined 17 mm apart	37
Oblique interlacing			Totora reed 2 × 2 interlacing; 7.5 cm high, 12 cm diameter, rim double	38
Twining	W		7 warps/cm in pairs which split; wefts twined Z 7–10 mm apart	39
Wrapping	R		Wooden loop 1.8 cm high; top wrapped in 16 loops V fiber; bottom wrapped in 3 loops R cotton	40
Linking			1-cm openings; body net from destroyed burial?	41
Linking			8-mm openings; organic stains; body net from destroyed burial?	42
Twining	BR Y, W	Y plied with W in warp; plain BR wefts	Wefts twined Z every 11 mm; 8 warps/cm in split pairs	43

Sector, Square	Specimen	Floor	Body/ Offering	Function	Fiber: Cotton, Vegetal	Spin Angle S	Spin Angle Z	Ply Angle S	Ply Angle Z	Thread Diameter (mm)
"	44	"		Bag	C	40			50	1
"	45	"		Bag	C	50			60	1
"	46	"		Belt	C	30			40	.5 – 1
"	47	"		Yarn	C	60			60	2 – 2.5
"	48	"		Yarn	C	30			40	1.4
"	49	"		Cord	V	30			30	8 – 10
"	50	"		Net	V	30			40	1
"	51	"		Mantle	C	40			60	1
"	52	"		Mantle	C	40			60	1
"	53	"		Mantle	C	30			50	1
"	54	"		Flat piece	⌈ C ⌊ V	40			30	1 ⌉ 1.5 ⌋
D-11:C-3	55	25		Belt	C	X			X	.5
"	56	"		Pad	V					
C-10:I-10	57	21		Mantle	C	X			50	1
"	58	"		Mantle	C	40			40	1
"	59	"		Bag	C	50			50	.8
"	60	"		Bag	C	10			40	1
"	61	"		Bag	C	30			30	.5
"	62	"		Belt	⌈ C ⌊ C	30 (wefts) 40 (warps)			30	.3 – .4 1
"	63	"		Basket	V					
C-10:E-10	64	26	I	Mantle	C	10			50	.5 – 1

Structure	Color: Red, Yellow, Black, White, BRown, Tan	Motif or Design	Remarks	Specimen
Linking	BR, W	Yes but unidentifiable	5 threads/cm; ribs 8 mm apart	44
Linking	W		Radiating rib pattern in base	45
Interlacing	BR, W, R	Warp face colors: 4 BR, 1 W, 2 R, 1 W, 2 R, 1 W, 2 R, 1 W, 2 R, 1 W, 5 BR, 1 W, 2 R, 1 W, 2 R, 1 W, 2 R, 1 W, 2 R, 1 W, 4 BR	48 cm long, 3.6 cm wide; 39 warps, both side selvages; BR wefts 2.5 mm apart, turn back, do not show; warp fringe at end	46
Spinning	BR, W	W and BR plied on some strands	16 strands	47
Spinning	Y, W		Y and W plied; loose hanks	48
Spinning			Hard fiber; pieces up to 17 cm long	49
Linking			5-mm squares; each 8 is 9 mm high	50
Interlacing, twining	W		1 × 1 interlace; 7 warps/cm; 5 wefts/cm; 3 warps bundled in 4 rows twining at selvage	51
Twining	W		Warp pairs; wefts 8.5 mm apart; 2 rows of twining at selvage	52
Twining		Decorated, design unidentified	Warp pairs intertwined; 9 warps/cm; wefts 10 mm apart	53
Interlacing			Cotton threads, 6/cm; totora reed strips, 6/cm	54
Interlacing	W		2.8 cm wide, both selvages; 48 warps; 4 wefts/cm	55
Random			Round pad 11 × 12 cm; made pocket for cotton fiber, achupalla leaf	56
Twining		Burnt	May be part of T.S. 58	57
Twining	W		Warp split pairs; 8 warps/cm; wefts 1 cm apart; selvage 4 rows twined tightly and fringe	58
Looping		Burnt	6 loops/cm; 5 rows/cm; selvage at rim	59
Linking	Y		Selvage; tab or handle	60
Linking	R, Y	Decorated, design unidentified	3-×-2.5-cm scrap; R joins parallel to ribs	61
Interlacing	BR, BR, Y	2 threads each color make zigzag warp stripes	1 selvage; BR wefts turn back	62
Twining, weaving			Totora reed piece of large basket, 13.5 × 11.5 cm	63
Twining	BR, Y, R	R and Y stripes in warp, BR wefts	Wefts .5 mm diameter, twined 5 mm apart	64

Sector, Square	Specimen	Floor	Body/ Offering	Function	Fiber: Cotton, Vegetal	Spin Angle S	Spin Angle Z	Ply Angle S	Ply Angle Z	Thread Diameter (mm)
"	65	"	"	Rope	C	25			60	1–2
"	66	"	13	Bag	C	20–30			50	.8–1
"	67	"	4	Yarn on spindle	C	40–50				1
"	68	"	II	Mantle	C	35–45			50	1.2–2
"	69	"	"	Shawl	C	20–30			50–60	1
"	70	"	III	Mantle	C	35–40			45	1
"	71	"	I	Mat	V, C					3
"	72	"	1	Bag	C	Too fragile to measure				
"	73	"	3	Bag	C	40			50	.7–1.2
"	74	"	5a	Bag	C	Too fragile to measure				
"	75	"	6	Bag	C	Too fragile to measure				.8
"	76	"		Bag	C	20–30			50	1
C-10:E-10	77	26	7	Bag	C	23–30			50	1
"	78	"	8	Bag	C	10–20			60	.5
"	79	"	9	Bag	C	25–35			40	1
"	80	"	5b	Bag	C	Too fragile to measure				
C-11:F-5	81	23		Net	V	40			45	1
"	82	"		Net	V		40			.7
"	83	"		Net	V	30			30–40	.7
"	84	"		Mantle	C	25–35 (wefts) 20–25 (warps)			30–50 40–50	.5–.7 1–1.5
"	85	"		Mantle	C	20 (wefts) 20 (warps)			40 50	.8 1.5
"	86	"		Flat piece	C	30–40			40–70	.5
"	87	"		Bag	C	10–50			30–55	.7–.8
"	88	"		Bag	C	20–60			50–60	.6–.8
"	89	"		Bag	C	30			30–50	.5
"	90	"		Bag	C	30			40	.5–1
"	91	"		Bag	C	30			50	.7

Structure	Color: Red, Yellow, Black, White, BRown, Tan	Motif or Design	Remarks	Specimen
Spinning	BR, W plied		28 cm long; 9 strands twisted together and 4 strands twisted together	65
Looping	B, Y	B snakes on Y	Encloses bottom basket in stack of baskets and gourd vessel	66
Spinning	Y to T		6.5 × 4 cm bundle on spindle with unspun cotton	67
Twining	T, Y	Split pairs	T and Y thread plied; wefts Z-twined 15 mm apart	68
Twining	R, Y, BR	R and Y stripes, BR wefts		69
Twining	W, BR	W warp in split pairs, BR wefts	Wefts 12 mm apart	70
Twining			Junco reed with cotton wefts 3.4 cm apart	71
Looping	W	Second color lost	In totora basket	72
Linking	Y, T		Ribs 7 mm apart; 7 threads/cm	73
Looping	Y, BR, B, R	S-shaped double-headed snake B on R		74
Linking	Y		9 threads/cm; in basket with plant bundles	75
Linking	Y		Ribs 7 mm apart; 7 threads/cm	76
Linking	Y, B	Y circles on B; sky pattern?		77
Looping	Y, BR	Zigzag lines BR on Y		78
Looping	R, BR, Y, T	Bird-wing design BR on Y	6 loops/cm; 4 rows/cm	79
Looping	Y, B	Wavy Y area and circles on B	Showing between baskets	80
Linking				81
Linking			2-mm openings	82
Linking			2-mm openings; selvage has 2 cords which close net as bag	83
Twining	BR	Warps split, change sides, turn back at selvage	7 warp threads/cm; wefts twined Z 6–7 mm apart	84
Twining	W	Warps split, cross, change sides	20 warp threads/cm; wefts 7 mm apart; selvage	85
Twining	W, BR, R, green	W linear human and geometric designs on BR; R stripe; green selvage	18 warps/cm; pairs split, change sides; wefts 2.5 mm apart; fine-textured flat cloth	86
Looping	R-BR, T	Frontal birds R-BR on T	7 loops/cm; 5 rows/cm	87
Looping	R-BR, T	Frontal birds, triangle border	4–6 loops/cm; 4 rows/cm	88
Looping	BR, T	Probably bird design	7–9 loops/cm; 6 rows/cm	89
Looping	R-BR, T	R-BR double birds on T; R triangle border	6–7 loops/cm; 4 rows/cm	90
Looping	BR, T	Human-like faces and bodies	6 loops/cm; 4 rows/cm	91

Sector, Square	Specimen	Floor	Body/ Offering	Function	Fiber: Cotton, Vegetal	Spin Angle		Ply Angle		Thread Diameter (mm)
						S	Z	S	Z	
"	92	"		Bag	C	30			40	.5–.8
"	93	"		Bag?	C	30			55–60	.7
"	94	"		Bag	C	40			50	1
"	95	"		Bag	C	25			45	.7–1
"	96	"		Thread	C	20			40	.5
"	97	"		Belt	C	40			60	.8·
"	98	"		Belt	C	20			30	1
"	99	"		Belt	C	30 (wefts) 30 (warps)			40	.5 1.3
"	100	"		Belt	C	20			40	.5
D-11:C-3	101	24	I	Mantle	C	20			40	.6
"	102	"	"	Mantle	C	20–30 (wefts) 30 (warps)			40 50	.5–.7 1–1.4
"	103	"	"	Mantle	C	30			50	1.5
"	104	"	"	Bag	C	20			30	.6
"	105	"	"	Bag	C	20			60	.8
"	106	"	"	Bag	C	40			45	.8
"	107	"	"	Hank of yarn	C	40			50	1.5
"	108	"	"	Belt	C	50 (wefts) 40 (warps)			55	.8
"	109	"	II	Mantle	C	50			60	.7–1
"	110	"	"	Mantle	C	10 (wefts) 20 (warps)			30 50	.5 1
"	111	"	"	Bag	C	30			50	.8
"	112	"	"	Bag	C	30			30	1
"	113	"	"	Bag	C	40			40	.7
"	114	"	"	Bag	C	30			50	.8
"	115	"	"	Bag	C	35			60	1.2

Structure	Color: Red, Yellow, Black, White, BRown, Tan	Motif or Design	Remarks	Specimen
Looping	R, T	Geometric birds? triangle border?		92
Looping	T, blue	Decorated in two colors	Scrap 4.5 × 2 cm	93
Linking	B, W	Stepped mountain	7 threads/cm	94
Linking	BR		9 threads/cm; fine texture	95
Spinning	BR		Ball of thread	96
Interlacing	W		> 2.5 cm wide; 1 side and 1 end selvage; warp face, 7/cm; wefts 3 mm apart, knotted in pairs at selvage	97
Interlacing	W		2 cm wide; both side selvages; warp face, 19 warp threads; 3 wefts/cm; wefts turn back at selvages	98
Interlacing	W		3 cm wide; both side selvages; warp face; unplied wefts, 5/cm	99
Interlacing	W		1 side selvage; warp face, 14 warps/cm; paired wefts, 6/cm	100
Twining			Warps in parallel pairs, 10 threads/cm; wefts 7 mm apart	101
Twining	Y, W		Wefts twined Z 7 mm apart Warps in split pairs, 8 threads/cm	102
Twining			Warps in parallel pairs, split at selvage; wefts 1 cm apart	103
Looping	BR, W	Yes but unidentifiable	6 loops/cm; 4 rows/cm	104
Looping	BR, Y	Yes but unidentifiable	6 loops/cm; 4.5 rows/cm; top selvage with ties	105
Linking	BR, Y, W	Yes but unidentifiable	6 threads/cm; ribs 7 mm apart	106
Spinning	T		61 threads 13 cm long	107
Interlacing	BR, T	BR diamonds on T	7.5 cm wide, both selvages; warp pairs, decoration in warp floats	108
Twining	W		Warp pairs; wefts 8 mm apart	109
Twining	BR		Warp in parallel pairs; wefts Z-twined 5 mm apart	110
Looping	W		6 loops/cm; 3.5 rows/cm	111
Looping	W		8 loops/cm; 4 rows/cm; same as 111?	112
Looping	W		6 loops/cm; 4.5 rows/cm; same as 111?	113
Looping	W		7 loops/cm; 8 rows/cm; spiral center of bag	114
Linking			6 threads/cm; ribs 6 mm apart	115

Sector, Square	Specimen	Floor	Body/ Offering	Function	Fiber: Cotton, Vegetal	Spin Angle S	Spin Angle Z	Ply Angle S	Ply Angle Z	Thread Diameter (mm)
"	116	"	"	Belt	C	40 (wefts)				.5
						20 (warps)			50	.8
"	117	"	III	Net	V		30			.9
"	118	"	"	Net	V	30			30–60	.6
"	119	"	"	Net	V	20			35	1.4–2.4
"	120	"	"	Net	V	20			20	.8
"	121	"	"	Mantle	C	30 (wefts)				.3–.5
						20 (warps)			40	.6
"	122	"	"	Bag	C	20			40	1
"	123	"	"	Bag	C	30			50	.8
"	124	"	"	Bag?	C	40–60			50–60	1
"	125	"	"	Bag	C	30			50	.8
"	126	"	"	Yarn	C	45			70	1.8–2
"	127	"	"	Thread	V	25			20	.5–.6
D-11:C-3	128	24	IV	Net	V	20			30	1
"	129	"	"	Mantle	C	20 (pairs)				.3–.5
						20 (singles)			30	.4
"	130	"	"	Mantle	C	10–20 (wefts)				.3–.5
							25 (warps)			.5–.7
"	131	"	"	Rope	V	20			30	10
C-12:D-1	132	18	I	Net	V	20			50–60	1
"	133	"	"	Net	V	20			30–40	.7
					C	40			50	1
"	134	"	A	Net	V	30			40–50	.5
"	135	"	"	Mantle	C	30 (wefts)			40	.5
						20 (warps)			30	.6
"	136	"	III	Mantle	C	40 (wefts)			40	.5–.7
						50 (warps)			50	.6–1
"	137	"	"	Mantle	C	30 (wefts)			40	.8
						35 (warps)			60	1
"	138	"	B	Mantle	C	20 (wefts)			40–50	.5–.7
						30 (warps)			40–55	.8–1.2
"	139	"	I	Mantle	C	50 (singles)				.8
						20 (pairs)			50	.8
"	140	"		Mantle	C	50 (wefts)				.7
						40 (warps)			50	.8–1

Structure	Color: Red, Yellow, Black, White, BRown, Tan	Motif or Design	Remarks	Specimen
Interlacing			No selvages; 2 cm wide; warp face, 10/cm; 5 wefts/cm	116
Linking			Body wrap; 5-mm square loops	117
Linking			3-mm squares; on back of head	118
Linking			10-mm squares; continuous	119
Linking			2-mm squares; continuous	120
Woven	W or T		Paired unplied wefts turn back at selvage; body wrap	121
Looping	R, T or Y	Yes, possibly bird	Base of bag, spiral; 7 loops/cm; 3.5 rows/cm	122
Looping	B, Y	Bird in B on Y	7 loops/cm; 3.5 rows/cm; perhaps same bag as T.S. 122	123
Linking	BR, W	Yes but unidentified	5.5 threads/cm; ribs 7 mm apart	124
Linking	T		8 threads/cm; ribs 6 mm apart	125
Spinning	W		8 pieces plied make cord, 7-mm diameter, 192 cm total length	126
Spinning			6 pieces of thread, total 104 cm long	127
Linking, looping			Looping on selvage only; linked squares open to 1 cm	128
Woven			10 pairs/cm; 9 singles/cm; cloth is equal face	129
Woven			All unplied, wefts S, warps Z; 8 weft pairs/cm; 8 single warps/cm; loose texture	130
Spinning			64 cm long	131
Looping			Figure 8, each 2 cm high	132
Looping			Figure 8, each 1 cm high, squares open 5 mm; cotton in selvage only	133
Looping			5 loops/cm; fine texture; 6 × 4 cm piece	134
Twining	BR		Wefts 3.5 mm apart; warps parallel pairs, 10 threads/cm	135
Twining	BR		Warps in parallel pairs; wefts 6 mm apart	136
Twining			8 warps/cm in split pairs; wefts 1 cm apart; selvage	137
Twining	BR, Y	BR and Y stripes in warp	10 warps/cm in split pairs; wefts 4–6 mm apart	138
Woven	BR		6 singles/cm; 5 pairs/cm; equal face	139
Woven	W		10 warps/cm in pairs; 6 wefts/cm; turn back at selvage	140

Sector, Square	Specimen	Floor	Body/ Offering	Function	Fiber: Cotton, Vegetal	Spin Angle S	Spin Angle Z	Ply Angle S	Ply Angle Z	Thread Diameter (mm)
"	141	"	A	Mantle	C	30 (wefts) 40 (warps)				.3–.7 .4–.7
"	142	"	I	Belt	C	40 (wefts) 20 (warps)			40	.3–1 .5–1
"	143	"	III	Belt	C	60 (wefts) 25 (warps)			50	.4 1
"	144	"	"	Bag	C	20			50	.7
"	145	"	"	Bag	C	20			40	.7–1
"	146	"	"	Bag	C	20			45	.5–.7
"	147	"	A	Bag	C	30			30	.5
"	148	"		Bag	C	X			50	.7
"	149	"		Bag	C	35			50	1
C-12:D-1	150	18		Cord	V	30			35	2
D-11:D-1	151	21		Bag	C	30			50	1
"	152	"		Purse?	V C C	25 (sewing) 35 (tie)			40 35	1.5 1.8
C-10:HJ-10	153	Below 20		Mantle	C	40			40	1
C-10:E-7	154			Mat	V					
D-12	155			Mantle	C	20			30–50	1
H-12:I-2	156			Flat piece	C	40 (wefts) 40 (warps)				.3 .2
C-11	157	13		Rope	V	X			20	5–8
"	158	"		Cord	C	30			50	3
H-11:B-9	159	Below 13		Flat piece	C	40 (pairs) 40 (singles)			40	.4–.5 1
"	160	"		Flat piece	C	40 (pairs) 35 (singles)			50	.4–.5 .6–1

Structure	Color: Red, Yellow, Black, White, BRown, Tan	Motif or Design	Remarks	Specimen
Woven			8 single warps/cm; 16 wefts/cm in pairs; both wefts in pair S-spun unplied	141
Interlacing	B, T	Oblique patterns in B floats on T	7.5 cm wide; both selvages; 12 warps/cm in pairs; 6 single wefts/cm	142
Interlacing	BR, W		9 warps/cm; warp face; 4 wefts/cm; turn back at selvage	143
Looping	W		5 loops/cm; 4 rows/cm	144
Looping	R, W	Yes but unidentified	6 loops/cm; 4 rows/cm	145
Looping	R, T	Yes but unidentified	6 loops/cm; 3 rows/cm	146
Looping	W or T	Yes but unidentified; second color lost	6 loops/cm; 8 rows/cm; very fine texture	147
Linking	W, R	R stripe 3 threads wide on W	Center and base of bag, rim lost	148
Linking	W, BR	Unidentifiable; BR largely decayed	6 threads/cm; ribs 7 mm apart	149
Spinning			2-ply cords twisted together to make cord 24 cm long	150
Looping	W		Complete bag 4.6 cm deep, 5 cm across; looping without foundation	151
Beaten Spinning Spinning ⎤	BR		Barkcloth folded to 17 × 5.8 cm, complete; sewn with BR thread; separate ties attached	152
Twining	W		8 warps/cm in split pairs; wefts 1 cm apart; selvage fringed	153
Twining			20 cm long junco in bundles, 3 cm diameter, twined with achupalla fiber	154
Twining	W		8 warps/cm in split pairs; wefts 9 mm apart	155
Warp twining			In looter debris; warp twined; warp face, 48 warps/cm; both warp and weft in pairs of unplied threads	156
Spinning			26 cm long	157
Spinning	W		35 cm long; 4-ply cord, replied S 20, then again S 10	158
Woven	W		7 singles/cm; 6 pairs/cm	159
Woven	BR, W	BR stripes in singles 6 and 12 mm wide	No selvage; 9 2-ply threads/cm; 6 pairs of 1-ply/cm	160

Sector, Square	Specimen	Floor	Body/ Offering	Function	Fiber: Cotton, Vegetal	Spin Angle S	Spin Angle Z	Ply Angle S	Ply Angle Z	Thread Diameter (mm)
H-11:D-10	161	Below 10		Flat piece	C	20–60			40	.5–.9
H-12:DE-1/2	162	Below 12		Rope	V	30			50	1
C-11:E-8	163	17		Net	V	10			50	1.4
"	164	"		Net	V	20			30	.8
"	165	"		Net	V	30			60	.6
"	166	"		Net	V	50–60				1.5
"	167	"		Mantle	C	20 (wefts) / 30 (warps)			30 / 40	.7 / .8
"	168	"	I	Mantle	C	20 (singles) / 20 (pairs)			40	.3–.5 / .7–.8
"	169	"		Flat piece	C	30			50	.7
C-11:E-8	170	17		Flat piece	C	50 (singles) / 20 (pairs)			40	.7 / .8
C-11:F-4	171	17		Flat piece	C	30 (wefts) / 40 (warps)			40	1.5 / 1
"	172	"		Bag	C	30			40–60	1
C-11:E-8	173	17	I	Bag	C	30			60	.5–.8
"	174	"	"	Bag	C	25			45	.8
H-12:A-6/7	175	15		Flat piece	C	20 (wefts) / 30 (warps)			40 / 30	.5 / .8
"	176	"		Flat piece	C	X			X	.4
"	177	"		Flat piece	C					
H-11:E-8	178	15		Flat piece	C	40	40 (wefts) / 40 (warps)			.2 / .8
"	179	"		Flat piece	C	40	40 (wefts) / 40 (warps)			.2 / .8
H-12:I-2	180	13		Belt	C		40			.5
H-12:A-6/7	181	15		Flat piece	C		30–50			N–.7
"	182	"		Flat piece	C		40			
"	183	"		Flat piece	C		20–40			.2–1

Structure	Color: Red, Yellow, Black, White, BRown, Tan	Motif or Design	Remarks	Specimen
Woven			25.5 cm loom width; weft pairs turn back	161
			14 cm long	162
Linking			5-mm loops; selvage; contains scrap of emerald-color fiber	163
Looping			5-mm loops	164
Linking			3-mm loops	165
Linking			Not body bags since these were extended burials	166
Twining	W		8 warps/cm in pairs, parallel or intertwined; wefts 1 cm apart	167
Woven		Blackened	6 singles/cm; 6 pairs/cm; equal face	168
Woven	T		6 threads/cm × 11 threads/cm; equal face	169
Woven			6 singles/cm; 5 pairs/cm	170
Woven	W		5 weft pairs/cm; 5 1-ply warps/cm	171
Linking	W		6-×-4-cm fragment with 1 cm of selvage	172
Looping	B, Y, R	Frontal anthropomorphic figure	At left side of man's head	173
Looping		Blackened	6 loops/cm; 4 rows/cm	174
Twining	BR		8 warps/cm in pairs; wefts 5 mm apart	175
Woven	W		10 cm loom width; 6 single warps/cm; weft in pairs; loose spin	176
Woven	BR, W	Plaid	6 single warps/cm; weft in pairs	177
Woven	W		24 cm loom width; 8 single warps/cm; 6 weft pairs/cm	178
Woven	W		28 cm loom width; 8 single warps/cm; 6 weft pairs/cm	179
Woven			9 cm loom width; 66 cm long; 1 end selvage; 9 single warps/cm; 7 weft pairs/cm	180
Woven	BR, W	Plaid	13 cm loom width; 13 single warps/cm over cord at end; 10 weft pairs/cm	181
Woven	W		17 cm loom width; 7 single warps/cm; 12 weft pairs/cm	182
Woven			> 18 cm loom width; 6 warps/cm; 8 wefts/cm	183

Sector, Square	Specimen	Floor	Body/ Offering	Function	Fiber: Cotton, Vegetal	Spin Angle		Ply Angle		Thread Diameter (mm)
						S	Z	S	Z	
H-11:DF-5/9	184	15		Flat piece	C	40	40 (weft)			.5
							40 (warps)			.5
H-12:A-6/7	185	15		Thread	C		40			.5
H-11:EF-8	186	15		Rope	V	20			40	15
H-12:A-6/7	187	15		Sandal	V	30 (sole)				2.4
						(ties)	30	20		3
H-11:H-9	188	11		Flat piece	C		30			.5
"	189	"		Flat piece	C	60	60			.8
H-11:C-9	190	11		Flat piece	V		35	60		3–4
"	191	"		Flat piece	C	50	50			.5
H-12:I-2	192	13		Flat piece	C	20–30 (wefts)				.25–1
							30 (warps)			.25–1
"	193	"		Flat piece	C	30 (warps)				.25
						30 (wefts)			30	.5
"	194	"		Flat piece	C	X	X (wefts)			
							X (warps)			
H-11:G-10	195	11		Flat piece	C	50	50 (wefts)			.2–.8
							50 (warps)			.3–.8
H-12:I-2	196	13		Flat piece	C	40 (wefts)			40	.3
						40 (warps)				.2
H-11:A-9	197	9		Flat piece	C	50	50			.3–1
"	198	"		Flat piece	C	50	50			.25–.5
"	199	"		Flat piece	C	50	50			
"	200	"		Flat piece	C	50	50			

Structure	Color: Red, Yellow, Black, White, BRown, Tan	Motif or Design	Remarks	Specimen
Woven	W		28 cm loom width; 8 single warps/cm; 7 weft pairs/cm	184
Spinning	W		32 unplied Z-spun threads 19 cm long, loosely S-twisted together	185
Spinning			13 pieces, total 2.80 m long	186
Twining			Toe of left sandal with ties between first 2 toes; note opposite spin on sole and ties	187
Woven	W		1 selvage; 10 single warps/cm; 8 weft pairs/cm	188
Woven	W		1 selvage; 9 single Z-spun warps/cm; 7 weft pairs/cm, S, Z	189
Twining			Maguey fiber; warps 4 cm apart; wefts plied S solidly on warps	190
Woven	W		S-spun warp; wefts in S and Z-spun pairs	191
Woven	W		3 loom widths sewn together: 20 cm, 23 cm, 23.5 cm; 7 single warps/cm; weft in S, S-spun pairs; tassels tied on side	192
Woven	T		35 single warps/cm; 7.5 weft pairs/cm, all S-spun	193
Woven	W		5 loom widths 20 cm wide sewn together; 6–8 single warps/cm; 6–7 weft pairs/cm, S, Z-spun pair; fringe and tassels; with cache including shell ornaments	194
Woven	W		8–9 single warps/cm; 16 wefts/cm in S, Z unplied pairs; with cache including shell ornaments	195
Warp twining			48 warp threads/cm; warp face of twined warp pairs; weft also in pairs of unplied threads; piece 9 × 8 cm	196
Woven	W, T		20 cm loom width; warps Z-spun, 10/cm; wefts paired S, Z, 5 pairs/cm; piece 20 × 80 cm	197
Woven	T		27 cm loom width; 12 single warps/cm; 14 S, Z weft pairs/cm	198
Woven	BR, T, R	BR and R weft stripes on T; 8-mm-wide BR stripes	27 cm loom widths sewn together; warps T singles; wefts S, Z pairs in T, singles in R and BR stripes	199
Woven			35 cm loom width; Z-spun single warps; S, Z weft pairs	200

Sector, Square	Specimen	Floor	Body/ Offering	Function	Fiber: Cotton, Vegetal	Spin Angle		Ply Angle		Thread Diameter (mm)
						S	Z	S	Z	
"	201	"		Flat piece	C	50	50			.2–.4
"	202	"		Flat piece	C	50	50 (wefts)			.5
							40 (warps)			
"	203	"		Yarn	C		30			.5
H-11:F-9	204	9		Flat piece	C	30	30 (wefts)			.8
							40 (warps)			.5
C-12	205	Surface		Mantle	C	30			40	1
"	206	"		Belt	C	40			30	
F-11	207	Surface		Cord	C, V	20			40	2
G-11	208	Surface		Flat piece	C	30			40	.8
C-11	209	Surface		Belt	C	20			30	1

Structure	Color: Red, Yellow, Black, White, BRown, Tan	Motif or Design	Remarks	Specimen
Woven	W		No selvage; Z-spun singles in warp, 11/cm; 15 S, Z pairs in weft	201
Woven	BR, W	BR weft stripes 2–4 weft pairs wide	26.5 cm loom widths sewn together with BR cotton yarn; 7 single Z-spun warps/cm; weft in S, Z pairs	202
Spinning	BR		6 single strands spun S 30 loosely twisted to sew T.S. 202 pieces	203
Woven	BR, W, T, B	Weft stripes: 6 W, 2 BR, 8 T, 2 BR, 5 W, 6 R-BR, 2 T, 6 W, 2 B, 6 T, 2 BR, 6 W, etc.	1 selvage; 7 single warps/cm; 7 S, Z weft pairs/cm	204
Twining	BR, W		12 warps/cm in split pairs, BR and W; wefts twined Z, 6 mm apart	205
Interlacing	W		Complete; 23 warps, warp face; 4.5 wefts/cm; warp fringe at end	206
Spinning	BR		C and V plied together S, Z, Z irregularly	207
Woven			No selvage; 7 single threads × 9 single threads; equal face; piece 5 × 13 cm	208
Interlacing	W		4.2 cm loom width; 35 cm long; unplied weft, plied warp; warp face	209

Bibliography

ADAMS, RICHARD NEWBOLD
1975   *Energy and Structure: A Theory of Social Power.* Austin: University of Texas Press.

ALLISON, M. J., E. GERSZTEN, J. MUNIZAGA, C. SANTORO, AND D. MENDOZA
1981   Tuberculosis in Pre-Columbian Andean Populations. In *Prehistoric Tuberculosis in the Americas,* edited by J. E. Buikstra, pp. 49–61. Evanston, Ill.: Northwestern University Archaeological Program.

ARNHEIM, RUDOLF
1964   *Art and Visual Perception.* Berkeley and Los Angeles: University of California Press.

BASS, W. M.
1971   *Human Osteology: A Laboratory and Field Manual.* Columbia: Missouri Archaeological Society, University of Missouri.

BASTIEN, JOSEPH
1973   *Qollahuaya Rituals: An Ethnographic Account of the Symbolic Relations of Man and Land in an Andean Village.* Cornell University Latin American Studies Program Dissertation Series, no. 56. Ithaca, N.Y.

BENFER, ROBERT A.
1984   The Challenges and Rewards of Sedentism: The Preceramic Village of Paloma, Peru. In *Paleopathology at the Origins of Agriculture,* edited by Mark N. Cohen and G. J. Armelagos, pp. 531–558. New York: Academic Press.

BENNETT, WENDELL C.
1954   *Ancient Arts of the Andes.* New York: Museum of Modern Art.

BIRD, JUNIUS BOUTON
1948a   Preceramic Cultures in Chicama and Viru. *Memoirs of the Society for American Archaeology,* no. 4, pp. 21–28. Menasha.
1948b   The Most Ancient Peruvian Farmers. *Transactions of the New York Academy of Sciences,* ser. 2, 10(5): 180–181.
1951   South American Radiocarbon Dates. In *Radiocarbon Dating,* edited by Frederick Johnson, pp. 37–49. Memoirs of the Society for American Archaeology, no. 8. Salt Lake City.
1952a   Appendix 3: Textile Notes. In *Cultural Stratigraphy in the Virú Valley, Northern Peru: The Formative and Florescent 2 Epochs,* edited by William Duncan Strong and Clifford Evans, Jr., pp. 357–360. Columbia Studies in Archeology and Ethnology, vol. 4. New York: Columbia University Press.
1952b   Before Heddles Were Invented. *Handweaver & Craftsman* 3(3): 5–7, 45, 50. New York.
1963   Pre-ceramic Art from Huaca Prieta, Chicama Valley. *Nawpa Pacha* 1:29–34. Berkeley: Institute of Andean Studies.

BIRD, JUNIUS BOUTON, JOHN HYSLOP, AND MILICA DIMITRIJEVIC SKINNER
1985   *The Preceramic Excavations at the Huaca Prieta, Chicama Valley,*

Peru. Anthropological Papers of the American Museum of Natural History. New York.

BISCHOF, HENNING
1984   Zur Entstehung des Chavín-Stils in Alt-Peru. *Beiträge zur Allgemeinen und Vergleichenden Archäologie* 6:355–452. Bonn: Deutschen Archäologischen Instituts.

BLUMBERG, J. E., W. L. HYLANDER, AND R. A. GOEPP
1971   Taurodontism: A Biometric Study. *American Journal of Physical Anthropology* 34:243–255.

BONAVIA, DUCCIO
1982   *Los Gavilanes: Precerámico peruano; mar, desierto y oásis en la historia del hombre.* Lima: Corporación Financiera del Desarrollo and Instituto Arqueológico Alemán.

BONAVIA, DUCCIO, AND A. GROBMAN
1978   El origen del maíz andino. In *Estudios americanistas I: Homenaje a H. Trimborn,* edited by R. Hartmann and U. Oberem. Coll. Inst. Anthro. 20. St. Augustin.

BONNIER, ELIZABETH, JULIO ZEGARRA, AND JUAN CARLOS TELLO
1985   Un ejemplo de crono-estratigrafía en un sitio con superposición arquitectónica—Piruru-Unidad I/II. *Boletín del Instituto Francés de Estudios Andinos* 14(3–4):80–101. Lima.

BOSERUP, ESTER
1965   *The Conditions of Agricultural Growth.* Chicago: Aldine.

BROTHWELL, D. R.
1963   *Digging Up Bones: The Excavation, Treatment and Study of Human Skeletal Remains.* London: British Museum (Natural History).

BUENO MENDOZA, ALBERTO, AND TERENCE GRIEDER
1979   Arquitectura precerámica de la sierra norte. *Espacio* 1(5). Lima.
1980   La Galgada: Nuevo clave para la arqueología andina. *Espacio* 2(9). Lima.

BURGER, RICHARD L.
1984   *The Prehistoric Occupation of Chavín de Huantar, Peru.* University of California Publications in Anthropology. Berkeley and Los Angeles: University of California Press.
1985   Prehistoric Stylistic Change and Cultural Development at Huaricoto, Peru. *National Geographic Research* 1:505–534.
1986   Unity and Heterogeneity within the Chavín Horizon. In *Peruvian Prehistory,* edited by Richard W. Keatinge. New York: Cambridge University Press.

BURGER, RICHARD L., AND LUCY SALAZAR BURGER
1980   Ritual and Religion at Huaricoto. *Archaeology* 33(6):26–32.
1985   The Early Ceremonial Center of Huaricoto. In *Early Ceremonial Architecture in the Andes,* edited by Christopher B. Donnan. Washington, D.C.: Dumbarton Oaks.

CÁRDENAS M., MERCEDES
1979   *A Chronology of the Use of Marine Resources in Ancient Peru.* Lima: Stiftung Volkswagen; Seminario de Arqueología, Instituto Riva-Agüero, Pontificia Universidad Católica del Perú.

COBO, BERNABE
1979   *History of the Inca Empire.* Translated by Roland Hamilton. Austin: University of Texas Press.

COE, MICHAEL D., AND RICHARD A. DIEHL
1980   *In the Land of the Olmec.* 2 vols. Austin: University of Texas Press.

CONKLIN, WILLIAM J.
1978   The Revolutionary Weaving Inventions of the Early Horizon. *Nawpa Pacha* 16:1–12. Berkeley: Institute of Andean Studies.

D'AQUILI, EUGENE G., CHARLES D. LAUGHLIN, JR., AND JOHN MCMANUS
1979   The Spectrum of Ritual: A Biogenetic Structural Analysis. New York: Columbia University Press.

DAVIDSON, JUDITH R.
1981 El *Spondylus* en la cosmología chimu. *Revista del Museo Nacional* 45:75–88. Lima.

DONNAN, CHRISTOPHER B.
1964 An Early House from Chilca, Peru. *American Antiquity* 30(2): 137–144.
1978 *Moche Art of Peru: Pre-Columbian Symbolic Communication.* Los Angeles: Museum of Cultural History, University of California, Los Angeles.

DONNAN, CHRISTOPHER B., AND CAROL J. MACKEY
1978 *Burial Patterns of the Moche Valley, Peru.* Austin: University of Texas Press.

DWYER, EDWARD B.
1979 Early Horizon Tapestry from South Coastal Peru. In *The Junius B. Bird Pre-Columbian Textile Conference,* edited by A. P. Rowe, E. P. Benson, and A.-L. Schaffer, pp. 61–82. Washington, D.C.: The Textile Museum and Dumbarton Oaks.

EDWARDS, D. S.
1984 Dental Attrition and Subsistence at the Preceramic Site of Paloma, Peru. Master's thesis, University of Missouri, Columbia.

ELIADE, MIRCEA
1964 *Shamanism: Archaic Techniques of Ecstasy.* Bollingen Series 76. Princeton: Princeton University Press.

EL-NAJJAR, M. Y.
1982 Skeletal Changes in Tuberculosis: The Hamann-Todd Collection. In *Prehistoric Tuberculosis in the Americas,* edited by J. E. Buikstra, pp. 85–97. Evanston, Ill.: Northwestern University Archaeological Program.

EMERY, IRENE
1966 *The Primary Structures of Fabrics: An Illustrated Classification.* Washington, D.C.: The Textile Museum.

ENGEL, FREDERIC
1957 Early Sites on the Peruvian Coast. *Southwestern Journal of Anthropology* 13(1):54–68. Albuquerque: University of New Mexico.
1960 Un Groupe humain datant de 5000 ans a Paracas, Pérou. *Journal de la Société des Américanistes,* n.s. 49:7–35. Paris.
1963 A Preceramic Settlement on the Central Coast of Peru: Asia, Unit I. *Transactions of the American Philosophical Society,* n.s. 53(3). Philadelphia.
1964 El precerámico sin algodón en la costa del Perú. In *Actas y Memorias del XXXV Congreso Internacional de Americanistas,* pp. 141–152. Mexico City.
1966 Le Complexe précéramique d'el Paraiso (Pérou). *Journal de la Société des Américanistes* 55(1):43–96. Paris.

FAZEKAS, I. G., AND F. KOSA
1978 *Forensic Fetal Osteology.* Budapest: Akademiai Kiado.

FELDMAN, ROBERT ALAN
1977 Life in Ancient Peru. *Field Museum of Natural History Bulletin* 48(6):12–17. Chicago.
1980 Aspero, Peru: Architecture, Subsistence Economy and Other Artifacts of a Preceramic Maritime Chiefdom. Doctoral dissertation, Harvard University.
1985 Preceramic Corporate Architecture: Evidence for the Development of Non-Egalitarian Social Systems in Peru. In *Early Ceremonial Architecture in the Andes,* edited by C. B. Donnan, pp. 71–92. Washington, D.C.: Dumbarton Oaks.

FEWKES, J. WALTER
1908 Ventilators in Ceremonial Rooms of Prehistoric Cliff-Dwellings. *American Anthropologist,* n.s. 10: 387–398.

FORBES, ROBERT JAMES
1964 *Studies in Ancient Technology,* 2d

rev. ed. 9 vols. Leiden: E. J. Brill.

FRISANCHO, A. R.

1976 Growth and Morphology at High Altitude. In *Man in the Andes: A Multidisciplinary Study of High-Altitude Quechua,* edited by P. T. Baker and M. A. Little, pp. 180–207. Stroudsburg, Pa.: Dowden, Hutchinson & Ross.

FURST, PETER

1966 Shaft Tombs, Shell Trumpets and Shamanism: A Culture-Historical Approach to Problems in West Mexican Archaeology. Doctoral dissertation, University of California, Los Angeles.

GENOVES, S.

1967 Proportionality of the Long Bones and Their Relation to Stature among Mesoamericans. *American Journal of Physical Anthropology* 26:67–77.

GILMORE, RAYMOND M.

1950 Fauna and Ethnozoology of South America. In *Handbook of South American Indians,* edited by J. H. Steward, 6:345–464. Washington, D.C.: Bureau of American Ethnology Bulletin 143.

GOLDMAN, IRVING

1963 *The Cubeo.* Urbana: University of Illinois Press.

GREENE, D. L., G. H. EWING, AND G. J. ARMELAGOS

1967 Dentition of a Mesolithic Population from Wadi Halfa, Sudan. *American Journal of Physical Anthropology* 27:41–55.

GRIEDER, TERENCE

1975 A Dated Sequence of Building and Pottery at Las Haldas. *Nawpa Pacha* 13:99–112. Berkeley: Institute of Andean Studies.

1978 *The Art and Archaeology of Pashash.* Austin: University of Texas Press.

1982 *Origins of Pre-Columbian Art.* Austin: University of Texas Press.

GRIEDER, TERENCE, AND ALBERTO BUENO MENDOZA

1981 La Galgada: Peru before Pottery. *Archaeology* 34(2):44–51.

1985 Ceremonial Architecture at La Galgada. In *Early Ceremonial Architecture in the Andes,* edited by C. B. Donnan, pp. 93–110. Washington, D.C.: Dumbarton Oaks.

GROBMAN, A., D. BONAVIA, D. H. KELLEY, P. C. MANGELSDORF, AND J. C. CAMARA-HERNÁNDEZ

1977 Study of Pre-ceramic Maize from Huarmey, North-Central Coast of Peru. *Bot. Mus. Leafl.* 25:221–242. Harvard University.

GROBMAN, A. D., AND R. RAVINES

1974 Maíz prehispánico del Valle de Cajamarca, Perú. *Revista del Museo Nacional* 40:135–137. Lima.

HILL, BETSY D.

1972–1974. A New Chronology of the Valdivia Complex from the Coastal Zone of Guayas Province, Ecuador. *Nawpa Pacha* 10–12:1–32. Berkeley: Institute of Andean Studies.

HOLLAND, WILLIAM R.

1964 Contemporary Tzotzil Cosmological Concepts as a Basis for Interpreting Prehistoric Maya Civilization. *American Antiquity* 29(3):301–306.

ISBELL, BILLIE JEAN

1978 *To Defend Ourselves: Ecology and Ritual in an Andean Village.* Latin American Monographs, No. 47. Institute of Latin American Studies, University of Texas at Austin.

IZUMI, SEIICHI, AND TOSHIHIKO SONO

1963 *Andes 2: Excavations at Kotosh, Peru, 1960.* Tokyo: University of Tokyo Press.

IZUMI, SEIICHI, PEDRO GUCULIZA, AND CHIAKI KANO

1972 *Excavations at Shillacoto, Huánuco, Peru.* University Museum Bulletin No. 3. Tokyo: University of Tokyo.

IZUMI, SEIICHI, AND KAZUO TERADA, EDS.
1972   *Andes 4: Excavations at Kotosh, Peru, 1963 and 1966.* Tokyo: University of Tokyo Press.

JOHNSTON, F. E.
1962   Growth of the Long Bones in Infants and Young Children at Indian Knoll. *American Journal of Physical Anthropology* 20:249–254.

KAJITANI, NOBUKO
1982   The Textiles of the Andes. *Senshoku no Bi* (Textile Arts), no. 20. Kyoto.

KANO, CHIAKI
1972   Pre-Chavín Cultures in the Central Highlands of Peru: New Evidence from Shillacoto, Huánuco. In *The Cult of the Feline,* edited by E. P. Benson, pp. 139–152. Washington, D.C.: Dumbarton Oaks.

1979   *The Origins of the Chavin Culture.* Studies in Pre-Columbian Art. Washington, D.C.: Dumbarton Oaks.

KLEIN, JEFFREY, J. C. LERMAN, P. E. DAMON, AND E. K. RALPH
1982   Calibration of Radiocarbon Dates: Tables Based on the Consensus of Data of the Workshop on Calibrating the Radiocarbon Time Scale. *Radiocarbon* 24(2):103–150.

KROGMAN, W. M.
1962   *The Human Skeleton in Forensic Medicine.* Springfield, Ill.: C. C. Thomas.

LATHRAP, DONALD W.
1970   *The Upper Amazon.* New York: Praeger.

LEACH, EDMUND R.
1967   Genesis as Myth. In *Myth and Cosmos: Readings in Mythology and Symbolism,* edited by John Middleton, pp. 1–13. Austin: University of Texas Press. (Reprinted from *Discovery,* May 1962.)

LUMBRERAS, LUIS G.
1974   *The Peoples and Cultures of Ancient Peru.* Translated by B. J. Meggers. Washington, D.C.:

Smithsonian Institution Press.
1977   Excavaciones en el Templo Antiguo de Chavín (Sector R): Informe de la Sexta Campaña. *Nawpa Pacha* 15:1–38. Berkeley: Institute of Andean Studies.

MACNEISH, RICHARD S.
1969   *First Annual Report of the Ayacucho Archaeological-Botanical Project.* Andover: R. S. Peabody Foundation for Archaeology.

MACNEISH, RICHARD S., A. NELKEN-TURNER, AND A. GARCÍA COOK
1970   *Second Annual Report of the Ayacucho Archaeological-Botanical Project.* Andover: R. S. Peabody Foundation for Archaeology.

MACNEISH, RICHARD S., T. C. PATTERSON, AND D. L. BROWMAN
1975   *Central Andean Interaction Sphere.* Papers of the R. S. Peabody Foundation for Archaeology, vol. 7. Andover.

MARCOS, JORGE G.
1979   Woven Textiles in a Late Valdivia Context (Ecuador). In *The Junius B. Bird Pre-Columbian Textile Conference,* edited by A. P. Rowe, E. P. Benson, and A.-L. Schaffer, pp. 18–26. Washington, D.C.: The Textile Museum and Dumbarton Oaks.

MASON, JOHN ALDEN
1960   *Mound 12, Chiapa de Corzo, Chiapas, Mexico.* Papers of the New World Archaeological Foundation, No. 9. Provo: Brigham Young University.

MATSUZAWA, TSUGIO
1972   Constructions. In *Andes 4: Excavations at Kotosh, Peru, 1963 and 1966,* edited by Seiichi Izumi and Kazuo Terada, pp. 55–176. Tokyo: University of Tokyo Press.

1978   The Formative Site of Las Haldas, Peru: Architecture, Chronology, and Economy. Translated by I. Shimada. *American Antiquity* 43(4):652–672.

MEGGERS, BETTY J., CLIFFORD EVANS, AND EMILIO ESTRADA
1965   *Early Formative Period of Coastal Ecuador: The Valdivia and Machalilla Phases.* Washington, D.C.: Smithsonian Institution.

MENZEL, DOROTHY
1964   Style and Time in the Middle Horizon. *Nawpa Pacha* 2:1–106. Berkeley: Institute of Andean Studies.

MERCHANT, V. L., AND UBELAKER, D. H.
1977   Skeletal Growth of the Protohistoric Arikara. *American Journal of Physical Anthropology* 46:61–72.

MOSELEY, MICHAEL EDWARD
1974   *The Maritime Foundations of Andean Civilization.* Menlo Park: Cummings.
1985   The Exploration and Explanation of Early Monumental Architecture in the Andes. In *Early Ceremonial Architecture in the Andes,* edited by C. B. Donnan, pp. 29–57. Washington, D.C.: Dumbarton Oaks.

MOSELEY, MICHAEL EDWARD, AND LINDA K. BARRETT
1969   Change in Preceramic Twined Textiles from the Central Peruvian Coast. *American Antiquity* 34(2): 162–165.

MOSELEY, MICHAEL EDWARD, AND LUIS WATANABE
1974   The Adobe Sculpture of Huaca de Los Reyes: Imposing Artwork from Coastal Peru. *Archaeology* 27(3): 154–161.

MOSELEY, MICHAEL EDWARD, AND GORDON R. WILLEY
1973   Aspero, Peru: A Reexamination of the Site and Its Implications. *American Antiquity* 38(4): 452–468.

MUELLE, JORGE C., AND ROGGER RAVINES
1973   Los estratos precerámicos de Ancon. *Revista del Museo Nacional* 39:49–70. Lima.

MURRA, JOHN V.
1962   An Archaeological "Restudy" of an Andean Ethnohistorical Account. *American Antiquity* 28(1): 1–4.

OLIVIER, G.
1969   *Practical Anthropology.* Springfield, Ill.: C. C. Thomas.

ORTIZ RESCANIÈRE, ALEJANDRO
1975   El orden Secoya o el árbol del universo. *Textual* 10:50–60. With the collaboration of J. Casanova, M.-F. Souffes, and Yaytrunbiá. Lima: Instituto Nacional de Cultura.

ORTLOFF, CHARLES R., MICHAEL E. MOSELEY, AND ROBERT A. FELDMAN
1982   Hydraulic Engineering Aspects of the Chimu Chicama-Moche Intervalley Canal. *American Antiquity* 47(3):572–595.

PATTERSON, THOMAS C.
1985   The Huaca La Florida, Rimac Valley, Peru. In *Early Ceremonial Architecture in the Andes,* edited by C. B. Donnan, pp. 59–69. Washington, D.C.: Dumbarton Oaks.
n.d.   The Historical Development of Andean Social Foundations on the Central Coast of Peru, 6000–1000 B.C. Ms., 1983.

PATTERSON, THOMAS C., AND MICHAEL E. MOSELEY
1968   Late Preceramic and Early Ceramic Cultures of the Central Coast of Peru. *Nawpa Pacha* 6:115–133. Berkeley: Institute of Andean Studies.

PEARSALL, D. M.
1978   Phytolith Analysis of Archaeological Soils: Evidence for Maize Cultivation in Formative Ecuador. *Science* 199:177–178.

PICKERSGILL, BARBARA
1969   The Archaeological Record of Chili Peppers (*Capsicum* spp.) and the Sequence of Plant Domestication in Peru. *American Antiquity* 34(1): 54–61.

POZORSKI, SHELIA, AND THOMAS POZORSKI
1979   Alto Salaverry: A Peruvian Coastal Preceramic Site. *Annals of the Carnegie Museum* 48, article 19. Pittsburgh.

POZORSKI, THOMAS GEORGE
1976   Caballo Muerto: A Complex of Early Ceramic Sites in the Moche Valley, Peru. Doctoral dissertation, University of Texas at Austin.

PRICE, BARBARA J.
1971   Prehispanic Irrigation Agriculture in Nuclear America. *Latin American Research Review* 6(3):3–60.

QUILTER, JEFFREY
1985   Architecture and Chronology at El Paraíso, Peru. *Journal of Field Archaeology* 12:279–297.

RAVINES, ROGGER, AND WILLIAM H. ISBELL
1975   Garagay: Sitio ceremonial temprano en el Valle de Lima. *Revista del Museo Nacional* 41:253–275.

REICHEL-DOLMATOFF, GERARDO
1971   *Amazonian Cosmos: The Sexual and Religious Symbolism of the Tukano Indians.* Chicago: University of Chicago Press.

ROE, PETER G.
1982   *The Cosmic Zygote; Cosmology in the Amazon Basin.* New Brunswick: Rutgers University Press.

ROWE, JOHN HOWLAND
1962a   *Chavín Art: An Inquiry into Its Form and Meaning.* New York: Museum of Primitive Art.
1962b   Stages and Periods in Archaeological Interpretation. *Southwestern Journal of Anthropology* 18(1):40–54. Albuquerque.
1967   Form and Meaning in Chavín Art. In *Peruvian Archaeology: Selected Readings,* edited by J. H. Rowe and D. Menzel, pp. 72–103. Palo Alto: Peek Publications.

ST. HOYME, L. E., AND R. T. KORITZER
1976   Ecology of Dental Disease. *American Journal of Physical Anthropology* 45:673–685.

SAMANIEGO, LORENZO, ENRIQUE VERGARA, AND HENNING BISCHOF
1985   New Evidence on Cerro Sechin, Casma Valley, Peru. In *Early Ceremonial Architecture in the Andes,* edited by C. B. Donnan, pp. 165–190. Washington, D.C.: Dumbarton Oaks.

SAUER, J.
1964   Revision of Canavalia. *Brittonia* 16:106–181.

SAUER, J., AND L. KAPLAN
1969   Canavalia Beans in American Prehistory. *American Antiquity* 34:417–424.

SHEPARD, ANNA O.
1965   *Ceramics for the Archaeologist,* 5th Printing with Foreword. Washington, D.C.: Carnegie Institution of Washington.

SMITH, C. EARLE, JR.
1980a   Chapter 5. Plant remains from Guitarrero Cave. In *Guitarrero Cave: Early Man in the Andes,* edited by T. F. Lynch, pp. 87–119. New York: Academic Press.
1980b   Chapter 6. Ancient Peruvian Highland Maize. In *Guitarrero Cave: Early Man in the Andes,* edited by T. F. Lynch, pp. 121–143. New York: Academic Press.

STEPHENS, S. G., AND M. E. MOSELEY
1973   Cotton Remains from Archaeological Sites in Central Coastal Peru. *Science* 180:186–188.

STINSON, S.
1985   Sex Differences in Environmental Sensitivity during Growth and Development. *Yearbook of Physical Anthropology* 28. New York: Alan R. Liss, Inc.

STRONG, WILLIAM DUNCAN, AND CLIFFORD EVANS
1952   *Cultural Stratigraphy in the Virú Valley, Northern Peru: The Formative and Florescent Epochs.* Columbia Studies in Archaeology and Ethnology, No. 4. New York: Columbia University Press.

TELLO, JULIO C.
1956 *Arqueología del Valle de Casma.* Lima: Editorial San Marcos.

TERADA, KAZUO
1985 Early Ceremonial Architecture in the Cajamarca Valley. In *Early Ceremonial Architecture in the Andes,* edited by C. B. Donnan, pp. 191–208. Washington, D.C.: Dumbarton Oaks.

TOKYO DAIGAKU
1960 *Andes: The Report of the University of Tokyo Scientific Expedition to the Andes in 1958.* Tokyo: Bijitsu Shuppan sha.

TOWLE, M. A.
1961 *The Ethnobotany of Pre-Columbian Peru.* Chicago: Aldine.

UBELAKER, D. H.
1978 *Human Skeletal Remains: Excavation, Analysis, Interpretation.* Chicago: Aldine.

URTON, GARY
1981 *At the Crossroads of the Earth and the Sky; An Andean Cosmology.* Austin: University of Texas Press.

VAILLANT, GEORGE C.
1944 *The Aztecs of Mexico.* Harmondsworth: Penguin.

WEBERBAUER, A.
1945 *El mundo vegetal de los Andes peruanos.* Lima: Ministerio de Agricultura.

WENDT, W. E.
1964 Die präkeramische Siedlung am Río Seco, Peru. *Baessler Archiv* 11:2255–2275.

WEST, M., AND T. W. WHITAKER
1980 Prehistoric Cultivated Cucurbits from the Virú Valley, Peru. *Economic Botany* 33:275–279.

WILLEY, GORDON R.
1953 *Prehistoric Settlement Patterns in the Virú Valley, Peru.* Bureau of American Ethnology Bulletin 155. Washington, D.C.

WILLIAMS, CARLOS
1980 Complejos de pirámides con planta en U, patrón arquitectónico de la costa central. *Revista del Museo Nacional* 44:95–110. Lima.
1985 A Scheme for the Early Monumental Architecture of the Central Coast of Peru. In *Early Ceremonial Architecture in the Andes,* edited by C. B. Donnan, pp. 227–240. Washington, D.C.: Dumbarton Oaks.

WITTFOGEL, KARL A.
1957 *Oriental Despotism.* New Haven: Yale University Press.

WU LEUNG, W. T., AND M. FLORES
1961 *Food Composition Tables for Use in Latin America.* INCAP and NIH.

YAMAMOTO, HIROYOSHI
1972 Bone and Shell Artifacts. In *Andes 4: Excavations at Kotosh, Peru, 1963 and 1966,* edited by Seiichi Izumi and Kazuo Terada, pp. 261–268. Tokyo: University of Tokyo Press.

Index

Adams, Richard N., 195, 198
altitude, 4, 5, **Fig. 10**
Alto Salaverry, 31, 148, 150, 151
Ancon, 150
    radiocarbon dates, 72
architecture
    mound-building, 197–198
    phases, 48, 201–203
    style, 59
art style, 208–209
    and art traditions, 215
Asia (continent), 31
Asia I site, Omas Valley, 209–210
Aspero, 24, 59, 71–72, 148, 150

barkcloth, 152, 154, 206, **Fig. 101**
    in burials, 78, **Fig. 69**
baskets, 152, **Figs. 100, 160**
Bass, W. M., 103
Bastien, Joseph, 18
bench, 36–37
Benfer, Robert A., 109–110, 121, 124
bird
    designs, 168–173
    designs on textiles, 201, **Figs. 130, 132,
        134, 136, 137, 139**
    petroglyphs, 183, **Fig. 155**
    symbolism, 207
Bird, Junius, 211
Black Chamber. See temple chambers and
        tombs: H-10:F-4
Bonavia, Duccio, 59
bone jewelry, 83, **Fig. 74**
Boserup, Ester, 192
Brothwell, D. R., 103, 104, 120
Burger, Lucy Salazar, 24, 58
Burger, Richard L., 24, 58

burials, 76–83, **Figs. 66–73**
    family crypt, infant burials, 196
Burned Tomb. See temple chambers and
        tombs: C-10:I-10

Castillo de Cocabal. See Early Horizon
ceramics, 1, 185–191, 202, 213, **Figs.
        157–159**
Cerro Sechín, 32, 212
Chavín de Huantar, 31
    ceramics, 191, 213
Chavín style, 211, 213, 215
Chiapa de Corzo, Mexico, 32
Chilca Valley, 105–110
Chillón Valley, 72
Chuquicara River. See Tablachaca River
circular courtyard, 24, 27, 30, 31, 197,
        Fig. 20
climate, 125
communication with other regions, 4, 144
Conklin, William J., 213–214
Cuicuilco, Mexico, 32

deer antler, 73, 75, **Fig. 63**
dental health, 121–124
diet, 145–146
Donnan, Christopher B., 22

Early Horizon
    at Castillo de Cocabal site, 9, 31, **Figs. 5, 9**
    Chavín style, 211
    at La Galgada, 37, 39
earplug, 75, 95, **Fig. 65**
Ecuador. See Valdivia culture of Ecuador
Edwards, D. S., 124

Fazekas, I. G., 103

feathers, 73, 75, **Fig. 64**
Feldman, Robert Alan, 24
firepit, 31, 43, 58, **Figs. 34–35, 53**
   fire in, 205
Forbes, R. J., 181

Gavilanes, Los, site, 24, 31, 32, 59
   radiocarbon dates, 71
Genoves, S., 103–104
gourds (*Lagenaria siceraria*), 141–143
   vessels, 102, **Figs. 94–95**
green stone
   petroglyphs, 182–184
   vault, 61–62
grid of site plan of La Galgada, 19, **Fig. 14**
Guañape site, Virú Valley, ceramics, 190–191
Guitarrero Cave, 150, 151

hair. *See* human hair
Haldas, Las, pottery, 190–191
hand prints, 35, **Fig. 29**
houses, 19, 22, 58, **Figs. 14–16**
Huaca Prieta
   carved gourds, 190, 213
   radiocarbon dates, 71
   style in textiles, 209–211
Huaricoto, 24, 31, 32, 58–59, 202
   ceramics, 190–191
   radiocarbon dates, 71
human figure design, 173, 178–179, 203,
   Figs. 140, 149–150
human hair, 76, 196–197, 206

Inca
   road, 9, **Fig. 17**
   settlement, 11, 144
Initial Period, 202–204, **Fig. 36**
   cache of jewelry in H-11:G-10, 92–95,
      Figs. 83–84
   style, 211–215
irrigation, 11, 22, 24, 138, 144, 192–194,
   Figs. 12, 17–18

jewelry, 83–95, 214–215
Johnston, F. E., 103

kiva (Southwestern U.S.), 31
Kosa, F., 103
Kotosh, 24, 31, 32, 59
   radiocarbon dates, 71
   Religious Tradition, 24, 58, 202
   temple style, 198
Krogman, W. H., 103

land use, 4–5
Leach, Edmund, 204–205
life expectancy, 105–110
litter, wooden, 78, 95, **Fig. 85**
Log-Roofed Tomb. *See* temple chambers and
   tombs: G-11:I-5

maize, 126, 147–148, 151
Malinalco, Mexico, 31
Matsuzawa, Tsugio, 53
Merchant, V. L., 103
mountain
   design in textile decoration, 166, 201, **Figs.
      122, 124**
   symbolism of design, 207
   symbolism of mound, 36
   terreform, symbolism of, 16, 18, 206,
      Fig. 13
Moxeke, 32, 212
myth, 204–205

Ojeda Ch., María J., 87
Olivier, G., 104
Omas Valley, 209–210
orientation of temple walls, 59, 202

Pallasca Province, 4, **Fig. 3**
Paloma, Chilca Valley, 105–110
Paraíso, El, Chillón Valley, radiocarbon dates,
   72
Paredes Botoni, Ponciano, 19
pathology of skeletons, 118–121
Piedra Parada, 31
plant down, 73, **Fig. 64**
pottery. *See* ceramics
Pozorski, Shelia, 148
Pozorski, Thomas, 148
Preceramic
   defined, 1, 204

phases, 195–199
style, 207–211
Price, Barbara J., 193

quarrystone, 32, 50, 58

radiocarbon measurements, 68–72
Reichel-Dolmatoff, Gerardo, 18
revetments, 44–50, **Figs. 42–45**
ritual chambers. *See* temple chambers and
    tombs
rituals, 24, 67, 75–82, 206
roof, 39, 53, **Fig. 54**
Rowe, John Howland, 213

Salinas de Chao, 31
Saltzman, Max, 181
sandal, 152, **Fig. 98**
San Lorenzo, Mexico, 32
Santa River, 4, 5, **Fig. 3**
Sawyer, Alan, 31
seasonal differences, 5
Sechín Alto, 31
serpent. *See* snake designs
shamanism, 75
shells, 83–87, 94, 213–215, **Figs. 74, 83–84**
    Spondylus, 89, 92, 94–95, 203
Shillacoto, 59
skeletons
    human, 103–124, 217–241
    monkey, 43
snake designs
    at Asia I, 209
    on ceramics, 187–190, **Figs. 158–159**
    on petroglyphs, 182–183, **Figs. 152–153**
    on textiles, 168, 169, 173, 182–183, 201,
        Figs. 128–131, 144–146, 153
Square Chamber. *See* temple chambers and
    tombs: C-11:I-3
square-in-circle design, 205
stature of humans, 110–118
stone artifacts, 96–102, **Figs. 88–93**

Tablachaca River, 4, 5, **Figs. 1, 3**
temple chambers and tombs
  C-10:E-10
    burials, 78, **Fig. 68**

gourd vessels, 102, **Figs. 94–95**
jewelry, 89–90, **Figs. 74, 79**
skeletal material, 224–226
textiles, **Fig. 109**; decorations, 173–175,
    Figs. 141–146
tomb contents, 244–245
C-10:I-10 (Burned Tomb)
  ceramic lid, 187–190, **Figs. 158–159**
  skeletal material, 230
  tomb contents, 90, 247–248, **Figs.**
    74, 81
C-11:E-8, Floor 17
  architecture, 62–63
  burials, 79–83, **Fig. 72**
  ceramic vessel, 187–190, **Figs.**
    158–159
  necklace, 90, **Fig. 80**
  skeletal material, 234–235
  tomb contents, 246
C-11:F-5, Floor 23
  architecture, 50, **Figs. 46–49**
  jewelry, 87–89, **Fig. 78**
  skeletal material, 226–229
  textiles, **Figs. 110, 113**; decorations,
    171–173, **Figs. 124, 135–140**
  tomb, 61–62
C-11:I-3, Floor 22 (Square Chamber)
  architecture, 53, **Figs. 46, 47, 49,**
    51–53
  tomb architecture, 62
C-12:D-1
  architecture, 63–66, 67, **Fig. 60**
  burials, 79, 82, **Figs. 71, 73**
  jewelry, 83, 90, **Figs. 74, 75**
  skeletal material, 230–234
  stone cup, 101, **Figs. 92–93**
  textiles, **Figs. 115, 116, 118**; decora-
    tions, 175–178, **Figs. 147–148, 151**
  tomb contents, 246–247
D-11:C-3, Floor 24
  architecture, 50, 67, **Figs. 46, 47**
  burials, 78–79, **Fig. 58**
  jewelry, 87, **Figs. 74, 76–77**
  skeletal material, 221–224
  textile decorations, 170, **Fig. 134**
  tomb, 63, **Figs. 57, 58**
  tomb contents, 245–246

D-11:C-3, Floor 25
  age, 69
  architecture, 50, **Figs. 46, 47, 49, 50**
  artifacts, 73
  disturbed burial, 96, **Fig. 86**
E-11:J-7
  architecture, 66, 67, 202, **Fig. 62**
  gourd vessel, 102, **Fig. 94**
  skeletal material, 235–241
F-12:B-2
  age, 69
  architecture, 27, 29, **Figs. 23, 24**
  basket, 205, **Figs. 100, 160**
  burials, 76–78, **Figs. 56, 66**
  jewelry, 83, **Fig. 74**
  skeletal material, 154, 217–220
  textile decorations, 166–171, **Figs.
    122–123, 125–133**
  textiles and matting, **Figs. 99, 100, 104,
    107**
  tomb, 61, **Fig. 56**
  tomb contents, 242–244
  wooden artifacts, 95–96, **Fig. 86**
Floor 10, North Mound, 44, **Figs. 34, 35,
    39, 40**
Floor 13, North Mound, 43, 44, **Figs. 34,
    35, 38**
Floor 30, North Mound, 32, **Fig. 26.** *See
    also* H-11:E-10
  earplug, 75, **Fig. 65**
G-11:I-5 (Log-Roofed Tomb), 63, 67, **Fig.
    59**
G-12:I-2, 35, **Figs. 27–29**
H-10:F-4 (Black Chamber), 27, **Figs. 21,
    22**
H-11:E-10, Floor 30
  age, 69–70
  architecture, 32, **Figs. 26, 31, 34, 35**
I-11:B-8, Floor 50
  age, 68–69

architecture, 30, 35, **Figs. 25, 26**
  tomb, 61
I-11:J-2, 60–61, 66, **Figs. 55, 61**
I-12:C-5
  architecture, 39, **Figs. 32, 33**
  items on floor, 73–75, **Fig. 64**
textiles, 152–181, 251–269
  decorations, 166–181
  dyes, 180–181
  loom, 162–165
  as offering, 199–200
  production, 203
  styles, 209–211
  techniques, 152–165
  for trade, 138, 148
tombs, 59–67
Towle, M. A., 128
trade route, 4, 16, 149
turquoise, 87, 92

Ubelaker, D. H., 103, 105
Urton Gary, 18
U-shaped temple or platform, 37–39, 58,
    202–203, **Figs. 38, 39**

Valdivia culture of Ecuador, 1, 16, 189–190,
    197, **Fig. 1**
vents, 30, 39, 43, **Figs. 37, 53**
Virú Valley, 190–191

waterworn stone (river cobbles), 24, 27, 32,
    58, **Fig. 25**
Whitaker, T. W., 141, 143
white finish for floors and walls, 30, 50, 59
Wittfogel, Karl A., 192, 194
wooden artifacts, 95–97, **Figs. 85–87**

yellow finish for walls, 50, 59, 198

www.ingramcontent.com/pod-product-compliance
Lightning Source LLC
Chambersburg PA
CBHW080414270326
41929CB00018B/3018